EAST BALI
Pages 100–123

LOMBOK
Pages 150–163

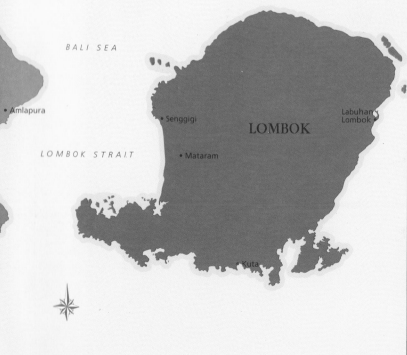

BALI SEA

• Amlapura

• Senggigi

LOMBOK

Labuhan
Lombok

LOMBOK STRAIT

• Mataram

• Kuta

EYEWITNESS TRAVEL

BALI
& LOMBOK

EYEWITNESS TRAVEL

BALI
& LOMBOK

DK

LONDON, NEW YORK,
MELBOURNE, MUNICH AND DELHI
www.dk.com

PRODUCED BY Editions Didier Millet, Singapore
EDITORIAL DIRECTOR Timothy Auger
PROJECT EDITOR Choo Lip Sin
ART DIRECTOR Tan Seok Lui
EDITORS Samantha Hanna Ascui, Marilyn Seow
SENIOR DESIGNER Felicia Wong Yit Har
DESIGNERS Nelani Jinadasa, Norreha Sayuti, Annie Teo Ai Min

CONTRIBUTORS
Andy Barski, Albert Beaucourt, Bruce Carpenter, John Cooke,
Jean Couteau, Diana Darling, Sarah Dougherty,
Julia Goh, Lorca Lueras, Tim Stuart, Tony Tilford

MAPS
ERA-Maptech Ltd, Ireland

PHOTOGRAPHERS
John Cooke, Koes Karnadi,
Tim Stuart, Tony Tilford, Richard Watson

ILLUSTRATORS
Anuar bin Abdul Rahim, Denis Chai Kah Yune, Chang Huai-Yan, Choong
Fook San, Koon Wai Leong, Lee Yoke Ling, Poo Lee Ming, Thomas Sui,
Peggy Tan, Yeap Kok Chien

Reproduced by Colourscan, Singapore
Printed and bound by Vivar Printing Sdn. Bhd, Malaysia

First American Edition, 2001
11 12 13 14 10 9 8 7 6 5 4 3 2 1

Reprinted with revisions 2005, 2007, 2009, 2011

Published in the United States by DK Publishing,
375 Hudson Street, New York, New York 10014

A CATALOGUE RECORD FOR THIS BOOK IS AVAILABLE FROM
THE LIBRARY OF CONGRESS.

Published in Great Britain by Dorling Kindersley Limited.

ISSN 1542-1554

ISBN 978-0-75667-029-0

THROUGHOUT THIS BOOK, FLOORS ARE REFERRED TO IN ACCORDANCE
WITH EUROPEAN USAGE, IE THE "FIRST FLOOR" IS ONE FLIGHT UP.

Front cover main image: Temples on the edge of Lake Bratan, Bedugul,
Tabanan

MIX
Paper from
responsible sources
FSC
www.fsc.org   FSC™ C018179

The information in this
DK Eyewitness Travel Guide is checked regularly.
Every effort has been made to ensure that this book is as up-to-date
as possible at the time of going to press. Some details, however,
such as telephone numbers, opening hours, prices, gallery hanging
arrangements and travel information are liable to change. The
publishers cannot accept responsibility for any consequences arising
from the use of this book, nor for any material on third party
websites, and cannot guarantee that any website address in this
book will be a suitable source of travel information. We value the
views and suggestions of our readers very highly. Please write to:
Publisher, DK Eyewitness Travel Guides, Dorling Kindersley, 80 Strand,
London WC2R 0RL, Great Britain, or email: travelguides@dk.com.

◁ Pura Bukit Sari in the monkey forest at Sangeh, West Bali

CONTENTS

HOW TO USE THIS
GUIDE 6

Ganesha statue at
Pura Luhur Uluwatu

INTRODUCING BALI AND LOMBOK

DISCOVERING BALI
AND LOMBOK
10

PUTTING BALI AND
LOMBOK ON THE MAP
12

A PORTRAIT OF
BALI AND LOMBOK
14

BALI AND LOMBOK
THROUGH THE YEAR
40

THE HISTORY OF
BALI AND LOMBOK
44

Freshly gilded temple parasols
drying in the sun

Gunung Agung, the most sacred volcano on Bali and a prominent feature in the landscape

BALI AND LOMBOK AREA BY AREA

BALI AND LOMBOK AT A GLANCE 54

SOUTH BALI 56

A pavilion in the grounds of Puri Agung Karangasem, Amlapura

CENTRAL BALI 78

EAST BALI 100

NORTH AND WEST BALI 124

LOMBOK 150

TRAVELLERS' NEEDS

WHERE TO STAY 166

WHERE TO EAT 180

SHOPPING IN BALI AND LOMBOK 192

ENTERTAINMENT 198

OUTDOOR ACTIVITIES 202

SURVIVAL GUIDE

PRACTICAL INFORMATION 214

TRAVEL INFORMATION 226

GENERAL INDEX 230

Pink lotus blossom, a symbol of grace and holiness in Bali

ACKNOWLEDGMENTS AND READING LIST 238

GLOSSARY 240

ROAD MAP
Inside Back Cover

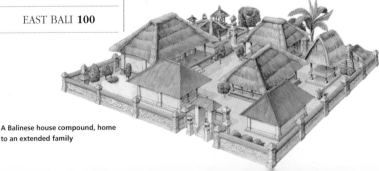

A Balinese house compound, home to an extended family

HOW TO USE THIS GUIDE

This guide helps you to get the most from your visit to Bali and Lombok. It provides detailed practical information and expert recommendations. *Introducing Bali and Lombok* maps the islands and sets them in their historical and cultural context. Features cover topics from festivals and music to wildlife and diving. Four chapters on Bali's regions, plus one on Lombok, describe sights of interest, using maps, photographs and illustrations. Restaurant and hotel recommendations can be found in *Travellers' Needs*. The *Survival Guide* has tips on everything from transport to safety.

BALI AND LOMBOK AREA BY AREA

The island of Bali is divided into four areas, each with its own chapter. A further chapter covers the island of Lombok. A map of these regions can be found inside the front cover of this book. All the sights are numbered and plotted on each chapter's *Regional Map*.

Each area can be quickly identified by its colour coding.

1 Introduction
The landscape, history and character of each region are outlined here, showing how the area has developed in the past and what it has to offer to the visitor today.

A locator map shows where you are in relation to other areas of the islands of Bali and Lombok.

2 Regional Map
This shows the road network and gives an illustrated overview of the whole area. The interesting places to visit are numbered and there are also useful tips on getting to, and around, the region by car and other means of transport.

Features and story boxes highlight special or unique aspects of a particular sight.

3 Detailed Information
The sights in each area are described individually following the numerical sequence on the Regional Map. Road map references, addresses, telephone numbers, opening hours, information on admission charges, as well as transport options, are provided where applicable.

4 Major Towns

An introduction covers the history, character and geography of the city or town. The main sights are plotted on the map and described in more detail.

A Visitors' Checklist gives transport and other useful information, plus details of facilities, local performances and festival dates.

The town map shows the major streets, main transport terminals and information centres.

5 Street-by-Street Map

This gives a bird's-eye view of a key area in a major town and points out interesting sights to visit, many of them shown in photographs.

A suggested route for a walk is shown in red.

For all the top sights, a Visitors' Checklist provides the practical information you will need to plan your visit.

6 Top Sights

These are given two full pages. Interesting temples or other important buildings are shown in a bird's-eye view, with major features highlighted. Areas of natural beauty such as national parks are shown in specially drawn graphics.

The gallery guide explains the layout of a museum or gallery and gives a summary of what the collections contain.

Stars indicate the sights or features that no visitor should miss.

INTRODUCING
BALI & LOMBOK

DISCOVERING BALI & LOMBOK 10–11
PUTTING BALI & LOMBOK ON THE MAP 12–13
A PORTRAIT OF BALI & LOMBOK 14–39
BALI & LOMBOK THROUGH THE YEAR 40–43
THE HISTORY OF BALI & LOMBOK 44–51

DISCOVERING BALI AND LOMBOK

Two compact, neighbouring islands nestling within the Indonesian archipelago, Bali and Lombok present visitors with a rare and idyllic holiday destination. Ancient volcanoes stand sentry over thick tropical jungle and deep river gorges, all fringed by fertile ricefields and seemingly endless beaches. These natural splendours are combined with an exotic history, defined by ancient palaces and sacred temples, and a diverse secular heritage of arts, music and crafts. These two pages highlight the best cultural, sporting and natural attractions in Bali's four regions and on Lombok, from ritual ceremonial customs and mountain trekking to surfing and a vibrant nightlife.

Hand-painted Balinese statue

SOUTH BALI

- High-performance surf beaches
- Bustling capital of Denpasar
- Historic Sanur
- Kuta & Seminyak resorts

The sweeping, white-sand beaches of South Bali offer world-class watersports facilities, including some of the best surf breaks (see pp208–9) in the world. It is also the location of Bali's busy capital city, **Denpasar** (see pp60–61), home to colourful street markets and indigenous art in the **Bali Museum** (see pp62–3).

The nearby historical village of **Sanur** (see pp64–5) was Bali's original tourist enclave; this restful, family destination is characterized by shady lanes, majestic trees and a 5-km (3-mile) shoreline within a gentle, reef-sheltered lagoon. The ambience is mellow and cosmopolitan. In contrast, the once sleepy

A festival procession in Ubud, renowned for ritual ceremonies

fishing village of **Kuta** (see pp66–9) is a cheerful jumble of closely packed pubs, discos, restaurants and juice bars. This is a good place for souvenirs and surf gear, and is also well served by money-changers and budget hotels.

Just north of Kuta, **Seminyak** (see p67) lays claim to the highest concentration of fine-dining restaurants on the island, together with a wide choice of chic cocktail bars and nightclubs. Elegant shops and luxury spa resorts also predominate here.

CENTRAL BALI

- Ubud's cultural traditions
- Exclusive retreats in Ayung River Gorge
- Elephant conservation

Central Bali is blessed with many of the quieter features that draw people to this beautiful island – dazzling, terraced ricefields, unspoiled villages, art and craft communities, and ancient temples

and palaces. The remarkable town of **Ubud** (see pp88–91) is the island's centre for musical and dance performances and numerous art galleries and craft shops line the streets. The town's **Museum Puri Lukisan** (see pp92–3) houses an inspiring collection of prewar and contemporary Balinese art and woodcarving, while its palace, **Puri Saren** (see p90), hosts traditional dance performances every evening. The annual Ubud Writers' & Readers' Festival attracts lovers of literature from all over the globe.

The spectacular **Ayung River Gorge** (see pp96–7) is renowned for its luxurious boutique hotels and exclusive hideaways, and the river is the setting for action-packed white-water rafting trips. The **Elephant Safari Park** (see p206), at Taro, in the jungles of Central Bali, is regarded as the best of its kind in the world, raising awareness of elephant welfare and conservation in the wild.

Relaxing on Kuta's palm-fringed sandy beach

◁ Terraced ricefields in the shadow of Gunung Agung volcano

Terraced ricefields of East Bali, with Gunung Agung in the distance

EAST BALI

- Sacred volcano, Gunung Agung
- Dive sites and coral gardens
- Ancestral stronghold of Tenganan

Dominating East Bali is the resplendent summit of **Gunung Agung** *(see p114)*, Bali's tallest and holiest volcano, dwelling place of the gods and a challenging trek. **Pura Besakih** *(see pp116–17)*, Bali's largest and most important temple, lies on its slopes.

The east coast winds around steep headlands and sheltered coves. This laid-back area features some of Bali's best coral reefs and dive sites *(see pp210–11)*, rich in marine life. Among them, **Candi Dasa** *(see p108)* is a quiet seaside destination

and a great base from which to visit the region's ancient sights, temples and palaces.

The neighbouring village of **Tenganan** *(see pp110–11)* is a 700-year-old walled community hidden within the hills, where residents practise a time-honoured lifestyle of ritual and ceremony. **Kintamani** village *(see p115)* offers spectacular views from the rim of the giant caldera which encircles Bali's most active volcano, **Gunung Batur** *(see pp120–21).*

NORTH AND WEST BALI

- West Bali National Park
- Dolphin-watching trips
- Ancient volcanic lakes
- Pura Tanah Lot sea temple

North Bali rests within the rain shadow of the central mountain range, while West Bali is the island's least-populated area, characterized by impenetrable highlands. **West Bali National Park** (Taman Nasional Bali Barat, *see pp136–7)* covers 77,000 ha (190,000 acres) of savannah, rainforest, coastal flats and coral reefs, and is home to numerous species of flora and fauna. On the north coast, **Lovina** *(see p147)*, has a pretty black-sand bay and the opportunity for early risers to spot dolphins off the coast.

Inland, the quiet waters of the picturesque **Lake Bratan** *(see p141)* lap around a mystical, tiered temple. Nearby, **Lake Buyan** and **Tamblingan** *(see pp140–41)*

border primeval rainforest. **Pura Tanah Lot** *(see p128)*, a venerated sea temple perched on a wave-lashed rock, is hauntingly beautiful at sunset.

LOMBOK

- Trekking Gunung Rinjani
- Sasak festivities
- Artisan handicrafts
- Marine life of the Gili Isles

Azure waters of Lake Segara Anak, below Gunung Rinjani

Only 35 km (22 miles) of sea separate Bali and Lombok, but the physical and cultural distinctions are considerable. Towering mountains, awesome waterfalls, magnificent coral reefs, a colourful Sasak culture, and a rare, unspoiled tranquillity are among Lombok's many charms. Its uncommercialized attractions include trekking the mighty **Gunung Rinjani** *(see pp158–9)*, which forms the second-highest peak in Indonesia.

Lombok's way of life exposes the integration of Sasak Muslim and Balinese Hindu traditions. Visitors are welcomed at splendid festivals such as the Sasak **Bau Nyale** ceremony *(see p42)*, when hundreds of people assemble on the beach to celebrate the annual spawning of the sea-worms.

Artisans produce remarkable handicrafts: decorative textiles, rattan basketware and distinctive, handmade pottery *(see pp36–7)*. The abundant marine life of the tiny **Gili Isles** *(see p156)* is a great attraction for divers.

Pura Ulun Danu Bratan temple, rising from an island on Lake Bratan

Putting Bali and Lombok on the Map

The island of Bali lies east of Java, separated from it by the Bali Strait. Bali is 5,633 sq km (2,253 sq miles) in area. Lombok lies east of Bali, with an area of 5,435 sq km (2,098 sq miles). Bali (population 3.8 million) is more developed than Lombok (population 3 million). The main airport for both islands is Ngurah Rai International Airport near Denpasar in Bali; most onward travel to Lombok is by domestic flight, or by ferry or fast boat from Padang Bai or Benoa Harbour. The road network reflects the islands' mountainous nature; many of the most important routes run along the coasts; roads across the islands follow the lie of the land.

KEY

✈ Airport

⛴ Ferry and boat service

═ Dual carriageway

▬ Major road

═ Minor road

-·- Provincial boundary

-·- Regency boundary

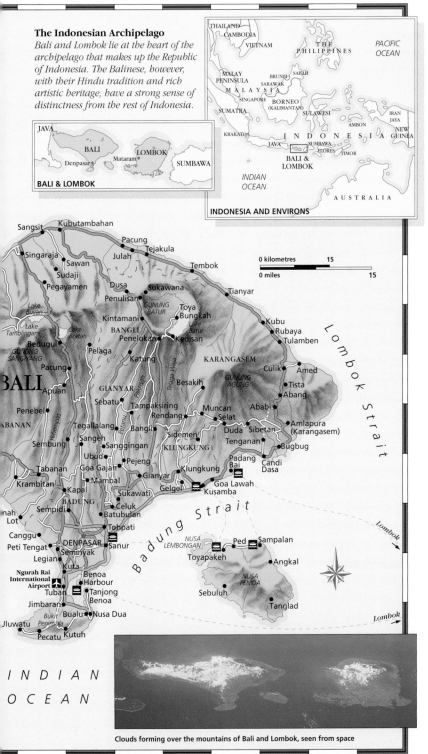

The Indonesian Archipelago

Bali and Lombok lie at the heart of the archipelago that makes up the Republic of Indonesia. The Balinese, however, with their Hindu tradition and rich artistic heritage, have a strong sense of distinctness from the rest of Indonesia.

THAILAND
CAMBODIA
VIETNAM
THE PHILIPPINES
PACIFIC OCEAN

MALAY PENINSULA
BRUNEI SABAH
MALAYSIA
SARAWAK
SINGAPORE
SUMATRA
BORNEO (KALIMANTAN)
SULAWESI
AMBON
IRAN JAYA
NEW GUINEA

KRAKATOA
I N D O N E S I A
JAVA
SUMBAWA
FLORES
TIMOR
BALI & LOMBOK

INDIAN OCEAN

AUSTRALIA

INDONESIA AND ENVIRONS

JAVA
BALI
LOMBOK
Denpasar
Mataram
SUMBAWA

BALI & LOMBOK

Sangsit
Kubutambahan
Singaraja
Sawan
Sudaji
Pegayamen
Pacung
Julah
Tejakula
Tembok
Sukawana
Tianyar

0 kilometres   15
0 miles   15

Lake Buyan
Lake Tamblingan
Lake Bratan
Bedugul
GUNUNG SANGYANG
Pacung
Apuan
Penulisan
GUNUNG BATUR
Kintamani
BANGLI
Penelokan
Pelaga
Katung
Toya Bungkah
Lake Batur
Kedisan
Kubu
Rubaya
Tulamben

BALI

GIANYAR
Sebatu
Tampaksiring
Rendang
Muncan
Selat
Besakih
KARANGASEM
GUNUNG AGUNG
Culik
Amed
Tista
Abang
Ababi
Amlapura (Karangasem)

Penebel
ABANAN
Tegallalang
Sangeh
Sembung
Ubud
Goa Gajah
Mambal
Pejeng
Bangli
Sidemen
Duda
KLUNGKUNG
Tenganan
Sibetan
Bugbug
Candi Dasa

Tabanan
Krambitan
Kapal
Sukawati
Gianyar
Klungkung
Padang Bai
Goa Lawah

Sanggingan
Celuk
BADUNG
Batubulan
Tobpati
Gelgel
Kusamba

nah Lot
Sempidi
Canggu
Peti Tengat
Legian
DENPASAR
Sanur
Semmyak
Kuta

Badung Strait

NUSA LEMBONGAN
Ped
Sampalan
Toyapakeh
Angkal

Lombok

Ngurah Rai International Airport
Tuban
Benoa Harbour
Tanjong Benoa
Jimbaran
Bualu
Nusa Dua
Bukit Peninsula
Jluwatu
Pecatu
Kutuh

NUSA PENIDA
Sebuluh
Tanglad

Lombok

Lombok Strait

I N D I A N

O C E A N

Clouds forming over the mountains of Bali and Lombok, seen from space

A PORTRAIT OF BALI AND LOMBOK

*T*he islands of Bali and Lombok are sufficiently close to be visible to each other on a clear day. They are both volcanic, are of similar size and have much else in common. However, they offer the visitor very different experiences. Bali – noisy, colourful, crowded and glamorous – is one of the world's most celebrated destinations; quiet Lombok was long a travellers' secret.

Geographically, Bali and Lombok are at the centre of the Indonesian Archipelago. This is a vast chain of islands stretching from the Indian Ocean to the Pacific. It lies across the ancient trade routes between Europe, the Middle East, India and China, and has absorbed influences from all these civilizations.

Bali is a province within the Republic of Indonesia, with its provincial capital at Denpasar. Lombok is part of the province of West Nusa Tenggara; Mataram, the provincial capital, is on the island. Both are mainly rural societies, despite the urbanization of southern Bali in the 1980s and

Stone statue from Klungkung

1990s. Facilities such as electricity and television came to most places only in the last quarter of the 20th century (despite this, the Internet is already widely used).

In daily life on Hindu Bali and mostly Muslim Lombok, great importance is attached to community matters, including social harmony. With Indonesia's move in the late 1990s from dictatorship to democracy, there is great awareness of the importance of religious tolerance, while at the same time each society takes pride in its own identity. Bali eagerly shares its flamboyant religious culture; the people of Lombok, however, are generally more reticent.

The Mayura Water Palace in Mataram, a legacy of Balinese rule in Lombok *(see p155)*

◁ A villager carrying her offering to an *odalan* (temple festival)

A Balinese family group carrying holy water to their house temple

THE BALINESE WAY OF LIFE

At the core of Balinese society is the village, a cohesive religious community organized around a group of temples. Village members are required to take part in temple rituals and assist in the community's funerary rites.

Religious practice in Bali entails music, theatre and elaborate offerings. The labour-intensive nature of rituals requires a high degree of social organization, which is visible in the village layout. Family house compounds are usually laid out on a north-south axis. The village core is dominated by temples, market, civic structures and often *puri*, houses of the nobility.

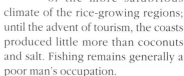
Painting of rice terraces

On Lombok, most of the indigenous Sasak people are orthodox Muslims *(see p23)*, their social life organized around the family and village mosque.

A road-side food stall near Candi Dasa

ECONOMIC DEVELOPMENT

Bali and Lombok were both prime rice-producers until land began to become scarce in the mid-20th century. Since then the government has encouraged crop diversification, particularly into commodity crops such as coffee, vanilla, cloves, tobacco and citrus fruits. Today, land is increasingly being used for tourism. There seem to be few alternatives. Marine and coastal resources have never been energetically developed, perhaps because of the more salubrious climate of the rice-growing regions; until the advent of tourism, the coasts produced little more than coconuts and salt. Fishing remains generally a poor man's occupation.

There has been little true industrialization. Some artisanal manufacturing has emerged in South Bali, particularly in the garment industry around Kuta; but although this does absorb some local labour, it also attracts workers from other, poorer islands who are willing to work for lower wages, compounding problems of unemployment with new social challenges.

On the other hand, cottage industry, in particular handicrafts, has allowed local economies within Bali and Lombok to shift away from agriculture without a great rural exodus.

ARTS AND HANDICRAFTS

Handicrafts and the production of art objects for secular use have become a vigorous export industry in Bali. Styles of painting, wood sculpture, jewellery and textiles have been adapted for sale to visitors and to export markets *(see pp36–7)*, and this has opened up several creative opportunities.

A sizeable expatriate community in Kuta, Sanur and Ubud has played an important role in developing this sector together with local entrepreneurs. Bali is also a marketplace for handicrafts, antiques and reproduction furniture from other islands of the Indonesian Archipelago.

Lombok has a venerable tradition of making low-fired domestic pottery *(see p154)*. The artisans are generally women, aided in the heavier chores and the marketing by their husbands. Lombok's hand-woven textiles and shapely rattan baskets have also found an eager international market. There are great hopes that tourism will further strengthen the island's local economy.

A beach in South Bali, the tourist centre of the island

TOURISM

Tourism came to Bali much earlier than to Lombok *(see p51)* and is far more developed here. On both islands there is awareness of its economic importance. On Bali, it has created an almost urban density in Kuta and Sanur; this is increasingly the situation in Ubud too, and density of road traffic is also now a problem. On Lombok, tourism is concentrated on the fertile west coast around Senggigi and the unspoilt Gili Isles *(see p156)*. The south coast of Lombok has splendid beaches that are still relatively pristine, although extensive development there is planned around the village also called Kuta *(see p162)*, where tourism is still on a small scale. For most travellers, even from outside Indonesia, access to Lombok is mainly by way of Bali.

Despite sporadic internal disturbances associated with broader political changes in Indonesia, Bali and Lombok remain places where social harmony is greatly prized and visitors are regarded as welcome guests.

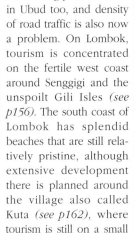

The rural landscape of Central Bali

Landscape and Wildlife of Bali and Lombok

Bali and Lombok have a rich flora and fauna. Human activity, including agriculture and tourism, has caused some loss of habitat diversity. Nevertheless, large areas are still unspoilt, and some are officially protected. There are few places better for the nature-lover than Bali and Lombok, where conditions for walking and exploring range from arid mountain slopes and high natural forests to the margins of rivers and rice-fields and the seashore.

Tree frog, common in Lombok

Giant golden orb weaver, common in lowland areas

FORESTS

Much of Bali and Lombok was once covered in forest, including large areas of lowland rainforest. Much has been destroyed; causes include volcanic eruptions, coffee and coconut cultivation and collection of firewood. Lush forests still grow on Bali's southern and western mountain slopes. On the drier, northern slopes the forest is deciduous.

VOLCANIC PEAKS

After volcanic ash is deposited by an eruption, centuries pass before the formation of soil capable of sustaining a rich plant life. However, the slopes are soon colonized by mosses, grasses and ferns, and there is a diverse bird life. On the arid northern and eastern slopes grows a grassland vegetation often punctuated by lontar palms.

The long-tailed macaque *monkey is often seen in forests, on roadsides and around temples.*

The mountain white-eye *gathers in treetops, uttering a characteristic high-pitched call.*

The helmeted friar bird *inhabits the arid mountain areas of Lombok.*

The black-winged starling *is an endangered species that lives in the deciduous forests of northwest Bali, as well as in open grasslands.*

The senduduk flower, *with its exotic pink petals, is found in mountain scrub.*

WALLACE'S LINE

Alfred Russel Wallace (1823–1913), a British naturalist, noted differences between the wildlife of the former tectonic landmasses of Asia and Australia – marked by a line that passes between Bali and Lombok at its southern extremity. The Australian group includes birds of paradise, and species such as the orange-banded thrush, which is seen in Lombok but not in Bali. The Asian group includes monkeys and the tiger (the latter last seen in Bali in the 1930s). Another example is the fulvous-breasted woodpecker, more often seen in Bali than in Lombok.

Orange-banded thrush

Wallace's Line

RIVERS AND RICEFIELDS

Some 150 rivers flow through the gorges of Bali and Lombok, assisting irrigation of the rice crops. Here birds, frogs, toads and spiders can live on planthoppers and other small pests which cause damage to the rice itself. The birds include egrets, herons, ducks and small finches.

The Java sparrow, *a red-billed native of Java and Bali, is found around river gorges and ricefields.*

Toads *live in damp habitats such as ricefields; here they survive on a diet of insects, including grasshoppers, beetles and crickets.*

COASTLINES

The beaches, coral reefs and shallow waters around these islands support a huge variety of marine life, even in developed areas such as Sanur. Although little true mangrove forest remains, mangroves still absorb the force of waves, helping to reduce coastal erosion.

The lionfish, *while visually attractive, is poisonous to touch. It lives in waters off the smaller islands around Bali.*

The green turtle *is endangered; it is hunted for its meat, sometimes used in Balinese ritual.*

Rice Cultivation

Rice goddess

The mountain lakes, the gentle climate and the volcano-enriched soils of Bali and Lombok are ideally suited for the growing of rice (*Oryza sativa*). Although some of the islands' rice-farming land is being converted to other uses, terraced ricefields are still the dominant feature of the rural landscape, and the cult and cultivation of rice remain much as they were in Neolithic times. Steep terrain makes mechanization difficult and poses a particular problem for "wet rice farming" – water flows far below the arable land, in deep river gorges. The Balinese solution, which dates from as early as the 9th century AD, is an ingenious and complex network of irrigation channels, tunnels and aqueducts that diverts water from sources high up in the mountains to water-sharing communities known as *subak*.

Padi Bali *is the generic term for several strains of traditionally grown rice, a tall, strong plant with a growing cycle of 210 days.*

The paddy field *is a basin of packed earth reinforced with intertwining grassroots. Irrigation water is let in and out of each field individually through a small gap in the earthen wall that can be opened or closed with a hoe. The water is drained off through channels that empty into rivers.*

Rice plants nearing full growth

RICEFIELD CEREMONIES

Across the island of Bali and among traditional farmers in Lombok, offerings are made in the ricefields at significant stages of the rice-growing cycle. These rituals reflect the central importance of rice cultivation in the traditional life of the islands. The most elaborate ricefield ceremony takes place when the rice grain begins to form on the stalk. A small shrine to honour Dewi Sri, the rice goddess (see p25), is built by the farmers in a corner of their ricefields and decorated with handmade palm-leaf festoons.

Bamboo shrines where offerings are given to the rice goddess

The rice barn, *once a common feature of houses in Lombok and Bali, is where sheaves of the older strains of rice are stored. The grain is threshed by hand as needed. These buildings are less frequently seen than in the past.*

Coconut, banana and bamboo grow along high ridges above the river valleys, concealing small village communities

RICE TERRACES

Bali's terraced ricefields have been described as an "engineered landscape", a collaboration between nature and human beings. Terracing allows rice to be planted on steep slopes and protects the land from erosion. Each terrace is irrigated by a complex series of channels, controlled by small dams.

River gorges can often be seen below rice terraces.

THE RICE-GROWING CYCLE

1. Rice seed *is planted in a protected bed. While the seedlings mature, farmers prepare the fields.*

2. The planting basin *is prepared by flooding, ploughing and levelling the field.*

3. Seedlings are transplanted *into flooded fields by hand. As the plants mature, the fields are alternately flooded and dried at specific stages to maximize growth, and they are periodically weeded.*

4. Harvesting *is done by women, who cut the stalks with a small knife concealed in their palms so as not to frighten the rice goddess.*

5. High-yield varieties of rice *are threshed directly in the fields and put in bags to be taken to a rice mill. Older strains of rice are kept on the cut stalks and gathered into bundles to be stored in a rice barn until needed.*

6. After harvest, *fields are burned off, producing a soil-protecting alkaline ash.*

The Islands' Religions

The majority of the Balinese are Hindu. Most of the Sasaks, the indigenous people of Lombok, practise orthodox Islam. However, permeating religious practice on Bali and Lombok are animistic beliefs and a sense of the supernatural *(see p24)*. Ancient agricultural and mountain cults are reflected in temple and village architecture, and in rural rituals. There are Muslim and Christian minorities in Bali's towns and coastal areas and a smaller number of Buddhists.

Temple offerings *are a prominent aspect of Hindu observance in Bali* (see pp38–9).

TRACES OF ANCIENT CULTS

In architecture and ritual practice, the forms and beliefs of prehistoric Indonesian societies are still visible today in modern Hindu Bali and the traditions of rural Lombok.

Temple shrine

A temple *in stepped-pyramid form suggests that a site predates Hindu times.*

Rice cult image made from palm leaves

A shrine *at the grave of folk hero Jayaprana, near Labuhan Lalang* (see p138), *draws petitioners for supernatural favours.*

HINDUISM

Balinese Hinduism has elements not only of the Shivaite cult, but also of animism and Buddhism. Deities are believed to visit the human realm on ritual occasions. Temples hold *odalan* (anniversary festivals), during which gods are honoured with offerings, music and dance *(see pp38–9)*.

Offerings of palm leaf and flowers

Sprinkler made of grass

Consecrated rice grains

Holy water, *the medium of the gods, is sprinkled on offerings and distributed along with rice grains to worshippers after prayers.*

Villagers carrying a temple effigy in a portable "ancestral spirit house" during a temple festival

ISLAM

Most people on Lombok are Muslims. Like the majority of Indonesians, they follow a traditional form of Islam which often incorporates underlying folk traditions. In some of the more isolated parts of the island, the Sasaks adhere to a form of Islam known as Wetu Telu, mixing Islamic beliefs with pre-Islamic, indigenous and Hindu-Buddhist elements. Like Balinese Hinduism, Wetu Telu ascribes great powers to the spirits that dwell within nature.

Many Muslims *in Bali and Lombok can be seen wearing the traditional* peci *cap, particularly on Friday, the day of prayer.*

A village mosque in Lombok

BUDDHISM

Although certain Buddhist cults flourished in Bali at around AD1000, it was not until late in the 20th century that mainstream Buddhism gained any significant presence here. Buddhists are still a small minority.

A gilded Buddha *dominates the interior of the Brahma Vihara Ashrama monastery, Banjar* (see p139).

CHRISTIANITY

Small communities of Protestants and Catholics are to be found in West Bali, where they resettled after conversion by missionaries in the early 20th century. Many Balinese people of Chinese descent are Christian.

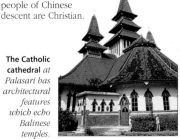

The Catholic cathedral *at Palasari has architectural features which echo Balinese temples.*

RELIGION IN COMMUNITY RITUALS

In Bali and Lombok religion plays a part in rituals such as weddings, funerals and coming-of-age ceremonies, which require the participation of an entire village *(see pp28–9)*. In Muslim Lombok, the most festive rituals are circumcision rites, undergone by boys around the age of eleven.

This palanquin (ceremonial litter) is in the form of a painted lion.

A gilded offering bowl holds ritual implements.

Hindu high priests *conduct a ceremony as part of the preparation for a royal cremation.*

At a circumcision rite, *a Sasak Muslim boy is paraded through the streets.*

Traditional Beliefs

Animism and ancestor worship are a strong undercurrent in Balinese life, even in local Hindu observance. The Balinese term *sekala niskala* ("visible-invisible") sums up the idea that the physical world is penetrated by a spirit world. The spirits, loosely described as "gods" and "demons", are honoured almost everywhere with offerings made of flowers and other materials. The invisible world is represented in many vivid symbols. Ancestors are deified in complex rituals and venerated at domestic and clan temples *(see p26).*

Temple statue

Figure of Rangda at Puri Saren, Ubud's royal palace *(see p90)*

ANIMISM

Large stones, trees and other powerful-looking natural objects are believed to be favoured dwellings for invisible beings. To keep these spirits content, a shrine or small temple may be erected for them. *Buta kala* (ground spirits) are demonic energies that cluster at crossroads, graveyards, rivers, in certain trees, or wherever there is an important life event such as a birth, a death or an accident. They are appeased with offerings that contain meat or strong drink.

Keris (dagger)

Parasols indicate that a deity is present.

The effigy of the god is presented with offerings.

Guardian spirits reside in demonic statues.

Objects *such as daggers and consecrated masks are seen as imbued with great spiritual power, and can give rise to trance possession.*

A shrine by a sacred tree, decorated on holy days when holy water and offerings are placed here

MAGIC

Fear of the supernatural feeds a widespread fear of witchcraft. Practitioners of Balinese "black" and "white" magic may engage invisible powers such as *buta kala* (ground spirits) to heal or harm. Household offerings are made to the spirits daily.

Daily flower offerings known as *canang*

A *tumbal,* a type of magical drawing often prepared by a witch doctor, is shown as protecting a man against the influence of a *buta,* or spirit.

Tumbal (Magical Amulet) (1938) by Anak Agung Gede Sobrat, Ubud

THE RICE GODDESS

The Hindu goddess of prosperity, Dewi Sri, became identified in Bali with the rice spirit of local belief, and she is honoured in the fields, the granary and the rice basket. Her image in offerings and textiles is known as the *cili* motif. According to tradition, after the daily meal has been cooked, tiny rice offerings must be set out before food can be consumed.

Bamboo shrines are built in the fields to honour the rice goddess during the growing cycle.

Offerings are consecrated with holy water.

Wooden ornament with *cili* motif representing the head of the rice goddess

BARONG AND RANGDA

The dragon-like Barong (representing order, harmony and health) and his demonic counterpart Rangda (associated with chaos, illness and harm) are guardian effigies. They are periodically "awakened" to restore the spiritual balance of a village by means of a ritual battle culminating in wild trance. Devotees of the Barong attack Rangda with their *keris* daggers. Rangda's power turns the daggers against the attackers; the Barong's power prevents the blades from piercing their bare skin.

Rangda, identifiable by her fangs, striped breasts and necklace of entrails

The Barong's beard is made of human hair.

The magical power *of the Barong and Rangda is concentrated in their masks, which are kept in a village temple and given offerings.*

"HIGH" AND "LOW" SPIRITS

The Balinese believe that human beings can help keep "high" and "low" spirits in balance through making ritual offerings to both. For the Balinese, the universe is dualistic in nature, a play of ever-shifting opposites. This opposition is symbolized by the black-and-white checked textile known as *poleng*, in which statues and other objects thought to be magically charged are often wrapped.

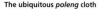

The ubiquitous *poleng* cloth

Guardian statues wrapped in *poleng* cloths, as often seen in Balinese temple forecourts

Balinese Temple Architecture

A Balinese *pura* (public temple) is a holy enclosure where Hindu deities are periodically invited to descend into *pratima* (effigies) kept in shrines. During *odalan* (festivals), temples are alive with music, dance and offerings *(see p.38)*. Otherwise they are rather quiet. Temples include the *kahyangan tiga* (the three village temples – *see pp28–9*), clan temples, market temples, irrigation temples, temples to nature deities, and "state" temples of former kingdoms. Temples are usually open to visitors during daylight hours.

The *padmasana* shrine *("lotus throne")*, in the most sacred corner of the temple, has an empty seat at the top open to the sky, signifying the Supreme God.

The *jeroan* (*inner courtyard*) has shrines to the temple's core deities and often to deities of the mountains, lakes and sea. It is often closed to visitors, but can usually be viewed from outside the walls.

The *bale gong* is a pavilion where ritual *gamelan* music may be played *(see p.32)*.

Pelinggih *are shrines or "seats" of the gods. The dark fibre used for the roof, which resembles human hair, is a product of the sugar palm.*

The *bale agung* is the village council pavilion.

The *kori agung* is a grand gateway usually reserved for gods and priests.

TEMPLE LAYOUT
The arrangement of Balinese temples follows a generally consistent pattern, with individual structures orientated along a mountain-sea axis. Degrees of sacredness are reflected in proximity to the mountain.

BALI'S MAIN TEMPLES

There are tens of thousands of temples on Bali, perhaps 200,000 including house temples. The locations of the most important ones are shown here. Visitors should observe temple etiquette *(see p219)*.

WHERE TO FIND THE PRINCIPAL TEMPLES

1. Besakih Temple Complex *(pp116–17)*
2. Pura Goa Lawah *(p108)*
3. Pura Kehen *(p104)*
4. Pura Luhur Uluwatu *(pp76–7)*
5. Pura Meduwe Karang *(pp148–9)*
6. Pura Taman Ayun *(pp130–31)*
7. Pura Tanah Lot *(p128)*
8. Pura Tirta Empul *(p99)*
9. Pura Ulun Danu Batur *(pp122–3)*

The *meru* shrine has 3, 5, 7, 9 or 11 tiers, depending on the importance of its deity. It symbolizes the Hindu holy Mount Meru, but can also represent other sacred peaks.

In the *jaba tengah* (middle courtyard) are secondary shrines and pavilions for a variety of practical purposes.

The *candi bentar* (split gate) is often used as a courtyard entrance. It represents the cosmic mountain split into the positive and negative forces of the universe.

The *kulkul* is a watchtower with a drum which is struck when deities are thought to descend to the temple.

Entrance

The *bale piasan* *is a sacred pavilion for placing religious offerings.*

Village Life

The Balinese village is one of the island's most visually distinctive features. It is essentially a religious community, organized around a core of temples. Village land is considered to be a bequest of the founding ancestors, who are worshipped as local deities. Private life is largely ruled by *adat* (village customary law). Every married couple is obliged to belong to the *banjar* (community association); among the *banjar*'s duties are funerary rites for village members. Not to belong to a *banjar* is to risk perdition in the afterlife.

Funerary rites *involve all village members, who will congregate in the spirit of* banjar suka duka *("together in happiness and woe").*

Village streets *are usually aligned with the mountain and the sea, an arrangement which the Balinese call* kaja-kelod *(mountainward-seaward).*

BALINESE VILLAGE LAYOUT

Traditional villages are orientated on a mountain-sea axis.

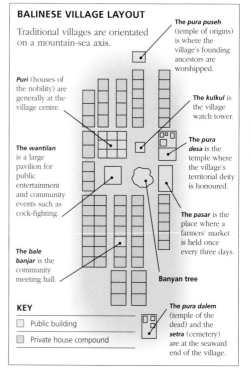

The *pura puseh* (temple of origins) is where the village's founding ancestors are worshipped.

Puri (houses of the nobility) are generally at the village centre.

The *kulkul* is the village watch tower.

The *wantilan* is a large pavilion for public entertainment and community events such as cock-fighting.

The *pura desa* is the temple where the village's territorial deity is honoured.

The *pasar* is the place where a farmers' market is held once every three days.

The *bale banjar* is the community meeting hall.

Banyan tree

KEY

☐ Public building

▨ Private house compound

The *pura dalem* (temple of the dead) and the *setra* (cemetery) are at the seaward end of the village.

The slit-log drum *in the* kulkul *tower summons* banjar *members to village duty, announces a death, and serves traditionally as a general alarm bell.*

The warung, *a family-run coffee-stall-cum-mini-shop, is at the heart of village social life, although it has no special location.*

A VILLAGE HOUSE COMPOUND

Village land is divided into uniform residential plots or compounds enclosed on all sides by a wall of clay or brick. Living quarters are enclosed pavilions for sleeping and storage, with large verandahs for work and socializing. The courtyards are generally floored with packed earth, and kept free of vegetation except perhaps for a few ornamental flowers or a decorative tree. Most compounds house extended families of the male line. They may not be sold. Upon the death of the occupant, if there is no heir the property reverts to the village.

A courtyard wall built of clay and capped with bamboo

Ancestors are honoured in the sanggah or merajan (house temple).

The **natah** (courtyard) is the symbolic centre of the domestic microcosm.

The **bale dangin** or *bale sakenam* ("eastern" open ceremonial pavilion) is used for rites of passage *(see p.38)*.

The **bale meten** is an enclosed pavilion for the household head or newly-weds.

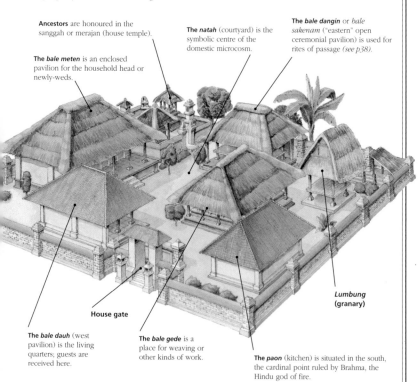

House gate

Lumbung (granary)

The **bale dauh** (west pavilion) is the living quarters; guests are received here.

The **bale gede** is a place for weaving or other kinds of work.

The **paon** (kitchen) is situated in the south, the cardinal point ruled by Brahma, the Hindu god of fire.

HOUSE GATES

The range of gates lining the narrow streets is one of the most striking features of a Balinese village. The gate is traditionally positioned towards the *kelod* (seaward, or downhill) end of the house compound. The degree of architectural elaboration generally reflects the material status of the family living in the house.

Simple house gate with *alang alang* grass thatch

Gate with tiled roof and minimal decoration

Gate with decorated roof and brickwork

Traditional Dance and Drama

The roots of Balinese dance are trance ritual and the Javanese theatrical forms known as *wayang*. Various performances take place at religious ceremonies, often late at night and several hours long. Shorter versions are put on for visitors in more convenient circumstances. In Lombok, the dances of the Sasak are ritual performances,

Wayang kulit shadow puppet

often involving men in competition or combat. Islam has favoured literary rather than performing arts, one reason why dance is less common in Lombok than in Bali.

Arja *is a dance-opera in which choreography, music, costume and singing styles are strictly defined for twelve core character roles.*

THEATRICAL PERFORMANCE

Various forms of dance and drama can be seen at the annual Bali Arts Festival *(see p41)*. Some tell a story; some are non-representational. Modern genres such as *sendratari* often contain elements of older traditions.

Servant-clowns   **Stage entrance**   **Offerings**

The oleg tambulilingan, *a dance created in the 1950s, is performed to the accompaniment of the Gong Kebyar gamelan orchestra (see p32).*

Noble hero

Sendratari *was devised in the 1960s as an art form without ritual function. The name is a contraction of the words for "art", "drama", and "dance".*

RITUAL AND TRANCE

Ritual-based performances range from dances performed for temple deities to complex dramas. They often contain elements of trance *(see p24)*. Even trance dances for visitors require ritual offerings.

Baris gede *is an old ritual dance performed by a regiment of soldiers to protect the deities.*

Kecak *is based on a* sanghyang *(trance) chorus formerly used in times of epidemic.*

MASK AND PUPPET THEATRE

Bali evolved its own style of the Javanese *wayang kulit* puppet theatre and *wayang wong* masked dance drama. Both are vehicles for the Indian epics *Mahabharata* and *Ramayana*. In *topeng*, the performer changes masks and costumes to show different characters.

Masks are often carved by the dancer.

Wayang kulit *(shadow puppet theatre) uses flat leather puppets which cast shadows on a screen. The puppet master manipulates the puppets with sticks.*

Servant-clowns interpret the Kawi (Old Javanese) speech of "high characters".

Topeng dancers *recount genealogical histories of dynasties through a series of masks. Players may be a troupe of three or more, or may perform solo.*

Servant-clowns *in topeng amuse the audience and make moral commentaries.*

Wayang kulit *characters are distinguished by headdress and manner of speech. These are the "prince" and the "demon".*

Wayang wong *characters wear masks and move like puppets. This is Garuda, a mythical bird.*

SASAK DANCES

In Lombok, the performing arts reflect both indigenous Sasak rites and Balinese traditions. Dances in Lombok are very often accompanied by drums; they often consist of a sequence of energetic movements alternating with slower actions and graceful poses. *Peresehan*, a dance which is often performed for festivals, is the ritual enactment of a duel between two Sasak warriors.

Peresehan, a traditional fight using poles and shields made of rattan.

Puspawresti *is a modern creation inspired by rejang. A dance addressed to the gods, rejang is performed by females, usually either young or past child-bearing age.*

Musical Instruments of Bali and Lombok

In Bali and parts of Lombok, traditional music is performed by a *gamelan* orchestra. This is a percussion ensemble consisting largely of bronze metallophones (instruments with tuned metal keys), led by drums; there are a few wind and stringed instruments. The music is based on rhythmic and melodic cycles punctuated by gongs. Many orchestras play for tourists. Most villages in Bali own at least one set of *gamelan* instruments for ritual occasions. Some sets are considered sacred and are played only during religious ceremonies.

Cengceng cymbals

The gamelan tingklik, *with bamboo keys, accompanies traditional dances.*

INSTRUMENTS OF THE GAMELAN

Most of the orchestra is made up of pairs of metallophones, which are tuned to a very slight but precise dissonance which gives the *gamelan* its piercing, shimmering sound. Each *gamelan* has its own unique internal tuning; instruments are not interchangeable between orchestras.

Bamboo resonators amplify sounds made by the bronze keys.

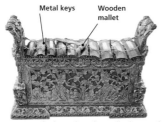

Metal keys   **Wooden mallet**

Gangsa, *which are keyed metallophones of various sizes, are played in syncopation to create a complex melodic texture.*

A pair *of "male" and "female" kendang (drums) conduct the orchestra.*

Bronze material is recycled from old gongs to make new ones.

Carved *pelawah* (instrument stands) are custom-designed for each orchestra.

GONGS

Bronze gongs of various sizes form the heart of the *gamelan* orchestra. They are struck with padded mallets or sticks to produce resonant sounds which punctuate the melodies made by keyed instruments.

Carved wooden frame

Pot gong

Kemong gong   *Kempur*   *Kempli*   *Gong Ageng*

Balaganjur, *a walking orchestra of cymbals and drums, has an exciting, crashing sound intended to scare off evil spirits in its path.*

DRUMS IN LOMBOK

Drums play an important role in the music of Lombok. The island's main musical traditions reflect Hindu-Buddhist forms which originated in Java and Bali, and others which developed from the traditions of Islam.

Kendang beleq ("big drum") at a cultural festival in Lombok

Celebration of a special occasion with the aid of drums

The use of drums and ceremonial dress at a wedding

The **terompong** is a series of inverted kettle gongs played by a single musician.

The **reyong** is a row of small gongs played by a group of two, three or four musicians.

THE GAMELAN ORCHESTRA

The Gong Kebyar is Bali's most popular and most complex form of *gamelan*. Its sound has been described as a "cascade of blazing gold".

Large bamboo musical instruments *are used by* gamelan jegog *orchestras, a type of ensemble associated particularly with West Bali.*

Suling *are bamboo flutes of various degrees of thickness and length. The players use a special breathing technique to produce a continuous stream of sound.*

Balinese Painting

Balinese art is a rich tradition very much alive today, especially in the villages of the Ubud-Mas-Batuan area of Central Bali. During the 20th century the influence of Westerners *(see p88)* was a factor in Balinese painting. However, themes and images still show traces of Bali's Javanese heritage, including Indian themes which pre-date the arrival of Islam in Java *(see p45)*. In the late 20th century, when some artists were educated in academies, what is known generally as "modern art" began to appear.

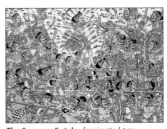

The "wayang" style *dominated pre-colonial painting; this anonymous canvas from Kamasan dates from the 19th century.*

One of the most gifted *Balinese artists of the mid-20th century was I Gusti Nyoman Lempad, who created expressive and stylized works such as* The Tantri Stories (1939). *Lempad took the art of drawing in Bali to new heights.*

Garuda, the mythical bird

A busy market scene

THE IDIOT BELOG WHO BECAME KING

The Batuan style, as in this work painted by Ida Bagus Made Togog in 1932, is typical of much Balinese painting in its full occupation of the canvas, repetition of patterned iconographic elements, fine detail and slightly monochromatic quality. Balinese painters often tell a story by showing scenes of everyday life. The basis of this story is not known.

REGIONAL STYLES

The Pita Maha association, which was centred around Ubud, led to the creation of the "Ubud Style". This stimulated the emergence of other local styles, such as that of Sanur in the south. The villages of Pengosekan and Penestanan, though both in the Ubud area, also developed distinct artistic identities.

The Community of Artists *in Pengosekan uses subtle colours, as in I Dewa Nyoman Batuan's* Cosmic Circle (1975).

The Sanur School *flourished in the 1930s.* Fighting Horses *(undated) by I Gusti Ketut Rundu is essentially decorative rather than narrative in nature.*

MODERN ART IN BALI

Academic art education has introduced a different, more analytical approach to Balinese art. Some painters have opted for academic realism; others have chosen a modernist look. I Nyoman Gunarsa combines the free brushstrokes of American Expressionism with exotic Balinese themes, such as traditional dancers and *wayang* figures. Painters such as Made Wianta and Nyoman Erawan have also produced art which is modern yet at the same time strongly Balinese in feeling.

Three Dancers (1981) by I Nyoman Gunarsa

A battle scene provides a sharp contrast to the peaceful scenes of daily life shown in the rest of the painting.

The Pita Maha *association was founded in 1936 by Cokorda Gede Agung Sukawati and European painters Walter Spies and Rudolf Bonnet. It encouraged local artists to create non-religious art using their own imaginative resources.*

The river at the centre of the painting gives it a strong graphic structure.

Farmers are shown working with their cows in the ricefields.

The Ubud Style, *as in* Balinese Stone-Craftsmen Working *(1957) by I Nyoman Madia, is characterized by themes of daily life and a way of showing anatomy influenced by Rudolf Bonnet.*

The Young Artists School *of Penestanan, influenced by Dutch artist Arie Smit, typically uses bright colours, as seen here in* Jayaprana Ceremony *(1972) by I Nyoman Kerip.*

Crafts and Textiles

Gold- and silversmithing, stone carving, wood-carving and weaving are all crafts that have survived from the age of Bali's opulent kingdoms. Today, a thriving handicraft industry produces goods mainly for tourism and export. Crafts are generally practised in specialist villages, and Bali is an important market for goods made on other Indonesian islands. Lombok has a long tradition of domestic pottery, and produces colourful handwoven textiles *(see p161).*

Garudas (mythical birds) carved in wood and painted in the villages around Ubud

CARVED ARCHITECTURAL ELEMENTS

The virtuoso carving of architectural elements, still practised today in Bali, blurs the distinction between crafts and fine arts. The works of craftsmen can be seen adorning many temples, palaces and houses; an industry has also developed producing items for general decoration.

Chinese-inspired motifs *decorate this door in Puri Agung (see p112), the work of Chinese artisans in the 19th century.*

Wall ornamentation *such as this example from Pura Tirta Empul (see p99) is carved from volcanic stone (paras).*

Wooden mallet and locally forged chisel

Stone sculpture *is a thriving industry as a consequence of strong local demand in the restoration of Bali's temples.*

LOMBOK POTTERY

Renowned for its simple designs and fine craftsmanship, Lombok pottery is made using simple, age-old techniques and fired in straw on open ground. Sasak women have been making pottery since the 14th century, when the skill was probably introduced by Majapahit migrants. Among Lombok's most prominent pottery villages are Penujak *(see p161),* Banyumulek *(see p154)* and Masbagik Timur.

Domestic pottery, *such as this water jar, is widely used in Lombok households for storage, cooking and bathing.*

Forms are built by hand.

Clay material comes from local riverbeds.

Lombok pottery, ranging from a terracotta colour to rich reddish-brown and black

ARTSHOP WARE

A large cottage industry has grown up in Bali, based on craft work. It provides employment to thousands of rural families who can no longer make a living by farming. The level of skill demonstrated by a sizeable part of the Balinese population is remarkable. Some craftsmen have an "artshop" in their home.

Painted wooden trinkets

Lacquer-painted baskets woven in Bali

Basketware *is widely made in Lombok using rattan, grass, bamboo and lontar. Designs vary between villages. Sometimes palm leaves are used for smaller boxes.*

Gold and silver *are imported to Bali from other islands and worked by members of the metal-smithing Pande clan.*

TRADITIONAL HANDWOVEN TEXTILES

The most common textiles are *endek* or warp *ikat* (made by dyeing the threads before weaving) and the more costly *songket* (gold tapestries). The Balinese are the only weavers in Southeast Asia to master double *ikat*, in the form of *geringsing* made in the village of Tenganan *(see pp110–11)*. Most of this work is woven on simple backstrap looms in the home.

The traditional hand-operated loom *is supported by the weaver who leans back to maintain the tension of the threads. Very complex pieces can take years to complete.*

Silk sarong made in North Bali in the 19th century, showing a mythological story enacted by shadow puppets

Detail of flower motif, part of a *geringsing* from Tenganan

Prada, a gold-painted fabric made in Bali

The rich design of *songket*, with a pattern of gold or silver thread

Festivals and Holy Days

Bali's holy days, often the occasion for extravagant celebrations, are calculated according to either a lunar calendar or the 210-day Balinese calendar. *Odalan* (temple festivals) are the anniversary celebrations of particular temples. There is almost always a temple festival taking place somewhere. Rites of passage and other religious holidays are mostly celebrated with guests at home in the family temple. Outsiders may watch more public occasions such as *odalan* and even cremations, provided they show due respect.

The ingredients *of offerings include palm leaves, flowers, fruit and other foodstuffs.*

Female devotees are dressed with a ceremonial waist sash and flowers for the occasion.

Offerings *are made by the women in the household. This skill is passed from mother to daughter. Older women are highly respected as* tukang banten *(offerings experts).*

TEMPLE FESTIVALS

At an *odalan,* the deities of a temple are honoured with offerings, prayers, and entertainment. Temples sometimes strike the visitor as rather quiet places, but they come alive during temple festivals, which generally last three days. The whole occasion has a carnival atmosphere, and demands elaborate preparations. All village members contribute labour and materials.

Male devotees, shown here praying, wear a white formal costume which includes a white headcloth.

In a Balinese cremation, *the corpse is placed in an animal-shaped sarcophagus.*

BALINESE RITES OF PASSAGE

Rites of passage ease a soul along the cycle which runs from before birth to after death. A person's *oton* is his or her birthdate on the Balinese calendar, and so occurs once every 210 days. A child's first and third *oton* are usually lavish occasions. A tooth-filing ceremony, in which the front teeth are filed even, marks the coming-of-age of an adolescent. A wedding ceremony takes place in the family home of the groom, where a high priest conducts prayers; a ritual bath is followed by a feast. A ritual cremation usually involves elaborate preparations by the community.

This guardian statue *has been elaborately decorated with flowers, cloth and offerings in preparation for a temple festival.*

Offerings are brought by worshippers from home and placed on a special platform.

The Balinese Calendar, each day represented by an appropriate image

THE BALINESE CALENDAR

Certain Balinese holy days are calculated according to the complex 210-day *pawukon* calendar. This is made up of 30 seven-day *wuku* (weeks), along with nine other overlapping *wewaran* (cycles) of different lengths. The most common *wewaran* are the three-day "market" cycle, the five-day cycle and the seven-day cycle. Many festivals fall when these cycles cross.

Saraswati and Renewal of the Cycle: On the last day of the 210-day cycle, Saraswati, the goddess of learning, is worshipped. Certain books are honoured with offerings laid on them and sprinkled with holy water. Children make offerings at school while adults bring gifts to healers and traditional teachers.

Banyu Penaruh: The first day of the 210-day cycle is one of ritual cleansing with holy water, usually at a spring temple or at the house of a high priest.

Pagerwesi: This is a day for spiritual strengthening; it is celebrated elaborately in North Bali with *penjor* and feasting as at Galungan. The name means literally "fence of iron".

Tumpek: Once every 35 days, offerings are made to specific categories of valued things, such as metal objects, trees, books, musical instruments, livestock and *wayang* puppets; in modern Bali, motorcycles, cars, computers and refrigerators may be included. There are six Tumpek days in the 210-day calendrical cycle.

Devotees receiving holy water during a religious festival

Decorated bamboo poles *known as* penjor *adorn Bali's village streets at Galungan.*

GALUNGAN AND KUNINGAN

Galungan occurs every 210 days, in the 11th week of the cycle. This holiday celebrates the creation of the universe. A period of festivity culminates ten days later in Kuningan, the Balinese "All Saints' Day".

BALI AND LOMBOK
THROUGH THE YEAR

The seasons in North Bali, South Bali and Lombok do not coincide precisely. In very broad terms the coastal areas are generally drier than those at higher altitudes. Any particular day can often differ from place to place: the situation in Ubud may well be different from that in Sanur. For precise dates of religious holidays and cultural festivals, visitors should check with tourist information offices

Buffalo racing in Negara, at its best from July to October

or consult the Internet – and be prepared for slight discrepancies. Many temples have festivals on the *purnama* (full moon). A few are mentioned below. The high season runs through July and August; the long weekends around Chinese New Year, Easter, Christmas and New Year are also particularly crowded. If you plan to travel then, book well in advance and expect to pay higher rates for accommodation.

***Ogoh-ogoh* (demonic effigies) in a Nyepi procession in April**

DRY SEASON

From April to October, occasional rain is normal. July and August are relatively cool and pleasant months, and nights in the highlands can even be chilly.

APRIL

Nyepi *(Mar/Apr)*. Falls on the day after the ninth new moon. At midday on the eve of Nyepi, massive offerings are set out at major crossroads; they are believed to have the power to exorcise evil spirits. That evening, there are noisy torchlit processions of huge *ogoh-ogoh* (demonic effigies). These are created each year by village youth groups, who compete to

make them as frightening, funny or outrageous as they can. At the end of the festivities, the effigies are burned.

On Nyepi itself, the Day of Silence, no one is allowed to go out on the street and no lights may be lit, until 6am the following day.

The growing impact of tourism and modern lifestyle on religious culture has caused some Balinese to become increasingly scrupulous about keeping the Day of Silence. Visitors are expected to observe these restrictions and remain indoors in their hotels. Special arrangements are made to look after guests, and sometimes include them in the festivities on the eve of Nyepi. During this 24-hour period airline travel is

suspended and Bali's international airport is closed. Travellers should check for details ahead of time.

Purnama Kedasa *(two weeks after Nyepi)*. To mark this, the full moon of the tenth month, there are large festivals at important Balinese temples, especially at Besakih *(see pp116–17)*, Pura Ulun Danu Batur *(see pp122–3)* and Pura Samuan Tiga *(see p87)*. These are opportunities to see offerings, music and sacred dance in their full cultural context.

MAY

Waisak *(Apr/May)*. The small Buddhist community of Bali visits the few Buddhist temples of the island on this holiday, which takes place

Balinese worshippers at a temple festival at Pura Taman Ayun

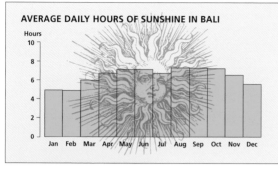

AVERAGE DAILY HOURS OF SUNSHINE IN BALI

Hours

Sunshine Chart
The island of Lombok typically receives about an hour less sunshine each day compared to Bali. Daylight hours are fairly constant throughout the year on both islands as they are close to the equator.

The annual Bali Kite Festival in South Bali

on the day of the full moon usually in May, according to the Buddhist lunar calendar.
Purnama Desta *(full moon).* Hindu temple festival held at Pura Maospahit in Denpasar *(see p61),* and Pura Segara, near Ampenan on Lombok.

JUNE

Pesta Kesenian Bali (Bali Arts Festival) *(mid-June to mid-July),* Denpasar. The height of Bali's secular cultural calendar, this is a two to four-week jamboree of mostly Balinese (but increasingly international) dance, theatre, music and cultural events at the Taman Werdhi Budaya (Bali Arts Centre) *(see p61).* The dates and duration vary somewhat from year to year. The opening-day parade is a spectacular procession in which the participating troupes perform as they move through the city streets, sometimes even going into a state of trance.

JULY AND AUGUST

This is the high season for visitors from Europe and North America. It is also

thought to be an auspicious time for cremations.
Bali Kite Festival *(Jun–Aug),* South Bali. An annual, international event which draws participants from all over Southeast Asia and Japan, the Bali Kite Festival takes place at the time of year when winds are most suitable for kite-flying. The festival inspires children throughout the countryside; they construct kites from plastic bags or any other materials they can find, often decorating them too, and fly them from drying rice fields and village streets.
Indonesia's Independence Day *(17 Aug).* In the week leading up to Independence Day, which is marked by events throughout Indonesia, Bali's traffic may be held up by ranks of schoolchildren marching along the roads, in preparation for the military-inspired ceremonies held on the big day itself in the provincial capital, Denpasar.

Mekepung *(Jul–Oct, dates variable).* Buffalo races held in Negara *(see p134).* A more modest version is put on for visitors all year round.

SEPTEMBER

In September, the weather is hot and dry, bringing out flowers in profusion.
Purnama Katiga *(full moon).* Temple festival at the Gunung Kawi Royal Monuments at Tampaksiring in Central Bali *(see p99).*

OCTOBER

Purnama Kapat *(full moon).* Festivals at many major temples, including Besakih *(see pp116–17),* Pura Ulun Danu Batur *(see pp122–3),* Pura Tirta Empul *(see p99),* Pura Pulaki *(see p138)* and Pura Tegeh Koripan *(see p115).*
Hari Raya Sumpah Pemuda *(28 Oct).* A working day commemorating the independence movement. It has come to be associated with political reform in Bali and elsewhere in Indonesia.

Kuta Beach during the high season in July and August

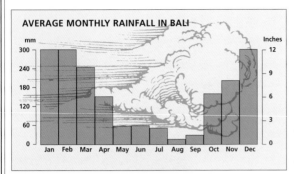

AVERAGE MONTHLY RAINFALL IN BALI

mm / Inches

300 — 12
240 — 9
180 — 6
120
60 — 3
0 — 0

Jan Feb Mar Apr May Jun Jul Aug Sep Oct Nov Dec

Rainfall Chart
The dry and rainy seasons fall in the same part of the year in both Bali and Lombok, although Bali experiences greater fluctuations in the amount of rainfall. The rainfall pattern has been somewhat distorted by the El Niño phenomenon in recent years.

Raindrops falling on an irrigated ricefield

RAINY SEASON

Monsoon weather brings rain from mid-October to mid-March, the wettest months being December and January. Several days of uninterrupted rain may be followed by a week without any rain at all. These are also the warmest months at the equator and rain brings relief from the heat. Sunny days during this period are hot and humid.

Bali and Lombok are not subject to typhoons, but in February there are normally a week or two of south-westerly wind and rain before the monsoon shifts direction and brings in cooler, drier weather from the northeast.

NOVEMBER TO DECEMBER

Purnama Kalima *(Nov)*. The full moon of the fifth month of the Hindu calendar is the occasion when Pura Kehen in Bangli *(see p104)* holds its temple festival.

The height of the rainy season comes in December

and January, when, according to local belief, people are at their most susceptible to illness. During this period many villages hold *melasti* processions, carrying statues of gods to the sea or to holy springs.

Purnama Kenam *(Dec)*. On the full moon of the sixth month, the temple festival takes place at Pura Lingsar in Lombok.

Siwa Latri *(Dec–Jan)*. "Shiva's Rite" is celebrated by Balinese Hindus two weeks after Purnama Kena, on the night before the seventh dark moon *(Tilem Kapitu)*. It involves a 24-hour vigil, usually held in a temple.

FEBRUARY TO MARCH

Chinese New Year *(Jan/Feb)*. Crowds of Chinese come to Bali from Singapore and Jakarta. Following the liberalization of government policy towards Indonesia's religious minorities, this holiday is likely to become increasingly characterized by Chinese ritual ceremonies. Like the Eve of Nyepi *(see p40)*, the Chinese New Year is celebrated with great fanfare, particularly in Denpasar.

Bau Nyale *(Feb)*. Sasak courtship rites take place on Kuta beach *(see p162)* in South Lombok, on the appearance of the *nyale* sea-worm, a traditional symbol of fertility.

Purnama Kesanga *(Feb/Mar)*. The temple festival of Pura Penataran Sasih in Pejeng *(see p97)*, near Ubud, takes place on the day of the full moon.

A street procession at a Muslim festival

Hindus praying during a temple festival at Pura Taman Pule in Mas

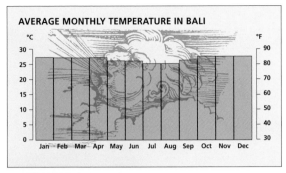

AVERAGE MONTHLY TEMPERATURE IN BALI

°C
30
25
20
15
10
5
0

Jan Feb Mar Apr May Jun Jul Aug Sep Oct Nov Dec

°F
90
80
70
60
50
40
30

Temperature Chart
Bali has an average temperature which is higher than Lombok by about one degree Celsius. Temperatures on Bali and Lombok fluctuate only marginally throughout the year, but it is generally cooler in the hill regions than in the areas near the coast.

Moving a musical gong in preparation for celebrating Galungan in Ubud

Calendar *(see p39)*. The most important of these is Galungan, which occurs in the 11th week. The whole of Bali is festively decorated, and people dress up in their best finery. Kuningan follows ten days after Galungan, on a Saturday, and marks the end of the holiday period. The day after Kuningan is Manis Kuningan, a big day for temple festivals at Pura Sakenan on Pulau Serangan, and Pura Taman Pule in Mas.

BALINESE HOLY DAYS

Between the major religious holidays and annual temple festivals, the 12-month lunar calendar is the framework for regular ritual celebrations and religious observance.

On the *tilem* (new moon) and *purnama* (full moon) of each month, special offerings are prepared and presented within the household and at local public temples.

The monthly celebration of *purnama* is particularly lively at certain "state" temples, such as the Pura Jagatnatha in Denpasar, Pura Kehen in Bangli and other regional capitals. It is marked by performances of shadow puppet theatre and readings of sacred poetry.

Other festivals are based on the 210-day Balinese

RAMADAN – MUSLIM MONTH OF FASTING

During Ramadan, the ninth month of the Islamic calendar, Muslims refrain from eating, drinking and smoking from dawn to dusk. Visitors to Lombok should avoid these activities in public in Ramadan.

At the end of Ramadan is **Idul Fitri**, a two-day holiday. Most Muslims return to their villages, causing massive air, sea and land traffic throughout the country.

Greeting cards for the Muslim festival of Idul Fitri

PUBLIC HOLIDAYS

New Year's Day (1 Jan)

Nyepi (Hindu New Year; 23 Mar 2012, 12 Mar 2013)

Hari Paskah (Good Friday/ Easter; 6 Apr 2012, 29 Mar 2013)

Hari Waisak (Buddhist holy day; 28 May 2012, 17 May 2013)

Ascension of Christ (17 May 2012, 9 May 2013)

Hari Proklamasi Kemer-dekaan (Independence Day; 17 Aug)

Christmas Day (25 Dec)

Hindu holidays based on Balinese 210-day calendar:

Galungan (1 Feb and 29 Aug 2012, 27 Mar and 23 Oct 2013)

Kuningan (11 Feb and 8 Sep 2012, 6 Apr and 2 Nov 2013)

Saraswati (16 Jun 2012, 12 Jan and 10 Aug 2013)

Muslim holidays based on Islamic 354- or 355-day calendar:

Idul Adha (26 Oct 2012, 15 Oct 2013)

Maulid Nabi Muhammed (4 Feb 2012, 24 Jan 2013)

Isra Miraj Nabi Muhammed Date varies

Idul Fitri (19 Aug 2012, 8 Aug 2013)

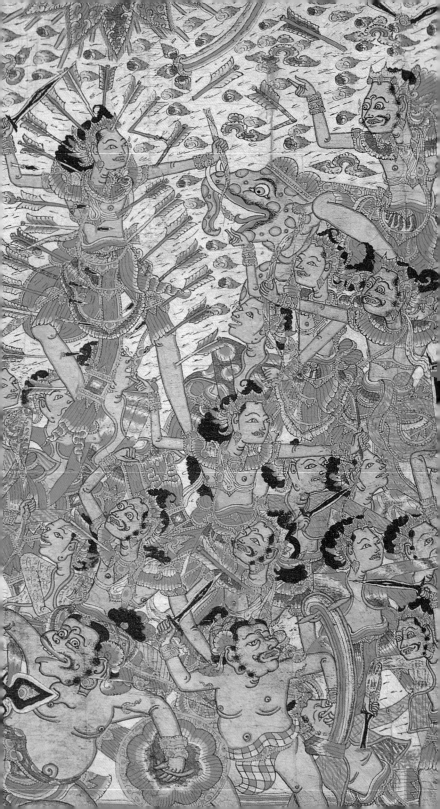

THE HISTORY OF BALI AND LOMBOK

*H*illtops and mountain gods are both prominent in Balinese legend. The landscape of the islands has deeply influenced their cultural, political and economic life for thousands of years. Old traditions have persisted remarkably, despite the successive impacts of colonialism, political strife and the travel industry.

The Balinese, and the Sasaks (the indigenous people of Lombok), are thought to be descendants of migrants from southern China who arrived around 2000 BC. Their legacy is believed to include the growing of rice as a staple crop, the craft of metal-working and the prevalence of mountain cults. These cultural traits, still clearly observable in traditional Balinese life today, suggest broad affinities with other peoples of Southeast Asia and the Pacific Ocean.

Keris (dagger) handle

EARLY KINGDOMS

There are few written records of Bali and Lombok before the 20th century, and none of Lombok before 1365; but ancient artifacts tell of Hindu kingdoms and the continuous influence of Java. An inscribed pillar in Belanjong, Sanur, dated to AD 914, implies that relations had been established before that date between Bali and the Buddhist Sanjaya dynasty of Central Java. In Central Bali there are relics of a Hindu-Buddhist kingdom, dating from the 10th–13th centuries, whose seat was near today's Pejeng and Bedulu. During the 11th century, the Gunung Kawi Royal Monuments

(see p99) were built in order to commemorate the king Anak Wungsu and his queen Betari Mandul. This king's edicts have been found in Sangsit on the north coast and as far as Klungkung in the south, implying that he was ruler of the entire island. Pura Tegeh Koripan *(see p115)* may have been built to venerate him. Anak Wungsu's reign, which began around 1025, was a period of close contact with Java. His mother was a Javanese princess; his father was the Balinese king Udayana; and his older brother was the great Airlangga, who ruled a large kingdom in East Java.

A contemporary of Anak Wungsu, Mpu Kuturan, is thought to have established the three-temple system common in Balinese villages *(see p28)*: the *pura puseh* (temple of origins), the *pura desa* (village temple), and the *pura dalem* (temple of the dead).

There was substantial Chinese influence in early Bali. *Kepeng* (Chinese coins) were in circulation from the 7th century onwards; the dragon-like Barong effigy *(see p25)* is thought to be of Chinese origin; and King Jayapangus of Bali married a Chinese princess in the 12th century.

TIMELINE

250,000 BC	10,000 BC	2,000 BC	1,000 BC	AD 1	AD 1000

250,000–10,000 BC
Upper Pleistocene era

Ancient pillar in Pura Belanjong, Sanur

AD 914 First written inscription, on a pillar in Pura Belanjong, of a Balinese royal name

2000 BC Migrations from China to Indonesia

Prehistoric bronze spearheads

AD 960 Holy spring temple of Pura Tirta Empul built

◁ **The Death of Abhimayu**, from the epic **Mahabharata**; late 19th century, Kamasan style (detail; artist unknown)

Shrine in Denpasar's Pura Maospahit, a temple established in the Majapahit era *(see p61)*

MAJAPAHIT BALI

Bali maintained its independence from the kingdoms of East Java until 1284. In that year the Singasari king Kertanegara sent an expedition to Bali, and as a consequence brought the island into the Javanese political sphere.

Kertanegara's successor in East Java, Raden Wijaya, founded the kingdom of Majapahit, which over the next two centuries became the largest empire ever in Southeast Asia. Bali was not truly subjugated by Majapahit until 1343, when the Javanese prime minister, Gajah Mada, defeated the king in Bedulu. Majapahit sovereignty was eventually established at Gelgel.

The Gelgel kings ruled with the help of local chieftains under a Majapahit lord. The people of some villages declined to adopt Majapahit's religious and social customs. These people, now known as the Bali Aga ("original Balinese"), remained isolated in their village settlements, and

Ceremonial bowl from around the 15th century

became a culturally distinct minority *(see p121)*. Majapahit shaped the culture that has survived in Bali to the present day, including architectural, dance and theatrical forms; literature written in Kawi script; and painting and relief sculpture influenced by *wayang* puppet theatre *(see p31)*. However, with time the imported culture gradually took on certain features of the more rustic Bali.

Majapahit also ruled Lombok. A 1365 Javanese chronicle mentions Lombok as a dependency. Lombok histories tell of Majapahit princes being sent to Bali, Lombok and Bima (present-day Sumbawa). The old Hindu-Buddhist elements in Lombok's culture can be traced to this period.

BALI'S GOLDEN AGE

By the end of the 15th century Bali had recovered its independence. Majapahit was seriously foundering, a decline accelerated by the rise of Islam in Java. The Balinese kingdom of Gelgel flourished in the mid-16th century under King Waturenggong, who extended it westward to Java, and over Lombok to Bima. Some Hindu Javanese nobles migrated to Gelgel, bringing a fresh infusion of Majapahit court culture. Waturenggong's reign was a time of rebirth in the Hindu arts, literature and religion.

Around the 1540s, two new streams of religious thought spread eastward from Java: Islam, which was never to become widely established in Bali; and a Hindu reformation movement led by Waturenggong's priest, Dang Hyang Nirartha. This Javanese brahman was a poet, architect and

TIMELINE

1050–1078 Reign of Anak Wungsu

1284 King Kertanegara of Kediri, Java attacks Bali

14th century coin from the Majapahit empire

| 1100 | 1200 | 1300 | 1400 |

1294 Raden Wijaya founds Majapahit kingdom in East Java

1343 Majapahit invasion of Bali by Gajah Mada

An edict written in old Balinese, 10th to 11th century

religious teacher. Among his reforms was the introduction of the *padmasana* shrine *(see p26)*, an altar to the Supreme God. He established, inspired or renovated many temples in Bali, including Pura Tanah Lot *(see p128)*. He preached in Lombok; and he is considered to be the ancestor of Bali's Brahmana Siwa clan, the island's main priestly kinship group.

Meanwhile, from the 16th century Lombok was embracing Islam. Two of the most important figures in the process were Sunan Prapen, a disciple of the Islamic saint Sunan Giri; and the possibly mythical Javanese prince, Pangeran Sangupati, whom the Sasaks consider founder of the mystical Islamic sect Wetu Telu *(see p23)*.

Kulkul tower at Pura Taman Ayun, built in Mengwi around 1740

RISE OF NEW POWERS

By 1597, which saw the first recorded visit to Bali by Europeans, the court at Gelgel was decadently rich. The dynasty was soon displaced by a new branch, founded around 1650 at Klungkung, the kings taking the title

Dewa Agung ("great lord"). Soon, the Klungkung dynasty began to break into smaller kingdoms. Over the next 250 years, warfare and intermarriage created a complex political landscape.

The 18th and 19th centuries saw the rise of other kingdoms that foreshadowed the regencies of Bali today. These were Klungkung, Karangasem, Buleleng, Jembrana, Bangli, Badung, Gianyar, Tabanan and Mengwi. Buleleng became a major power under Panji Sakti, who ruled from 1660 to 1704; in the 18th century it was rivalled by Mengwi and Karangasem. Mengwi was split up among its enemies in the late 1890s, but a trace of its former glory remains at the royal temple complex Pura Taman Ayun *(see pp130–31)*. Although the territory ruled by Klungkung was smaller than the other great kingdoms, the Dewa Agungs retained prestige because their realm included the important temple at Besakih *(see pp116–17)*.

The kingdom of Karangasem in eastern Bali occupied Lombok in 1740; Balinese settlers lived in the western part of the island. There was resistance in the centre and the east from the Sasak nobility and Bugis migrants *(see p135)*. Conversely, contacts with Islam increased in Bali itself. By the end of the 18th century all of the kings on Bali had hired Muslim mercenaries. This is why many "Balinese-Muslim" villages still exist near what were formerly important court centres.

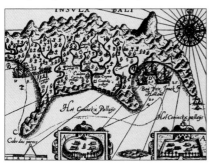
Dutch map of Bali, c.1597, clearly showing volcanic peaks

c.1540 Sunan Prapen sent as a Muslim missionary to Bali and Lombok	**c.1550–70** Reign of Waturenggong in Gelgel – Bali's Golden Age	**1619** Founding of Batavia in West Java	*Puri Agung, grand palace of the 18th-century Karangasem dynasty*
		c.1650 Establishment of Klungkung dynasty	**1740** Karangasem conquers Lombok
1500	**1600**	**1700**	**1800**
c.1540 Hindu reformer Nirartha reaches Bali	**1597** First recorded visit of Europeans to Bali	**1602** Founding of the United East India Company (VOC) *(see p48)*	**c.1700** Rise of Mengwi **c.1680** Rise of Karangasem	**1800** VOC is dissolved; Dutch colonial government installed
		c.1660–1704 Rise of Buleleng	

ARRIVAL OF THE EUROPEANS

The 17th century saw a new player on the scene. The Dutch set up the United East India Company (VOC) in 1602, a trading company succeeded in 1800 by the Dutch East Indies colonial administration.

Until the mid-19th century, Dutch colonial attention was concentrated in Batavia (now Jakarta), on the island of Java. Bali had little contact with the Dutch, except for trade in opium and slaves. Balinese kings sold debtors and prisoners of war; the Dutch sold opium.

The raja of Buleleng, mid-19th century

A TUMULTUOUS CENTURY

The 19th century brought enormous suffering to Bali and Lombok, as a consequence of volcanic eruption, famine, disease and war. There were military incursions by the Dutch and petty wars between the kingdoms. Thomas Stamford Raffles (later the founder of Singapore) showed some interest in Bali during the British interregnum in

Java (1811–16), a consequence of the Napoleonic Wars – this caused some concern to the Dutch. The Dutch were to become far more militant after their victory over the Javanese, who were led by the prince Dipanagara, in the Java War of 1825–30. They also found themselves in conflict with Balinese kings over salvage from shipwrecks: the kings regarded cargo as a just reward for saving ship and crew. One such dispute with the king of Buleleng in 1845 led to the landing of Dutch troops on Balinese soil. The Balinese, led by the brilliant tactician Gusti Jelantik, resisted three military expeditions before they were finally defeated in 1849 at Jagaraga; Jelantik fled to Karangasem where he was killed in a palace intrigue.

The Dutch now had direct control of the northern Balinese kingdoms of Buleleng and Jembrana. Rivalry prevented a lasting alliance among the

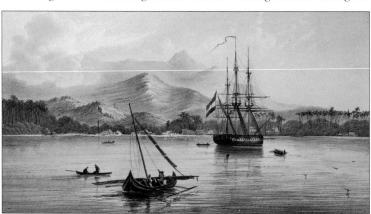

View of the harbour of Ampenan, Lombok, c.1850

TIMELINE

1808–1816 French and British interregnum

1815 Eruption of Gunung Tambora in Sumbawa

Accession of Raja Ratu Ketut Ngurah Karangasem, ruler of Lombok, 1855

1810	1820	1830	1840	1850

1811–16 T S Raffles becomes Lt-Governor of Java

Mayura Water Palace, built by the Balinese dynasty which ruled in Lombok until 1843

1825–30 Java War

1846–9 Buleleng expeditions; *puputan* at Jagaraga

1843 Lombok accepts Dutch sovereignty

Dutch cavalry in Lombok, 1894

other kingdoms; most aspired to Dutch help against their neighbours. The Balinese ruler in Lombok during this time had accepted Dutch sovereignty in 1843. In 1849 he sided with the Dutch against Buleleng by attacking Buleleng's ally Karangasem, his own ancestral home. Thus Karangasem became a vassal of Lombok.

THE FALL OF BALI'S OLD KINGDOMS
Dutch control over Lombok was not fully asserted until the end of the 19th century. In 1894, seizing the pretext of a Sasak revolt against their Balinese masters, the Dutch attacked and subdued the whole island, in the process acquiring Karangasem as well. In 1900, Gianyar put itself under Dutch control, while Bangli hesitated. Three kingdoms remained independent – Badung, Tabanan and Klungkung.

The occasion for the next and decisive Dutch attack was another dispute over a shipwreck – the pillage of a

small Dutch ship which had run aground off Sanur. The matter escalated and became a political stand-off. In September 1906, a large Dutch fleet arrived. In Denpasar, kings, princes and brahmans dressed in white and had their ritual weapons blessed. As the Dutch advanced towards the town, they were met by hundreds of men, women and children emerging from the Denpasar palace. The Balinese ran towards the Dutch guns and were mown down. The survivors turned their weapons on themselves in an orgy of suicide. That afternoon a similar tragedy took place at the nearby Pemecutan palace. The king of Tabanan surrendered with his son; two days later they committed suicide in their cell. In Klungkung, the Dewa Agung and his court were shot down in another *puputan* in 1908. Bali was then wholly incorporated into the Dutch East Indies.

COLONIAL RULE
Royal houses were stripped of property and power as the Dutch recruited surviving "rajas", as junior personnel, into their bureaucracy. With a *modus vivendi* established, The Netherlands were to conserve Bali as a "living museum" of classical culture, a show

Interior of the Karangasem royal palace, built c.1900

The Ruins of Denpasar *(1906)*
by W O J Nieuwenkamp

1860	1870	1880	1890	1900

1860–88 Epidemics and plagues in Bali

1882–1900 Inter-kingdom wars in Bali

1888 Major earthquake in Bali and Lombok

1906 Dutch expedition against Badung; *puputan* in Denpasar; Tabanan falls

1894 Dutch conquest of Lombok

case for enlightened Dutch colonialism. The restoration of the role of the rajas as custodians of ritual matters gave the appearance of cultural continuity.

At the same time the Dutch used compulsory labour, formerly a royal prerogative, to improve irrigation and build a network of roads

King and visitor at the gateway of Puri Gianyar, 1910

across the island. They streamlined village laws and class structure; new taxes rewarded loyal nobility but impoverished the peasantry, and were especially harsh on Lombok. These actions created tensions that were to erupt later, when post-colonial governments raised popular expectations but were not able to resolve certain fundamental social problems.

Photograph of Balinese people, taken by G P Lewis in the 1920s and coloured for publication

THE LAST PARADISE

To visitors from abroad, however, Bali was a paradise. Early images by Dutch illustrator W O J Nieuwenkamp, and German photographer Gregor Krause, inspired Westerners to visit the island. The Dutch cautiously encouraged tourism. Some visitors stayed on more permanently, settling mainly in Ubud and Sanur, and presented to the outside world an image of Bali as "the island of the gods" where "everyone is an artist".

Meanwhile, a modern bureaucracy was growing, whose members soon constituted, with Chinese, Arab and Muslim traders, the core of a new urban intelligentsia. Together with other Indonesians from Java, Sumatra and the eastern islands, they formed the pan-archipelago political networks which later gave rise to Indonesian nationalism. In 1928, the *lingua franca* of the archipelago, Malay, was declared the official language of the Dutch East Indies, Bahasa Indonesia.

WAR AND INDEPENDENCE

In 1942 Japan invaded and occupied the Dutch East Indies. Requisition of crops led to deprivation. Non-Indonesians were imprisoned by the Japanese or deported. The occupation spurred on the forces of nationalism. Leading the nationalists was Javanese intellectual Sukarno, who proclaimed independence on 17 August 1945, two days after the Japanese surrender.

However, the Dutch returned to reclaim their colonies. They met fierce resistance. In Bali they achieved a

TIMELINE

1908 Klungkung *puputan*; Dutch control all of Bali		1928 Opening of Bali Hotel in Denpasar	1936 Founding of the Pita Maha art movement (*see p35*)	1942 Japanese invasion; Dutch withdraw from the archipelago	1949 Transfer of sovereignty to Republic of Indonesia	1963 Eruption of Gunung Agung
Klungkung's king in 1908, Dewa Agung Semarabhawa						

1910	1920	1930	1940	1950	1960

	1917 Earthquake; eruption of Gunung Batur			1946 Dutch return; *puputan* at Margarana	1965 30 September coup attempt; Anti-Communist purges begin
	The title page from Island of Bali	1937 Publication of *Island of Bali*, a classic travel work, by Miguel Covarrubias	1945 Indonesia proclaims independence; Sukarno becomes president	
1914 Opening of Bali to tourism					

Balinese judges under the colonial regime, 1935

AUTOCRACY AND REFORM

On 30 September 1965, an alleged coup attempt took place in Jakarta. Sukarno was displaced by the little-known general Suharto, who then led a "cleansing" campaign in which thousands of communists and suspected communist sympathizers were murdered, and countless internal conflicts brutally settled. Suharto's "New Order" eventually brought prosperity to Bali with the resurgence of tourism.

The first modern tourists were travellers on the "hippie trail" of the late 1960s and 1970s. The Australians discovered Bali as a nearby holiday destination. The coconut groves of Kuta were gradually replaced by "art-shops" and small hotels. In the 1980s and 1990s, South Bali was transformed by a building boom. There were just a few hundred hotel rooms in 1965, and 30,000 by 1999.

In the Suharto era, development took place at the expense of civil liberties, a trade-off destroyed by the financial crisis of 1997. In May 1998, Suharto was forced to resign. Suppressed social pressures erupted.

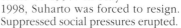
Pro-democracy banner, 1999

political foothold amongst the former nobility. Pro-republican youths waged guerrilla war until November 1946, when a band of 94 freedom-fighters, led by Gusti Ngurah Rai, died in a *puputan* at Marga *(see p132)*. Despite this victory, the Dutch were in an unsustainable position. Three years later they withdrew from Indonesia, transferring sovereignty on 27 December 1949.

The prosperity promised by independence did not materialize for many years. Guerrilla bands roamed the islands of the archipelago. Successive governments, powerless or over-nationalistic, deterred foreign investors. Thought to be extinct, Bali's highest volcano Gunung Agung erupted in 1963, killing thousands of people, devastating East Bali and causing famine. Political polarization worsened.

In Bali, after the 1999 elections, some public buildings were burned down. Later, Lombok suffered unrest, apparently provoked by outsiders; tourists were unharmed. Megawati Sukarnoputri, favoured by the majority of Balinese as presidential candidate, became vice-president. Terrorist bombings in 2002 and 2005 brought tragedy to Bali in the new millennium; the two men responsible for the 2002 attack were executed in 2008.

Suharto in Bali, 1979

1966 Bali Beach Hotel is opened
Nusa Dua Beach Hotel

1998 Economic crisis causes riots in Jakarta; Suharto resigns

2009 Susilo Bambang Yudhoyono is the first Indonesian president ever to be re-elected

2010 Number of foreign tourists visiting Bali reaches a record 2.5 million

1970	1980	1990	2000	2010	2020

1983 Opening of Nusa Dua Beach Hotel, part of a 5-star resort complex

1999 PDI-P party led by Megawati Sukarnoputri wins 80 per cent of vote in Bali; Abdurrahman Wahid becomes president of Indonesia

2002 On 12 October a terrorist bomb in Kuta kills over 200 people

2008 The bombers responsible for the 2002 terrorist attacks are executed

1967–98 Suharto's New Order; dramatic rise of tourism

BALI & LOMBOK AREA BY AREA

BALI AND LOMBOK AT A GLANCE 54–55

SOUTH BALI 56–77

CENTRAL BALI 78–99

EAST BALI 100–123

NORTH AND WEST BALI 124–149

LOMBOK 150–163

Bali and Lombok at a Glance

The attractions of Bali and Lombok are varied, appealing to visitors with an interest in cultural heritage, natural beauty, and sports. South Bali has the greatest concentration of beach resorts and nightlife; Central and East Bali are particularly rich in history and artistic interest. Throughout both islands there is wonderful scenery, from volcanic peaks and lakes to rice terraces and a beautiful coastline, in many areas quite undeveloped.

Bali Bird Park (see pp84–5) *is home to nearly 1,000 birds of over 250 species displayed in a fine tropical garden.*

Pura Meduwe Karang (see pp148–9) *is a temple noted for its stone sculptures, wall carvings and reliefs.*

Ubud *(see pp88–95)* and the nearby villages are at the heart of Bali's cultural life.

Singaraja *(see pp146–7)* retains the atmosphere of an old port and colonial capital.

Taman Nasional Bali Barat *(see pp136–7)* is a large nature reserve which includes the Bali Starling Breeding Facility and the coral reefs of Menjangan Island.

NORTH AND WEST BALI
(see pp124–149)

CENTRAL BALI
(see pp78–99)

0 kilometres   20

0 miles   10

Bali Museum (see pp62–3) *is noted both for its fine collection of artifacts and for its architecture.*

SOUTH BALI
(see pp56–77)

Denpasar *(see pp60–61)* is Bali's administrative capital and commercial centre.

Pura Taman Ayun (see pp130–31) *is a royal temple with an inner and an outer moat.*

Kuta *(see pp66–9),* the most developed tourist centre in Bali, is crowded with hotels, shops, bars and restaurants.

Pura Luhur Uluwatu (see pp76–7) *is set high on the edge of a cliff at the end of South Bali's Bukit Peninsula.*

◁ Ruins of Puri Taman Ujung water palace

Taman Nasional Gunung Rinjani (see pp158–9) *is a national park and trekking area encompassing Lombok's highest volcano and the crater lake Danau Segara Anak.*

Gunung Batur (see pp120–21), *an active volcano, and Lake Batur are enclosed within a spectacular caldera within which are several historic temples and some trekking routes.*

Besakih Temple Complex *(see pp116–17)* contains 22 temples built on the lower slopes of the sacred volcano Gunung Agung.

EAST BALI
(see pp100–123)

LOMBOK
(see pp150–163)

Tenganan *(see pp110–11)* is a village where the minority Bali Aga ("original Balinese") still live according to their own, ancient traditions.

Senggigi *(see p156)* is a popular beach resort area set in a sandy bay.

Taman Gili (see pp106–107) *is a royal compound with beautiful ceiling paintings in its two main pavilions.*

Pura Lingsar (see p154) *in Sweta is a temple with 300 years of history. Apart from the temple's importance to worshippers, the lotus ponds in the precincts give pleasure to local children.*

SOUTH BALI

A blend of history, culture and tourism, South Bali offers many contrasts. Budget travellers have flocked to the beaches here since surfers first arrived decades ago; at the other extreme, lavish hotels and resorts have created a more glamorous and exotic version of Bali. Meanwhile, despite modern development, temples and village communities still maintain their cultural and artistic traditions.

At the heart of South Bali is Denpasar, the island's provincial capital since 1958 and today a busy, modernizing city, Bali's administrative and commercial hub. Denpasar used to be a royal capital – the kingdom of Badung dominated the southern part of Bali from the late 18th to the beginning of the 20th century, and its heritage is to be seen in several of its older buildings. Two important cultural centres are here: the Bali Museum *(see pp62–3)* and Taman Werdhi Budaya (Bali Arts Centre) *(see p61)*.

The city lies within Bali's most important tourist area, a triangle formed by the beach resorts of Kuta, Legian, Seminyak and Canggu on the west coast, Sanur on the east coast, and Nusa Dua to the south.

Kuta is Bali's leading tourist centre. The beaches are famous. There are hotels of every standard, exciting restaurants and clubs, water sports, pulsating night life and shops to suit every budget. Sanur has many of the attractions of Kuta, but in a gentler, less raucous style. Nusa Dua, a development planned specially for visitors, offers the manicured gardens of a 5-star resort-hotel complex complete with an 18-hole golf course.

The highland peninsula of Bukit in the far south is arid and stands in stark contrast to the verdant gardens and rice terraces that enriched the rajas of old. One of Bali's holiest temples, Pura Luhur Uluwatu, is set high on a cliff at the Bukit's southwest extremity, with a spectacular view of the ocean.

The sea is never far away in South Bali. Surfers come for the waves, divers and snorkellers for the reefs and underwater life. Everyone comes for the beach life, which has few rivals in Asia or further afield.

Fishermen off the South Bali coast in their light outrigger boat

◁ Woodcarving of a Garuda (a mythical bird), an example of the craft work typical of South Bali

Exploring South Bali

Most visitors arrive at Denpasar's airport at the centre of South Bali. The most important resort areas, with their beaches and nightlife, are only a short taxi ride away. Some people feel no need to venture further afield, but communications are good to other parts of Bali, and to Lombok. South Bali is therefore a good base for further exploration; it is easy to make all the practical arrangements here. This is the least mountainous part of the island, but much of the landscape is lush with gardens and ricefields, and the Bukit Peninsula in the south offers a more rugged contrast. Offshore to the east lie the islands of Nusa Lembongan and Nusa Penida, usually reached from Benoa Harbour.

SIGHTS AT A GLANCE

Benoa Harbour **7**
Canggu **2**
Denpasar pp60–61 **1**
Jimbaran **11**
Kuta and Legian pp66–9 **4**
Nusa Dua **10**
Nusa Lembongan **13**
Nusa Penida **14**
Pulau Serangan **8**
Pura Luhur Uluwatu
   pp76–7 **12**
Sanur **3**
Seminyak **5**
Tanjung Benoa **9**
Tuban **6**

Kuta Beach, a popular spot for sunbathing, surfing and other water sports

GETTING AROUND

All flights to Bali land at Ngurah Rai International Airport, south of Tuban. Bali's first dual carriageway, Jalan Bypass Ngurah Rai, runs from Nusa Dua to Kuta (via the airport), up to Tohpati (via Sanur) before continuing its coastal route as far as Kusamba. Transport is plentiful, in the form of *bemo*, taxis, and tourist shuttle-buses. Buses run from Denpasar to other parts of the island, and to the inter-island ferry terminals at Gilimanuk and Padang Bai. These cater more for locals than visitors.

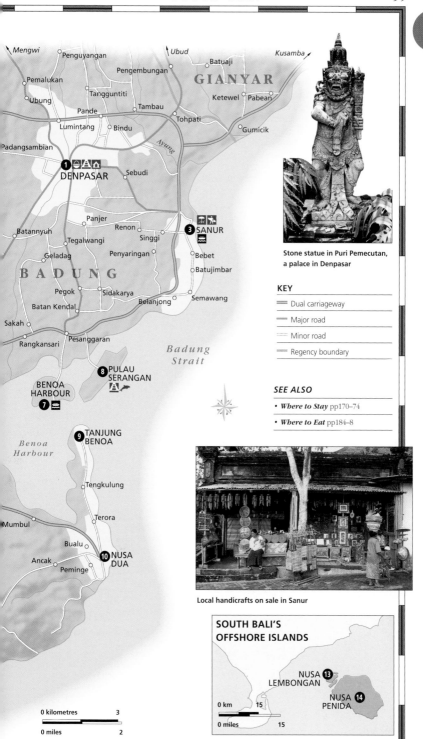

Stone statue in Puri Pemecutan,
a palace in Denpasar

KEY

━━━ Dual carriageway

━━━ Major road

┄┄┄ Minor road

━━━ Regency boundary

SEE ALSO

• **Where to Stay** pp170–74

• **Where to Eat** pp184–8

Local handicrafts on sale in Sanur

**SOUTH BALI'S
OFFSHORE ISLANDS**

NUSA
LEMBONGAN

NUSA
PENIDA

0 km   15

0 miles   15

0 kilometres   3

0 miles   2

Denpasar ●

Denpasar is Bali's bustling provincial capital. Some older buildings predate the Dutch invasion of 1906 *(see p49)*, and there are still some white-walled, red-tiled structures dating from colonial times. On the streets can be seen several statues commemorating heroes of Indonesia's struggle for independence.

Detail of wall carving Around the main street, Jalan Gajah Mada, are shophouses built by Chinese, Arab and Indian traders. Shopkeepers from all over Bali buy wholesale here.

Bronze statues in Taman Puputan commemorating *puputan* heroes of 1906

▣ Pasar Badung
Jalan Gajah Mada. ○ *daily.*
This is a lively, open-air market full of colour and excitement; sellers from all over Bali do a brisk trade all day. The extensive flower section is not to be missed – exotic blossoms used in religious offerings *(see p38)* are a major commodity on Bali.

The fruit, vegetable and fish market is full of spectacular tropical harvests. Bargains can be found among the textiles, baskets, mats and traditional dancers' costumes.

▣ Jalan Hasanudin
Gold jewellery in Balinese, Indonesian and Western designs is sold here.

▣ Jalan Sulawesi
This three-block stretch houses a myriad of fabrics and textiles. Everything from cheap batiks to imported silks and brocades can be found here. This is where the Balinese come to buy their temple clothing, and the delicate lace used for *kebaya* (a traditional tight-fitting ladies' blouse).

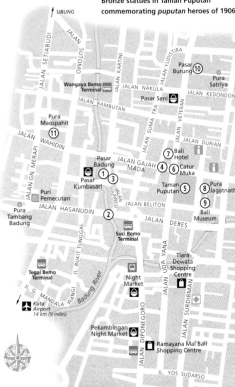

Colourful textiles for sale on Jalan Sulawesi

▣ Jalan Gajah Mada
Several interesting Chinese apothecaries with an array of herbal medicines can be found on this busy street. One of the largest is Toko Saudara. Other stores sell electronics, sporting goods, handicrafts, batik and *ikat* textiles. Many traders of Arab and Indian descent have businesses here.

For hotels and restaurants in this region see pp170–74 and pp184–8

✕ Taman Puputan

Jalan Udayana and Jalan Surapati.

Puputan translates as "ritual fight to the death", and this large square in the middle of town (once the site of Denpasar's palace) has a huge bronze statue which commemorates the *puputan* of 1906 *(see p49)*. Nowadays the square is much more peaceful, making a pleasant green oasis amid the bustle and noise of Denpasar.

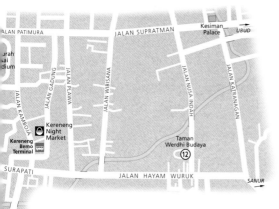

Statue of Ngurah Rai *(see p51)*

🏨 Inna Bali Hotel

Jalan Veteran 3. **Tel** *(0361) 225 681.*
www.innabali.com

Built in 1928, and once the only luxury accommodation in Bali, this hotel has welcomed famous guests such as Charlie Chaplin and Noel Coward. The open pavilion on the opposite side of Jalan Veteran was built to stage dances for guests.

Seen here were many great performers who helped to make Balinese dance world-famous.

🏛 Pura Maospahit

Jalan Sutomo, Grenceng.
🚫 to public.

This temple dates from the time between the 13th and 15th centuries, when the Majapahit ruled over Bali *(see p46)*. The style of the statuary and brickwork developed at that period. The restrained ornamentation is delightful. Although the temple is closed to visitors, the architecture can be seen from outside.

Pura Maospahit, one of Bali's oldest temples

🏛 Taman Werdhi Budaya

Jalan Nusa Indah. **Tel** *(0361) 222 776.* **Fax** *(0361) 247 722.* 🕐 8am–5pm Tue–Sun. 🚫 public hols.
Also known as the Bali Arts Centre, this is an attractive if under-used complex with extensive gardens, an art museum, several indoor theatres and an outdoor amphitheatre. There are frequent dance and music performances, but no set programme.

The centre is a good place to come to during the heat of the day. The permanent collection of sculptures and paintings reflects the art world of the 1970s and 1980s. More recent works are shown in rotating exhibitions.

Information can be found in the *Bali Post* newspaper and tourist magazines.

DENPASAR

Bali Museum ⑨
Catur Muka ⑥
Inna Bali Hotel ⑦
Jalan Gajah Mada ④
Jalan Hasanudin ②
Jalan Sulawesi ③
Pasar Badung ①
Pasar Burung ⑩
Pura Jagatnatha ⑧
Pura Maospahit ⑪
Taman Puputan ⑤
Taman Werdhi Budaya ⑫

🏨 Catur Muka

Northwest corner of Taman Puputan.
On the traffic island adjacent to Taman Puputan is a representation of Wisnu, the four-headed Hindu god, shown in the form of a stone statue 20 m (65 ft) tall, dating from the 1970s. The name means "four faces".

🏛 Pura Jagatnatha

Taman Puputan, Jalan Letkol Wisnu.
🕐 daily. 🎫 donation.
This temple was built in the 1970s for the worship of Sang Hyang Widhi Wasa, the Supreme God. It is crowded on the full and new moons, and on Kajeng Kliwon, which falls every 15 days in the Balinese calendar *(see p39)*. It has a very tall *padmasana* shrine *(see p26)*.

🏛 Bali Museum

See pp62–3.

🐦 Pasar Burung

Off Jalan Veteran. 🕐 daily.
At this lively bird market many species of birds and other animals can be seen. The Balinese love song-birds, and those with exceptional voices can sell for very high prices. There is also trade in dogs, tropical fish, fighting crickets and fighting cocks.

---

0 metres 500

0 yards 500

Key to Symbols see back flap

Denpasar: Bali Museum

Ritual Bronze Age axe

The Bali Museum houses one of the world's best collections of Balinese art. Completed and opened in 1931 by architect P J Moojen, its attraction is not only the items on show but also the buildings and setting. The exterior walls, gates and courtyards were executed in the manner of an old Denpasar royal palace, while the Tabanan, Karangasem and Buleleng *gedung* (pavilions) are built in the style of the regions after which they are named.

Ceremonial Gate
Fine brickwork without mortar is combined with volcanic-stone reliefs.

Carved Palace Doors
On display are these carved, gilded doors from the 19th century.

★ Stone Sculptures
Lining the verandah of the pavilion are stone statues from the 16th to the 19th centuries. The one shown here depicts motherhood.

Masks
Ritual masks, such as this 19th-century example from South Bali, are shown with puppets and musical instruments.

Bronze Cannons
This 17th-century gun, with monster-head muzzle, is one of a pair made for a Denpasar prince.

The gazebo has a base decorated with fine stone motifs.

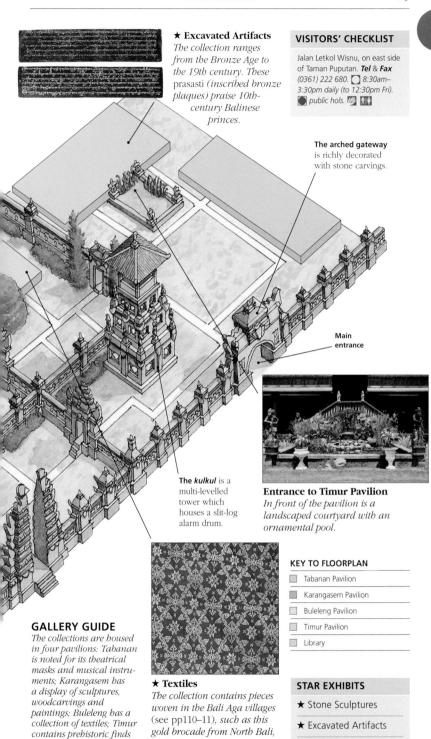

★ **Excavated Artifacts**
The collection ranges from the Bronze Age to the 19th century. These prasasti *(inscribed bronze plaques) praise 10th-century Balinese princes.*

VISITORS' CHECKLIST

Jalan Letkol Wisnu, on east side of Taman Puputan. *Tel* & *Fax* (0361) 222 680. ☐ *8:30am–3:30pm daily (to 12:30pm Fri).* ☐ *public hols.* ☒ ☒

The arched gateway is richly decorated with stone carvings.

Main entrance

Entrance to Timur Pavilion
In front of the pavilion is a landscaped courtyard with an ornamental pool.

The *kulkul* **is a** multi-levelled tower which houses a slit-log alarm drum.

KEY TO FLOORPLAN

- ☐ Tabanan Pavilion
- ☐ Karangasem Pavilion
- ☐ Buleleng Pavilion
- ☐ Timur Pavilion
- ☐ Library

GALLERY GUIDE
The collections are housed in four pavilions: Tabanan is noted for its theatrical masks and musical instruments; Karangasem has a display of sculptures, woodcarvings and paintings; Buleleng has a collection of textiles; Timur contains prehistoric finds and, upstairs, some antique woodcarvings.

★ **Textiles**
The collection contains pieces woven in the Bali Aga villages (see pp110–11), such as this gold brocade from North Bali, and examples of geringsing *double* ikat *from Tenganan.*

STAR EXHIBITS

- ★ Stone Sculptures
- ★ Excavated Artifacts
- ★ Textiles

Canggu ❷

Road Map C4. ℹ *Denpasar (0361)*
756 176. 🚻 🏪 🌊

In the absence of nightlife,
the quiet atmosphere of
Canggu is a complete contrast
with that of Kuta *(see pp68–9).*
This is a place for walks on
the quiet, windswept beach.
Behind the beach is a landscape of coconut palms,
ricefields and modern villa
developments. One can walk
all the way along the beach
from Canggu to Seminyak.

This area was discovered by
surfers in the early 1970s, and
remains a favourite surfing
spot. The waves are too big
for good swimming.

Those interested in the
use of traditional elements
in architectural design will
appreciate the vacation houses
and villas, which combine
Balinese style with modernity.

**Farmers harvesting rice in Canggu
with vacation homes nearby**

There are several distinctive
"boutique hotels" *(see p166).*
They include the Tugu *(see
p170),* a self-styled "museum
hotel", furnished with antiques. The pieces range from
dragon doors made by Dayak
headhunters in Borneo to
colonial Art Deco furniture.
The villas are themed on
artists who lived in Bali, such
as Walter Spies and Adrien Le
Mayeur *(see p50).* It is worth
visiting the hotel just to eat
in the Chinese restaurant,
set inside an 18th-century,
wooden Chinese temple
moved here from North Bali.

Sanur ❸

**Sculpture of Hindu
deity Ganesha at
Pura Segara**

Bali's longest-established resort, Sanur
has a quiet charm. At its heart is an old
Balinese community. The simple layout of
Sanur's streets and its tranquil atmosphere
appeal to families and those seeking a
relaxed vacation with the convenience
and facilities of a beach resort, but
without the intrusiveness of Kuta's
hawkers and traffic. The shops are
pleasant and sell goods from Bali and
elsewhere in Indonesia. Many of the
unpretentious cafés and pubs aim to
attract visitors of a particular nationality
or lovers of a particular sport. The nightlife is enjoyed
by both visitors and locals.

Exploring Sanur

Jalan Danau Tamblingan,
Sanur's main artery, is lined
with restaurants, and shops
selling locally made fashion
and craft goods. It runs some
5 km (3 miles) parallel to the
beach from old Sanur village,
to the formerly distinct villages
of Blanjong and Mertasari.
Half-way is Bale Banjar Batu
Jimbar, a community centre
where musicians practise and
women make flower and
palm-leaf offerings. At Pasar
Sindhu, sarongs and other
products can be bought at
bargain prices; it operates
early in the morning.

**Jalan Danau Tamblingan, lined with
shops and restaurants**

🏛 Pura Desa

Jalan Hang Tuah. ⭕ *daily.*
This fine village temple was
probably built early in the last
century, although its brickwork
has been restored since. It is in
Sanur's oldest neighbourhood,
which is famous for the
spiritual power of its priests.

🏛 Museum Le Mayeur

Jalan Hang Tuah, via Grand Bali
Beach Hotel. **Tel** *(0361) 286 164.*
⭕ *8am–2pm Tue–Sun.* 📷 🎫 ♿
Built in the 1930s by
Adrien Jean Le Mayeur
– Belgian painter and
one of Sanur's first
European residents –
the house became a
museum and gallery
on the artist's death in
1958. Now a little
faded, some of the
buildings are wooden,
with interesting carved
decorations. The court-
yard garden features in

Le Mayeur's work. Le Mayeur's
wife, the famous Balinese
dancer Ni Polok, is the subject
of several paintings on show.

🏨 Grand Bali Beach Hotel

Jalan Hang Tuah. **Tel** *(0361) 288 511.*
www.innagrandbalibeach.com
Bali's only high-rise hotel was
refurbished after a fire in 1992
and is now adorned with giant
Balinese-style statues. After it
was built in 1964, the religious
authorities issued a famous
edict outlawing structures
taller than coconut palms.
Such buildings were deemed
offensive due to the spiritual
value attributed to the trees.

Grand Bali Beach Hotel complex

For hotels and restaurants in this region see pp170–74 and pp184–8

Sanur Beach, as seen from the Bali Hyatt Hotel

Sanur Beach

The beach runs virtually the full length of the town; along much of it is a paved walk. Offshore, enormous breakers crash into a reef. The calm waters between the reef and the white sands are good for swimming except at low tide. Beyond the reef the currents are strong. Activities include diving, fishing trips and an evening sail on a *jukung*, a traditional outrigger. The beach is a place to explore for marine life, such as sea grass, starfish, sea cucumbers, hermit crabs, *Fungia* corals and sea urchins. It is regarded as an excellent place to watch the sunrise.

Pura Segara

Jalan Segara Ayu, or from Sanur Beach. ○ *daily.* 🖼 *donation.* Set in the grounds of Segara Village Hotel, but accessible to the public, this is one of the best of several beach temples built of coral. The pyramid shape of the offering houses is unique to Sanur, and suggests origins in prehistoric times.

Bali Hyatt Hotel

Jalan Danau Tamblingan. **Tel** *(0361) 281 234.* **www**.bali.resort.hyatt.com Even non-residents should visit the Bali Hyatt (*see p173*) for a drink or a meal, if only to enjoy the gardens. Here Australian landscape architect Made Wijaya developed a style of Balinese garden design which has influenced designers worldwide.

Pura Belanjong

Jalan Danau Poso. ○ *daily.* 🖼 *donation.* In this plain-looking temple is an ancient stone column, the Prasasti Blanjong. On it is carved the oldest edict so far found in Bali (AD 914). The inscription is written in a form of Sanskrit, although it is not all decipherable. It suggests Sanur was a lively trading port more than 1,000 years ago.

SANUR TOWN AND BEACH

Bali Hyatt Hotel ⑥
Grand Bali Beach Hotel ③
Museum Le Mayeur ②
Pura Belanjong ⑦
Pura Desa ①
Pura Segara ⑤
Sanur Beach ④

0 metres   1,000
0 yards   1,000

Key to Symbols *see back flap*

DENPASAR
Sanur Paradise Plaza ①
Pura Desa ①
JL. HANG TUAH
Bemo Terminal
Bali Beach Golf Course
Museum Le Mayeur ②
Grand Bali Beach Hotel ③
Sanur Beach ④
JALAN DANAU BERATAN
JALAN DANAU BUYAN
JALAN SEGARA AYU
Pura Segara ⑤
Art Market
JALAN TEGEH AGUNG
JALAN SINDHU
Art Market
Art Market
BYPASS NGURAH RAI
JALAN PUNGUTAN
GANGBIMI AYU
JL. PANTAI KARANG
JALAN DANAU TAMBLINGAN
Bale Banjar Batu Jimbar
Bali Hyatt Hotel ⑥
JALAN DUYUNG
KUTA & LEGIAN
BYPASS NGURAH RAI
JALAN DANAU POSO
Pura Belanjong ⑦
Bemo Terminal
Puri Santrian
Kuta Airport 14 km (9 miles)

Kuta and Legian ❹

The beach at Kuta is long and sandy. However, the dollar-a-night homestays which attracted young backpackers and surfers in the 1970s have been replaced by a resort strip, which is now world-famous *(see Street-by-Street, pp68–9)*. Besides the beach and water sports, the principal attractions are shopping and nightlife. Development has spread beyond the original Kuta Beach, including Legian, and has now enveloped Tuban in the south and Seminyak in the north.

Surfers at Kuta Beach, a location suitable for all levels of ability

Exploring Kuta and Legian

As Bali's main tourist hub, Kuta is a good base for relaxation and organizing trips to other parts of the island. Away from the beach, shopping is perhaps the most tempting activity around these parts; there are no major cultural or historic sights in either Kuta or Legian.

A good rest-stop is **Made's Warung I** *(see p185)*, casual and cool, and one of Kuta's most famous restaurants. Both Legian and Seminyak *(see opposite)* are now as built up as Kuta proper. However, Legian's labyrinth of back streets offers a wide range of low-priced accommodation options.

🏖 Kuta Beach

The beach is flat and sandy, and stretches for over 3 km (2 miles), backed by some sizeable hotels. Hawkers sell their wares and refreshments are available all day long. Surfboards can be rented – this is a good place for the novice surfer, although one should watch out for the rip tides. Because of currents, swimmers should stay between the safety flags. Kuta Beach becomes Legian Beach north of Jalan Melasti. Legian Beach's famous nightspots are **Kama Sutra**, Double Six and Bacio.

Relaxing on the golden sands of Kuta Beach

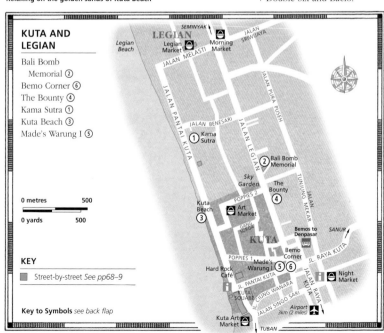

KUTA AND LEGIAN

Bali Bomb
   Memorial ②
Bemo Corner ⑥
The Bounty ④
Kama Sutra ①
Kuta Beach ③
Made's Warung I ⑤

0 metres   500
0 yards   500

KEY

◼ Street-by-street *See pp68–9*

Key to Symbols *see back flap*

Poppies Lanes I & II

These two narrow lanes are lined with small shops, stalls, hotels and bars. One of the first hotels was Poppies, from which the lanes took their name. The network of alleys in this part of Kuta offers a refuge from the traffic, pollution and noise of the main streets.

Jalan Legian

This is the commercial artery of Kuta, running parallel with the beach. At the southern end is **Bemo Corner**, a busy intersection. Jalan Legian is the place to find banks, travel agencies, car-rental outlets and the like. Pubs, bars and nightclubs proliferate – some, such as **The Bounty** and **Sky Garden**, are landmarks in themselves. Also on Jalan Legian, the **Bali Bomb Memorial** is a poignant reminder of the 202 victims of the Kuta bomb blast of October 2002.

Bima monument on Jalan Bypass

Environs

On the outskirts of Kuta, on Jalan Bypass Ngurah Rai at Simpang Siur roundabout, is an ornate modern statue of Bima, hero of the Hindu *Mahabharata* epic. It is one of several public monuments erected by the authorities for the benefit of visitors.

Shop in Jalan Legian, selling craft goods from Bali and elsewhere

Pool volleyball at the Waterbom Park & Spa, Tuban

Seminyak ➎

Road Map C5. 🚌 *from Kuta.* 🛈 *Kuta, (0361) 756 176.* 🍽 🖥 📷 🍴

Seminyak extends north of Kuta and Legian. The further northward one goes, the more peaceful the atmosphere becomes, although Seminyak is now an important tourist centre. Some good fashion boutiques can be found here, selling inexpensive but stylish clothes made in the region.

The luxurious **Oberoi Hotel** (*see p173*) has very attractive gardens overlooking the beach. Further north still, development on the palm-lined beach has been less aggressive, although this may change with time.

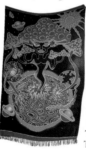

Colourful scarf for sale in Seminyak

Environs

A short walk up the beach north of Seminyak is the **Pura Petitenget** ("magic chest") temple, raised some 8 m (26 ft) above road level. Founded by the 16th-century priest, Dang Hyang Nirartha (*see pp46–7*), it is considered one of Bali's most mystically charged temples.

The area from Seminyak to Kerobokan, 5 km (3 miles) to its north, is a furniture-making centre (*see p194*). Galleries line the main road.

🏛 Pura Petitenget

Jalan Kayu Aya. ⬜ *daily.* 🖼 *donation.*

Tuban ➏

Road Map C5. 🚌 *from Kuta.* 🛈 *Kuta, (0361) 756 176.* 🍽 🖥 📷 🍴

It is hard to know where Kuta ends and Tuban begins. However, the streets of Tuban are laid out on a slightly larger scale, and the effect is a sense of greater order than in Kuta. By the beach is a series of large luxury hotels with spacious gardens. Shopping in Tuban has an international feel, especially in the modern beach-front Discovery Mall. Some people may find it a welcome respite from the bustle that often accompanies shopping in Bali. The northern limit of Tuban is the Matahari department store, selling a huge range of practical items, T-shirts and handicraft goods.

Near the Matahari store it is possible to take a ride on a *dokar*, one of the colourful carts pulled by small, hardy horses originally brought in from Sumba Island.

A very popular attraction for visitors is the **Waterbom** Park and Spa (*see p201*) which has an array of slides and pools. It is also a good place to relax and eat.

Tuban is one of the departure points for surfers making their way to the break at Kuta Reef, off Jimbara (*see p74*). Fishermen with motorized outriggers can be chartered for the trip.

Street-by-Street: Kuta

Kite for sale on the beach

Kuta is the most developed visitor destination in Bali. Thirty years ago the beach was set against coconut groves and banana plantations. It is still a great attraction today; however, a few steps away, there are now streets lined with businesses catering for visitors – bars, restaurants, hotels, nightclubs and department stores. Packed along the narrow lanes are shops and stalls selling many kinds of product likely to appeal to travellers from around the world, as well as *losmen* offering budget accommodation *(see p166)*. Commercialized Kuta may be, but it is a vibrant place, and caters for all budgets.

A local artisan at work on one of the many handicraft stalls in the area

★ Poppies Lane II
Along this narrow alley are shops, stalls, restaurants and reasonably priced accommodation.

To Legian

JALAN PANTAI KUTA

★ Kuta Beach
The sandy beach, which stretches northwards towards Seminyak and beyond, is a place to surf, swim, and relax in the sun.

★ Poppies Lane I
This is a good area for travellers on a budget, with several inexpensive hotels as well as casual dining places.

STAR SIGHTS

★ Poppies Lanes I & II

★ Kuta Beach

★ Kuta Square

For hotels and restaurants in this region see pp170–74 and pp184–8

VISITORS' CHECKLIST

Road Map C5. 🚌 🚐
ℹ *Jalan Raya Kuta,*
Tel *(0361) 756 176,*
www.badung.go.id;
Jalan Pantai Kuta 2,
(0361) 756 176. 🍴 🏨 📷 🛍

Made's Warung I
(see p185) is one of
Kuta's first and most
famous restaurants.

Bemo Corner
Busy shopping streets
radiate from this intersection,
which is Kuta's central hub.

L E G I A N

**To Jalan Bypass Ngurah
Rai, Denpasar, Sanur
and Nusa Dua**

J A L A N   P A N T A I   K U T A

T A N E T

J A L A N   T E G A L   W A N G I

J A L A N   K A R T I K A   P L A Z A

**To
Tuban →**

★ **Kuta Square**
This is a major shopping
complex housing hundreds
of small retailers, the large
Matahari emporium and
Kuta Galleria (see p195).

KEY

— — — Suggested route

| 0 metres | 100 |
| 0 yards | 100 |

**Hard Rock Café
and Hotel**
This, the only
Hard Rock hotel
in Asia, has the
largest swimming
pool in Bali.

Kuta Art Market
Here it is possible to buy
basketware and other craft
goods made in Bali and
the nearby islands of the
Indonesian Archipelago.

Cruise vessels in Benoa Harbour

Benoa Harbour ❼

Road Map C5. 🚌 🚐 *from Denpasar (shuttle bus services available to Benoa from hotels).* 🚢 *to Lembar on Lombok.* ▢

Benoa Harbour will appeal to boat-lovers. Among the commercial and privately owned vessels, there is often an interesting variety of traditional craft from the Indonesian Archipelago. These include *pinisi*, broad-beamed sailing cargo boats from South Sulawesi; and brightly coloured fishing boats from Madura, off north-east Java. There is a multitude of boat-charters and tours on offer. Day trips to Nusa Lembongan (*see p74*) are recommended. A yacht or traditional Bugis can be hired for a day-trip; longer trips go as far as Komodo and the Lesser Sunda Islands.

Nearby, on the Jalan Bypass Ngurah Rai, is the Mangrove Information Centre (0361 728 966), which aims to preserve the 15 species of coastal mangrove in its natural forest.

Pulau Serangan ❽

Road Map C5. 🖼️

The island of Serangan is separated from the southern curve of Sanur beach by a mangrove area known as Suwungwas. The name "Turtle Island" is sometimes used, because of the sea turtles that used to lay their eggs here. The island has been greatly extended by reclamation during construction works for a hotel. A bridge now links it to mainland Bali. Local people maintain an unofficial guard post, and charge visitors a small fee for access to the island. Besides the Balinese, there is an old Bugis community (*see p135*); their ancestors migrated from South Sulawesi, in the 1600s.

Here also is one of the six most sacred temples in Bali, **Pura Sakenan**, said by some to have been founded by the 16th-century reformist priest Dang Hyang Nirartha (*see pp46–7*). Others believe the temple was founded in the 11th century by the Javanese Buddhist priest Mpu Kuturan. Within the inner courtyard is a stepped pyramid built of white coral, reminiscent of temples in Polynesia. During Manis Kuningan (*see p43*), a vibrant festival takes place here on the temple's anniversary.

The island is a good vantage point from which to watch vessels returning to Benoa Harbour at the end of the day. There are views of the islands and great sunsets.

🏛 Pura Sakenan
Pulau Serangan. ⏱ *daily.*
💰 *donation.* 🎭 *Manis Kuningan.*

Tanjung Benoa ❾

Road Map C5. 🚌 🚐 *from Nusa Dua.* ℹ️ *Badung, (0361) 756 176.* 🍴 🛍 🏨 ♻

Tanjung (meaning "Cape") Benoa is a long, narrow, sandy spit, with a small fishing village built on it. The cape is separated from Benoa Harbour by a narrow stretch of water. The village was once a trading port, and some Chinese and Bugis as well as Balinese still live here. There are some Balinese temples built of carved limestone, as well as a mosque. At an ancient Chinese temple built by sailors and traders, fishermen of all religions consult with the fortune-teller in the hope of finding a good catch.

There is now a modern road leading to the tip of the peninsula from Nusa Dua. Hotels, spas and restaurants specializing in grilled seafood have grown up along both sides of the road. One quirky landmark is the stone pine-apple motif marking the entrance to the Novotel.

Wall motif in a mosque in Tanjung Benoa

Despite development, Tanjung Benoa still attracts those in search of a relaxing beach off the beaten track. There are facilities for water sports, such as water-skiing, banana-boat rides, fishing and paragliding. Cruise operators offer trips out to sea for snorkelling in waters rich in corals and tropical fish.

An ancient Chinese temple on Tanjung Benoa

◁ **The *kecak* dance, in which a chorus of men chant an accompaniment as the *Ramayana* story is enacted**

The world-renowned Bali Golf and Country Club, and beyond it the resorts of Nusa Dua and the sea

Nusa Dua ⑩

Road Map C5. 🚗 🚌 🚶 *Denpasar*
(0361) 223 602. 🍴 🏪 🏨 🏩 ⚓ 🏊

The Nusa Dua (literally "Two Islands") area is named after the two peninsulas along its coast. It consists primarily of luxury resorts run by major hotel chains. The beaches are sandy and clean. The entrance road is lined with

Split gate at the entrance garden of the Nusa Dua Beach Hotel

rows of statues; it leads through a large *candi bentar* (split gate), on each side of which carvings of frogs serve as guardian figures.

Inside, there is an air of gentility and order. The hotels are built on a big scale. Their grandiose entrances have been described as "Bali Baroque" or "expanded traditional" in style – they are of interest to architecture enthusiasts. Young visitors will love the fish ponds of the

Ayodya Resort, with thousands of brightly-coloured *koi* (a type of carp first bred in Japan) swimming among water lilies.

The Bali Golf and Country Club *(see p204)* has a championship course over three types of terrain (highland, coconut grove and coastal). Other facilities at Nusa Dua include the Bali International Convention Centre, the Bali Collection Mall, restaurants and the Pasifika Art Museum. There are also regular dance and other cultural activities held here.

Environs

Bualu is a bustling village outside the gates of the Nusa Dua complex. Several streets are lined with restaurants offering fresh fish and shops selling handicrafts.

Between the Sheraton Laguna and Grand Hyatt hotels a headland with native flora and several Balinese shrines juts out into the sea. The views from here are good.

Geger Beach is sheltered by a reef, making it ideal for families, safe for swimming and the best location for kite surfing. Camel safaris through the arid hills are offered at the Nikko Hotel. One beach near the Nikko is popular with surfers.

Beautiful beaches line the southern coast. Most require a hike or climb; many are popular surfing spots, but they can be dangerous for beginners, with big waves and strong currents.

West of Nusa Dua, on the road to Uluwatu, is the **GWK** (Garuda Wisnu Kencana, or "Golden Garuda Vishnu") cultural centre. The main feature is a statue of the head of the mythological bird Garuda and the upper body of the Hindu god Vishnu. Exhibitions and performances can be seen here.

🎫 **GWK**
Jalan Raya Uluwatu, Bukit Ungasan, Jimbaran. *Tel (0361) 703 603.*
☐ *daily.* 📷 🏪 ⬛
http://gwk-culturalpark.com

The Amanusa, a boutique hotel overlooking the golf course at Nusa Dua

For hotels and restaurants in this region see pp170–74 and pp184–8

Sun loungers at the Four Seasons Resort, Jimbaran

Jimbaran ⓫

Road Map C5. *Kuta, (0361) 756 176.* www.badung.go.id

Jimbaran is a large village consisting of many family compounds laid out on traditional Balinese lines *(see pp28–9)*. There are no individual buildings of great interest to visit, but Jimbaran is a good place for those who like to see scenes of local everyday life. Several of Bali's most luxurious resorts have been built nearby. The most famous is the Four Seasons Resort *(see p170)*.

There is a very attractive beach, from which the sunsets and the views are spectacular. On a clear day the profiles of all Bali's volcanoes and hills are visible from here, including the three peaks of Gunung Batukau to the west *(see p133)*, and Gunung Batur *(see p120–21)*, Gunung Agung *(see p114)*, Gunung Abang *(see p121)* and Gunung Seraya *(see p103)* to the east. On the beach itself, it is possible to rent sailing-boats and take part in other water activities.

Jimbaran is a good place to eat. The beach is lined with thatch-roofed eating places, where customers choose their fresh seafood which is then grilled over coconut husks and delivered to the table.

There is a large fishing settlement here, consisting of simple huts built near the waterfront. Many of the fishermen are not of Balinese origin, but migrants from the islands of Java and Madura. The brightly painted boats with their impressive bows and sterns can be seen all day long bobbing at anchor in the surf off the coast. As the sun begins to set, the fishing craft set off into the dusk with lamps burning – it is an unforgettable sight.

Surfing at Kuta Reef, off the west coast of South Bali

Environs
Kuta Reef is one of Bali's famous surfing points. The reef break which lies off the coast of Tuban is one of the surfing spots in the sea around the Ngurah Rai International Airport. It can be reached by paddling for some time, or chartering an outrigger at Tuban *(see p69)* or at Jimbaran.

The **Bukit Peninsula** is the southernmost part of Bali, making up most of the area south of Jimbaran. Much of the coast is a series of limestone cliffs. The Bukit is now home to some of the most luxurious holiday rental villas and boutique hotels on the island.

Pura Luhur Uluwatu ⓬

See pp76–7.

Nusa Lembongan ⓭

Road Map E4. *from Sanur, Kusamba & Padang Bai.* *Klungkung, Jalan Untung Surapati 3 (0366) 21 448.*

This small island has pristine beaches for sunlovers and good coral reefs for divers and snorkellers. Bird-lovers will find a variety of species.

Day trips to the island have been available since the early 1990s. In operation now are several jet catamarans, the best-known of them being the *Bali Hai (see p207)*; as a consequence the island is visited by larger groups than hitherto. Trips to the island are also offered by some local boat owners. The boats include *pinisi*, a type of Indonesian sailing vessel originating in the island of Sulawesi to the northeast.

Most boat-operators rent water-sport equipment, and snorkelling and diving gear.

On the island is an extensive underground house, known as the **Cavehouse**. It was dug by a Balinese priest after he was instructed in dreams to live in the belly of Mother Earth. He has passed away but the cave remains a popular curiosity.

For those who like pristine islands with no cars, Nusa Lembongan is a good place to stay a night or two. There are some good homestays for budget travellers. After the daytrippers go, silence reigns; only some overnighters and the locals remain.

Ideal conditions for snorkelling off Nusa Lembongan

For hotels and restaurants in this region see pp170–74 and pp184–88

KEY

▭ Ferry service

🏄 Surfing

🐬 Diving or snorkelling

0 kilometres   10

0 miles   6

The coastal temple Pura Batu Kuning, on Nusa Penida

Nusa Penida ⑭

Road Map E5 & F5. 🛳 *from Sanur, Kusamba & Padang Bai.*
ℹ *Klungkung, (0366) 21 448.*
🍴 🏠 ♻

This quiet, undeveloped island, once the penal colony of the Raja of Klungkung, appeals mainly to hardy adventurers. Here, Balinese language and art have been less subject to change than on the mainland. The island is the legendary home of Ratu Gede Mecaling, the Balinese "King of Magical Powers". It is somewhat feared by many Balinese.

In general the landscape is dry, even arid, resembling the limestone hills of the Bukit Peninsula. Towards the south coast, with its tall white cliffs, there are a few lusher hills.

Some cotton is grown here. From it is woven the *cepuk*, a form of *ikat* textile *(see p37)* thought to have magical, protective powers. Other local occupations include seaweed farming.

There are several interesting temples here. One is the **Pura Ped**, in the village of Toyapakeh. The temple is built on an island in a large lotus pond. Among the carvings in **Pura Kuning**, near Semaya, are some explicitly erotic reliefs. The *pura desa*, or village temple, of the inland village of **Batumadeg** also has some interesting decorative reliefs. They show a number of sea creatures, including crabs and a variety

of shellfish. The main gate is especially imposing.

A short distance south of Suana there is a sacred limestone cave, **Goa Karangsari**.

In general there are few facilities of any kind on Nusa Penida. Visitors must take even basic supplies with them. Simple homestays are the only accommodation. The roads are not good. The best way to get about is by motorcycle or on foot. It is also possible to rent a car with a driver or take a *bemo*.

The waters off the coast of Nusa Penida are crystalclear, although the currents are often strong. Here experienced divers will be able to see to see many large and rare species of underwater life. There are fine coral formations, especially off the south coast, where the sea is also famous for its rare but spectacular concentrations of giant sunfish *(see pp210–11)*; in December and January they float in the water like large hot-air balloons. Sailfish and the whale shark can occasionally be seen. Off the northern half of the island the waters, while also clear, are shallower and calmer, especially in the strait between Nusa Penida and Nusa Lembongan. Most people who dive off these islands make their arrangements with operators in Sanur.

For those who want to explore Nusa Lembongan there is a ferry that runs from Toyapakeh, and fast boats from Sanur and Serangan.

Stone sculpture at Pura Ped

Diving off the coast of Nusa Penida

Pura Luhur Uluwatu ⑫

Local monkeys

Pura Luhur Uluwatu is not only one of Bali's most sacred places of worship but also one of the most beautiful examples of classical Balinese architecture. It is connected in legend to two figures important in the history of Balinese religion, Mpu Kuturan, thought to have built it in the 11th century, and the reformer priest Dang Hyang Nirartha (later deified as Betara Sakti Wawu Rauh) *(see pp46–7)*, who rebuilt it some 500 years later. Until the beginning of the 20th century only the princes of Denpasar were allowed to worship here. It is best to visit during the late afternoon when the sea breezes rise, and then enjoy the sunset.

★ Three-tiered Meru
The pagoda is dedicated to Nirartha who achieved enlightenment here.

This courtyard is reserved for worshippers.

View of the Temple
From several points the temple can be seen in its full glory as the surf crashes onto the rocks below. It is sometimes possible to see turtles and dolphins in the sea.

STAR FEATURES

- ★ Three-tiered Meru
- ★ Main Gate
- ★ Candi Bentar

Stairways
These stepped paths along the cliff rise 200 m (600 ft) above the sea.

★ **Main Gate**
The unusual arched doorway has the shape of Meru, the Cosmic Mountain of Hinduism. Surmounting it are three finials and a kala head – this is a fanged demon with bulging eyes, thought to ward off evil spirits.

Guardian Statues
These Ganesha, elephant-headed guardian statues, wearing a belt with a clasp in the form of a cyclops, are masterpieces of Balinese sculpture.

The *jero tengah*, or central courtyard, offers spectacular views of the sunset.

★ **Candi Bentar**
At the top of the stairs leading to the temple is a candi bentar (split gate) decorated with elaborate carvings.

The *astasari* is a shrine for festival offerings.

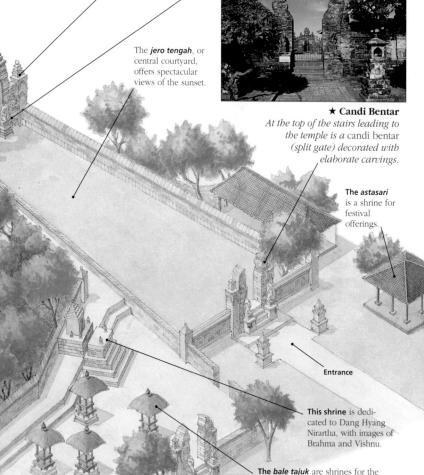

Entrance

This shrine is dedicated to Dang Hyang Nirartha, with images of Brahma and Vishnu.

The *bale tajuk* are shrines for the spiritual guardians of Nirartha.

CENTRAL BALI

*B*ali's broad southern slopes, with their terraced ricefields and hundreds of villages, were the cradle of traditional Balinese society. This area coincides with the regency (and former kingdom) of Gianyar, made up of many puri (noble houses) whose former glory lives on in the courtly arts of sculpture, painting, gold- and silversmithing, music, dance and theatrical performance.

Gianyar is bounded on its western side by the tumultuous Ayung River and to the east by the Melangit River. A number of other rivers slice through the intervening landscape. Between the Petanu and Pakrisan Rivers are the remains of one of Bali's oldest civilizations. Here is the village of Ubud, a cultural centre and former kingdom, which attracts many visitors today.

From the 9th to the 11th century, Bali was ruled by Hindu-Buddhist kingdoms centred near present-day Pejeng and Bedulu, a short distance from Ubud. After the Majapahit conquest in the 14th century, power shifted to Klungkung but it returned here in the 18th century. At that time branches of the Klungkung dynasty grew into rival kingdoms, two of which were based

in Sukawati and Gianyar. Satellite *puri* competed in architectural and ritual display.

Inter-kingdom warfare at the end of the 19th century gave Ubud much of Gianyar's land. Politically, Puri Gianyar remained on top, partly because of its early incorporation into the Dutch colonial regime.

Ubud became internationally famous as a gateway into Bali's cultural heartland, when several Western artists and intellectuals settled here in the 1930s. Today, many farmers are turning to tourism and handicrafts for economic reasons. Local cultural traditions are being preserved as a consequence.

The climate of Central Bali cools noticeably as one ascends from the coastal region into the foothills, and can be chilly north of Tegallalang.

View across the Ayung River valley from the Alila Ubud Resort

◁ Densely carved temple gate of the Pura Desa (village temple) in Peliatan

Exploring Central Bali

Central Bali, rich in history, is famous for
craft production and the performing arts.
Ubud is an important artistic centre, and a
good base for exploring the area. Many
ot her villages and monuments of historic
and cultural interest are located on the
roads running between the coastal plain
and the slopes of Gunung Batur. The river
gorges, separated by ridges and rice
terraces, provide beautiful landscapes,
and exciting white-water rafting. Near
Singapadu are the attractively laid-out
Bali Bird Park and Bali Reptile Park.

Pura Pengastulan, a temple in Bedulu

GETTING AROUND

The main route through Central Bali leads
through several arts and crafts villages:
Batubulan, Celuk, Sukawati, Batuan, Mas and
Ubud. A parallel, more westerly road runs
through Singapadu. Most of these roads can be
travelled by *bemo*. Taxis are not as frequent as
in South Bali. North of Ubud three parallel roads
climb, via the villages of Payangan, Tegallalang
and Tampaksiring towards Gunung Batur and
Kintamani. Bicycles and motorcycles are not
pleasant ways of travelling on main roads south
of Ubud, because of the density of traffic,
although they are more satisfactory further north
and on back roads. Public buses between
Denpasar and Singaraja ply the main north-south
route; however, tourist shuttle buses run
frequently between South Bali's resorts and
Ubud, and are much more comfortable.

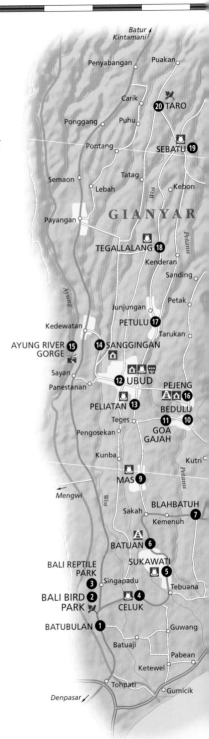

Tilem gallery selling woodcarvings in the village of Mas

SIGHTS AT A GLANCE

Ayung River Gorge **15**
Bali Bird Park pp84–5 **2**
Bali Reptile Park **3**
Batuan **6**
Batubulan **1**
Bedulu **10**
Blahbatuh **7**
Celuk **4**
Gianyar **8**
Goa Gajah **11**
Gunung Kawi Royal
Monuments **21**

Mas **9**
Pejeng **16**
Peliatan **13**
Petulu **17**
Pura Tirta Empul **22**
Sanggingan **14**
Sebatu **19**
Sukawati **5**
Taro **20**
Tegallalang **18**
Ubud pp88–95 **12**

SEE ALSO

• *Where to Stay* pp174–6
• *Where to Eat* pp188–9

KEY

━━ Dual carriageway

━ Major road

--- Minor road

━ Regency boundary

0 kilometres 3
0 miles 2

Coconuts being collected near Ubud

Keris trance, one of the energetic ritual dance performances which can be seen in Batubulan

Batubulan ❶

Road Map C4. 🚌 🚐 🚹 *Gianyar, (0361) 943 401.* 📧 🚻 ♿

Although Denpasar's urban sprawl is enveloping Batubulan and the main road is lined with shops selling "antique" furniture, this large village is still a centre of traditional stone carving. Craftsmen can be seen in countless workshops sculpting mythological and religious figures or highly imaginative modern forms, apparently oblivious to the heavy traffic passing by on the main road.

The village temple, **Pura Puseh**, is a good example of the use of *paras*, Bali's ubiquitous grey stone, which is in fact volcanic tuff, quarried from river gorges. *Paras* is used both for sculpture and as a building material. Its soft texture makes it very easy to carve.

Batubulan is also home to several venerable Barong and Keris dance theatre troupes. During alternate weeks the Pura Puseh is the pleasant venue of a daily Barong and Keris dance performance by the celebrated **Denjalan** troupe; in intervening weeks the location is Batubulan's *bale banjar*, or community pavilion. A few other troupes perform at around the same time. Daytime performances were developed in the 1930s,

in response to the desire of visitors to take photographs. However, this exorcistic drama still has ritual significance.

🏛 **Pura Puseh**
Main Road, Batubulan. ◯ *daily.* 🖼 *donation.*

🎭 **Denjalan**
Tel *(0361) 298 038 or (0361) 298 282. Performances: 9:30am daily.* 🖼

Bali Bird Park ❷

See pp84–5.

Bali Reptile Park ❸

Jalan Serma Cok Ngurah Gambir, Singapadu. Next to Bali Bird Park. **Road Map** D4. **Tel** *(0361) 299 344.* ◯ *daily.* ● *Nyepi.* 🖼 📧 🚻 🍴

A visit to the Bali Reptile Park (Rimba Reptil) is easily combined with a visit to the Bali Bird Park nearby. The two are conceived in a similar style. Although somewhat smaller in area than the Bird Park, the Reptile Park is also set in lush, botanically interesting gardens. The landscaping concept is that of an ancient archaeological site, excavated and restored to its former glory. All the significant reptile species of Indonesia can be seen in the

collection. They include Komodo dragons, four species of crocodiles, and what is claimed to be the largest known python in captivity. Many venomous snakes from around the world are well displayed in glass cages. Among them are a king cobra, a Malayan pit viper and a death adder.

Celuk ❹

Road Map D4. 🚌 🚐 🚹 *Gianyar, (0361) 943 401.* 📧 🚻 ♿ *(limited).*

The village of Celuk is devoted almost entirely to gold- and silversmithing. Much of the jewellery sold in Bali originates here. The workers belong to the caste clan of Pande Mas, traditionally practitioners of various metal crafts. Grand jewellery shops line the main road; smaller ones selling cheaper goods occupy the narrow side streets. Several studios produce traditional and modern designs of ornamental jewellery as well as *keris* daggers and religious items. Jewellery can be made to order. Buyers should be aware that at the larger outlets, prices may include a commission (often 40–60 per cent) passed on to tour guides.

Silver earrings from Celuk

Sukawati ❺

Road Map D4. 🚌 🚐 ℹ️ *Gianyar,*
(0361) 943 401. 🅿️ 📷 ♿ *(limited).*

Sukawati is worth visiting primarily as a handicrafts centre. Opposite the farmers' market on the east side of the main road through the town is the **Pasar Seni** ("Art Market"). It is housed in a complex of two-storey buildings packed with stalls selling craft goods. Behind it is a market selling woodcarvings, open until 10am daily.

To the people of Bali, Sukawati is important as the ancestral seat of many of the region's *puri* (noble houses), and as a centre of the sacred shadow puppet theatre, *wayang kulit (see p31)*. In the early 1700s an off-shoot of the royal house of Klungkung was established here. The palace, on the northeast corner of the main intersection, is much reduced; and the temples, further north on the main road and nestling in side streets to the east, are not generally open to visitors.

Stone sculptures of mythological figures in a shop at Sukawati

Batuan ❻

Road Map D4. 🚌 🚐 ℹ️ *Gianyar,*
(0366) 93 401. 🍴 🅿️ 📷 ♿ *(limited).*

The history of Batuan goes back almost 1,000 years. The population contains more nobility than commoners; and it is celebrated for its artistic excellence in the fields of not only dance but also painting and architecture. Painters' studios are prominent in the village. The Batuan school of painting is known for its dense graphics, dramatically restricted colour palette and astute observation of human life *(see pp34–5)*.

The **Pura Puseh**, the magnificent village temple, welcomes visitors. Extensively renovated, its opulent shrines and carvings are proof that Bali's traditional building arts are thriving. *Gambuh* performances are held at the temple on the 1st and 15th of each month, a rare opportunity to see this ancient court dance. Among the dance troupes of Batuan are practitioners also of *topeng* and *wayang wong (see p31)*. These are, like *gambuh*, performed to traditional music during temple festivals.

🏛️ **Pura Puseh**
🕐 *daily.* 💰 *donation.* 💃 *Gambuh dance: 7–9pm, 1st & 15th monthly.*
♿

Blahbatuh ❼

Road Map D4. 🚌 🚐 ℹ️ *Gianyar,*
(0361) 943 401. 🅿️ 📷 ♿ *(limited).*

The village of Blahbatuh is marked by a huge stone statue of a baby, which was erected in the early 1990s and said by some to be the village giant Kebo Iwo as an infant. Others whisper that the women of a nearby village urged their husbands to build the statue to placate a demon who they believed had been claiming the lives of their children.

Vihara Amurva Bhumi Blahbatuh, a large Chinese temple *(klenteng)* with Buddhist and Hindu elements which has undergone grand expansion, is a little-known but increasingly popular centre of worship for Chinese Buddhists from throughout South Bali.

Giant baby statue near Blahbatuh

Environs

On the main north-south road between Blahbatuh and the Bedulu road is the large workshop and showroom of the **Sidha Karya Gong Foundry**, established by the renowned gongsmith I Made Gabeleran. A full array of traditional musical instruments and dance costumes is on sale here.

At **Kutri**, 3 km (2 miles) north of Blahbatuh, is a hill at the base of which is the temple complex **Pura Bukit Dharma Kutri**. On the hilltop, from which there are good views, is a shrine that houses a partly effaced, but still fine, relief carving of the goddess Durga killing a bull. It is thought to be a portrait statue of an 11th-century Balinese queen.

Kemenuh, 1.5 km (1 mile) west of Blahbatuh, is a woodcarving centre where you can see woodcarvers at work and choose from a selection of ritual and ornamental pieces including effigies, masks and statues.

🏛️ **Vihara Amurva Bhumi Blahbatuh**
Blahbatuh. 🕐 *daily.* 🚻

🏛️ **Sidha Karya**
Jalan Raya Getas-Buruan, Blahbatuh.
Tel *(0361) 942 798.*

🏛️ **Pura Bukit Dharma Kutri**
Kutri. 🕐 *daily.* 🚻

Pura Bukit Dharma Kutri, a temple named after a hill near Blahbatuh

Bali Bird Park ❷

Built on what was originally an expanse of ricefields, Bali Bird Park, or Taman Burung, is a place where visitors can see a profusion of exotic wildlife at close quarters. There are almost 1,000 birds here, many of them in big, walk-in aviaries. There are 250 species not only from Bali and Lombok, but also from the rest of Indonesia, Africa, Australia and the Americas. Many of the birds are rare and endangered, and some of these are bred here. Among the inhabitants is Bali's only endemic bird, the Bali starling *(see p137)*. Besides the birds, there are more than 300 exotic trees and plants on display in a beautifully landscaped setting.

Edward's fig parrot

★ Birds of Paradise
The lesser bird of paradise, from New Guinea, has been hunted close to extinction.

Bali Aviary

★ Papua Rainforest Aviary
This huge, walk-in aviary has a raised walkway. The birds here include many birds of paradise, the toco toucan, and sun conures from South America.

Australian Pelican
This large waterbird sometimes wanders as far as Indonesia.

Victoria Crowned Pigeon
This aviary has one of the three crowned pigeon species from New Guinea; also the Nicobar pigeon; the pink-necked pigeon; and the great argus pheasant.

INDONESIAN OWLS

These nocturnal birds can rarely be seen in the wild and the buffy fish owl and the barred or Sumatran eagle owl are therefore a highlight of the Bali Bird Park. They are both large and feed on rodents. In all there are 38 recognised species of Indonesian owl – many of them found only on small islands. Their secretive nature and, in some cases, preference for inhospitable habitats are reasons why little is known about them.

Buffy fish-owl

KEY

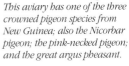

P	Parking
	Souvenir shop
♿	Wheelchair access
▢	Café
🚻	Toilet

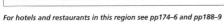

Komodo Dragons
These carnivorous creatures are the world's largest lizards, endemic to Komodo in Indonesia.

Hornbills
The Asian pied hornbill has a very distinct, loud, raucous call.

Birds of Bali and Java

0 metres 50

0 yards 50

To Bali Reptile Park

Live shows

Entrance

Parrots and cockatoos

Cassowary enclosure

Breeding centre

Birds of South America

The African Grey Parrot
This species can often be trained to mimic.

★ Toraja House
This typical house from Sulawesi is nearly 100 years old. It was dismantled, moved and re-assembled here.

Major Mitchell's Cockatoo
Apart from this species from Australia, several parrots and cockatoos native to Indonesia (of which there are over 75 species) are bred in this bird park.

STAR SIGHTS

★ Papua Rainforest Aviary

★ Birds of Paradise

★ Toraja House

Puri Gianyar, a palace of the royal family of the former kingdom of Gianyar, restored to its past glory

Gianyar ❽

Road Map D4. 🚗 🚌 ℹ *Jalan Ngurah Rai 21, (0361) 943 401.* 🛏 🏪 ♿ *(limited).* ⛽

This town is a centre of administration rather than of the tourist industry. The people of Bali shop here for farm produce, household appliances and paraphernalia for ceremonies; there is also a large market. This is a good place to buy jewellery and hand-woven and hand-dyed textiles, many of them made locally. During the day, there are food stalls at the Bale Banjar Teges (community association meeting hall) at the town centre; the *babi guling* (roast pig) is famous.

On the north side of the town square is the impressive **Puri Gianyar**. Although the palace is closed to visitors, its grand outer walls and gates

Local food stalls at the night market in Gianyar

give a sense of the power of the former kingdoms. After damage by an earthquake in 1917, the *puri* was restored as a replica of the original 17th-century construction.

Environs

Southwest of Gianyar are several villages whose livelihood is increasingly based on craft products from plant materials. Although these are sold for export and in shops around Bali, visitors can buy for better prices at source. **Bona**, 3 km (2 miles) southwest of Gianyar, specializes in hand-woven objects made from the leaves of the lontar palm. About 2 km (1 mile) southwest of Bona is the village of **Blega**, which is a centre for the production of bamboo furniture.

Mas ❾

Road Map D4. 🚗 🚌 ℹ *Gianyar, (0361) 943 401.* 🍴 🛏 🏪 ♿ *(limited).* ⛽

The village of Mas is most famous not for teak furniture, as the number of roadside shops selling it

might suggest, but for fine wood sculpture and *topeng* masks *(see p31)*. The brahmans of Mas have been master-carvers for many generations; sculpture has been produced for the art market since the 1930s *(see pp36–7)*. Among the best-established studio-galleries are Siadja & Son, the Njana Tilem Gallery and Adil Art-shop. Tantra Gallery and I B Anom (for masks) are well-known. Brahmans come to Mas from all over Bali every Manis Kuningan festival *(see p39)* to honour their ancestor, the Hindu priest Dang Hyang Nirartha (also known as Dwijendra) at the temple **Pura Taman Pule**. The large old tree in the temple is regarded as holy. According to local belief, a gold flower once grew from it. The tree is dressed up in ceremonial colours during the festival. On the evening of the festivities there is usually a ritual performance of *wayang wong (see p31)*.

Elaborately carved gateway at Pura Taman Pule, Mas

🏛 Pura Taman Pule

🕐 *daily.* 🎭 *wayang wong: during festivals.* 🎉 *Kuningan (see p43).*

Bedulu ⑩

Road Map D3. 🚗 🚌 🚹 *Gianyar,*
(0361) 943 401. 🍴 🖃 ♿ *(limited).*

This large, quiet village
was at the centre of the
Pejeng kingdom of the
10–13th centuries. The
monumental relief carvings
on a large rock wall at the
Yeh Pulu spring, south of
the village, are thought to
date from the mid-14th-
century Majapahit conquest
(see p46). The carvings –
about 25 m (80 ft) long with
an average height of 2 m (6
ft) – are thought to be the
work of a single artist. Myth
attributes the work to the
legendary 14th-century giant
Kebo Iwo. The stories can be
"read" by looking at the
vigorously carved images
from left to right. Among
them are heroic scenes
showing humans fighting
demonic beasts.

The large **Pura Pengas-**
tulan temple *(see p80)* has
grand gates built in the art-
deco style made fashionable
by the artist I Gusti Nyoman

**The village of Bedulu decorated
for the Galungan festival**

Lempad *(see p34)*, who was
born in Bedulu.

Lempad's style may be seen
also in the nearby **Pura
Samuan Tiga**. This name
derives from a legend. In the
11th century, a meeting
(*samuan*) is said to have
been held here among the
gods of three (*tiga*) warring
religious sects after they had
defeated the demon king
Mayadanawa.

The annual festival around
Purnama Kedasa *(see p40)* is
a brilliant 11-day celebration;
but even when empty, Pura
Samuan Tiga has a great,
quiet strength. The grand
inner gate by Lempad is
particularly impressive, as is
the cockfighting pit on the
east side of the first courtyard.

🛕 **Yeh Pulu**
⭕ *daily.* 🖼 *donation.*

🅰 **Pura Pengastulan**
⭕ *daily.* 🚫

🅰 **Pura Samuan Tiga**
⭕ *daily.* 🖼 *donation.* 🎭 *Perang
Sampian: 1pm during festival.*
🎏 *Purnama Kedasa (Apr, variable).*

Carved rocks at the entrance to Goa Gajah, the "Elephant Cave"

Goa Gajah ⑪

Bedulu. **Road Map** D3. 🚗 🚌
🚹 *Gianyar, (0361) 943 401.*
⭕ *daily.* 🖼 🅿 🚻 🎎

The Goa Gajah ("Elephant
Cave") became known to
Westerners only in 1923. It is
thought to date from the 11th
century. Steps lead down to
the temple and other monuments, about 15 m (50 ft)
below road level. The large
springs, excavated in 1954,
were intended probably for
bathing and as a source of
holy water. The cave itself,
with a large face in the exu-
berantly carved surrounding
rock, is a small, rather airless,
T-shaped chamber in which
are niches containing Shivite
and Buddhist statues.

Outside the cave is a shrine
to the Buddhist child-protector
Hariti, depicted as the Balinese
Men Brayut, a poor woman
with too many children. In a
ravine a little to the south are
a spring and more shrines.

THE LEGEND OF BEDAULU

The name Bedulu comes from the 14th-century
sorcerer-king Bedaulu, who was said to remove his
head (*hulu*) to achieve more efficient meditation.
One day he was disturbed in this practice and
hastily took the head of a passing pig (*beda* means
"different"). Thereafter it was forbidden to look at
the king, lest his ugly secret be discovered, and he
ruled from a tower, raised above eye level.
However, the Majapahit general Gajah Mada tricked
him during a feast. As Gajah Mada tipped back his
head to drink, he looked up, glimpsed the king's
true nature and so was able to overpower him.

The King of Bedulu in his Tower **(1934) by I Tomblos**

Street-by-Street: Ubud ⑫

Almost everywhere in Ubud one is conscious of the town's artistic traditions. Since most shops stay open until around 9pm, the best time for strolling around is the early evening. By then the traffic has abated, the cafés and restaurants are invitingly lit, and the cool air is often filled with *gamelan* music from cultural performances. The main street, Jalan Raya Ubud, is the setting for several buildings of architectural interest. The streets running off it to the north and south lead to village neighbourhoods, and are lined with family-run shops, small businesses catering for visitors, and art galleries.

Pura Taman Saraswati
This temple is set by a lotus pond.

★ **Museum Puri Lukisan**
A fine collection of Balinese art is on show here (see pp92–3).

JALAN RAYA UBUD

JALAN KAJENG

MONKEY FOREST

Ary's Warung
This restaurant is run by a minor Ubud palace family, on land either side of the house gate.

Monkey Forest Road
is lined with galleries, restaurants and hotels.

INFLUENTIAL VISITORS OF THE 1930S

Bali owes much of its fame to foreign guests of Ubud's royal family in the 1920s and '30s. Through their films, books and photographs, these visitors projected to the world an exotic image of Bali. Among the most influential were German painter and musician Walter Spies and Dutch painter Rudolf Bonnet, who helped found the Pita Maha artists' association *(see p35)*; and Mexican artist Miguel Covarrubias, who wrote the classic *Island of Bali* (1937). The anthropologists Margaret Mead and Gregory Bateson lived in Sayan, just outside Ubud; their neighbours were composer Colin McPhee and his wife, ethnographer Jane Belo.

Walter Spies, who settled in Ubud in 1927

To Monkey Forest Sanctuary

0 metres   100
0 yards   100

KEY

– – – Suggested route

STAR SIGHTS

★ Museum Puri Lukisan

★ Puri Saren

★ Pasar Ubud

★ **Puri Saren**
*Ubud's palace has a shady
forecourt where visitors can
relax during the day and see
traditional dance every evening.*

VISITORS' CHECKLIST

Road Map C3. 🚌 *from
Denpasar & Kuta.* 🚐
ℹ️ *Ubud Tourist Information,
Jalan Raya Ubud, (0361) 973
285.* 🎭 *Balinese performances:
daily, details posted at Ubud*
ℹ️🍴🏛️📷🛍️

★ **Pasar Ubud**
*A farmers' market
takes place here
in the morning.
Shops and stalls
sell all kinds of
crafts, snacks and
sundries through-
out the day.*

**Ubud Tourist
Information Centre**

The *wantilan* is a hall
where local people can
gather and cultural
events take place.

**Seniwati Women's
Art Gallery**

JALAN SUWETA

JALAN RAYA UBUD

JALAN SRIWEDARI

**To Peliatan
and Bedulu**

Lempad House was
once an artist's home
and studio *(see p90).*

JALAN HANOMAN

JALAN DEWI SITA

**To Pengosekan,
Batubulan and
Denpasar**

Jalan Dewi Sita is a street around
which have been established many
popular boutiques, art galleries
and restaurants.

Jalan Hanoman
*Temples, shops, art studios, and
homestays can be found here.*

Exploring Ubud

Rangda mask

Ubud has long been known as the "village of painters". In the 1930s, the encouragement of the *puri* (royal family) attracted foreign artists and intellectuals seeking the "real Bali", and so the village's international reputation was born. A peaceful hamlet until the 1980s, Ubud developed rapidly into a village of "cultural tourism". Now it is a small town, packed with galleries, craftshops, restaurants, bars and hotels. However, Ubud spends much of its prosperity on ritual ceremonies and conservation of traditional art forms.

A palace gate in Puri Saren

ℹ Ubud Tourist Information Centre

Jalan Raya Ubud.
Tel (0361) 973 285. ◯ *daily.*
The centre is a reliable source of information about tours, transport, dance performances, and current cultural events. It provides information about local ceremonies and encourages foreigners to observe dress etiquette when visiting temples or rituals *(see p218).*

⌂ Museum Puri Lukisan

See pp92–3.

▣ Pura Taman Saraswati

Jalan Raya Ubud. ◯ *daily.*
This temple was built in the 1950s by I Gusti Nyoman Lempad *(see p34)* at the command of Ubud's prince, in honour of Saraswati, the deity of learning and the arts. It is set in a water garden, with a lotus pond as the centrepiece. The temple has fine carvings by Lempad: a 3-m (10-ft) statue of the demon Jero Gede Mecaling; and the *padmasana* shrine in the northeast corner,

dedicated to the Supreme God *(see p26).* The temple is normally closed, but admission may be gained via the adjacent Café Lotus.

⛩ Puri Saren

Jalan Raya Ubud. **Tel** (0361) 975 057.
▣ *Traditional dances 7:30pm daily.*
www.ubudvillage.com
The grandeur of Ubud's royal palace dates from the 1890s, the time of warlord Cokorda Gede Sukawati. The present walls and resplendent gates are largely the work of master artist I Gusti Nyoman Lempad *(see p34).* The *puri,* which owns several hotels, remains influential in Ubud's religious and cultural life, and spends lavishly on local ceremonies.

◨ Pasar Ubud

Jalan Raya Ubud. ◯ *daily.*
At the huge Pasar Ubud (Ubud Market) there are sellers of agricultural produce and dry goods on the ground floor and between the buildings. The main attraction for visitors is the all-day handicraft market. The food market is held every three days on *pasah.*

⛩ Lempad House

Jalan Raya Ubud. **Tel** (0361) 975 618.
◯ *daily.*
This is the family compound of I Gusti Nyoman Lempad *(see p34),* perhaps Bali's most celebrated artist. Some works by Lempad are on display in the courtyard, although the Neka Art Museum *(see p96)* holds a better collection of his work. Lempad was also an architect and builder in the traditional style, and the handsome north and east pavilions of the house were designed by him.

A group of woodcarvers at work near the Lempad House

⌂ Seniwati Gallery Art by Women

Jalan Sriwedari 2B.
Tel (0361) 975 485. ◯ *daily.*
www.seniwatigallery.com
Pondok Pecak Jalan Monkey Forest.
Tel (0361) 976 194. ◯ *Mon–Sat.* ▣
This is one of the few galleries exhibiting women's art in Asia. They work with 72 mostly Balinese artists, who paint in modern and traditional styles. Their library and bookshop, **Pondok Pecak Library and Learning Centre**, offer language and arts classes.

Pura Taman Saraswati facing Café Lotus across an ornamental pond

For hotels and restaurants in this region see pp174–6 and pp188–9

🏛 Pura Gunung Lebah
Campuhan.

To the west of Ubud, Jalan Raya descends into the valley known as **Campuhan**, where two rivers meet *(campuh)*. A bridge built by the colonial Dutch survives next to the modern traffic bridge. From it can be seen the spring temple Pura Gunung Lebah (Pura Campuhan), which was founded in the 8th century. This has been a foreigners' residential neighbourhood since the 1930s, when Walter Spies *(see p88)* built his house at what is now the Tjampuhan Hotel and Spa.

Coconut palms surrounding rice plantations in the valley west of Ubud

Environs
At the end of a long street known as Monkey Forest Road is the **Monkey Forest Sanctuary**, offering protection to three troupes of long-tailed

A long-tail macaque in the Monkey Forest Sanctuary

monkeys (*Macaca fascicularis*). It is advisable to heed the warnings against feeding the monkeys – they can become aggressive. In the forest, there is an important temple complex and a graveyard. The large **Pura Dalem Agung** is a "temple of the dead"; its carved decorations are appropriately frightening. Close by is a spring temple, renovated in the 1990s with extra carvings.

Padang Tegal, on the southern outskirts of Ubud, is a large village notable for its

many painters and intellectuals, and offers numerous homestays. South of Padang Tegal is the small village of **Pengosekan**, home to many painters and woodcarvers. In the village of **Tebesaya**, east of Padang Tegal, there are many good places to eat, shop and stay. West of Pengosekan is **Nyuh Kuning**, a woodcarving centre.

🐒 Monkey Forest Sanctuary
Monkey Forest Road, Jalan Wana Wanara. **Tel** *(0361) 971 304.*
⏰ *8am–6pm daily.* 🎫
www.monkeyforestubud.com

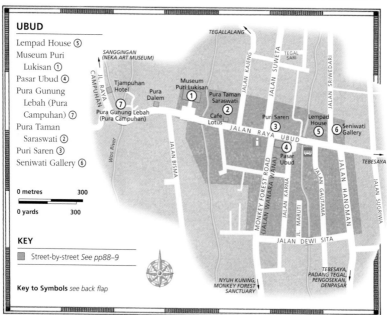

UBUD

Lempad House ⑤
Museum Puri Lukisan ①
Pasar Ubud ④
Pura Gunung Lebah (Pura Campuhan) ⑦
Pura Taman Saraswati ②
Puri Saren ③
Seniwati Gallery ⑥

0 metres   300
0 yards   300

KEY
▪ Street-by-street *See pp88–9*

Key to Symbols *see back flap*

TEGALLALANG

SANGGINGAN (NEKA ART MUSEUM)

Tjampuhan Hotel
Pura Dalem
Pura Gunung Lebah (Pura Campuhan) ⑦

Museum Puri Lukisan ①
Pura Taman Saraswati
Cafe Lotus
Puri Saren ③
Lempad House ⑤
Seniwati Gallery ⑥

Pura Taman Saraswati ②

JALAN RAYA UBUD

Pasar Ubud ④

JALAN KAJENG
JALAN SUWETA
TEGAL SARI
JALAN SRIWEDARI
JL. RAYA CAMPUHAN
Wos River
JALAN BISMA
MONKEY FOREST ROAD (JALAN WANARA WANA)
JALAN KARNA
JL. MARUTI
JALAN GAUTAMA
JALAN HANOMAN
JALAN SUGRIWA
JALAN DEWI SITA

TEBESAYA

NYUH KUNING, MONKEY FOREST SANCTUARY

TEBESAYA, PADANG TEGAL, PENGOSEKAN, DENPASAR

Ubud: Museum Puri Lukisan

Museum Puri Lukisan ("Palace of Painting"), was the brainchild of Ubud's prince Cokorda Gede Agung Sukawati, and Dutch painter Rudolf Bonnet *(see p88)*. It was conceived in 1953 out of concern that Bali's finest works of art were disappearing into private collections around the world. The museum's holdings are mainly 20th-century Balinese painting and wood sculpture, including important collections from the 1930s. The grounds, with their gardens and ponds, are a shady, tranquil oasis in the centre of Ubud.

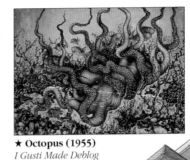

★ Octopus (1955)
I Gusti Made Deblog is known for his fine ink-wash technique.

Building I

Dharmaswami
(1935)
This work by Ida Bagus Gelgel is in the Balinese tradition of painting fables and tales.

★ Dewi Sri *(1960)*
The woodcarver Ketut Djedeng depicts the rice goddess with a grain of rice in her hand.

Birds Dancing the Gambuh *(1940)*
A bas-relief showing the gambuh dance inspired this painting by Ida Bagus Sali.

Building II

LOOKING AT BALINESE PAINTINGS

The density of Balinese painting is extraordinary. Even with little or no background in the arts, the viewer can enter the imaginative world of Balinese culture as represented by both traditional and modern painting. It is a good idea to look at a Balinese work from a distance at first, to see its graphic composition before moving nearer to inspect the details of the content. Close inspection reveals tiny scenes being enacted by the inhabitants of the canvas.

Tiger with Monkey (undated), artist unknown

VISITORS' CHECKLIST

Jalan Raya Ubud.
Tel (0361) 971 159.
⬜ 9am–5pm daily.
⬤ public hols. 🎫 🏛 ♿
www.museumpurilukisan.com

GALLERY GUIDE

Building I houses woodcarving and pre-World War II painting, including the Pita Maha and Lempad collections (see pp34–5). Building II has contemporary Balinese art. Temporary exhibitions are housed in Building III.

Building III

★ Balinese Market
(detail, 1955)
Anak Agung Gede Sobrat, a leading Ubud school painter, explores a modern theme here.

Ticket office

Entrance steps

Parking

★ Kala Rau *(1974)*
I Ketut Budiana, of Padang Tegal, Ubud, paints the lunar eclipse of Balinese myth.

STAR EXHIBITS

- ★ Dewi Sri
- ★ Octopus
- ★ Balinese Market
- ★ Kala Rau

A Walk in the Ubud Countryside

Lacewing butterfly

The ricefields and ridges around Ubud are very suitable for walking. Two routes are shown here. They can be followed separately, or one after the other forming a longer route. The ricefield walk is 6 km (4 miles) long but can be shortened to 4 km (nearly 3 miles) by omitting the northern loop. The 5-km (3-mile) ridge walk runs between two rivers, the Wos Timur and the Wos Barat. Walkers may cross ricefields provided they behave with due consideration. Wildlife sightings may include the iridescent blue Java kingfisher among other birds, the golden orb weaver spider, and a colourful variety of butterflies.

View from Pura Ulun Sui

Jalan Raya Sanggingan ⑫
On this busy road, *bemo* transport can be found back into central Ubud.

Bridge ⑪
Near the bottom of the gorge, a bridge crosses the river to a steep road leading up to the village of Payogan.

Warung in Artists' Settlement ⑩
A small, isolated community of painters lives in this village, from which there are dramatic views along the Wos River gorges. Further north the landscape opens up to reveal ricefields.

Alang Alang Grass ⑨
After Pura Campuhan, a setting for some important religious ceremonies, the path continues through alang alang, a grass used for thatching roofs.

Large Banyan Tree ⑧
The ridge walk starts near the Ibah Luxury Villas, leading past an old banyan tree to a footbridge hanging over the river gorge.

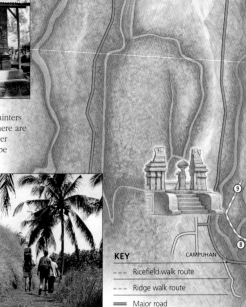

Bangkiang Sidem

Payogan

KEDEWATAN

SANGGINGAN

CAMPUHAN

KEY

- - - Ricefield walk route
- - - Ridge walk route
▬▬ Major road
═══ Minor road
═══ Track

Rice Harvest ⑤
According to the season, rice farmers may be planting or harvesting. Across a narrow bridge carrying irrigation water is an attractive *subak* temple *(see pp20–21).*

Pura Ulun Carik ⑥
From here there is a view of the Wos Timur gorge, where chestnut and black coucal birds abound.

Jalan Raya Ubud ⑦
The path back to the main road passes a palace complex.

Pura Pejenenang ④
Crossing the Wos Timur river to this temple cuts off the northern part of the walk, creating an optional shorter route.

Ricefield Shrines ③
Offerings are placed at these shrines to the rice goddess, who will bless the growing crops.

Pura Ulun Sui ②
This is also known as Juwukmanis Temple. Adjacent to it is a *subak* office with a map explaining the irrigation system of Bali.

Café Lotus ①
The ricefield walk starts at Café Lotus in central Ubud, running north along Jalan Kajeng towards the ricefields.

| 0 metres | 500 |
| 0 yards | 500 |

UBUD

TIPS FOR WALKERS

Start point: Café Lotus, in Ubud.
End point: Jalan Raya Sanggingan.
When to go: All year, but in the wet season, trails can be slippery.
Precautions: River gorges are prone to flash flooding and should be crossed by the bridges. Do not descend into gorges without an experienced guide. Avoid the small trails down to the stone quarries in the Wos River gorge – they are slippery and prone to landslides. Care should be taken walking along the edges of ricefields. Walking shoes and sneakers are suitable footwear.

The south pavilion of the Agung Rai Museum of Art, Peliatan

Peliatan ⑬

Road Map D3. 🏠 🚌 *from Ubud.*
🛈 *Ubud, (0361) 973 285.* 🎭 *kecak,
legong and Barong dance; women's
gamelan.* 🍴 🔲 🗒 🏠 🤝

The village of Peliatan, once
the seat of an offshoot of the
royalty of Sukawati, is
renowned for artistic activities.
It was known among
foreigners for its artistic
traditions even earlier than
Ubud. Today, Peliatan's
gamelan and dance troupes
(see pp30–33) travel abroad
as cultural ambassadors, and
perform locally in traditional
rituals and for visitors.

Peliatan is also a centre of
painting and woodcarving.
Many artists' studios can be
found along its main street
and back lanes. The collector
Agung Rai established the
successful Agung Rai Gallery
and the impressive **Agung Rai
Museum of Art** (usually
referred to as ARMA), in
southwest Peliatan, which has
collections of classical and
contemporary Balinese and
Indonesian painting as well as
temporary exhibitions. The
Rudana Museum houses an
extensive painting collection.

The northern part of Peliatan,
known as Andong, has some
interesting craft shops.

🏠 **ARMA**
Jalan Pengosekan. *Tel (0361) 975
742.* ◯ *daily.* 🔲 ☑ 🔲 🔲
www.armamuseum.com

🏠 **Rudana Museum**
Jalan Cok Rai Pudak 44. *(0361)
975 779.* ◯ *daily.* 🔲

Sanggingan ⑭

Road Map C3. 🚌 *from Ubud.*
🛈 *Ubud, (0361) 973 285.* 🍴 🔲
🗒 🏠 🤝

The road running through the
village of Sanggingan is lined
with art shops, art galleries,
restaurants and small hotels.

The excellent **Neka Art
Museum**, founded in 1976 by
local collector and former
teacher Sutéja Neka, houses
one of the best collections of
Balinese and Indonesian
paintings on the island.
The collection is displayed in
seven buildings numbered
according to the chronological
sequence of the works
displayed. Moving through the
buildings gives a good
overview of Balinese art
history and its Indonesian
context today. Some works
are offered for sale. Of
particular interest to visitors
are the classical *wayang*-style
paintings, anonymous works
of great graphic sophistication;
and also the Lempad collection *(see p34)*, consisting of
superb pen-and-ink drawings.

🏠 **Neka Art Museum**
Jalan Raya Campuhan. *Tel (0361) 975
074.* ◯ *daily.* ● *public hols.* 🔲 🚫
🔲 🔣 **www.museumneka.com**

Portrait of Sutéja Neka (1991) by
Arie Smit, Neka Art Museum

Ayung River Gorge ⑮

Road Map C3. 🚌 *from Ubud.*
🛈 *Ubud, (0361) 973 285.* 🍴 🗒 🤝

Between Kedewatan and
Sayan, the east bank of the
spectacularly beautiful
Ayung River Gorge, flanked

The Ayung River Gorge viewed from the ridge at Sayan village

For hotels and restaurants in this region see pp174–6 and pp188–9

White-water rafting in the rapids of the Ayung River Gorge

by rice terraces, is discreetly populated with some attractive luxury hotels and private houses. Several companies offer white-water rafting from points on both sides of the river *(see p203)*.

Environs
In the village of **Penestanan**, just east of the Gorge, there are studios making painted batik and beadwork. This is also the centre of the Young Artists movement *(see p35)* which emerged in the 1960s.

Pejeng 16

Road Map D3. 🚌 *from Ubud & Gianyar.* 🛈 *Ubud, (0361) 973 285.*
🛇 🍽 📷 🏠 ⌔

Pejeng, a village on the road from Bedulu to Tampaksiring, lies at the heart of the ancient Pejeng-Bedulu kingdom, and there are many interesting relics from that time to be seen. The **Museum Purbakala** (Archaeological Museum) displays prehistoric objects in bronze, stone and ceramics, including several turtle-shaped stone sarcophagi.

A short walk from the museum are three temples of particular interest for their sacred stone sculptures. **Pura Arjuna Metapa** ("Arjuna Meditating" Temple) is a small pavilion standing alone in the ricefields, sheltering a cluster of stone sculptures that were probably once part of a spring temple. In accordance with the *wayang* tradition that recounts tales from the *Mahabharata*, Arjuna is attended by a stone-relief servant character. About 100 m (110 yards) north is **Pura Kebo Edan** ("Crazy Giant" Temple). The demonic

WOODCARVING IN BALI

The surprising abundance of Balinese woodcarving reflects not only an intense decorative tradition but also the fact that Bali's wilderness is forest (still inhabited by tigers in the early 20th century). Trees have a ritual anniversary and must be given offerings before being felled. Traditional woodcarving is of two main sorts: ritual objects such as effigies and masks; and ornamental carving, especially of architectural elements. The liberalizing art movement of the 1930s *(see pp34–5)* encouraged woodcarvers to sculpt freely for a foreign market. The main centres of woodcarving today include Peliatan and several other villages in Gianyar regency, including Tegallalang *(see p98)* and Mas *(see p86)*.

Sleeping Woman (1956), by Ida Bagus Njana

statuary suggests that this was a cult-temple of Bhairava Buddhism. The chief figure is a masked 3.6-m- (12-ft-) high giant, dancing on a corpse. The beautifully proportioned **Pura Pusering Jagat** ("Navel of the World" Temple) has numerous pavilions housing similar tantric stone figures. The "Pejeng Vessel", a cylindrical stone urn carved with cosmological figures, is kept in a shrine in the southeastern corner of the temple.

About 2 km (1 mile) north of Pejeng, **Pura Penataran Sasih** houses the "Pejeng Moon" (*sasih* means moon), a bronze drum 186 cm (74 inches) long, of unknown age. Considered sacred, it is kept in a tall pavilion. Temple guides sometimes encourage visitors to stand on the base of an adjacent shrine; from here can be glimpsed the drum's fine geometric patterning. The design is associated with

the Dong-son culture of southern China and northern Vietnam around 1500 BC.

🏛 **Museum Purbakala**
Pejeng. **Tel** (0361) 942 347.
🕐 Mon–Fri. 📷 donation.

🏯 **Pura Arjuna Metapa**
Across the road from Museum.
🕐 daily. 📷 donation.

🏯 **Pura Kebo Edan**
Pejeng. 🕐 daily. 📷 donation.

🏯 **Pura Pusering Jagat**
Pejeng. 🕐 daily. 📷 donation.

🏯 **Pura Penataran Sasih**
Pejeng. 🕐 daily. 📷 donation. 📷

Petulu 17

Road Map D3. 🚌 *from Ubud & Pujung.* 🛈 *Ubud, (0361) 973 285.*

This village is known for its white-plumed egrets and Java pond egrets, generically called *kokokan* in Balinese. They feed all over the island and return here in the late afternoon to roost in the trees lining the road. It is not known why the birds suddenly settled in Petulu in 1965. The best place to view them is the road from the Jununganung direction through the ricefields; seen from here the V-formations of birds at sunset are an unforgettable sight.

Prehistoric turtle-shaped stone sarcophagi at the Museum Purbakala in Pejeng

Woodcarver at work in Kenderan, a village near Tegallalang

Tegallalang ⑱

Road Map D3. ▦ *from Ubud.*
ℹ *Ubud, (0361) 973 285.* 🍴 ▢
🏛 🎨

Plain-looking Tegallalang village, once the seat of a kingdom, is interesting as a centre of the woodcarving industry. As in most of the villages along this road, many people are engaged in producing cottage-craft wood products wholesale, retail, "antique" and made-to-order.

Environs
Kebon is a pretty village on a steep side road 3 km (2 miles) north of Tegallalang. At the junction with the main road is the excellent Kampung Kafe *(see p188).* **Kenderan**, also on a back road, is a former micro-kingdom with several small *puri* (houses of the nobility).

The small village of **Manuaba**, about 4 km (2 miles) north of Kenderan, is notable for the important

Brahman temple **Pura Griya Sakti**, with its refurbished *wantilan* performance pavilion. A visit to see the huge intertwined trees behind the inner courtyard requires permission of the temple attendant.

There is an interesting holy spring, **Telaga Waja**, in Kapitu, 1 km (half a mile) south of Kenderan. Access is by way of a 200-m (220-yard) foot-path and a long, steep flight of steps. At the site itself, there are traces of meditation niches which suggest that Telaga Waja was once a Buddhist retreat; it is possibly over 1,000 years old.

🏛 **Pura Griya Sakti**
Manuaba. ◯ *daily.* 🎫 *donation.*

Sebatu ⑲

Road Map D3. *from Ubud.*
ℹ *Ubud, (0361) 973 285.* 🍴 ▢

Sebatu village, part of a larger area of the same name, is highly regarded among the Balinese not only for its painted wood sculpture but also for its dance, music and classical dance costumes. Easily explored on foot, the village is laid out on a grid of three north-south streets, with the temples and *bale banjar* (community pavilion) at the northern end. The western-most street is lined with studios making woodcarvings for sale to visitors.

In a little valley on the western outskirts of Sebatu itself is the lovely spring temple **Pura Gunung Kawi**, not to be confused with the royal monuments of the same name near Tampaksiring *(see p99)*. The bathing springs are worth seeing (but should not be photographed if they are in use), as is the carp-filled spring pool in the northwest corner. In the centre of the pool is a handsome shrine. There are some interesting sculptures, some of them new and some old, among the small, colourfully painted pavilions in the central courtyard.

Stone sculpture in Pura Gunung Kawi

🏛 **Pura Gunung Kawi**
◯ *daily.* 🎫

Pura Gunung Kawi, Sebatu's tranquil spring temple

For hotels and restaurants in this region see pp174–6 and pp188–9

Taro ⓴

Road Map D3. 🛈 *Ubud, (0361) 973 285.* 🏨 ♿

On a well-marked (but often rough) road to the west of Pujung is Taro, said to be one of the very earliest settlements in Bali.

At the village centre is the large temple **Pura Gunung Raung**. Over its walls it is possible to admire the long *bale agung* pavilion, and a glowering three-tier *meru* pagoda. The latter represents the East Javanese mountain Gunung Raung; from here the legendary sage Rsi Markandya and his followers set out in the 8th century on a mission to Bali.

Taro is the source of Bali's albino cattle; these animals are valued for their importance in large rituals.

An albino cow, revered in Bali

Formerly they were sacrificed; today they are merely borrowed for the ceremony and then returned. The herd has now multiplied greatly and wanders freely in the forest south of the village.

The well-run **Elephant Safari Park** *(see p206)*, created in the late 1990s, enables visitors to view the landscape from the back of a Sumatran elephant. Attractions include elephants that have been trained to paint, a museum of elephants and their history, a large restaurant, luxurious accommodation and a spa.

Gunung Kawi Royal Monuments ⓳

Tampaksiring. **Road Map** D3. 🚌 *from Bedulu & Gianyar.* 🛈 *Ubud, (0361) 973 285.* ◯ *daily.* 📷 🚻

To the east of the small town of Tampaksiring, bordering the Pakrisan River, is a valley into the sides of which are carved nine immense monuments. They are shaped like *candi* (Buddhist-Hindu shrines), and are carved into

Gunung Kawi Royal Monuments, *candi* **shrines set in natural rock walls**

niches in a natural rock wall in the hill. At their heart are a temple and a holy spring. A flight of stairs leads to the monument complex, which straddles the river. Commonly called "tombs", these are in fact memorial shrines, associated with the legendary 11th-century king Anak Wungsu *(see p45)* and his wives. To the south of the main complex are the "Second Cloisters" on the east bank, and the "Third Cloisters", which are believed to be monuments dedicated to the queens of Anak Wungsu or his descendents. The "Tenth Tomb", to the west, is reached by a short walk along the edges of some ricefields.

On the steps leading to the tombs, craftsmen from Tampaksiring sell their wares, including some exquisite bone carvings.

Pura Tirta Empul ⓶

Manukaya. **Road Map** D3. 🚌 *from Bedulu & Gianyar.* 🛈 *Ubud, (0361) 973 285.* ◯ *daily.* 📷 🚻 ⚠

This sacred spring temple, near the source of the river Pakrisan, is a major tourist stop, but it is a pleasant place to visit. The main feature is a series of courtyards containing rectangular bathing-pools. The spouts dispense specific kinds of holy water, which devotees request with elaborate ritual offerings. The temple is thought to date from the 10th century; the present walls are recent. The pavilions are in an on-going state of restoration, an indication of the temple's importance. People come from all over the island for holy water and ritual ablutions, particularly on the day of the full moon *(purnama)*.

Pura Tirta Empul, a spring temple and source of holy water

EAST BALI

The old kingdoms of Eastern Bali wielded influence and power beyond their lofty mountains and lush green valleys. What remains of their palaces and temples is still a window into a world of ceremony and tradition, focused around Gunung Agung, centre of the Balinese universe, and, high on its steep volcanic slopes, Besakih, one of the most important temples in Bali.

The East Bali area corresponds to the three regencies of Klungkung, Bangli and Karangasem. It is an area of natural beauty and stark contrasts. Not far from its high volcanic peaks are some of Bali's best beaches. Just over 3,000 m (almost 10,000 ft) high, the active volcano of Gunung Agung dominates the landscape, its foothills covered with green ricefields. East Bali was devastated by Agung's eruption in 1963 *(see p115)* and by an earthquake in 1974. In many places great lava flows transformed the landscape.

In East Bali are some of the island's most important temples and palaces. Extravagant temple complexes stand on ancient sites endowed with cosmic significance, for example at Besakih and around the volcanic lake in the vast crater of Gunung Batur. At Tirtagangga, in the hills north of Amlapura, a luxurious water palace was built by descendants of the last king as late as the 1940s. This tradition of royal grandeur dates back ultimately to the 15th century, when the court of the first king of Gelgel was established. Around the courts and palaces of the region the arts flourished and villages of skilled artisans grew up. This tradition of craftsmanship survives in many places today.

In the 14th century the Javanese kingdom of Majapahit brought to Bali a new social order and caste system. Some communities resisted it, and their descendants, known as the Bali Aga (original Balinese), still live here in culturally distinct villages such as Tenganan and Trunyan.

Klungkung's royal house came to an end in 1908, when the king and members of his court committed *puputan (see p49)*, rather than submit to Dutch colonial control. However, many architectural relics still remain as reminders of pre-colonial times.

Ricefields of East Bali overlooked by the sacred volcano, Gunung Agung

◁ Using the process of evaporation, traditional salt production on Bali's east coast

Exploring East Bali

East Bali is dominated by the mighty volcano Gunung Agung, upon whose slopes is the important Besakih Temple Complex. To the west is Gunung Batur, with its own temples and a crater lake. To the south is historic Klungkung, and the royal pavilions of Taman Gili. From here the road runs eastwards to some good trekking country near Manggis and Tirtagangga, and on to the dive sites of Amed and Tulamben on the coast. The arid, lava-strewn eastern slopes of Gunung Agung are austerely beautiful. Tenganan, not far inland from the resort area of Candi Dasa, is one of the island's Bali Aga ("original Balinese") villages, which are culturally distinct from the rest of Bali.

SIGHTS AT A GLANCE

Amed **15**

Amlapura **12**

Bangli **1**

Besakih Temple Complex
pp116–17 **18**

Candi Dasa **8**

Gelgel **5**

Goa Lawah Bat Cave **6**

Gunung Agung **17**

Gunung Batur pp120–21 **19**

Gunung Lempuyang **14**

Iseh **2**

Kintamani **20**

Klungkung pp105–7 **4**

Padang Bai **7**

Pura Tegeh Koripan **22**

Pura Ulun Danu Batur
pp122–3 **21**

Sidemen **3**

Tenganan Bali Aga Village
pp110–11 **10**

Tirtagangga **13**

Tulamben **16**

Ujung **11**

Walk

Tenganan to Tirtagangga **9**

SEE ALSO

• *Where to Stay* pp176–7

• *Where to Eat* pp189–90

0 kilometres   5

0 miles   3

Lush green ricefields around Tirtagangga

GETTING AROUND

A car, rented with or without driver, is the best way of getting around. Roads are mostly good, although signposting is poor. Because of the many bends, journeys often take longer than one anticipates. *Bemo* run between villages, but taxis are scarce. Although public buses ply the coastal roads, tourist shuttle buses are more comfortable. Public transport is virtually non-existent at night. Padang Bai, on the southern coast, is the ferry port for Lombok.

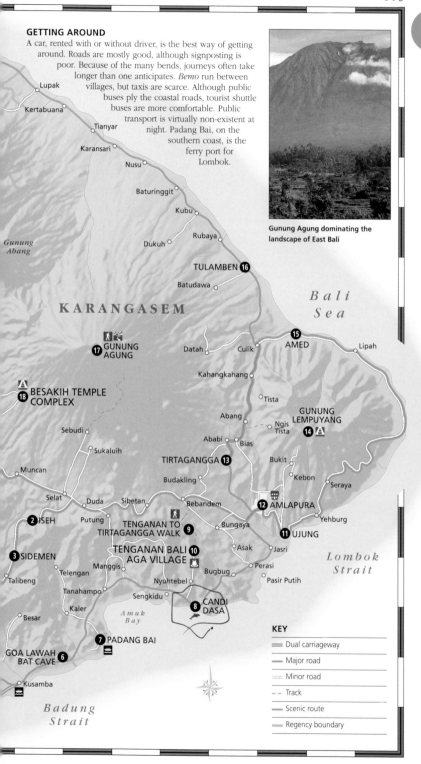

Gunung Agung dominating the landscape of East Bali

Lupak

Kertabuana

Tianyar

Karansari

Nusu

Baturinggit

Kubu

Rubaya

Dukuh

Gunung Abang

TULAMBEN **16**

Batudawa

KARANGASEM

Bali Sea

Datah

Culik

15 AMED

Lipah

17 GUNUNG AGUNG

Kahangkahang

Tista

18 BESAKIH TEMPLE COMPLEX

Abang

Ngis Tista

GUNUNG LEMPUYANG

Sebudi

Ababi

Bias

14

Sukaluih

TIRTAGANGGA **13**

Bukit

Muncan

Budakling

Kebon

Seraya

Selat

Duda

Sibetan

Bebandem

12 AMLAPURA

2 ISEH

Putung

TENGANAN TO TIRTAGANGGA WALK **9**

Bungaya

Yehburg

11 UJUNG

3 SIDEMEN

TENGANAN BALI AGA VILLAGE **10**

Asak

Jasri

Lombok Strait

Talibeng

Manggis

Perasi

Telengan

Bugbug

Tanahampo

Nyuhtebel

Pasir Putih

Kaler

Sengkidu

8 CANDI DASA

Amuk Bay

Besar

7 PADANG BAI

GOA LAWAH BAT CAVE **6**

Kusamba

Badung Strait

KEY

═══ Dual carriageway

─── Major road

═══ Minor road

- - - Track

─── Scenic route

─── Regency boundary

Bangli ❶

Road Map D3. 🏠 🚌 🛈 *Jalan Brigjen Ngurah Rai 30, (0366) 91 537.* 🍴🛍🏛🛒

A royal court city from the 14th to the 19th century, Bangli is one of Bali's oldest towns, a small, well-ordered and tidy community. Set some way up the hills towards Gunung Batur, the town is ideal for a walk in the cool mountain air.

Pura Kehen, a place of worship since the 12th century, steps impressively up a hillside in a series of eight terraces, enclosing a huge banyan tree in the first courtyard of the complex. High in the banyan's branches is an almost invisible *kulkul* with an alarm drum. Fine statuary lines the steps leading to the *padmasana* shrine *(see p26)* with a multi-tiered *meru* roof in the inner sanctuary. The shrine is covered with elaborate ornamentation. The gold-painted doors of the temple are beautiful.

Pura Penyimpenan ("the temple for keeping things") contains three ancient bronze inscriptions which imply that the area was considered holy long before the present temple complex was built.

Images of heaven and hell, the latter imaginatively grim, cover the walls of **Pura**

Mythological figure in Pura Dalem Penungekan, a temple of the dead

Dalem Pengungekan, a temple dedicated to the dead, and inside are shrines to Brahma, Shiva and Vishnu.

🏛 **Pura Kehen**
Jalan Sri Wijaya. ⬜ *daily.* 💰 *donation.* 🎭 *Pagerwesi (dates vary).*

🏛 **Pura Penyimpenan**
Jalan Sri Wijaya. ⬜ *daily.* ⬤ *for ceremonies.* 💰 *donation.*

🏛 **Pura Dalem Pengungekan**
Jalan Merdeka. ⬜ *daily.* ⬤ *for ceremonies.*

Environs
From the wooded **Bukit Demulih**, some 4 km (2 miles) west of Bangli, there are glorious views of Gunung Agung, and, on a clear day, as far as Nusa Penida and Sanur. At Bunutin, 7 km (4 miles) south of Bangli, **Pura Penataran Agung** has two small shrines on islands in a lake filled with water lilies.

Iseh ❷

Road Map E3. 🚌 *from Bangli and Klungkung.* 🛈 *Amlapura, (0363) 21 196.* 🖼

The area around Iseh is remarkable for glorious landscapes. Some of the best can be seen on the road eastward from Bangli via Muncan and Duda, which carves its way east through great volcanic valleys. The terraced ricefields are lush and green. Iseh itself is a small village with little in the way of tourist facilities. Walter Spies *(see p88)* built a house here, which is still standing today, and it was this location that inspired some of his most beautiful paintings.

Environs
At **Putung**, 6 km (4 miles) east of Iseh, there are some great lookout points and a couple of homestays *(see pp166–7)*. A further 4 km (2 miles) to the east is the village of **Sibetan**, the best place to buy *salak (see p183)*, a small, crisp, tart-tasting fruit with a scaly exterior that looks rather like snakeskin.

Ricefields and coconut groves at Iseh, a good setting for a walk

Sidemen ❸

Road Map E3. 🚌 *from Bangli and Klungkung.* 🛈 *Amlapura, (0363) 21 196.* 🎎 ▢ ◇

Sidemen is set in some of the most beautiful country in East Bali. The views from the slopes of Gunung Agung stretch out like a green patchwork with an impressive mountain backdrop. The town is a retreat from the hustle and bustle elsewhere, and there are some good homestays *(see pp166–7)* overlooking ricefields. In Sidemen one can visit work-shops making *songket*. This work is historically the pre-serve of higher castes, and still implies high social status.

Street corner in the town centre of Klungkung

Klungkung ❹

Road Map D4. 🚗 🚌 🛈 *Jalan Untung Surapati 3, (0366) 21 448.* 🎎 ▢ 🏠 ♿ *(limited).* ◇

Klungkung, also known as Semarapura, is a district capital and an important trading point. The most important historic sight in Klungkung is a pair of pavilions set in an ornamental moat, known as **Taman Gili** *(see pp106–7)*. Adjacent to Taman Gili is the small **Museum Daerah Semarapura** in which can be seen a collection of bronze and marble sculptures, and paintings by Italian modernist Emilio Ambron, as well as photographs of the royal

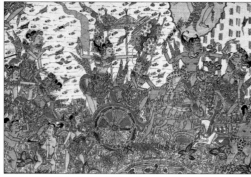

***Wayang*-style painting by an artist from Kamasan village**

family and the palace dating back to the early 1900s.

On the south side of Taman Gili is a large gateway, which is thought to be the entrance to the inner courtyard of the old palace. Legend has it that these massive wooden doors have remained stuck together since the *puputan* of 1908, when 200 members of Klung-kung's royal court committed ritual suicide *(see p49)*. This event is marked by the **Puputan Monument** across the road from Taman Gili. At the same road junction, a large indoor market sells temple and ritual para-phernalia, local handicrafts and food. It is one of Bali's best markets for textiles.

Environs
Less than 1 km (half a mile) south

The Puputan Monument in Klungkung

of Klungkung is the "artists' village" of **Kamasan**; here painters can be seen at work. The artists of Kamasan have largely defined the style of traditional Balinese art *(see pp34–5)*. As you travel from Klungkung to Kamasan, a turning on the left leads to **UD Kamasan Bali** (tel: 0366 24 781), where you can see *kereng* (Chinese coins) being forged. A small shop here sells all kinds of sacred coins and accessories. About the same distance to the northeast is the temple of **Pura Taman Sari**. In the temple's large, uncluttered compound is an eleven-roofed *meru* tower built on a stone turtle surrounded by a moat.

TEXTILES OF EAST BALI

In Bali great importance is attached to textiles and their making, and nowhere more so than in East Bali. This area is famous for a type of double *ikat* weave called *gering-sing*, produced only in the Bali Aga village of Tengana *(see pp110–11)*. *Geringsing* cloths are credited by the Balinese with protective spiritual powers. In Sidemen, complex, decorative motifs in gold and silver threads are woven into cloth to create a rich brocade textile known as *songket*. This is often worn by the Balinese at religious or social events, and as part of the costume of traditional dancers.

***Songket* fabrics woven in a Sidemen workshop**

Klungkung: Taman Gili

Built originally in the early 18th century, Taman Gili ("moated garden") is what remains of Klungkung's royal palace, most of which was destroyed in 1908 during the Dutch conquest. The main features are two raised, open meeting halls, or *bale*, with intricately painted ceilings. The paintings have undergone restoration and repainting several times in the last hundred years, but remain fine examples of the *wayang* style *(see p35)*, in which the figures resemble shadow puppets. The Kerta Gosa was originally the setting for the royal "high court". The present structure of the Bale Kambang dates from the 1940s.

The Moat
The surrounding moat gave the Bale Kambang its name, meaning "floating pavilion".

Kerta
Gosa

Entrance

★ Kerta Gosa Ceiling Paintings
There are 267 painted panels arranged in several tiers. At the apex is a carved lotus flower surrounded by gilded doves, representing the goals of enlightenment and salvation.

The demon Wirosa pursuing sinners

A scene from the *Tantri* stories

A stage in the ascent to enlightenment and salvation

KERTA GOSA CEILING PAINTINGS

The main series shows part of the *Bhima Swarga* narrative, which was incorporated into Balinese tradition from the Indian *Mahabharata* epic. There are also scenes from the *Tantri* stories (a Balinese version of a series of Indian moral fables), and some based on an astrological calendar, showing earthquakes and eruptions.

VISITORS' CHECKLIST

Puri Semarapura, corner of Jalan Surapati and Jalan Puputan, Klungkung. ☐ 7am–6pm daily. ⦿ public hols. 🔲 ✓ ⚏

★ Bale Kambang Ceiling Paintings
These depict scenes from Balinese myths, including the story of Sutasoma, a Buddhist saint symbolizing strength without aggression.

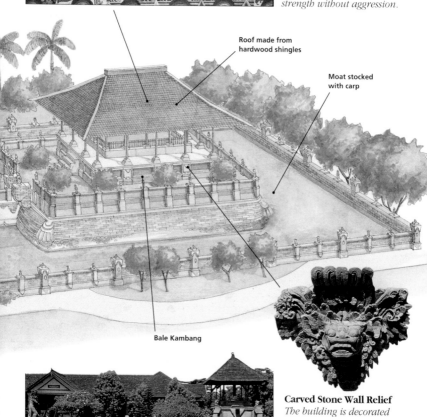

Roof made from hardwood shingles

Moat stocked with carp

Bale Kambang

Carved Stone Wall Relief
The building is decorated with carved reliefs of mythical creatures.

Museum Daerah Semarajaya
West of the Bale Kambang, the museum (see p105) has objects relating to the dynasties of Klungkung and Gelgel.

STAR FEATURES

★ Kerta Gosa Ceiling Paintings

★ Bale Kambang Ceiling Paintings

Temple entrance at the Goa Lawah Bat Cave

Gelgel **❺**

Road Map E4. ▣ *from Klungkung.*
ℹ *Klungkung, (0366) 21 448.*
🎭 *Purnama Kapat (Oct).*

The royal court of the
Majapahit rulers of Bali
(see p46) was established in
Gelgel in the 14th century by
Dewa Ketut Ngulesir, son of
Bali's first Majapahit king. A
reminder of the former
kingdom is Gelgel's very
ancient royal temple of **Pura
Dasar**, with its large outer
courtyard, and several tall
meru towers.
    The **Pura Penataran** is one
of a number of other temples
that can be seen along
the village's broad streets.

Goa Lawah
Bat Cave **❻**

Road Map E4. ▣ ▣ **ℹ**
Klungkung, (0366) 21 448. ◯ *daily.*
🎭 🎭 ⛩ ⛩

Thought to be more than
1,000 years old, Goa Lawah
is important to temple rituals
pertaining to the after-life.
The main feature of the
temple is a cave inhabited
by tens of thousands of fruit
bats. Local legend has it that
the cave stretches 30 km (19
miles) back into the
mountain, as far as Besakih,
(see pp116–17) and is the
home of a giant dragon-like
snake called Basuki who
feasts on bats.
    For visitors there are some
good eateries outside the cave
that have fine views over the
ocean towards Nusa Penida
and Lombok. However, it is
also renowed for hawkers.

Environs
Kusamba, 4 km (3 miles)
southwest of Goa Lawah, is a
busy little fishing village with
a black-sand beach. *Jukung*
(outrigger fishing craft) line
the shore, and are available for
chartered day trips to nearby
islands. The boats can feel
vulnerable as the ocean swell
picks up. Salt production pans
can be seen on the coast here.

Colourful *jukung* (outriggers) on the
black-sand beach at Kusamba

Padang Bai **❼**

Road Map E4. ▣ ▣ ⛴ *to Nusa
Lembongan, Nusa Penida & Lembar,
Lombok.* **ℹ** *Amlapura, (0363)
21 196.* ⛩ ▣ ⛩ ⛩

This is a relaxed beach resort,
a good base for the
exploration of East Bali. It is
also the main port for ferries
to Lombok, and therefore the
traffic from Denpasar is quite
heavy. In the village are
numerous restaurants, hotels,
guesthouses, bars, tour guides
and dive shops.

Environs
Within walking distance to the
west of Padang Bai is **Biastugal**, an unspoiled white-sand
bay where sunworshippers
gather. A little further along the

coast one can rent outriggers
for diving and snorkelling.
At the eastern end of the bay,
a 20-minute walk away, there
are several temples. They
include **Pura Silayukti**,
associated with Mpu Kuturan,
who introduced the three-
temple system to Balinese
villages in the 11th century
(see p28).

🏯 Pura Silayukti
◯ *daily.* 🎭 *dates vary.*

Candi Dasa **❽**

Road Map E4. ▣ ▣ **ℹ** *Jalan
Candi Dasa, (0366) 41 204.* ▣ ⛩ ⛩

Originally a fishing village,
Candi Dasa has now grown
into a popular resort. However, since the reef which
once lay offshore was largely
destroyed by exploitation as a
raw material, the beach has
been almost completely
eroded. Candi Dasa is
still a good base for
exploring the region,
and for diving and
snorkelling. There are
some reputable diving
schools, and good dive
sites near the offshore
islands. There is a wide
range of *losmen* and
other accommodation,
restaurants and bars. The
local dish is *bebek
betutu*, succulent duck
cooked with herbs and
spices *(see p182)*.
    The name Candi Dasa is
said to be derived from the
Balinese "Cilidasa", which
means "ten children". In the
centre of the village, overlooking a lagoon with water
lilies, is **Pura Candi Dasa**,
a temple dedicated to Hariti,
the goddess of fertility.

🏯 Pura Candi Dasa
Jalan Candi Dasa. ◯ *daily.*

Environs
About 2 km (1 mile) east of
Candi Dasa and up a steep
flight of steps is **Pura Gomang**,
where there are great views
of the coast. Further east is
Pasir Putih, a secluded bay
hemmed in on one side by a
sheer rock face, and used as a
harbour by *jukung* outriggers.

Walk from Tenganan to Tirtagangga ❾

The walk from Tenganan to Tirtagangga reveals some of the most scenic terrain of Bali's interior, and many glimpses of traditional Balinese life along the way. The 6-km (4-mile) walk takes about three hours. From the higher points there are impressive views of Bali's mountains; the route passes also through terraced ricefields and peaceful hillside

Ricefield toad

villages. This is a good way to see village temples, local schools, tiny mountai *warung* (shops) and weavers of basketware. In the early morning vendors sell *tuak*, a sour-tasting alcoholic drink made from the flower of the *jaka* palm tree. These trees can be recognized by the enormous grape-like buds jutting from their trunks.

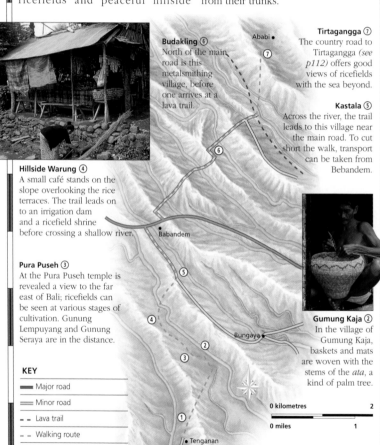

Budakling ⑥
North of the main road is this metalsmithing village, before one arrives at a lava trail.

Ababi •

Tirtagangga ⑦
The country road to Tirtagangga (*see p112*) offers good views of ricefields with the sea beyond.

Kastala ⑤
Across the river, the trail leads to this village near the main road. To cut short the walk, transport can be taken from Bebandem.

Hillside Warung ④
A small café stands on the slope overlooking the rice terraces. The trail leads on to an irrigation dam and a ricefield shrine before crossing a shallow river.

Babandem

Pura Puseh ③
At the Pura Puseh temple is revealed a view to the far east of Bali; ricefields can be seen at various stages of cultivation. Gunung Lempuyang and Gunung Seraya are in the distance.

Bungaya •

Gumung Kaja ②
In the village of Gumung Kaja, baskets and mats are woven with the stems of the *ata*, a kind of palm tree.

KEY

▬	Major road
═	Minor road
– –	Lava trail
- -	Walking route

• Tenganan

0 kilometres   2

0 miles   1

Tenganan Village Gate ①
From the village, a stone-paved path leads to a temple complex and then to the edge of the forest. Here a wall marks the beginning of a half-hour climb to the primary school at Gumung.

TIPS FOR WALKERS

Start point: *Tenganan.*
End point: *Tirtagangga*
Getting there: *Bemo to Candi Dasa, then own transport.*
When to go: *Any time, but trails are slippery in rainy season.*
Walking time: *3 hours.*

Tenganan Bali Aga Village ⑩

Wall motif
in clay

The Bali Aga, or "original Balinese" *(see p46)*, maintain a distinct cosmology and social organization. For example, villagers must marry in the community or live on the outskirts of the village. They make fine basketware, and this is the only place in Southeast Asia where *geringsing* double-*ikat* textiles *(see p37)* are made. Tenganan is the best preserved of the Bali Aga villages. It is closed to outsiders after dark.

Detail of double-*ikat* geringsing textile

Market

Public baths

Village Temple

In the village's "temple of origins", outside the village walls, the community joins in rituals reflecting a dualistic cosmology based on principles of complementary opposites.

The *wantilan* is a large, open pavilion where village members meet for social activities.

THE LEGEND OF TENGANAN

It is said that in the 14th century, King Bedaulu, the ruler of Bali, lost his favourite horse and offered a reward for its return. The horse was eventually found dead near Tenganan and the villagers asked to be granted land as a reward. The King sent his minister to draw the boundaries of the area to be given to them, instructing the minister to include all of the land where he could smell the dead horse. Accompanied by the village chief, who had hidden some of the rotting horse meat in his clothes, the minister performed his duties and drew generous boundaries which remain today.

Land at Tenganan, owned communally according to Bali Aga tradition

Village Houses

A short flight of steps leads up to each house which also has a small courtyard.

STAR FEATURES

★ Bale Petemu

★ Main Street

VISITORS' CHECKLIST

Road Map F3. 🚌 *from Candi Dasa.* 🛈 *Amlapura, (0363) 21 196.* ◯ *daylight hours.* 💰 *donation.* 🎭 *Rejang Dewa (dance) (Feb); Usaba Sambah and Mekare-kare (stick fight) (Jun–Jul).* 🚻 🏪 👪

★ Bale Petemu
This is the meeting hall of one of three associations of unmarried village men.

★ Main Street
The main streets are partly cobbled and rise in tiers, connected by ramps.

Fighting Cocks
Birds are often kept in cages in front of the houses; most fights take place outside the village.

0 metres 30

0 yards 30

Entrance

The kitchen of the *bale agung* is where large numbers of pigs are killed and cooked for ceremonial purposes.

The bale agung is the hall for meetings of the village council, composed of all the married couples.

Ujung ⓫

Road Map F3. 🚌 🚐 *from Amla-pura.* ℹ️ *Amlapura, (0363) 21 196.*

Ujung, meaning literally "at the end", is an appropriate name given the remote location of this fishing village. The **Puri Taman Ujung** is a water palace built in 1919 by the last raja of Karangasem, Anak Agung Anglurah Ketut. The buildings were all but destroyed in the 1976 earthquake but have been restored to their former grandeur.

Environs
The narrow road winding east from Ujung around the eastern tip of Bali is very scenic, with spectacular views of the ocean and Gunung Seraya. Before taking this road, one should check its condition with the locals.

🏛️ **Puri Taman Ujung**
⭕ *daily.* 🖼️ *donation.* 🔲

Puri Taman Ujung, the royal water palace before renovation

Amlapura ⓬

Road Map F3. 🚌 🚐
ℹ️ *Jalan Diponegoro, (0363) 21 196.*
🍴 🔲 🛍️

The small but busy trading town of Amlapura is a district capital with an active market serving the area. The town was given its present name after reconstruction in the aftermath of the 1963 eruption of Gunung Agung. It is still often referred to by its former name, Karangasem.

Karangasem became an important power in the late 17th century. The royal families of Karangasem had strong political links with the nearby island of Lombok. In the mid-18th century they ousted the powerful kings

The Maskerdam Building, a royal residence furnished in Dutch style

of Sulawesi from Lombok and then divided the island up among themselves.

The Balinese of Karangasem remained in power in western Lombok until 1894, although facing continuous challenges from the Sasak nobles. Karangasem became a vassal of Lombok in 1849, when the Lombok king attacked his own ancestral land. It placed itself under Dutch rule in 1894, after the Dutch conquest of Lombok.

Puri Agung, a royal palace of the kings of Karangasem, was built at the turn of the 20th century. It was the birthplace of the last king. The palace compound is no longer inhabited, descendants of the royal family preferring to live in the palaces of Puri Gede and Puri Kertasurahe across the road (unlike Puri Agung, they are not open to the public). Architecturally, Puri Agung is an eclectic mix of European and Balinese styles. It has a particularly impressive entrance gateway.

The main attraction is the **Maskerdam Building**, so-called as a tribute to the Dutch ("Amsterdam" as pronounced by the locals). Behind its carved doors are pieces of furniture donated by Queen Wilhelmina of the

Dutch royal family. Another building in the compound is known as the Bale London, as some of its furniture bears the British royal family's coat-of-arms. There are two *bale* (open halls) beside ornamental ponds in front of the Maskerdam Building. These were used for ceremonies and meetings. Over one of the *bale* entrances is a photograph of the raja, taken in 1939 when the district was granted limited self-rule by the Dutch.

🏛️ **Puri Agung**
Jalan Gajah Mada. ⭕ *daily.* 🖼️ 🔲

Tirtagangga ⓭

Ababi. **Road Map** F3. 🚌 🚐
ℹ️ *Amlapura, (0363) 21 196.* ⭕ *daily.*
🖼️ 🔲 🍴 🔲 ♿ *(limited)* ♻️

Tirtagangga (meaning "holy water from the Ganges") is the best surviving example of Bali's royal water palaces. It was built in 1947 by Anak Agung Anglurah Ketut, the last king of Karangasem, and restored after damage sustained in the 1963 eruption of Gunung Agung. The complex consists of a sacred spring, a cold spring-fed pool and several other ponds. Bathing is permitted in the pools. A small fee is charged at the spring-fed pool, which has simple changing rooms. The pools and fountains are set in well-maintained gardens.

Tirtagangga has a cool climate, and is a good base for walks in the area. There are several homestays here.

Gardens surrounding the bathing pools in Tirtagangga

Plantations beside the scenic route around Gunung Lempuyang

generations, salt is made from brine poured into wooden frames, gathered in sacks and laid out by the road for sale.

Divers come to this area, and in particular to the bay at Jemeluk to the east of Amed, to enjoy underwater views of colourful coral gardens and a spectacular variety of fish.

The east coast round Amed is hot, dry and economically rather poor. Barren hills pinned with thirsty-looking *lontar* palms stand in stark contrast to the green mountain slopes behind. The arid, harsh landscape is distinctly different from the lushness of most of East Bali.

Environs
Some 5 km (3 miles) east of Amed is the quiet coastal village of **Lipah**, where tourist facilities are rapidly developing, happily in reasonable taste and at reasonable prices.

Gunung Lempuyang ⑭

Drive through villages of Tista, Abang and Ngis Tista. **Road Map** F3. ⊟
▣ ⃘ *Amlapura, (0363) 21 196.* ▣

At just over 1,000 m (3,300 ft), Gunung Lempuyang is worth a full day's trip, especially when there is a temple ceremony. Getting there is part of the attraction – the road from Tirtagangga runs northeast along a valley, with Gunung Agung to the west and Gunung Lempuyang to the east, carving its way through lush ricefields. The mountain itself is then reached via a side road.

At the top stands **Pura Lempuyang Luhur**. There has probably been a temple on this remote and sacred site since pre-Hindu times. The temple is important to Balinese today because of its location – at the top of the island's easternmost mountain. The temple is not large; there is just a single courtyard with a few simple *bale* (pavilions). The views of Gunung Agung are spectacular. Reaching the temple involves a two-hour climb up 1,700 stone steps, passing the smaller temple

of Pura Telagamas at the bottom. There are several strategically located resting places along the way.

🛕 **Pura Lempuyang Luhur**
◯ *daily.* 🎏 *temple anniversary festival (Manis Galungan, 1 Feb & 29 Aug 2012).*

Amed ⑮

Road Map F2. ▣ ▣ ⃘ *Amlapura, (0363) 21 196.* ▮▮ ▢ ◨ ◿

A sleepy little fishing-town, Amed is of interest for its dive sites and salt-production. In a simple evaporation process little changed for

Boats for diving or snorkelling trips off the coast around Amed

Lontar palms in the coastal region of Tulamben

Tulamben ⑯

Road Map F2. ▣ ▣ *from Amlapura & Singaraja.* ⃘ *Amlapura, (0363) 21 196.* ▮▮ ▢ ◨ ◿

Tulamben is a nondescript little village, but it is of interest as the location of the wreck of the American cargo ship *Liberty*, 120 m (396 ft) long and torpedoed southwest of Lombok during World War II. It lies 40 m (44 yards) offshore and, at its deepest point, some 60 m (198 ft) down. The water provides great diving and snorkelling. Day trips off Tulamben can be arranged with dive operations (*see p202*). Boats can be rented locally.

Gunung Agung ⑰

Gunung Agung is a 3,014-m- (9,888-ft-) high, active volcano, the dominant feature of East Bali. It has a profound significance in the life of every Balinese. Communities orientate their houses, temples and even beds in relation to this sacred place, where the spirits of ancestors are believed to dwell. Visitors climbing the mountain should observe rules for temple dress (*see p218*) or risk offending local sensibilities.

TIPS FOR CLIMBERS

Start point: *Either of two base camps: Besakih ①; and Pura Pasar Agung ②, north of Selat.*
Getting there: *Bus or bemo to Besakih from Denpasar, Gianyar and Amlapura. Own transport to Pura Pasar Agung.*
When to go: *Off-limits during the rainy season (Oct–May), when there are dangerous mud slides and swollen rivers, as well as ceremonies (Mar–Apr).*
Guide: *Visitors are strongly advised to engage a reliable guide (see p205), because the climbs from both base camps are steep and require early-morning starts. The lower slopes are heavily forested. Changes in weather can be dramatic and sudden. Attitudes of local people to climbers may be unfriendly.*
Length of climb: *Six hours starting from Besakih; three hours from Pura Pasar Agung.*

From Besakih ①
This climb, the longer of the two routes, goes right to the top of the volcano, where there are spectacular views of Bali and Lombok when the weather is clear.

KEY

- – – Trekking route
- ▬▬ Major road
- ══ Minor road

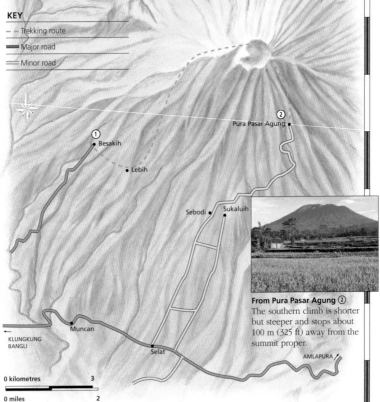

From Pura Pasar Agung ②
The southern climb is shorter but steeper and stops about 100 m (325 ft) away from the summit proper.

0 kilometres   3

0 miles   2

THE 1963 ERUPTION OF GUNUNG AGUNG

Although Gunung Agung had long been thought extinct, in 1963 it erupted dramatically, shooting boulders and ash high into the sky. In all, the event lasted six months. Whole villages were buried; nearly 2,000 people died; and much arable land was laid waste. The rock-filled rivers of East Bali and Agung's bare eastern flank still bear witness to the event. According to local belief the disaster happened because spiritual leaders wrongly timed the performance of Eka Dasa Rudra. This is a Hindu spiritual purification ceremony which takes place every hundred years. Ancient texts suggest that the ceremony should have taken place not in 1963, but in 1979.

Eruption of Gunung Agung (1968)
by Ida Bagus Nyoman Rai

Besakih Temple Complex ⑱

See pp116–17.

Gunung Batur ⑲

See pp120–21.

Kintamani ⑳

Road Map D2. 🚌 🚐 🏛 *Penelokan, (0366) 51 370.* 🍴 📷 🅿 🛍

One of the most popular destinations for visitors in Bali is Kintamani, notable above all for its view of a volcano within a caldera. The air here is fresh and the view from Kintamani into the caldera of Gunung Batur (*see pp120–21*) is perhaps the most famous on the island, as the tourist buses testify.

Kintamani is one of three small villages set high on Batur's caldera rim. Penelokan and Batur are the other two. It is hard to distinguish where one ends and the next begins, as they have now merged together to form a ribbon of development catering for the many visitors who come here. The whole road is transformed into a parking lot when the tour buses arrive. The hawkers can be particularly persistent.

However, people do not come to look at the village of Kintamani itself – they come to stand in awe of the view. It is worth stopping here just to get a real sense of the scale of the landscape from a high vantage-point; here it is easy to see the relative positions of Gunung Batur, the Bali Aga village of Trunyan (*see p121*) down on the shore of the lake, and Gunung Abang on the eastern side of the lake facing Gunung Batur.

There are many places to eat along most of the 10 km (6 miles) of the main road along the crater rim; most of them have good views. There is also a market selling fresh local produce.

Pura Ulun Danu Batur ㉑

See pp122–3.

Pura Tegeh Koripan ㉒

Road Map D1. 🚌 🚐 *from Kintamani.* 🏛 *Penelokan, (0366) 51 370.* 🕐 *daily.* ⚫ *during ceremonies.* 📷 *donation.* 🎎 *temple festival (Oct).*

Pura Tegeh Koripan (also known as Pura Sukawana or Pura Penulisan) is one of the oldest temples in Bali, dating from the 11th century or earlier (*see p45*). Set at more than 1,500 m (4,950 ft) on the side of Gunung Penulisan, it is certainly one of the highest (*see p120*). It does not get very much tourist traffic and, therefore, has a peaceful atmosphere.

It is in fact a complex of five temples. Its pyramidal structure, set on eleven levels of terraces along the slope, suggests that it dates from the pre-Hindu-Buddhist era, and is associated with the megalithic culture of Bali.

The main temple, Pura Panarajon, is over 300 steps up and at the highest position in the complex. Inside, there are some stone inscriptions and statues thought to date to the 10th century.

From the slopes of Gunung Penulisan there are good views: on clear days one can see as far as Java to the east, and the Bali Sea to the north.

An ancient shrine in Pura Tegeh Koripan

Shop and *warung*, typical of those which line the road to Kintamani

For hotels and restaurants in this region see pp176–7 and pp189–90

Besakih Temple Complex ⑱

Pura Besakih is a grand complex of 22 temples spread over 3 sq km (1 sq mile) on the slopes of Gunung Agung (see p114), where the Balinese believe the spirits of their ancestors live. Said to have been founded in the late 8th century by the Javanese sage, Rsi Markandya, it later came under the jurisdiction of the Klungkung kingdom. All but two shrines were destroyed in an earthquake of 1917, and it underwent several major renovations in the 20th century, escaping damage in the 1963 eruption of Gunung Agung. Now it is an important focus of modern Indonesian Hinduism.

Stone wall carving

★ **Eleven-tiered Meru**
The tall meru *(pagodas) are shrines for deified kings, ancestral spirits and nature gods.*

★ **Main Courtyard**
This is the main focus of worship at the temple. A padmasana tiga *(triple lotus shrine) is dedicated to Brahma, Shiva and Vishnu.*

Terraced Entrance
The terraces at the entrance to Pura Penataran Agung are an echo of the stepped pyramids of Indonesian prehistory.

Stairs
Only worshippers are allowed to use the entrance stairway.

Footpaths connect the temples in the complex.

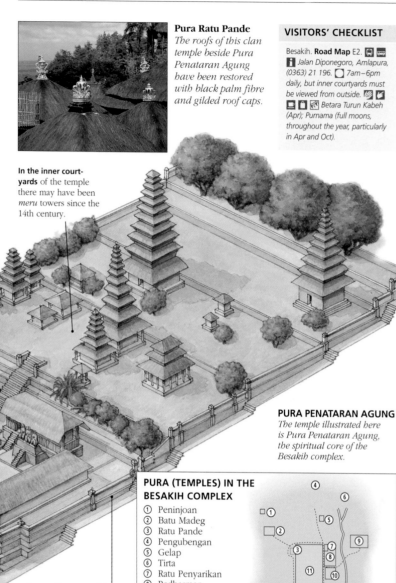

Pura Ratu Pande
The roofs of this clan temple beside Pura Penataran Agung have been restored with black palm fibre and gilded roof caps.

VISITORS' CHECKLIST

Besakih. **Road Map** E2. 🚌 🚐
🛈 *Jalan Diponegoro, Amlapura,
(0363) 21 196.* 🕐 *7am–6pm
daily, but inner courtyards must
be viewed from outside.* 🎫 🚻
🚽 🏪 🎭 *Betara Turun Kabeh
(Apr); Purnama (full moons,
throughout the year, particularly
in Apr and Oct).*

In the inner court-yards of the temple there may have been *meru* towers since the 14th century.

PURA PENATARAN AGUNG
The temple illustrated here is Pura Penataran Agung, the spiritual core of the Besakih complex.

Low walls surround the temple complex; visitors can view the shrines by walking along the footpaths and looking over the walls.

PURA (TEMPLES) IN THE BESAKIH COMPLEX

① Peninjoan
② Batu Madeg
③ Ratu Pande
④ Pengubengan
⑤ Gelap
⑥ Tirta
⑦ Ratu Penyarikan
⑧ Pedharman
⑨ Kiduling Kreteg
⑩ Ratu Pasek
⑪ Penataran Agung
⑫ Dukuh Segening
⑬ Basukian
⑭ Merajan Kanginan
⑮ Goa
⑯ Bangun Sakti
⑰ Ulun Kulkul
⑱ Manik Mas
⑲ Pesimpangan
⑳ Dalem Puri
㉑ Merajan Selonding
㉒ Jenggala

KEY

--- Footpath

STAR FEATURES

★ Main Courtyard

★ Eleven-tiered Meru

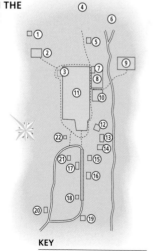

Irrigated ricefield at Tirtagangga, with Gunung Agung in the distance ▷

Gunung Batur ⑲

Although Gunung Batur (Mount Batur) is not the largest volcano in Bali, it is the most active. It is surrounded by a spectacular caldera, which implies that it was once much larger than now, having blown off its top in an eruption. It has erupted on a large scale more than 20 times in the last 200 years. The most devastating occasion was in 1917 when more than 1,000 people died and over 2,000 temples were destroyed. Volcanic activity has made the slopes of Gunung Batur bare and dry, in contrast to the vegetation which covers the slopes of Gunung Abang, on the opposite side of Lake Batur.

Gunung Batur Eruptions
Minor but noisy eruptions occur frequently day and night, and can be watched from the road running through Kintamani.

TIPS FOR WALKERS

Walking up to one of the four craters of Gunung Batur takes an hour from **Serongga***, or three hours from* **Kedisan***.*
  A local cartel, the HPPGB, discourages trekking alone, and climbers are advised to take a licensed guide with them. An information centre is located at **Toya Bungkah***, where there is also losmen accommodation.*
  The air can be quite chilly before daybreak, and warm clothing is highly recommended for night treks. Care should be taken to avoid the hot steam issuing from fissures in the rocks.
  The slopes of the volcano can be slippery and dangerous, and trekking is not recommended from October to April.

Gunung Penulisan
SINGARAJA
Pura Tegeh Koripan (see p115)
Kintamani
Pura Ulun Danu Batur (see pp122–3)
Batur
Penelokan
UBUD
TAMPAKSIRING AND UBUD
BANGLI

0 kilometres		3
0 miles		2

KEY

━━━ Major road

- - Footpath

Ferry/boat service

Ⓐ Temple

ℹ Tourist information

☀ Viewpoint

The Western Slopes of Gunung Batur
The area at the foot of the volcano is covered with lava deposited by old eruptions. The vegetation is sparse here.

For hotels and restaurants in this region see pp176–7 and pp189–90

Lake Batur
This lake is the main irrigation source for much of the agriculture of Central and East Bali. It is said to be protected by the lake goddess, Ida Betari Dewi Ulun Danu.

Shrines on Gunung Abang
In the forest on the peak of Gunung Abang is a temple containing some small, brightly painted shrines.

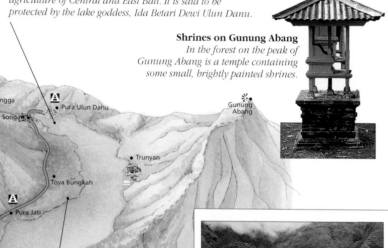

Trunyan, on the eastern shore of Lake Batur, reachable most easily by water

TRUNYAN BALI AGA VILLAGE

One of the culturally isolated Bali Aga villages (*see p46*), Trunyan is still most easily accessible by boat. Villagers here practise customs found nowhere else in Bali, even in other Bali Aga villages. These include the treatment of their dead bodies, which are placed in pits, and covered by cloth and shabby bamboo canopies. The influence of an ancient tree is said to preserve the corpses from putrefaction. The cemetery is the main feature of interest to visitors. Trunyan is the home of Da Tonta, a 4-m- (13-ft-) high statue of Dewa Ratu Gede Pancering Jagat, patron guardian of the village, which is brought out at the Berutuk festival (usually October). The people here tend to expect "donations" from visitors, whom they now regard as a source of income.

Toya Bungkah
This village near a hot spring has simple restaurants and losmen *accommodation.*

Pura Ulun Danu Batur ㉑

This temple is one of the most important on Bali because of its association with Lake (*danu*) Batur, which supplies the irrigation system of Gianyar and Bangli through a series of underground springs. From a distance the temple's silhouette can be seen on the rim of the vast Batur caldera. Adjoining this temple are others in the process of enlargement, making up a quite extensive complex.

Stone sculpture

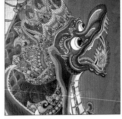

Temple Flags
Deities and mythical beasts are often depicted in rich colours on temple flags and sculptures.

Third Courtyard
The third courtyard is the most sacred. Three gateways lead from one courtyard to the next.

Garuda
The figure of Garuda, a bird from Hindu mythology, is depicted in this stone relief on the courtyard wall.

★ **Central Courtyard**
The great quadrangle, shown here occupied by a festive structure of bamboo and straw, is the occasional setting for a baris gede dance (see p30).

OFFERINGS TO THE LAKE GODDESS

Offerings of fruits and flowers

Devotees from all over Bali present elaborate offerings at this temple, which is dedicated to Ida Betari Dewi Ulun Danu, the goddess of Lake Batur. The respect accorded to the goddess is reinforced by events in the temple's history. At its former location closer to the lake, the temple was miraculously saved from destruction in the volcanic eruption of 1917, when the lava flow stopped just short of its walls. Another eruption, in 1926, prompted the villagers to move the temple to its present location.

VISITORS' CHECKLIST

Batur. **Road Map** D2. 🚗 🚌 🛈
Penelokan, (0366) 51 370.
🕐 *7am–6pm daily.*
🎟 *donation.* 🛕 *temple anniversary (Apr & Oct Purnama).*

★ **Gold-painted Doors**
The great timber doors of the main temple gateway are reserved for the use of priests on important occasions.

Side Gate
This tall, slender gate, built in a combination of brick-work and paras stone decoration, leads to another temple.

The bale gong is a pavilion housing the temple's set of gamelan instruments, including a great gong believed to have a magical history.

Entrance

STAR FEATURES

★ Central Courtyard

★ Gold-painted Doors

NORTH AND WEST BALI

*A*t the heart of North and West Bali is a mountainous, volcanic hinterland. This is ringed by coastal plains where most of the population live. Before the Dutch took over Southern Bali in the early 20th century and a harbour was built at Benoa in the 1920s, most contact between the Balinese and the rest of the world took place in this Northern and Western region of the island.

North and West Bali corresponds to the regencies of Tabanan, Jembrana and Buleleng, of which the administrative capitals are Tabanan, Negara and Singaraja respectively. To the west of Tabanan regency rice-growing gradually gives way to dry fields and forests. The population is increasingly Muslim as one moves west; the older Muslim settlements were established by Bugis sailors in the 17th century. The landscape of Buleleng regency on the north coast consists of steep mountain slopes plunging down to a narrow stretch of dry land which is generally impervious to irrigation – the exceptions are the relatively fertile hinterland of Singaraja town and the plantation area of Munduk and Busungbiu further inland.

The history of this part of Bali has been influenced as much by the sea as by the traditions of the courts: both Singaraja and Negara have the flavour more of Javanese coastal trading towns than of the Balinese centres of aristocratic power. North Bali is more heavily marked by the Dutch colonial presence than the rest of the island, which was colonized later. Following their brutal takeover of Buleleng in 1849, the Dutch set up a Residentie (prefecture) in Singaraja in 1855. Singaraja shows evidence of its Dutch past in its old offices and mansions and the airy, shady atmosphere of the town. Temples evolved an original, even at times humorous, style of bas-reliefs and sculptures where Europeans, cars, boats and other signs of modernity often appear in the places taken by demons and abstract flower motifs in temples further south.

New converts to Christianity were resettled by the Dutch in the hinterland of Negara. Later, several settlements were established along the coast by Madurese migrants.

Ducks being farmed on the coastal plains of Western Bali

◁ Pura Tanah Lot *(see p128)*, a Balinese temple situated on a rocky outcrop by the ocean

Exploring North and West Bali

West Bali has areas of great natural beauty. The mountains, black-sand beaches, coconut plantations and ricefields make up some idyllic landscapes. The eastern part is known for its many impressive temples, and for Gunung Batukau, surrounded by Bali's last remaining primary forest. Near the hill-resort area of Bedugul is a string of mountain lakes in an ancient caldera. On the north coast lies Singaraja, once the Dutch colonial capital. A great expanse of territory is occupied by the Taman Nasional Bali Barat (West Bali National Park), and the adjacent area of protected scrub forest.

Clear waters at Pantai Gondol

SEE ALSO

- **Where to Stay** pp177–9
- **Where to Eat** pp190–91

SIGHTS AT A GLANCE

Banjar ㉒
Blayu ❼
Gilimanuk ⑯
Gitgit ㉚
Gunung Batukau ⑫
Jagaraga ㉛
Kapal ❷
Krambitan ❹
Lake Bratan and Bedugul ㉗
Lake Buyan ㉖
Lovina ㉙
Makam Jayaprana ⑲
Marga ❾

Medewi Beach ⑬
Mengwi pp129–31 ❻
Menjangan Island ⑱
Munduk ㉔
Negara ⑮
Pantai Gondol ㉑
Pejaten ❸
Pemuteran ⑳
Pengambangan ⑭
Pupuan ㉓
Pura Gangga ⑪
Pura Meduwe Karang
    pp148–9 ㉜

Pura Tanah Lot ❶
Sangeh ❽
Singaraja pp144–6 ㉘
Tabanan ❺
Taman Nasional Bali Barat
    pp136–7 ⑰
Tejakula ㉝
Yeh Panas ❿

Tour
Lake Tamblingan pp140–41 ㉕

Ricefield being planted near Tabanan

GETTING AROUND

A car is the ideal means of travelling around North and West Bali, as the distances are relatively great, and public transport is non-existent in remoter places. Along the very busy main road from Denpasar via Mengwi to the port of Gilimanuk, there are branches off to sights including the mountain Gunung Batukau and the coastal temples of Tanah Lot. The main route from Denpasar to Singaraja gives access to sights such as Pura Taman Ayun and Bedugul. Both these major roads are served by *bemo* and public buses, as is the north-coast road from East Bali to Gilimanuk via Singaraja.

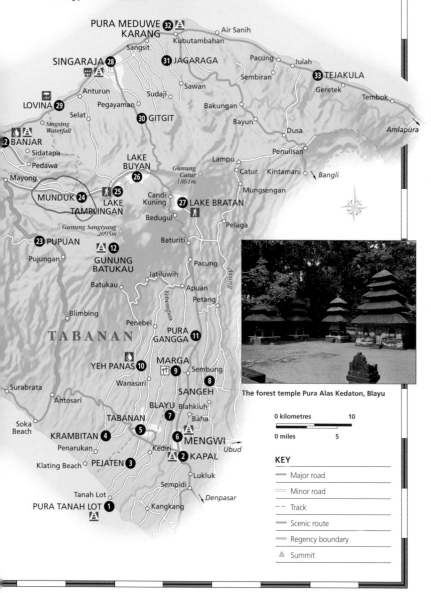

PURA MEDUWE KARANG 32

Air Sanih
Kubutambahan
Sangsit

SINGARAJA 28

JAGARAGA 31

Pacung
Julah
Sembiran

TEJAKULA 33
Geretek
Tembok

Anturun
Sudaji
Sawan

LOVINA 29
Pegayaman
Selat

GITGIT 30

Bakungan
Bayun

Singsing Waterfall

Dusa

Amlapura

BANJAR 2
Sidatapa
Pedawa

LAKE BUYAN 26

Lampu
Penulisan

Mayong

Gunung Catur 1861m

Catur
Kintamani

Bangli

Mungsengan

MUNDUK 24
LAKE TAMBLINGAN 25

Candi Kuning

LAKE BRATAN 27

Pelaga

Bedugul

Gunung Sangiyang 2095m

Baturiti

PUPUAN 23

GUNUNG BATUKAU 12

Baturiti

Pacung

Pujungan

Jatiluwih
Apuan
Petang

Batukau

Blimbing

Penebel

PURA GANGGA 11

TABANAN

YEH PANAS 10

MARGA 9

Sembung

Wanasari

SANGEH 8

Surabrata

BLAYU 7

Blahkiuh

The forest temple Pura Alas Kedaton, Blayu

Antosari

TABANAN 5

Baha

KRAMBITAN 4

MENGWI 6

Penarukan

Kediri

KAPAL 2

Ubud

Soka Beach

PEJATEN 3

Lukluk

Klating Beach

Sempidi

Tanah Lot

Denpasar

PURA TANAH LOT 1

Kangkang

0 kilometres   10

0 miles   5

KEY

— Major road

═ Minor road

-- Track

— Scenic route

— Regency boundary

▲ Summit

Crossing the rocky approach to Pura Tanah Lot at low tide

Pura Tanah Lot ❶

Tanah Lot. **Road Map** B4.
🚌 🚐 from Denpasar & Kediri.
ℹ️ Tabanan, (0361) 811 602.
🕐 daily. 💰 donation. 🎭 temple
anniversary. 🍴 🏪 🏧 ♻️

One of Bali's most heavily
promoted landmarks, Pura
Tanah Lot is a temple set
dramatically on a small island
about 100 m (100 yards) off
the coast. It can get very
crowded, and to visit the
temple proper it is best to
arrive well before sunset,
when there are not too many
visitors around. As the sun
goes down, the shrines make
a magnificent silhouette
against a glowing horizon –
a memorable sight despite
the throngs of visitors at this
time. The many handicraft,
souvenir and refreshment
stalls at Tanah Lot are a major
source of income for the
region's women and children.

The islet – a promontory
until the beginning of the
20th century – is accessible
on foot only at low tide. It is
quickly being eroded by the
onslaught of the sea. The
cliffs around the island have
been carefully reinforced
with concrete, and tripods
have been sunk into the sea
to act as breakwaters.

As its name suggests, the
temple is situated at the
meeting-point of land (tanah)
and sea (lot). The part that
faces the sea is dedicated to
the Balinese goddess of the
sea, Betara Tengah Segara,
while the landward side is
thought to be the seat of the
gods from Gunung Batukau
(see p133). The temple is

associated with the saint
Dang Hyang Nirartha (see
pp46–7). He is said to have
advised its construction in
order to protect Bali
against scourges and
epidemics; these de-
structive forces were
thought to originate
from the sea.

Environs
Along the nearby coast,
numerous temples and
shrines have been built
to protect Tanah Lot.
They include **Pura
Pekendungan, Pura
Jero Kandang, Pura
Galuh** and **Pura Batu Bolong**.
The latter stands on a small
promontory linked to the
mainland by a natural bridge.

Kapal ❷

Road Map C4. 🚌 🚐 from Kediri
and Denpasar. ℹ️ Tabanan, (0361)
811 602. 🏧

The most conspicuous
feature of Kapal is
hundreds of shops
selling ready-made
temple shrines and
somewhat "kitsch"
cement
statues.

There is also some attractive
earthenware pottery here.

In a quiet street leading off
the main road is **Pura Sada**,
the temple of origin of the
royal house of Mengwi (see
p47). Damaged during an
earthquake in 1917, it was
rebuilt in the 1960s by a team
of Indonesian archaeologists
based on the 17th-century
original. The most interesting
part is the 11-tier stone *meru*
built in the style of a Javanese
candi. Such towers are
known as *prasada,* and
are very rare in Bali. This
example is a reminder of the
kings' claimed descent from
the Majapahit (see p46). The
tall, 16-m- (53-ft-) high phallic
form emphasizes its
dedication to the
Hindu god Shiva.
Affixed to the sides
of the tower are
images of the eight
lords of the compass
directions. Vishnu
and Brahma with
Shiva, the deities of
the Hindu Trimurti
(triad), are portrayed
on the eastern side.
On the lower base
of the tower are
represented the seven seers
of the Hindu-Balinese
cosmos. The *candi bentar*
(split gate) is decorated with
sets of Boma (guardian
spirit) heads on the front and
back; these are split like the
gate itself. The closely packed
rows of mini-shrines in the
temple yard are said to
commemorate the crew of
a ship that sank while trans-
porting to Bali the sacred
effigy of a Majapahit king.

Statuary for
sale at Kapal

📷 **Pura Sada**
Banjar Pemebetan, near Banjar
Celuk, Kapal. 🕐 daily. 💰 donation.

Cluster of small shrines at Pura Sada in Kapal

Pejaten ❸

Road Map B4. 🚗 🚌 *from
Denpasar & Tanah Lot.* 🛈 *Tabanan,
(0361) 811 602.*

The village of Pejaten is home
to a considerable cottage
industry that produces
terracotta roof tiles,
earthenware, pots with
coloured glazes, and
other decorative objects
often attractively naive
in character. It is a
good place to browse
and bargain.

Environs

About 3 km
(2 miles) northeast
of Pejaten is the village of
Kediri, with an ornate white
statue marking its centre. Kediri
is important locally for its
cattle market and colourful
fabrics. The road from here
south to Tanah Lot crosses
enchanting rural landscapes.

*Earthenware pot
produced in Pejaten*

Krambitan ❹

Road Map B4. 🚗 🚌 *from Tabanan.*
🛈 *Tabanan, (0361) 811 602.* 🌿

The small town of Krambitan
was an old agrarian kingdom
until the turn of the 20th
century. It still has a village-
like atmosphere and some
old architecture. Krambitan is
an important repository of
Balinese classical culture.

Two palaces, **Puri Anyar**
and **Puri Agung Wisata**,
operate as guesthouses.
Occasionally, "royal parties"
of Balinese dances take
place, complete with torches
and *tektekan*, a form of
gamelan music in which
cengceng (cymbals) are
augmented by bamboo sticks
or wooden cowbells.

🎪 **Puri Anyar and
Puri Agung Wisata**
Tel *(0361) 812 774/668.* 🔵 *daily.*
🔴 *public hols.* 🏷 *donation.* 🔳

Environs

Klating Beach, on the coast
6 km (4 miles) south of
Krambitan, is an unspoiled
black-sand beach with some
simple *losmen* accom-
modation available nearby.

Tabanan ❺

Road Map C4. 🚗 🚌 *from
Denpasar.* 🛈 *Jalan Gunung Agung,
(0361) 811 602.* 🍴 💻 🔳 🌿

This is a bustling commercial
town. The interesting, if
somewhat rundown,
Museum Subak has
mock-ups of the *subak*
irrigation systems of Bali
(see pp20–21), whereby
associations are formed
by owners of land
irrigated by a common
water source. Some
traditional farming
implements are
also displayed.

🏛 **Museum Subak**
Jalan Raya Kediri, Sanggulan.
Tel *(0361) 810 315.* 🔵 *daily.*
🔴 *public holidays.* 🏷 *donation*

Environs

Located in Wanasari, 7 km
(4 miles) north on the road
to Gunung Batukau, **Taman
Kupu Kupu** is a small butterfly
park, home to some rare
species. Black-sand beaches
line the coastal road to
Negara *(see p134)*. **Surabrata**,
also called Balian Beach,
30 km (19 miles) west of
Tabanan, is charming. It has
a fishing village set by a cliff,
and a small river called
"Sacred River" – a name
intended to appeal to visitors.
The surfing is good and basic
accommodation is available.

🦋 **Taman Kupu Kupu**
Jalan Batukau, Sandan Wanasari.
Tel *(0361) 814 282.* 🔵 *daily.*
🔳🔳

Mengwi ❻

Road Map C4. 🚗 🚌 *from
Denpasar & Bedugul.* 🛈 *Tabanan,
(0361) 811 602.* 🍴 🔳

This quiet town was for a
long time the seat of the most
important kingdom in West
Bali. It held sway over the
eastern tip of Java for most
of the 18th century *(see p47)*.
The lanes of the town are a
pleasant setting for a stroll. At
Mengwi is a temple set in a
water-garden, **Pura Taman
Ayun** *(see pp130–31)*.

Environs

The road from Mengwi to
Sangeh offers views of ricefields and temples. **Baha**, 5 km
(3 miles) north of Mengwi, is
a village restored to its traditional state, with house compounds and temples typical
of a Balinese community.

Ricefields in the regency of Tabanan

Mengwi: Pura Taman Ayun

The Taman Ayun ("Vast Garden") temple, in its moated setting, symbolizes the Hindu world set in the cosmic sea. Its *meru* towers represent the mountains, residence of the gods. Located on an axis connecting the mountains with the sea, Pura Taman Ayun is thought to ensure the harmonious circulation of water from the mountains of Bali to the ricefields, then to the sea, and back to the mountains. Originally established in 1740, the temple was restored in 1937. In it there are ancestral shrines of the former ruling Mengwi family and their dependants, as well as shrines dedicated to particular mountains, to the sea and to agricultural deities.

★ **Eleven-tiered Meru**
The tallest meru *symbolizes the mountain Gunung Batukau (see p133).*

Water from the inner moat is used to cleanse the temple during festivals such as *odalan* (temple anniversaries).

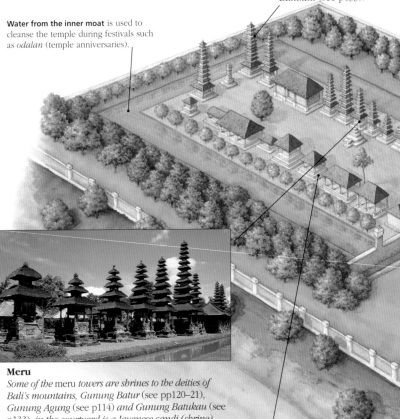

Meru
Some of the meru *towers are shrines to the deities of Bali's mountains, Gunung Batur (see pp120–21), Gunung Agung (see p114) and Gunung Batukau (see p133); in the courtyard is a Javanese candi (shrine).*

Outer moat

Bale
Several bale *(wooden pavilions) are built on carved stone bases. One contains a lotus throne on which Hindu deities Shiva, Brahma and Vishnu are believed to sit.*

STAR FEATURES

★ Eleven-tiered Meru

★ Kori Agung

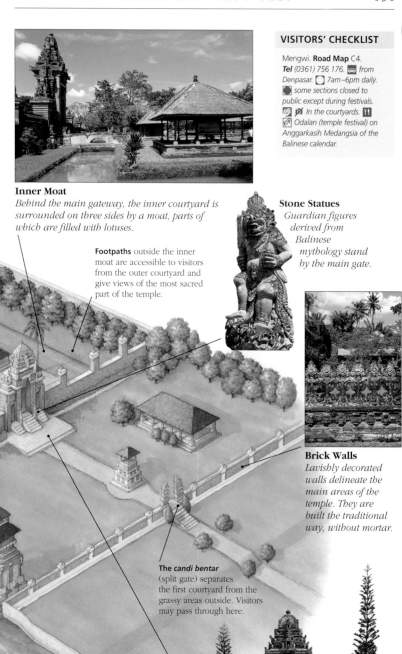

VISITORS' CHECKLIST

Mengwi. **Road Map** C4.
Tel (0361) 756 176. 🚌 *from
Denpasar.* ⬭ *7am–6pm daily.*
⬤ *some sections closed to
public except during festivals.*
📷 🚫 *In the courtyards.* 🔟
📅 *Odalan (temple festival) on
Anggarkasih Medangsia of the
Balinese calendar.*

Inner Moat
*Behind the main gateway, the inner courtyard is
surrounded on three sides by a moat, parts of
which are filled with lotuses.*

Footpaths outside the inner
moat are accessible to visitors
from the outer courtyard and
give views of the most sacred
part of the temple.

Stone Statues
*Guardian figures
derived from
Balinese
mythology stand
by the main gate.*

Brick Walls
*Lavishly decorated
walls delineate the
main areas of the
temple. They are
built the traditional
way, without mortar.*

The *candi bentar*
(split gate) separates
the first courtyard from the
grassy areas outside. Visitors
may pass through here.

★ Kori Agung
*On the lintel of the kori agung (main gate)
is a rare carving of Sai, a guardian figure,
with gods and godly seers to each side. The
doors are open only during ceremonies.*

Blayu ❼

Road Map C3. 🚌 *from Denpasar & Kediri.* 🛈 *Tabanan, (0361) 811 602.*

Blayu, like nearby Mambal, is a scenic village on a road lined with beautiful *kori* house gates typical of the area. Near the village is the monkey forest of Alas Kedaton. In the temple, **Pura Alas Kedaton**, is an ancient statue of Ganesha, the Hindu god of knowledge.

⚐ Pura Alas Kedaton
🕐 *daily.* 📷 ✓ 🎭 *Anggarkasih Medangsia.*

Meru tower at Pura Alas Kedaton, in the monkey forest near Blayu

Sangeh ❽

Road Map C3. 🚌 *from Denpasar.* 🛈 *Tabanan, (0361) 811 602.*
📷 🛍 ♿

Monkeys are found in many gorges and mountains around Bali, and a good place to see them is the monkey forest of Sangeh. It consists of palahlar trees, some as high as 30–40 m (100–130 ft). Monkeys can be seen around a small temple, **Pura Bukit Sari**, deep in the woods, but signposted on the main road. The monkeys are considered sacred, a tradition deriving from the Hindu *Ramayana* epic, in which Prince Rama allied himself with the monkey kings Subali and Hanoman to attack the evil king Rawana.

The monkeys should be approached with caution. People will be greeted with mischievous grins, but it is not advisable to get too friendly – the monkeys may

try to climb up on visitors' shoulders, and will not get down unless given something to eat. Brusque movements can provoke them to bite. The animals may even take spectacles or money, in which case a *pawang* (monkey tamer) will retrieve the stolen object using a banana as an incentive.

⚐ Pura Bukit Sari
Sangeh. 🕐 *daily.* 📷

The memorial tower at Margarana

THE BATTLE OF MARGA

In February 1946, after the Japanese surrendered at the end of World War II, the Dutch strove to reestablish their colonial authority in Bali. Local nationalists led a guerrilla war against them. On 20 November 1946, 94 Balinese fighters under the command of Gusti Ngurah Rai were trapped by Dutch troops west of Marga. Surrounded on the ground and strafed from the air, they fought to the last, in a modern repeat of the ritual *puputan (see p51)*. After this bloody defeat, resistance waned and Bali was to remain effectively under Dutch control until the end of 1949.

A monkey in Sangeh

Marga ❾

Road Map C3. 🚐 🚌 *from Denpasar & Mengwi.* 🛈 *Tabanan, (0361) 811 602.*

The village of Marga is the site of a battle between the Dutch and the Balinese guerrillas in 1946. On the western side of the village is the Margarana Monument. Besides the graves of the 94 guerrillas fallen at the battle *(rana)* of Marga, the garden contains monuments to 1,372 heroes of the War of Independence in the 1940s. The graves do not resemble Christian, Muslim or even Hindu graves: they are small, *meru*-shaped structures reminiscent of ancient temples from the Javanese empire of Majapahit *(see p46)*.

The central monument, not to be mistaken for a Balinese *meru* shrine, is designed as it is to symbolize the day of the proclamation of independence, 17 August 1945. The four steps and five small pillars at its foot represent the year (45); the eight tiers of its roof give the month (August); and the height of 17 m (56 ft) gives the day (17). A statue of Gusti Ngurah Rai *(see p51)* completes the scene.

At Marga, shrines to independence fighters at the Margarana monument

The hot-spring resort and hotel in Yeh Panas

Yeh Panas ⑩

Penatahan, near Penebel.
Road Map C3. 🚌 from Denpasar & Tabanan. **Tel** (0361) 262 356. ⏰ 6am–8pm daily. 🛏 🍴 🖥 🌿 ♿

It is worthwhile dropping by the Yeh Panas hot springs on the road to Gunung Batukau from Tabanan or Penebel. There are several sulphurous springs in this area. The main hot springs have been turned into a spa, which also has a hotel; those which are open to the public are clearly indicated by signs. There is also a spring temple here.

Hot springs are also to be found in the village of Angsri near Apuan. They are in a pleasant, natural setting, but have no modern facilities.

Pura Gangga ⑪

On a small road leading through Perean to Apuan and Baturiti.
Road Map C3. 🛈 Tabanan, (0361) 811 602. 🚫 to visitors. 🖥

Pura Gangga is a temple on the main highway to Bedugul. It is named after the holy river Ganges (Gangga) in India, and is set on the lush banks of a small river. The temple has a seven-tier *meru* with a stone base. It is unusual in that the base is open at the front, rather than entirely closed in the usual fashion. Although the temple is not open to visitors, its atmospheric compound and architectural features can easily be viewed from outside the precincts.

Gunung Batukau ⑫

Road Map B2. 🚌 from Denpasar & Tabanan. 🛈 Tabanan, (0361) 811 602. 🖥 🛏 🌿

Gunung Batukau is the second highest peak in Bali (Gunung Agung being the highest). On its slopes is the last remaining true rainforest on the island. The mountain is much revered by the Balinese as the source of irrigation water for areas to the south and west of it.

The temple of **Pura Luhur Batukau** is located among the lofty trees at its foot. It is seen as very important by the Balinese because of its geographical position at Bali's highest western peak. There is a constant stream of worshippers performing rites or requesting holy water from the temple priests.

The charm of the temple's setting lies in a blend of artifice and nature: the spires of its *meru* shrines and other dark-thatched pavilions appear to be engulfed by the forest. Trees, bushes and grass are all in various shades of green, which contrast with the black and reddish profile of the roofs and walls of the temple. Hence the origin of the name given to the central deity of the temple: Sang Hyang Tumuwuh, "The Ultimate Plant Grower".

In the centre of a nearby artificial pool is a small shrine, dedicated to the Lord of Gunung Batukau and the goddess of nearby Lake Tamblingan (*see pp140–41*).

🛕 **Pura Luhur Batukau**
⏰ daily. 💷 donation. 🚫 some areas.

Environs
To the east of Pura Luhur Batukau on the road to Baturiti are the famous rice terraces of **Jatiluwih**, stretching down to the sea in the far distance. Rice granaries line the road in the local villages. Other beautiful rice terraces are to be seen in **Pacung**, at the turn-off to Jatiluwih and Batukau.

Rice-producing lands in Jatiluwih, near Gunung Batukau

Pura Rambut Siwi, a temple on a promontory west of Medewi Beach

Medewi Beach ⓭

from Denpasar. Negara, (0365) 41 060.

Medewi is a surfers' haunt on the west coast of Bali. The long, rolling breakers can be 7 m (23 ft) high. The beach is composed of black sand, over which are scattered small black stones. The beach is a memorable sight when the stones glitter under the rays of the setting sun. On the horizon is the shape of the Javanese coast. Visitors will find some basic hotels and restaurants here.

Environs
The **Pura Rambut Siwi** temple complex is built on a promontory, 6 km (4 miles) west of Medewi Beach. The setting offers a fine panorama over the sea. The main temple was established to venerate the priest Dang Hyang Nirartha (pp46–7), after he cured the local villagers of a deadly illness. There is a single, three-tiered *meru*. A lock of hair (*rambut*), believed to be a relic in the pavilion shrine, or *gedong*. The temple entrance faces the sea and is guarded by a superbly carved statue of the demonic figure, Rangda (see p25). There are other smaller temples in caves along the nearby cliff.

Pura Rambut Siwi
6 km (4 miles) west of Medewi Beach, then 500 m (1,650 ft) south.
daily. donation.

Pengambangan ⓮

Negara, (0365) 41 060.

This Muslim settlement lies on the bank of the Ijo Gading river. Lined up along the shore are brightly painted Bugis boats. Each one has a miniature mosque on top of its mast, a reminder of the Islamic traditions of the Bugis. Not far away is a full-sized mosque, with Islamic arches and a shining dome. Music with a Middle Eastern flavour often blares from the coffee shops here; the place has a particular atmosphere.

Environs
The village of **Perancak**, on the other side of the river, has a mosque with tiered roof in the traditional Indonesian style.

Negara ⓯

from Denpasar & Gilimanuk.
Jalan Ngurah Rai, (0365) 41 193.

The real charm of Negara lies in the Bugis origin of its urban core. On both sides of the Ijo Gading River, south of the central bridge on Jalan Gatot Subroto, is the Bugis community of Loloan. A walk on its streets evokes the atmosphere of Sulawesi, where many early Bugis migrants originated (see box). Wooden houses with elaborately carved balconies line the streets. The most beautiful are at the end of Jalan Gunung Agung and on nearby Jalan Puncak Jaya. Loloan boasts several traditional *pesantren* (Islamic boarding schools); many shipowners' sons were trained as *ulema* (religious scholars) in the holy city of Mecca.

Negara is also known for its *jegog*, *gamelan* orchestras playing huge bamboo instruments (see p33). A sport which was introduced to West Bali by the descendants of the Madurese of East Java is the *mekepung*. This is a race in which jockeys compete in decorated two-wheeled chariots drawn by a pair of water buffaloes. The most exciting races can be seen from July to October.

The *mekepung* buffalo race, a regular event in Negara

Environs
A small road 4 km (2 miles) west of Negara leads to the

The mosque in Perancak, across the river from Pengambangan

North of Negara, the large Catholic church at Palasari

quiet beach of **Rening**, 8 km (5 miles) away, where bungalows are available. From the nearby Cape Rening there is a beautiful sunset view over the mountains of eastern Java. Another good beach is Candi Kusuma, 13 km (8 miles) west of Negara.

To the north are two Christian villages: **Palasari** (Catholic) and **Blimbingsari** (Protestant). These were established at the end of the 1930s on State land passed by the Dutch to Balinese converts to Christianity, who were excluded from their own community. The architecture in both villages is an interesting mix of Balinese and Dutch-Nordic styles. Near Palasari an irrigation reservoir provides tranquil landscapes.

Gilimanuk 🔟

🚌 🚐 *from Denpasar & Singaraja.*
🚢 *from Ketapang, Java.* ℹ️ *Negara,*
(0365) 41 210. 🚻 🏪 📷 ♻️

Gilimanuk is the ferry port to Java. There are many *warung* here catering for travellers who sometimes have to wait hours for a ferry.

The main architectural feature is an enormous arched "gateway to Bali", surmounted by four flaming dragons facing in the cardinal directions, with a throne of heaven in the centre.

Environs
North of Gilimanuk at Cekik, the **Museum Purbakala** (Archaeological Museum), displays some sarcophagi and neolithic tools excavated from a nearby funerary site. Some promising archaeological discoveries have been made here showing signs of pre-Bronze Age human settlement in this area. Also in Cekik is the headquarters of the Taman Nasional Bali Barat *(see pp136–7)*, the nature reserve covering a substantial area of West Bali.

🏛 **Museum Purbakala**
Jalan Raya. No phone. ⬜ *Mon–Sat.*
📷 ♿

The arched "gateway to Bali" at Gilimanuk

THE BUGIS IN BALI

The Bugis, who are Muslims, are a seafaring people known for their adventurousness. They originated in Sulawesi, one of the Greater Sunda islands north of Bali. After Makasar in Sulawesi fell to the Dutch in 1667, thousands fled, many of them sailing to Java and Bali. East Java was in turmoil at the time. In both Java and Bali the Bugis were often hired as mercenaries. The estuary of the Ijo Gading River in the Balinese kingdom of Jembrana was a good anchorage, and in the 1680s a company of Bugis offered their services to the king. In due course they moved up-river, and settled next to the king's palace at Negara. Other Bugis communities settled on Bali's north coast. Bugis mercenaries helped the king of Buleleng, Panji Sakti, occupy Blambangan, Java, in 1697.

As late as the end of the 19th century, a group of Bugis in South Bali were operating as pirates from Pulau Seranga *(see p72)* near Denpasar.

The Bugis controlled Bali's trade with Java until the mid-20th century, when the opening of the ferry link in Gilimanuk destroyed their economic power. Most of them are now impoverished fishermen.

Bugis boats painted in the traditional bright colours

Taman Nasional Bali Barat ⓱

Heliconia flower

The far west of Bali is occupied by the Taman Nasional Bali Barat ("West Bali National Park"). This is a wildlife preserve established by the Dutch in 1941, bordered by a large area of protected, productive land. The preserve aims to safeguard Bali's remaining wilderness and provides sanctuary for some threatened species. Permits are required for anyone who wants to stay overnight or to penetrate deeply into the park. Only travel on foot is allowed.

★ **Mangroves and Wetlands**
Mangrove roots protect the coast from erosion; the wetlands are home to fish, mudskippers and crabs.

The Bali Starling Breeding Facility is a haven for the endangered birds.

GUNUNG PRAPAT AGUNG
332 m (1,100 ft)

Labuhan Lalang

Banyuwedang

Teluk Terima

Pemuteran   Pura Pulaki

Gilimanuk

NATIONAL PARK

Makam Jayaprana

Cekik

GUNUNG KELATAKAN
698 m (2,300 ft)

GUNUNG BAKUNGAN
603 m (1,900 ft)

GUNUNG SANGIANG
1,004 m (3,300 ft)

GUNUNG MERBUK
1,385 m (4,550 ft)

Blimbingsari

Sumbersari

GUNUNG MESEHE
1,344 m (4,450 ft)

Palasari

Malaya

Negara

Mendoy

Perancak

Reefs and Marine Life
The park includes the marine environment around Menjangan Island (see p138), a good diving site rich in fish and coral.

Nature Walk
A short trek, taken with a guide from the park head-quarters, passes by rivers and through rainforest. Close to the route are several forest shrines including one with a hilltop view.

STAR SIGHTS

★ Savanna

★ Mangroves and Wetlands

★ Sambar Deer

★ **Savanna**
Along the north slopes of the central mountain range grow deciduous acacia, palm trees and arid shrubs. Plants live for long periods without rain on this dry savanna grassland.

Grasslands

Fertile grasslands stretch out towards the sea near the quiet beach of Pantai Gondol. A fishery research project is located here.

★ Sambar Deer

The forested mountain slopes are the habitat of these deer, which roam freely in the park.

VISITORS' CHECKLIST

Administered by the Indonesian Forestry Service (PHPA). Visitors must apply for permits at these offices. **City Office:** Jalan Suwung 40, Box 329, Denpasar. **Park Headquarters:** Jalan Raya Gilimanuk, Cekik. **Tel** *(0365) 61 060.* ◯ *8am–2pm Mon–Thu, 8–11am Fri, 8am–noon Sat.* **Ranger Station and Branch Office:** Labuhan Lalang. ◯ *8am–6pm daily.*

KEY

▬▬	Major road
═══	Minor road
– –	Walking trail
▬▬	Wildlife preserve boundary
☼	Viewpoint

B A L I   S E A

SINGARAJA

Seririt

GUNUNG MUSI
▲
1,244 m
(4,100 ft)

Munduk

GUNUNG PATAS
▲
1,412 m
(4,650 ft)

PUPUAN

PROTECTED PRODUCTION LAND

Pekutatan
Medewi
Beach

DENPASAR & TABANAN

0 kilometres   10

0 miles   5

THE BALI STARLING

The Bali starling *(Leucopsar rothschildi)*, also known as Rothschild's mynah, is the only surviving bird endemic to Bali and one of the world's most endangered bird species. In 2005 it was estimated that there were fewer than ten Bali starlings surviving in the wild.

The conservation project in the West Bali National Park is an internationally supported attempt to save the species, by breeding the birds in captivity before releasing them to the wild. At the breeding facility, Bali starlings are protected from poaching, the principal cause of their declining numbers in the wild.

The endangered Bali starling

Balinese Sapi

These local cattle, descended from the wild banteng, now rare, have been domesticated for heavy work in the ricefields.

Shrine dedicated to a romantic hero at Makam Jayaprana

Menjangan Island ⑱

🖼️ 🚌 to Labuhan Lalang from Denpasar & Seririt. 🚢 from Labuhan Lalang. 🅸 Labuhan Lalang, (0365) 61 060. 📠 📧

For diving and snorkelling in a pristine environment, Menjangan Island is not to be missed. Technically part of Taman Nasional Bali Barat (*see pp136–7*), it owes its name to the Java deer (*menjangan*), which wander across from the mainland at low tide. There are eight main diving points around the island, each with its own marine life. The best is perhaps the Anchor Wreck, named for the encrusted anchor on the reef.

Labuhan Lalang, on the bay of Teluk Terima, is Bali's nearest point of access to Menjangan Island. Boat tickets may be bought at the office of the Department of Forestry here. The last boats leave for Menjangan Island at 11am and return at dusk. There is basic accommodation at Labuhan Lalang.

Makam Jayaprana ⑲

Teluk Terima. 🖼️ 🚌 from Denpasar & Seririt. 🅸 Singaraja, (0362) 25 141. ⭕ daily. 📠 📧

The Makam Jayaprana ("Jayaprana Mausoleum") is also a temple. It has to be reached by a climb from the road (*see p136*); however, the

panoramic view over Gunung Raung in Java, Menjangan Island and Gilimanuk is ample reward for the effort. The shrine was built on the burial site of Jayaprana, a romantic hero of Balinese folklore. According to legend, Jayaprana had married a woman named Layonsari, of such extreme beauty that the Lord of Kalianget decided to get rid of him and marry her.

The king pretended that Bugis pirates had landed in Gilimanuk and sent Jayaprana with a body of soldiers to repel them. When they came to their destination the soldiers killed Jayaprana. However, resisting the advances of the king, Layonsari killed herself to rejoin her beloved Jayaprana in death.

A lionfish and coral off Menjangan Island

Today, suitors ask for favours of love at the grave. It is decorated with statues of Jayaprana and Layonsari.

Pemuteran ⑳

🖼️ 🚌 🅸 Singaraja, (0362) 25 141. 🍴 🛏️ 🏊

Pemuteran is a fast-growing coastal resort and fishing village with the best white-sand beach in North Bali. It has beautiful coral reefs with a profusion of tropical fish. There are good diving and snorkelling spots, and a turtle sanctuary. It is a convenient place for visitors to Menjangan Island to stay overnight; a boat can be rented here.

Environs

A little west of Pemuteran is the small bay of **Banyuwedang**. The name is Balinese for "hot springs". There are many springs along this shore, supposedly with curative powers. They are alternately covered and exposed by the tide. A spa resort, **Mimpi Resort Menjangan** (*see p178*), has been built over one of them.

Pura Pulaki, about 5 km (3 miles) east of Pemuteran, is a coastal temple near a point where a mountain ridge plunges abruptly into the sea, almost blocking the coastal passage. It is associated with the priest Dang Hyang Nirartha (*see pp46–7*) who is said to have turned the local inhabitants into *gamang* (ghosts). Living around it are monkeys, often mischievous; they are regarded as holy.

🅰️ **Pura Pulaki**
Banyu Poh. ⭕ daily. 📧 donation. 📷 certain areas.

Pantai Gondol ㉑

6 km (4 miles) west of Grogak, across the field next to the Fisheries Research Project (Perikanan). 🖼️ 🚌 🅸 Singaraja, (0362) 25 141.

Gondol beach is located at the foot of a small promontory, the Gondol Cape. With beautiful white sand and coral, it is a good, uncrowded spot for snorkelling and diving. However, there are no visitor facilities here.

The beach at Pantai Gondol, still pleasantly undeveloped

For hotels and restaurants in this region see pp177–9 and pp190–91

Air Panas at Banjar, a natural hot spring popular with visitors

Banjar ②

Road Map A1. ☐ ☐ to Seririt, then own transport. ℹ Singaraja (0362) 25 141. ☐ ☐ ☐ ☐

Banjar is a town of historic significance, set on the coastal plain with the North Bali uplands as a backdrop. In 1871, when still a semi-independent kingdom run by a brahman family, it put up strong resistance to Dutch encroachment. This confrontation is known as the Banjar War. The ruling family was eliminated in one of Bali's first recorded *puputan*, or "fights to the last" *(see p48)*.

The brahmans from Banjar are famous for their literary talents. In the 19th century they adapted texts from classical Kawi (Old Javanese) into common Balinese.

Brahma Vihara Ashrama *(see p23)* is a Buddhist monastery built in 1970 by a powerful local brahman, Bhikku Giri Rakhita, who converted to Theravada Buddhism, the form of Buddhism prevalent in Thailand. The temple contains many Thai iconographic features. There is an impressive view from the monastery over a nearby valley and the shoreline.

Another highlight of Banjar is the **Air Panas** hot spring, popular with both locals and visitors from nearby Lovina.

There are three pools; in the highest one the water is hot. Eight carved dragon-heads spurt out greenish-yellow, sulphurous water believed to be therapeutic for complaints of the skin. The hot water is considered sacred by the locals – a temple has been built around the spring, which is set in cool and shady surroundings.

Environs

From Banjar one can visit **Pedawa**, 10 km (6 miles) inland. This remote place is a Bali Aga village *(see p46)*. It was one of the villages which rebelled against the Javanese occupation of 1343, and has retained Hindu cultural features dating from before that time. Indeed, the Hindu triad of Brahma-Vishnu-Shiva was unknown here until recently. While the Balinese generally build a whole range of shrines for gods and ancestors behind their houses, the people of Pedawa build a single bamboo structure.

There are two routes from Banjar to Pedawa: both run through stunning mountain and plantation landscapes.

In **Sidatapa**, a village on another road running inland from Banjar, there still remain some interesting old houses constructed of bamboo.

🏛 **Brahma Vihara Ashrama**
Between Banjar and Pedawa.
Tel (0362) 92 954. ☐ 8am–6pm daily. 🌀 donation. ☐

♨ **Air Panas Banjar**
☐ 8am–6pm daily.
🌀 donation. ⛩

The Buddhist monastery of Brahma Vihara Ashrama at Banjar

A large bunutan tree spanning the road en route to Pekukatan from Pupuan

Pupuan ㉓

Road Map B2. 🚗 🚌 *from Denpasar & Singaraja.* ℹ️ *Tabanan, (0361) 811 602.* 🔟

Pupuan is Bali's vegetable-growing centre, situated in the rainiest part of the whole island. The area around it is cool and mountainous. The road from Seririt to Antosari travels through some of Bali's most beautiful landscape, with excellent coastal views. It climbs steeply via Busung-biu, Pupuan, and through a forested pass 790 m (2,600 ft) high into lush spice-growing countryside. It then winds down to Blimbing and Bajra before passing rice terraces, with rice barns along the road. The road southwest to Pekukatan passes a coffee plantation area, and at one point is arched by the roots of a huge bunutan tree.

Environs
At **Blimbing**, 12 km (7 miles) to the south, is the nearest accommodation, panoramic views and a restaurant.

Munduk ㉔

Road Map B2. 🚗 🚌 *from Singaraja & Seririt.* ℹ️ *Singaraja, (0362) 25 141.* 🔟 🏠 ♻️

Munduk is a highland village amid plantations of coffee and cloves. It is set on a high ridge near the volcanic lakes of Tamblingan, Buyan and Bratan. In the area there are still a few rest-houses from the 1920s, built in a mixed Dutch Colonial-Chinese style. In the village it is possible to visit the workshop of I Made Trip, Bali's most famous maker of bamboo instruments.

Munduk is an ideal base for exploring on rented bicycles, for mountain walks to Pedawa, for ricefield walks to Uma Jero, or for a tour of Lake Tamblingan and Lake Bratan. There are several waterfalls in the area – the most spectacular, 30 m (100 ft) high, can be found 1 km (half a mile) along the road eastwards to Bedugul.

Lake Tamblingan Tour ㉕

This tour of the mountain lakes incorporates a boat trip, a walk and a scenic drive. From Gubug, fishermen take visitors across Lake Tamblingan in a dugout canoe, skirting the north shore where dense forest descends to the edge of the water. The lake is the most unspoiled one on the island and is located in a volcanic caldera. It is surrounded by primary forest with monkeys and many species of birds to discover. The forest resounds with birdsong, especially that of barbets.

Pura Ulun Danu Tamblingan ③
The walk begins with a flight of steps to the temple. From a courtyard the trail leads into the forest.

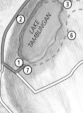

Sacred Spring ②
Inside a cave, marked by parasols and only accessible by water, there is a sacred spring.

Gubug ①
A *warung* in the village of Gubug gives information on the area. There is no trail along the north shore and travel by canoe is necessary to see parts of Lake Tamblingan.

Dugout canoe crossing Lake Tamblingan

Parasailing, one of the water activities available at Lake Bratan

Lake Buyan 26

Road Map B2 & C2. 🚗 🚌 *from Singaraja*. 🛈 *Singaraja, (0362) 25 141.* 🍴 🍵 ♨

There are great views over the lake from the mountain road – dense forest scrub vanishes at the shoreline into the water. Boats can be hired from fishermen and treks organized to a cave on the slopes of Gunung Lesong, to Gesing or to Munduk.

Lake Bratan and Bedugul 27

Road Map C2. 🚗 🚌 *from Singaraja & Denpasar.* 🛈 *Tabanan, (0361) 811 602.* 🍴 🏨 🍵 ♨

Lake Bratan offers a variety of water activities such as parasailing and water-skiing. Visitors can hire boats, and there are guides for treks to peaks such as Gunung Catur and Gunung Puncak Manggu. The lake is the setting for

the 17th-century **Pura Ulun Danu Bratan** temple, built on a small island and dedicated to the goddess of the lake, Dewi Danu. There is a small stupa-shaped shrine for Buddhist worshippers, with statues of Buddhas occupying niches that mark the four points of the compass. The panorama includes an 11-tiered *meru* located on the shore across a wooden bridge.

The 155-ha (390-acre) **Eka Karya Botanic Gardens** contain 320 species of orchids, a fern garden, a herbarium and a collection of plants used for making *jamu* (traditional medicines). Also here is the Bali Treetop Adventure Park.

To the north of Lake Bratan, the well-manicured Bali Handara Kosaido Country Club *(see p204)* boasts one of the world's best golf courses.

🏌 Eka Karya Botanic Gardens
Kebun Raya, west of Candi Kuning.
Tel *(0368) 21 273.* ◯ *daily.* 🖥 👫
Bali Treetop Adventure Park
Tel *(0361) 852 0680.* ◯ *daily.*

SINGARAJA

LAKE BUYAN

BEGUGUL

Pura Pekemitan Kangin ④
This temple on the ridge, up a long winding flight of steps, overlooks the narrow forested isthmus separating the two lakes.

Rainforest ⑤
Many trails lead into the dense tropical rainforest extending towards Lake Buyan. The vegetation is characterized by vines, creepers and massive trees with huge buttress roots.

Gubug ⑦
From here, the tour continues by car on the ridge-top road.

Pura Dalem Gubug ⑥
A short trail leads to this lakeside temple, which has a tall *meru* on a small promontory. A path then leads through open pasture back to Gubug.

Lake Buyan ⑧
As you travel along the road, you can enjoy views of the lakes from the caldera rim.

KEY

– –	Boat trip
– –	Walk route
▬▬	Drive route
═══	Minor road
⎓⎓	Track (some inaccessible)

0 kilometres _____ 2

0 miles _____ 1

TIPS FOR WALKERS

Start point: *Gubug by canoe.*
End point: *Return to Gubug on foot and proceed by pre-arranged vehicle on the scenic road along the top of the ridge, heading west to Bedugul.*
Getting there: *Own transportation via Bedugul or Munduk.*
When to go: *Mornings. Avoid the rainy season when trails are slippery and infested with leeches.*
Tour time: *2–3 hours.*

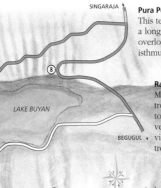

Street-by-Street: Singaraja ㉘

Ornament sold
in the market

With its waterfront mosques, temples, market and well-ordered streets, Singaraja is a pleasant place to stroll around. The harbour has not been dredged for 60 years and its business has mostly shifted to Celukang Bawang, 38 km (24 miles) to the west. However, this area is still one of the most interesting parts of the town, occupied by communities of trading minorities – Chinese, Bugis *(see p135)* and other Muslims. The Balinese community lives further east, while the modern commercial centre is near the market, Pasar Anyar, around Jalan Ahmad Yani and Jalan Diponegoro.

This bustling commercial area is where banks and businesses are concentrated.

To Lake
Bratan and
Bedugul

View of River Buleleng
From the bridge, the old residential houses of Singaraja can be seen along the river banks.

★ Chinese Temple
This temple with its classical red roof tiles, decorated with tablets in gold calligraphy, betokens the presence and influence of the Chinese trading community in this part of Singaraja.

To bus
terminal

Buleleng River

STAR SIGHTS

★ Chinese Temple

★ Masjid Nur

★ Independence Monument

KEY

– – – Suggested route

◁ **Pura Ulun Danu Bratan, a temple dedicated to the lake goddess (see p141)**

Masjid Agung Jamik
The minaret and gleaming dome are prominent features of this mosque set within a large compound.

Pasar Anyar
is a food and crafts market with a wealth of busy stalls housed in four buildings.

★ Masjid Nur
This mosque was built in a style influenced by Indian architecture.

JALAN DIPONEGORO

JALAN ERLANGGA

Pabean Harbour
The old harbour attracted settlements of traders from elsewhere in the Indonesian Archipelago; their descendants still live here.

★ Independence Monument
The statue commemorates Ketut Merta. During the independence struggle just after World War II, he was shot from a patrol boat as he raised an Indonesian flag in place of the Dutch colours.

0 metres 50

0 yards 50

Exploring Singaraja

Singaraja, north Bali's main commercial centre, was the administrative capital of Bali in colonial times. Colonial-style architecture remains in streets south of the centre, but buildings erected under the New Order *(see p51)*, such as the Pura Jagat Natha temple, combine monumental scale with traditional style. *Singa* means "lion"; *raja* means "king". The city's identity is expressed in the prominent modern statue of a winged lion where Jalan Veteran meets Jalan Ngurah Rai. The former palace of the kingdom of Buleleng, housing the administrative offices of the regency, was damaged by fire in the brief political disturbances of 1999.

A street scene in Singaraja

🔲 Pura Jagat Natha
Jalan Pramuka. 🖾 *donation.*
Pura Jagat Natha, the territorial Hindu temple of the Buleleng regency, is a large complex of buildings covered in fine stone carvings; its towering *padmasana* shrine *(see p26)* is typical of Balinese temples built from the 1970s on. There are *gamelan* rehearsals in the evenings in one of the courtyards.

🏯 Gedong Kertya
Jalan Veteran 20 & 22. **Tel** (0362) 22 645. ◯ 8am–3:30pm Mon–Thu, 8am–1pm Fri. 🖾 *donation.*
Gedong Kertya is a library founded by the Dutch in 1928 for the preservation of Balinese *lontar* manuscripts.

These are specially cut palm leaves inscribed with a stylus and rubbed with blacking to make the script legible. The same technique is used to make *prasi*, illustrations of traditional stories. Gedong Kertya, which contains many thousand such manuscripts, is frequented mainly by Balinese in search of their genealogical origins or potent medicinal recipes.

🏯 Puri Sinar Nadiputra
Jalan Veteran, next to Gedong Kertya. ◯ *Mon–Thu & Sat.*
In a former palace is the Puri Sinar Nadiputra weaving factory, where one can look at the textile-making process, and buy the products.

Silk and cotton *ikat* cloth is sold in the adjacent shop.

Environs
In the village of **Nagasepaha**, 8 km (5 miles) south of Singaraja, glass-painting is practised. Its initiator was a local puppetmaster, Jero Dalang Diah. He used to carve the characters for his stories out of buffalo or cow leather before painting them. In 1950, he was inspired by a Japanese glass-painting and began to paint on glass, using images from Balinese *wayang* stories *(see p30)*. Now, his descendants and several neighbours practise this art-form and sell their works.

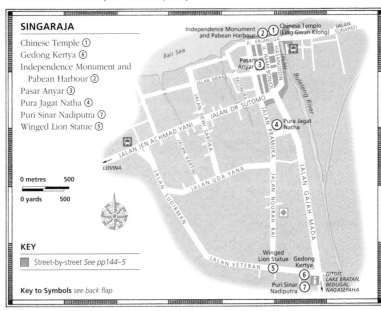

SINGARAJA

Chinese Temple ①
Gedong Kertya ⑥
Independence Monument and
    Pabean Harbour ②
Pasar Anyar ③
Pura Jagat Natha ④
Puri Sinar Nadiputra ⑦
Winged Lion Statue ⑤

Independence Monument and Pabean Harbour ②
Chinese Temple (Ling Gwan Kiong) ①
Bali Sea
Pasar Anyar ③
Buleleng River
Pura Jagat Natha ④
JALAN ERLANGGA
JALAN SURAPATI
JALAN MERAK
JALAN PATTIMURA
JALAN DR SUTOMO
JALAN DEWI SARTIKA
JALAN DEWI SARTIKA
JALAN JEN ACHMAD YANI
JALAN KARTINI
JALAN UDA YANA
JALAN PRAMUKA
JALAN NGURAH RAI
JALAN GAJAH MADA
JALAN SUDIRMAN
JALAN VETERAN
LOVINA

0 metres   500
0 yards   500

Winged Lion Statue ⑤
Gedong Kertya ⑥
Puri Sinar Nadiputra ⑦

GITGIT, LAKE BRATAN, BEDUGUL, NAGASEPAHA

KEY

▨ Street-by-street *See pp144–5*

Key to Symbols *see back flap*

Lovina ㉙

Road Map B1. 🚌 🚏 ℹ️ *Kalibukbuk, (0362) 41 910.* 🍴 🏨 🏪 🛍️

The name Lovina means "I love Indonesia", and is often used for a long stretch of the coast encompassing a series of villages, from Tukadmungga in the east to Kaliasem in the west. The beach resort area has quiet, black-sand coves lined with coconut trees. Outriggers add to the nostalgic charm, and dolphins can often be seen in the sea. For snorkellers, there are still pristine coral reefs.

The tourist facilities of Lovina are on Jalan Binaria, which leads to a modern sculpture of dolphins. To the north are ricefields, coconut groves and hotels; to the south, roads lead to villages with the mountain looming in the background. From the village of Temukus, you can trek to the **Singsing Waterfall**.

Gitgit ㉚

Road Map C1. 🚌 🚏 *from Singaraja & Bedugul.* ℹ️ *Singaraja, (0362) 25 141.* 🏞️ *to waterfall.* 🍴 🏪 🛍️

This village is the location of an impressive waterfall, 45 m (149 ft) high, about 400 m (450 yds) from the main road and surrounded by lush vegetation. Another waterfall, 1 km (half a mile) up the hill, is not quite as high, but there are fewer visitors there.

At Gitgit, Bali's highest waterfall, a refreshing stop for sightseers

Pura Beji, a highly decorated temple in Sangsit, near Jagaraga

Environs
Pegayaman, just north of Gitgit, maintains 17th-century Javanese traditions. On the Prophet's birthday *(see p43)*, villagers parade a *tumpeng* (mountain-shaped offering).

Jagaraga ㉛

Road Map C1. 🚏 *from Singaraja.* ℹ️ *Singaraja, (0362) 25 141.*

Jagaraga was the site of a battle in 1849, in which the war hero Patih Jelantik held the Dutch to a long stand-off before he was defeated. The relationship between the Balinese and the Dutch is reflected in the lively reliefs of the local temple of the dead, **Pura Dalem**. These were carved in the early decades of the 20th century. The subjects include aircraft, ships and a European in a car being held up by an armed man.

🅰️ Pura Dalem
Jagaraga. 🕐 *daily.* 🎟️ *donation.* 📷

Environs
The central gate of **Pura Beji** in **Sangsit**, 4 km (3 miles) from Jagaraga, is famous for its ornamentation. Garudas (mythical birds) are carved half in the round, half in low relief. The nearby **Pura Dalem** has some grim depictions of the tortures in hell inflicted on those who infringe moral rules.

The country around **Sawan**, 4 km (3 miles) south of Jagaraga, is said to produce some of Bali's best rice. There are impressive river gorges in the area. Sawan is also known for its northern dance and music tradition. **Air Sanih**,

12 km (8 miles) from Sangsit, is a small beach resort named after a spring. There is a pleasant beach restaurant and basic accommodation.

🅰️ Pura Beji
Sangsit. 🕐 *daily.*

Relief in the Pura Dalem, Jagaraga, showing a man driving a car

Pura Meduwe Karang ㉜

See pp148–9.

Tejakula ㉝

Road Map D1. 🚌 🚏 *from Singaraja.* ℹ️ *Singaraja, (0362) 25 141.* 🛍️

The old village of Tejakula is famous for its silver jewellery and its ancient *wayang wong* dance *(see p31)*. This eastern part of the regency of Buleleng is one of the most unspoiled areas of Bali. At Tejakula itself there are some quiet black beaches and idyllic coconut groves.

Environs
Nearby are several Bali Aga villages *(see p46)*. One of them, **Sembiran** (a short way up the mountain road west of Tejakula), has the characteristic stone-paved roads, some megalithic remains, and good views down to the north coast.

Pura Meduwe Karang 32

The large temple is notable for its statuary and carved panels which can be examined at close quarters. Although not the most extreme example, the temple shows a flowery style of decoration characteristic of North Bali. There are successive split gates and a set of two symmetrical *gedong*, or pavilions. The highest point is the towering, elaborately decorated Betara Luhur Ing Angkasa shrine.

Frangipani flower

Split Gates
At each level of the temple the ascent to the main shrine passes through a candi bentar (split gate) decorated with relief carvings.

Elaborately carved *paduraksa* (stone posts)

The long pavilion at the side of the forecourt is used for gatherings during festival celebrations.

Terraces at different levels are linked by steps.

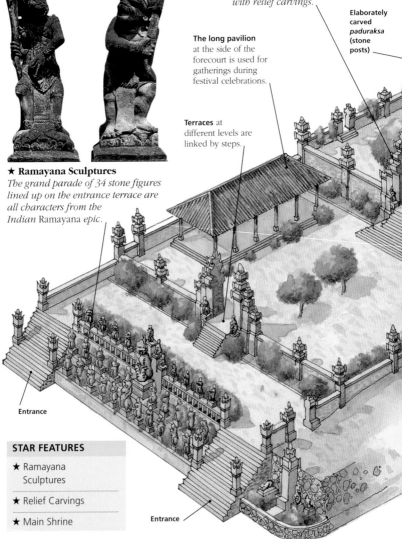

★ Ramayana Sculptures
The grand parade of 34 stone figures lined up on the entrance terrace are all characters from the Indian Ramayana epic.

Entrance

Entrance

STAR FEATURES

- ★ Ramayana Sculptures
- ★ Relief Carvings
- ★ Main Shrine

The Cyclist
A westerner on a bicycle is depicted on the side of the main shrine. He is believed to be the Dutch artist W O J Nieuwenkamp, who came here in 1904.

★ **Relief Carvings**
This local priest is typical of the subject matter of reliefs adorning the courtyard walls, which show people and scenes from everyday life.

Ornate columns in place of walls distinguish this temple from others in Bali.

The walls of the courtyard are reinforced at intervals by pillars topped with carved decorations.

Wall Sculpture
With subjects taken from Balinese legend, these decorate the walls round the central courtyard.

★ **Main Shrine**
The impressive Betara Luhur Ing Angkasa shrine honours the "Lord possessing the ground". Offerings are also made at the shrine to the sun-god Surya and to Mother Earth for fertility of the agricultural land.

LOMBOK

Glistening paddy fields, verdant hills, rugged mountains and long stretches of white sandy beach make up the landscape of Lombok. A mix of Muslim Sasaks and Hindu Balinese provides a rich diversity of cultures. In terms of both the local economy and facilities for visitors, Lombok is much less developed than Bali, but easily accessible and rewarding to visit.

The Sasaks are the indigenous people of Lombok. Numbering about three million, they are thought to be descended from a hilltribe of North India and Myanmar. The minority Balinese population, about 100,000, live mostly near the west coast.

Lombok's identity has been formed by two major influences. Javanese arrivals in the 14th century brought Islam and Middle-Eastern influences, while the Balinese Hindus, who were the colonial masters of the island from the 16th century until the 1890s, have been an important presence.

The Sasaks and the Balinese provide the island with a rich heritage of dialects and languages, traditional dance, music, rituals and crafts. Beautiful pottery is made and cloth woven, using skills passed down through the generations. The influence of Javanese, Hindu and Islamic cultures can be seen in architecture and ceremonies. While Muslim Javanese architectural influences can best be seen in the mosques, the Sasaks provided the distinctive shape of the *lumbung* (rice barn), more rarely seen now than in the past.

Lombok appeals to visitors for its natural beauty more than for its architectural heritage. The island's varied geography provides ideal conditions for trekking, wave- and wind-surfing, diving, snorkelling and game-fishing. A chain of volcanic mountains in the north is dominated by Gunung Rinjani, which offers good trekking country. Sandy beaches punctuated by extinct volcanic peaks and huge cliffs plunging straight into the Indian Ocean make for a spectacular south coast. The east coast is blessed with calm seas, peaceful beaches, sheltered coves and beautiful coral islands.

Sunset over the Lombok Strait seen from Senggigi beach, a resort area on the west coast

◁ A mosque set in a plantation near Sapit, southeast of Gunung Rinjani

Exploring Lombok

Not far from the ferry terminal at Lembar is Mataram, the provincial capital. From here a road runs from west to east taking in the sights of Narmada, Lingsar, and the hill-station area of Tetebatu. A road to the south coast leads to Kuta, a surfing spot and ideal base for exploring the rugged southern coast, which has many beautiful and remote beaches. Lombok's main resort area is Senggigi beach, north of Mataram. Easily accessible from Senggigi are the Gili Isles, an excellent diving and snorkelling location. North central Lombok is dominated by Gunung Rinjani, a huge volcanic peak surrounded by a national park, with opportunities for trekking in remote areas.

A mosque in the town of Selong

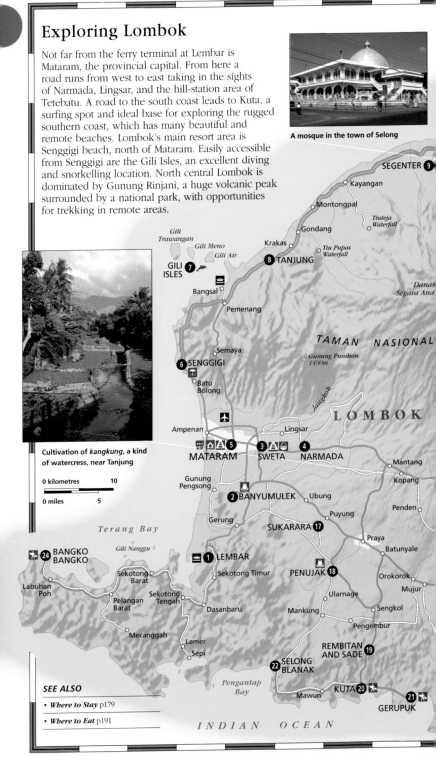

Cultivation of *kangkung*, a kind of watercress, near Tanjung

0 kilometres	10
0 miles	5

Map locations:

- SEGENTER 9
- Kayangan
- Montongpal
- Gondang
- Krakas
- 8 TANJUNG
- Tiu Pupas Waterfall
- Tiuteja Waterfall
- Danau Segara Ana
- Gili Trawangan
- Gili Meno
- Gili Air
- GILI ISLES 7
- Bangsal
- Pemenang
- TAMAN NASIONAL
- Gunung Punikan 1490m
- Semaya
- 6 SENGGIGI
- Batu Bolong
- LOMBOK
- Ampenan
- Lingsar
- MATARAM 5
- 3 SWETA
- 4 NARMADA
- Mantang
- Kopang
- Gunung Pengsong
- 2 BANYUMULEK
- Ubung
- Puyung
- Penden
- Gerung
- SUKARARA 17
- Praya
- Batunyale
- Terang Bay
- Gili Nanggu
- 1 LEMBAR
- Sekotong Timur
- PENUJAK 18
- Orokorok
- Mujur
- 24 BANGKO BANGKO
- Sekotong Barat
- Ularnage
- Labuhan Poh
- Pelangan Barat
- Sekotong Tengah
- Dasanbaru
- Mankung
- Sengkol
- Pengembur
- Mecanggah
- Lemer
- Sepi
- REMBITAN AND SADE 19
- 22 SELONG BLANAK
- Pengantap Bay
- KUTA 20
- Mawun
- 21 GERUPUK
- INDIAN OCEAN

SEE ALSO

- *Where to Stay* p179
- *Where to Eat* p191

GETTING AROUND

There are bus and *bemo* services on some main roads in Lombok, particularly the main east-west route from Mataram, and the road to Senggigi. There is little transport elsewhere, even on the road south to Kuta. Independent travellers are strongly recommended to rent their own vehicle, preferably with a driver. Remoter roads can be steep, narrow, or badly surfaced.

The majestic landscape of Taman Nasional Gunung Rinjani

Traditional Sasak dance

KEY

— Major road

═ Minor road

-- Track

— Scenic route

△ Summit

SIGHTS AT A GLANCE

Bangko Bangko ㉔
Banyumulek ❷
Gerupuk ㉑
Gili Isles ❼
Kuta ⑳
Labuhan Lombok ⑭
Lembar ❶
Mataram p155 ❺
Narmada ❹
Penujak ⑱
Pringgasela ⑮
Rembitan and Sade ⑲
Sapit ⑬

Segenter ❾
Selong Blanak ㉒
Sembalun ⑫
Senaru ❿
Senggigi ❻
Sukarara ⑰
Sweta ❸
Taman Nasional Gunung Rinjani pp158–9 ⑪
Tanjung ❽
Tanjung Luar ㉓
Tetebatu ⑯

Panoramic view from the hilltop of Gunung Pengsong

Lembar ❶

🚍 🚌 ⛴ from Padang Bai & Benoa Harbour. 🛈 ferry terminal. 🛗

Lombok's main sea port, in a bay surrounded by hills, is the gateway to the island for passenger car-ferries and a jetfoil from Bali. Crowds of merchants and other travellers mill around Lembar's ferry terminus. Much lively haggling takes place over prices of seats in overloaded buses and vans travelling to other destinations on Lombok. There is a small tourist office, some phones and a few food stalls. At the docks, beautiful Bugis schooners (see p135) and small steamers load and unload cargo.

Environs
The roads around Lembar run through lush, rural scenery. The coast road, skirting the peninsula towards **Sekotong** some 10 km (6 miles) to the south, has good views of the bay and its *bagan*, stationary fishing platforms standing in the sea. Fishermen lower huge nets into which they attract fish with the aid of lanterns. From here skiffs take passengers to

the remote coral islands of Gili Gede and Gili Nanggu. Accommodation on the islands is basic, and visitors mostly provide their own entertainment and food.

Banyumulek ❷

🚌 from Mataram. 🛈 Mataram, (0370) 634 800. 🛗

This village of wooden huts with thatched roofs is a centre for the production of handmade terracotta pots. Here, visitors can see how they are made and roam among the displays of pots, some decorated with textiles and rattan. Buyers of pots too large to carry can have them shipped abroad if necessary.

Environs
About 3 km (2 miles) west of Banyumulek, an easy climb up **Gunung Pengsong** leads to a good view. From the Hindu shrine at the top, Bali's Gunung Agung and Lombok's Gunung Rinjani are visible in opposite directions. On one side the plain of Mataram stretches to the sea and on the other is an arc of rugged mountains.

Sweta ❸

🚍 🚌 🛈 Mataram, (0370) 634 800 or (0370) 632 723. 🍴 🖥 🛗

One of Lombok's oldest temples, **Pura Lingsar**, is in Sweta. First built in 1714, the large complex has both Balinese Hindu and Sasak Wetu Telu (Muslim) shrines, as well as a pond containing sacred albino eels. At the **Bertais Market**, fruits, vegetables and spices – onions, garlic, bright red chillies in every size imaginable – are displayed in all their colours. One can also bargain for baskets, textiles, bamboo products, and bridles and stirrups.

The bus terminal serving Mataram is at Sweta.

🏛 **Pura Lingsar**
North of Sweta. 🕐 daily. 🎫
🎊 Perang Topat (Rice Cake War) & Pujawali (Nov–Dec).

Narmada ❹

🚍 🚌 🛈 Mataram, (0370) 634 800 or (0370) 632 723. 🕐 daily. 🎊 Duck Catching Festival (17 Aug).

Narmada, built in 1805, was originally a raja's (king's) summer palace. In the gardens is a lake said to represent the crater lake of Gunung Rinjani (see pp158–9). When no longer able to climb the mountain and see the lake, the raja gazed on its likeness. Lotus-filled ponds and terraced gardens recall royal splendours of the past.

Lotus pond in Narmada, a 19th-century royal water palace

LOMBOK'S POTTERY TRADITION

Vase from Penujak

Pottery is the main product of several villages. Traditionally no potter's wheel is used. Some pots are formed by hand using tools known as "stone and paddle", others are built up by coiling lengths of clay. Water decanters, decorated plates and saucers, vases, huge water containers and lamps are all created by hand. Banyumulek's pots are simple in design and devoid of embellishments; Masbagik specializes in distinctive geometric patterns; and Penujak (see p161) produces pots decorated with animal motifs.

Mataram ⑤

City tourism logo

Mataram, Ampenan and Cakranegara run together without a break; the whole conurbation is commonly known as Mataram. Mataram proper is the capital of the Indonesian province of West Nusa Tenggara. Its large, white-washed, high-roofed houses hark back to Dutch colonial days. Ampenan, to the west, was once Lombok's main port and a vital link in the spice trade. Cakranegara, to the east, was the royal capital until a century ago; today, it is a bustling commercial centre.

VISITORS' CHECKLIST

🛬 Selaparang Airport. 🚌 Sweta.
🏢 ℹ Department of Tourism, Art & Culture, Jalan Singosari 2, Mataram, (0370) 634 800.
🎭 Peresean (stick fight)(Aug).
🍴 🏨 🛍 🏧 ⚓

Exploring Mataram

Mataram is characterized by its parks and wide, tree-lined streets with buildings which echo traditional Sasak styles. There are several monuments, such as the **Kencana Warga Mahardika**, a tribute to outstanding citizenship.

Along the winding streets of Ampenan are homes and businesses of Arab and Chinese merchants. Some of the buildings, now turned into attractive restaurants and cafés, show an Art Deco influence. At sunset, visitors head down to the bustling beach and have a drink in the old colonial bank building.

At the **Lombok Pottery Centre** *(see pp194–5)*, pottery and other handicrafts are sold.

🏛 Museum Negeri

Jalan Panji Tilar Negara 6. **Tel** *(0370) 637 503.* ◯ *8am–2pm Tue–Thu & Sat–Sun, 8–11am Fri.* ● *public hols.* 🔲 🎫

The provincial state museum displays local textiles and ceramics, copperwork and woodcarvings, as well as artefacts relating to the islands of West Nusa Tenggara and paintings representing the variety of ethnic cultures.

🏯 Mayura Water Palace

Jalan Selaparang, Cakranegara. **Tel** *(0370) 624 442.* ◯ *daily.* 🎫

This complex was built in 1844 under the Balinese Karangasem dynasty. The centrepiece is a lake, surrounded by a park dotted with shrines and fountains.

🛕 Pura Meru

Jalan Selaparang, Cakranegara. ◯ *daily.* 🎫

With its three slender, multi-tiered shrines representing the Hindu Trimurti of Vishnu, Shiva and Brahma, this is Lombok's largest Hindu temple complex.

Pura Meru seen from the Mayura Water Palace

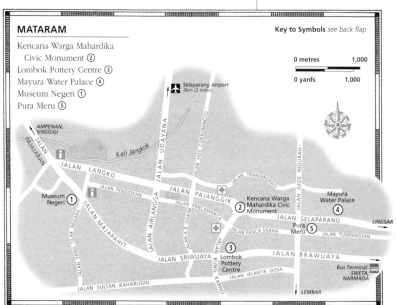

MATARAM

Kencana Warga Mahardika
   Civic Monument ②
Lombok Pottery Centre ③
Mayura Water Palace ④
Museum Negeri ①
Pura Meru ⑤

Key to Symbols *see back flap*

| 0 metres | 1,000 |
| 0 yards | 1,000 |

The beach resort area in Senggigi, a major tourist centre of Lombok

Senggigi **6**

from Lembar & Mataram.
Mataram, (0370) 640 691.
Cultural Appreciation Month
(Aug).

Senggigi is the most popular resort in Lombok, attracting visitors with its white sandy beaches and small palm-fringed bays. Although very much less developed than Kuta in Bali, Senggigi has a broad range of accommodation, restaurants and entertainment facilities.

Although Senggigi Beach is strictly speaking two glistening bays, separated by a thrust of white coral jutting out into the ocean, the area now known as Senggigi is a 6-km (4-mile) strip of road and beachfront. Restaurants and small cafés line the colourful main beach road.

The views up and down the coast, and out across the sea to Bali, which can be enjoyed from the coastal road, are majestic. Swimming off the beach is safe; and waves suitable for less experienced wave-riders peel to the left and right off the reef. Many people also windsurf here.

Around the reef itself is a variety of marine life and beautiful coral. This is a good spot for relaxed snorkelling.

Environs
An atmospheric temple shrine stands on a black outcrop of rock reaching out into the sea at **Batu Bolong**, 3 km (2 miles)

from central Senggigi. Here, Hindu devotees make their offerings at dusk. The crimson sunsets are beautiful, with the silhouette of Bali's Gunung Agung also faintly visible in the distance.

Gili Isles **7**

from Senggigi & Mataram
to Bangsal. from Bangsal.
Mataram, (0370) 640 691.

These three islands, each no more than 2–3 km (1–2 miles) across, are visited primarily because of the diversity and abundance of colourful marine life in the coral reefs and crystal clear waters around them. They are all accessible from Bangsal by a short boat trip. The best time for diving here is late April to late August.

Gili Air ("ai-year"), closest to the mainland and with the largest resident population, is quiet around the secluded hotels, but elsewhere on the island the local village life is quite lively. A few bars are mixed in with the tropical trees and shrubs, and lodging tends towards the upper end of the range. This is a good place for families.

Gili Meno, which offers a real sense of escape, is the smallest and least developed of the islands. It has fewer accommodation options, but the places to stay are mostly more up-market than those on the other two islands.

Gili Trawangan, the largest and furthest from the mainland, is the party island. A foreshore strip of bars and restaurants tucked in among many simple *losmen* (see p166) and hotels churn out music till the early hours. The other side of the island is quieter. There is a wide range of accommodation and restaurants, drawing a broad spectrum of visitors.

MARINE LIFE IN THE GILI ISLES

Divers *(see pp210–11)* who want to see sharks can generally do so within a day's diving off the Gili Isles. Reef sharks, which have no interest in humans, are often encountered. The coral is fine, despite damage caused by fish-bombing in past years. Over 3,500 species of marine life survive around the Gilis, compared with 1,500 off the Great Barrier Reef. In these waters can be seen the orange-and-white striped clown fish, the brightly coloured parrot fish and the majestic moorish idol. There are two endangered turtle species, the green turtle and the hawksbill, living in these waters. Divers at all levels of ability will find a rich variety of reef fish and other underwater life.

Brightly coloured coral in the waters off the Gili Isles

For hotels and restaurants in this region see p179 and p191

A drum known as a *kecimol*, at a Muslim wedding in Tanjung

Tanjung ⑧

🚗 🚌 *from Mataram.* 🛈 *Mataram, (0370) 640 691.* 📅 📷 🛍️ 🍴

Tanjung's livelihood is based on fishing as well as the agricultural products of the countryside. It is a large village on the road north to the Gunung Rinjani foothills, with a twice-weekly cattle market. It is surrounded by lush country in which coconut groves alternate with ricefields and vegetable gardens. In the river shallows grows *kangkung* (a leafy vegetable rather like watercress), one of Lombok's favourite dishes.

Environs
The road north runs along the black-sand beach and the terrain becomes distinctly arid. Four km (2 miles) from Tanjung on the coast is **Krakas**, famous for fresh, cool spring water. The spring is located under water 400 m (1,320 ft) offshore at a depth of about 10 m (33 ft). Local fishermen, who will take visitors out in their boats for a small fee, collect the water, which is drinkable. Further north, just past the small town of Gondang, are the **Tiu Pupas** waterfall and seven caves.

Segenter ⑨

🚌 *from Mataram.* 🛈 *Mataram, (0370) 640 691.* 🕘 *9am–5pm daily.* 💰 *donation.*

The small settlement of Segenter is a typical, traditional Lombok community, a good place to wander, and see the people going about their daily lives. The inhabitants are less pushy and commercially minded than those around Senggigi.

In the late morning, many villagers can be seen resting in the "guest huts", open structures with platforms raised above ground level, set between rows of the larger thatched houses which make up the village as a whole.

The people of Segenter lead an almost self-sufficient life; they produce most of the staple food necessary for their daily needs and plant cotton, rice and tobacco to sell at the market.

A house in Segenter, constructed from parts of the coconut palm

Senaru ⑩

🚌 *from Sweta & Tanjung.* 🛈 *Mataram, (0370) 640 691.* 🚻 📷 🛍️ 🍴

At a height of over 400 m (1,320 ft) on the lower slopes of Gunung Rinjani, Senaru is braced by cool refreshing air. From here one will be rewarded with perfect views of Rinjani to the south and the ocean to the west.

Once a secluded mountain settlement sheltered from the outside world, this village with its traditional-style houses is fast becoming a weekend escape from the heat of the coastal regions.

Senaru has many simple guesthouses and restaurants. It is the most popular departure point for treks and climbs up the mountain *(see pp158–9)*. Arrangements for a trek through the Gunung Rinjani national park and up the volcano can be made: camping equipment, tent and sleeping-bag rental are available, and food and other necessities can be bought. Porters and guides can be engaged here.

Environs
An easy 30-minute walk to the west of Senaru leads to the dramatic 40-m- (132-ft-) high **Sendanggile Waterfalls**, where water comes straight off one of the highest peaks in Southeast Asia. Here is the chance to wade in what must be the cleanest and freshest water in Indonesia. A little further uphill is the **Tiu Kelep** waterfall, with a lovely pool perfect for swimming.

Another short 30-minute walk from the village centre is **Payan**, with thatched huts and a megalithic appearance: this is one of Lombok's few remaining Wetu Telu villages *(see p23)*. Although somewhat commercialized, it is an example of Lombok's aboriginal village traditions. The women wear traditional sarongs and black shirts for weaving and during Muslim ceremonies. The Muslim practices observed here contain both Balinese and Hindu elements.

The Sendanggile Waterfalls near Senaru

Taman Nasional Gunung Rinjani ⓫

This national park is a magnet for experienced trekkers, and for nature lovers. Gunung Rinjani is a volcano 3,726 m (12,224 ft) high, important in the religions and folklore of both the Hindus and the Sasaks of Lombok. Rinjani itself is not active; the smaller Gunung Baru has erupted several times over the last 100 years. In 1995, the skies rained ash, tremors shook the island, and activities in the National Park were halted. There have been no such problems since. The tourist information office at Mataram can advise on current conditions. Climbs to the caldera rim and to the summit, which are quite challenging, can be arranged in Mataram, Senggigi or Senaru. Sembalun Lawang is another starting point, but there are fewer facilities here.

The ebony leaf-monkey, frequently seen in Lombok

Trekking from Senaru
Climbs can be arranged with many operators working out of local homestays.

BATU KOQ & BAYAN — Batu Koq
Senaru — Sindang Gila Waterfall
Rinjani Trek Centre

Base Camp
Campsite
GUNUNG SENKEREANG JAYA
2,919 m (9,577 ft)
Hot Springs
Campsite
Tiuteja Waterfall
GUNUNG PLAWANGAN
2,612 m (8,600 ft)
GUNUNG E
2,363 m (7,752 f

GUNUNG BUANMANGGE
1,916 m (6,300 ft)
GUNUNG TANAKLAYUR
2,664 m (8,800 ft)

BUKIT KETIMUNAN
1,602 m (5,200 ft)

0 kilometres   5
0 miles   3

★ **Danau Segara Anak**
The blue-green waters of this lake are surrounded by the steep walls of the volcanic crater. Trails lead down to the small, active volcano of Gunung Baru within the caldera.

Mountains near Sembalun
*The range of mountains rising on the eastern side of the
Sembalun Valley is an impressive sight, particularly seen
from the direction of Gunung Kanji.*

Black-naped Oriole
*This bird has bright
yellow-and-black
plumage and a
rich call note.
Other bird
species seen
in the park
include
lorikeets,
pigeons
and
thrushes.*

BAYAN
& ANYAR

Sajang

Sembalun Lawang

Sembalun Bumbung

GUNUNG ATAS TIMUR
2,238 m
(7,400 ft)

GUNUNG KANJI
2,045 m
(6,750 ft)

GUNUNG NANGI
2,330 m
(7,700 ft)

psite

GUNUNG PROPOK
2,077 m
(6,850 ft)

GUNUNG RINJANI
3,726 m
(12,300 ft)

Sapit

AIKMEL &
LABUHAN LOMBOK

KEY

══	Major road
──	Minor road
	Trekking route
☀	Viewpoint

Sembalun Valley
*Sweeping views of plantations and
small villages nestling in the valley
can be seen from the mountain
pass, 2,000 m (6,600 ft) high, on
the road south to Sapit.*

★ View from Gunung Rinjani
*From the highest point on Lombok, the view stretches
beyond the dry volcanic slopes to the coastal plains.*

STAR SIGHTS

★ Danau Segara Anak

★ View from
  Gunung Rinjani

Gunung Rinjani towering over plantations near Sapit

Sembalun ⓬

🚌 from Mataram & Tanjung. ℹ Mataram, (0370) 634 800. 🍴 🛒

Lying in a valley surrounded by mountains is Sembalun, a village consisting of single-storey wooden buildings. Visitors are few here, and there are only a couple of basic places to stay. However, there is a pleasant sense of remoteness. The air is fresh, and can be quite cold at night. This is a good place for walks in the countryside. The growing of shallots is a major source of income here, and a pungent, but not unpleasant, scent pervades in the valley.

From here the view of Gunung Rinjani is very vivid. The mountain seems to be almost within an arm's reach. Sembalun is the starting point of a Rinjani climb route more direct than that from Senaru (*see pp158–9*), but the facilities here are not as good.

Environs
The road east to Sapit runs across one of the highest mountain passes in Indonesia. The hairpins and gradients give good views over the Sembalun Valley.

Sapit ⓭

🚌 from Sweta. ℹ Mataram, (0370) 634 800. 🍴 🛒

Sapit is situated on the eastern slopes of Gunung Rinjani at about 800 m (2,640 ft) above sea level. It is a refreshingly cool mountain resort commanding views of eastern Lombok, and of Sumbawa across the sea beyond. Blanketing Rinjani's lower slopes around Sapit are emerald-green rice terraces and tobacco plantations.

The village is basic, but gardens and flower-beds make a fresh, orderly impression. There are some inexpensive but clean guest-houses here.

Vessels at a jetty at Labuhan Lombok

Labuhan Lombok ⓮

🚐 🚌 from Mataram. ⛴ from Mataram and Sumbawa. ℹ in ferry terminal. 🍴 🛒

The bay around Labuhan Lombok forms a natural harbour. A road runs parallel with the shore, and between it and the waterside are the settlements of Bugis fisher-men consisting of houses on stilts. Colourfully painted trawlers are moored nearby. The forebears of this community came from South Sulawesi (*see p135*). The town's Sunday market sells all

House on stilts in the coastal village of Labuhan Lombok

For hotels and restaurants in this region see p179 and p191

manner of produce and daily needs. At one end of the bay, 2 km (1 mile) from the town, is the ferry jetty for services running east of Lombok to Sumbawa, the next island in the Lesser Sundas group.

Pringgasela ⓯

🚌 *from Sweta & Labuhan Lombok.* ℹ️ *Mataram, (0370) 634 800.* ▫️

In the cool, quiet foothills of Gunung Rinjani is the shady village of Pringgasela. A mountain stream runs through it beside the road. Many villagers here are weavers, and they are happy for visitors to watch them at work. By tradition, girls in the village learn to weave from around the age of ten. Outside many of the houses textiles are displayed for sale, and the overall impression is colourful. The patterns and colours, with blacks and reds predominant, are characteristic of Lombok.

Basket produced in Loyok

Environs
In the hills south of Pringgasela is another craft centre, **Loyok**, the premier basketware, bamboo and palm-leaf handicraft village in Lombok. The road from Loyok runs parallel to a fast-flowing stream that weaves through a series of beautiful forests and valleys.

Tetebatu ⓰

🚌 *from Mataram.* ℹ️ *Mataram, (0370) 634 800.* 🍴 ▫️ 🛍️

The hill-station village Tetebatu, with its views of Gunung Rinjani, is a good place for relaxation. The village itself is quite modest, but over an area running 3–4 km (2–3 miles) up the mountain slope there are a number of guesthouses, set among ricefields.

Pleasant walks are to be had in the mountain air, passing large-leaved tobacco plantations. One hike runs to a small river into which flows the Jeruk Manis waterfall – the route is quite strenuous but can be tackled by fit children over ten, as well as adults. Other walks lead to isolated villages and a tropical forest inhabited by monkeys. It is advisable to engage one of the guides who offer their services in the village.

Sukarara ⓱

🚌 *from Sweta.* ℹ️ *Mataram, (0370) 634 800.* ▫️

Many people in Sukarara earn their living by weaving *songket* textiles *(see p37)*. The tourist trade is rather evident here. Large numbers of shops display and sell many varieties of cloth from around the region. Village women dressed in black will demonstrate their expertise with the loom and are willing to pose for photographs.

Penujak ⓲

🚌 *from Sweta.* ℹ️ *Mataram, (0370) 634 800.* ▫️

Along with Banyumulek *(see p154)* and Masbagik, Penujak is one of Lombok's main pottery-producing villages, and perhaps the best place to see the process, which the villagers will explain. Traditionally, women made the pots by hand while the men marketed them. Now that export sales have led to increased output, men join in the production process. Each village produces its own distinct pottery decoration and colour, but all the designs are available in all three places.

Traditional earthenware pottery produced in Penujak

TEXTILES IN LOMBOK
Hand-woven textiles, of very high quality, are produced in Lombok using traditional backstrap looms. The villages which specialize in textile-weaving are Sukarara, Pringgasela, Rembitan and Sade *(see p162)*. There is some larger-scale production around Mataram. In the villages, the entire process of cloth-making can be watched by visitors, from the boiling of barks and roots to make dyes, and the soaking of cotton threads, to the weaving of original patterns on the hand-operated loom. The villagers use only natural plants for the dyes. Yellow dye, for example, is made from an extract of turmeric root, while blue comes from the indigo plant. Roots and bark are pounded and boiled; the cotton threads are immersed for 24 hours, and, when dry, are arranged on the loom in the manner demanded by the pattern of the textile.

A weaver at work on a hand-operated loom in Sukarara

Typical Lombok sarong

Rembitan and Sade ⑲

ℹ️ Mataram, (0370) 634 800.
📷 donation. 🔲 🔲 🔲

The farming villages of Rembitan and Sade, about 3 km (2 miles) apart from one another, are both attractively set against the hillside. Despite the fact that many visitors stop here, and therefore sellers of souvenirs abound, Rembitan and Sade remain good places to catch a glimpse of traditional Sasak life, in which weaving textiles, growing rice and rearing goats and cattle are major occupations. A distinctive feature is the *lumbung*, a bonnet-shaped rice barn. Once a symbol of Lombok, these barns are now rare. The walls of the thatch-roofed barns and houses are made of bamboo or palm-leaf ribs.

Kuta's rugged coastline, a paradise for surfers and sun-lovers

Kuta ⑳

🚌 from Sweta. ℹ️ Mataram, (0370) 634 800. 🔲 🔲 🔲 🔲 🛐 Nyale fishing festival (Feb–Mar).

Lombok's Kuta is mostly undeveloped, in complete contrast to its namesake in Bali. The coastline around it is ruggedly beautiful. Kuta bay has dazzling white sand, and few people. The ocean swells form perfect waves for the surfers who come here.

The village of Kuta consists of a scattered collection of wooden buildings which provide homes for the fishing community and also some visitor accommodation.

A landmark to the east of the village is the Novotel Coralia Lombok (*see p179*), which has been designed to fit in with the building style typical of this part of Lombok.

Environs
There are two other superb beaches not far from Kuta. **Mawun** beach is 8 km (5 miles) west, and attractively isolated. The same distance to the east is **Tanjung Aan**, a wide, sandy bay. Waves crash on rocky outcrops at each end of the bay, but the water on the beach itself is smooth and turquoise.

Gerupuk ㉑

ℹ️ Mataram, (0370) 634 800. 🔲 🏂

The village of Gerupuk is situated on the edge of a long bay. The village's main income, apart from fishing, comes from seaweed cultivation. The seaweed, used as an ingredient in food products for farm animals, grows on semi-submerged bamboo frames in the waters off the beach. After being harvested it can be seen drying in neat bundles along the roadside.

Gerupuk is home to one of south Lombok's most popular surf breaks. In the bay, swells from the Indian Ocean build up and break on coral reefs, creating fine waves. Surfers hire a small skiff for the short trip to the break; the journey gives breathtaking views of the nearby cliffs and rocky crags. The skiffs anchor a short distance from the break and await the surfers' return.

The waves here are considered more user-friendly and forgiving than others on this coast, where the sea can often be rough. They break on coral deep enough not to cause undue worry to board riders, unlike the shallow breaks and steep take-off points of Maui near Selong Blanak to the west. While the waves mostly break right, left breaks also peel off, although less regularly. The surf is best early in the morning before any wind gets up – usually before 9am; but even later in the day when crosswinds blow offshore, the waves are fine. The surfers are mostly Japanese, Australians and locals from Kuta village itself; there is a smattering of Brazilians and French. They generally find accommodation at Kuta Beach.

The waves at Gerupuk, one of the best surfing spots on Lombok's coast

For hotels and restaurants in this region see p179 and p191

Selong Blanak ㉒

ℹ *Mataram, (0370) 634 800.*

Marked at each end by rocky promontories, Selong Blanak is a tranquil bay with a fishing settlement. Lined up on the beach are multi-coloured outrigger canoes. Most people come here to surf at a nearby beach known as **Maui**. The waves are exceptionally fast. Because of the steep take-offs and the fact that the waves are ridden over very shallow coral, this is a place for very experienced surfers only.

Tanjung Luar ㉓

ℹ *Mataram, (0370) 634 800.*

The village of Tanjung Luar earns its living from the sea. It is a minor port – travellers from nearby islands land here by means of an inter-island taxi service which uses small outriggers. Many occupations to do with fishing and the sea are represented here. There is a busy fish market. Fishermen return to port after spending several days afloat, and sell their

Coastal landscape near Selong Blanak

catch beside the water's edge. It is possible to watch huge sharks being brought to shore. Contributing to the lively atmosphere are the salt-sellers, the children fishing off the main jetty, and the people giving their boats a new coat of paint.

A short walk from the fish market, lining the beach-front, live some Bugis communities *(see p135)*, their wooden houses raised on stilts. Colourful Bugis schooners, with their distinctive high prows, lie at anchor here.

For many people in Tanjung Luar, *cidomo* are the only form of transport. These are small horse-drawn buggies, brightly painted and often decorated with bright red pompoms and tassels.

Buggy at Tanjung Luar

Bangko Bangko ㉔

🚌 *from Lembar.* **ℹ** *Mataram, (0370) 634 800.*

A popular place for fishing and surfing, Bangko Bangko lies at the end of a peninsula at the south-west extremity of Lombok. A location rather than a village, it can be reached only along a dirt road. The reward for this trip off the beaten track is some spectacular scenery.

Some surfers have named the area Desert Point. The waves that peel to the left off a coral shelf, before slamming into the base of the cliff-face, provide great conditions for experienced riders. The un-predictable, often dangerous seas are good for game fish-ing. A fishing trip can be booked through tour-opera-tors in Lembar *(see p154)*.

Harbour scene at Tanjung Luar, with Bugis houses raised on stilts

TRAVELLERS' NEEDS

WHERE TO STAY 166–179

WHERE TO EAT 180–191

SHOPPING IN BALI AND LOMBOK 192–197

ENTERTAINMENT 198–201

OUTDOOR ACTIVITIES 202–211

WHERE TO STAY

Set among tropical gardens and gently swaying palm trees, even the largest of Bali's hotels have a Balinese flavour. This is re-inforced by the staff and the island's cultural ambience. The range of accommodation has expanded with the emergence of a category of inti-mate, exclusive hotels known as

Hotel porter

"boutique hotels", in addition to the resorts that now dot the island. For groups, villas can offer more sense of privacy than hotels. Lombok is less developed than Bali, but offers a good variety of accommodation. There is little provision specifically for the disabled in the hotels of either Bali or Lombok.

LOSMEN AND HOMESTAYS

The most common type of low-budget accommodation in Bali is the *losmen*. The term is derived from the colonial-era word *"logement"* – and once implied little more than a room in a Balinese household. Today the name is applied to a category of small, inexpensive lodgings, in many places the only accommodation available. *Losmen* and true homestays are not formally organized, and are usually not included in hotel listings. You usually cannot reserve, and so you must find a place to stay on reaching your destination.

Losmen generally consist of simple rooms built around a central area. Mosquito nets, a fan, and sometimes a bath-room are provided, but rarely toilet paper. Some *losmen* offer air-conditioning and hot water, but charge more. Break-fast is almost always included. Large numbers of *losmen* are to be found in Kuta (Poppies Lane II), Central Ubud (Jalan Bisma and Jalan Kajeng), the village of Lembongan on Nusa Lembongan and Candi Dasa (the main street); and near the beaches at Lovina, Padang Bai and Amed.

Pool facilities in a resort at Senggigi Beach, Lombok

HOTELS AND RESORTS

Bali's many resorts and hotels tend to be concentrated in the more developed tourist areas of South and Central Bali. They span a broad price range, and in many cases good package deals can be booked in your home country. The choice of hotels and resorts in Lombok is much more limited than in Bali. They are concentrated in the west, around Senggigi and on the Gili Isles.

The dramatically increasing number of resorts in Bali and the growing popularity of boutique hotels and villa

vacations are incentives for hotels and resorts to offer good value for money, so it is worth shopping around for the best deal. The large resorts are particularly suita-ble for families with young children or visitors looking for a complete, all-inclusive holiday. They offer a luxuri-ous experience insulated from the hustle and bustle of the islands' daily life, and usually provide baby-sitting services, or in-house programmes for children.

Nusa Dua, on Bali's south-ern tip, was conceived as a comprehensive 5-star resort area with a full infrastructure including a magnificent golf course and a large shopping mall (*see p73*). White sand beaches add to the allure of Nusa Dua, and many visitors find they have no reason to venture further afield.

Elsewhere on the island, large, self-contained resorts offer both privacy and social opportunities. Many of them have been designed and are managed by major operators in the hospitality industry. They offer world-class service and facilities such as tennis courts and gyms, spas, pools, beautiful gardens, first-class restaurants and nightly cultural performances.

Prices vary according to room, region and season. Most hotel rooms will be equipped with fans and bathrooms. However, expect to pay more for hotel rooms with air-conditioning.

The Bali branch of the **PHRI** (Persatuan Hotel dan Restaurant Indonesia, or Indonesian Hotel and Restaurant Association) publishes hotel listings and a star rating, but they tend

Simple losmen accommodation in Lombok

◁ **The two-tiered pool of The Legian hotel in Seminyak**

Furnished in Balinese style, a villa with private pool and courtyard

to be neither complete nor up to date. In theory the association should help with problems, but it is usually more effective to submit any complaints direct to the hotels themselves.

SPECIALITY HOTELS AND RESORTS

Some hotels and resorts cater to visitors interested in certain types of activity, food or cultural experience. For example, those situated on mountains will generally offer trekking. A number of small homestays in Kintamani, and those close to Gunung Agung, offer trekking to the volcanoes.

For snorkelling and diving, excellent choices are the resorts around Amed and Tulamben on the east coast, those on the island of Nusa Lembongan, the North Bali resorts (from which trips can be made to the underwater gardens of Taman Nasional Bali Barat), and those on Gili Trawangan (accessible from Lombok). Cooking courses are offered by several resorts.

For visitors interested in spiritually orientated holidays, Ubud is a popular centre. Some hotels in Ubud and elsewhere offer the opportunity to become involved in local village life, and visitors can try their hand at cooking, weaving, and other local crafts.

PRIVATE VILLAS

For people travelling with children, villas can be a good choice, as they are generally fully staffed with housekeepers, babysitters, gardeners, security and often a cook. They will feature a pool and gardens, satellite television and several bedrooms. For families or groups of friends, villas can offer great savings and give opportunities for private relaxation and entertainment that a hotel cannot match. Pool parties, cocktail parties and barbecues can all be a part of a villa holiday.

Some Bali-based agents offer a selection of villas and will work to find something to suit your budget, personal needs and number of guests. The largest operators are **Elite Havens**, **BHM**, **Prestige Bali Villas** and **Private Homes and Villas**.

Fountain at Inter-continental Resort Bali

TRAVELLING WITH CHILDREN

Bali is a wonderland for the young. The Balinese have a particular fondness for children, and hotel staff will take an interest in them. All the large 5-star resorts and many of the smaller ones have good facilities for children, so that parents can sit back and relax. Some of the facilities on offer are baby-sitting services, organized children's activities, children's clubs and family suites.

RESERVATIONS

The internet is a good means of booking direct or investigating a hotel or resort before making a decision. Bypassing the travel agency can mean good discounts, but you may find you have no recourse if all is not as promised at your hotel.

Many resorts have their own websites, and Bali-based agents have also set up similar services for hotels, private villas and tours. A number of websites are given in the Directory (*see p169*). Keying in "accommodation bali" on a search engine will bring up more sites. You can compare prices given on the websites with those quoted by a travel agent, and in some cases even go on a virtual tour of the resorts.

Westin Resort, a large resort with full family facilities at Nusa Dua

Spas and Spa Resorts

Aromatic flowers

One of the most prominent facilities offered by Bali hotels to their guests is the spa. Traditional health and beauty treatments derived from local, natural ingredients have been used in Indonesia for many centuries, but it is only in more recent years that they have been made widely available to visitors. Some of Bali's top spas have been rated as among the best in the world. However, visitors on a budget can also indulge – although the smaller salons cannot match the luxury of the most expensive places, some of them offer a range of similar treatments at a fraction of the cost.

Spa and massage room at the Four Seasons Resort, Sayan

TRADITIONAL TREATMENTS

Bali's spas aim to provide pleasure and relaxation rather than clinical therapy. They are intended not to treat health problems, but rather to calm the mind and beautify the body. Many of the spas have been designed with couples in mind; with the exception of the local beauty parlours, they offer treatments for both men and women.

A complete treatment will include a full body exfoliation called the *lulur*, an aromatic beauty therapy that has been popular for generations with the Javanese. Other enjoyable experiences include the traditional Balinese massage, a gentle process characterized by long, sweeping hand movements; and the relaxing and therapeutic cream bath, which includes an hour-long head-and-shoulder massage and a natural hair treatment. These are popular with both men and women.

Western influence has made itself felt, particularly through the addition of aromatherapy. Indonesia has an abundance of natural herbs and flowers, and an industry has grown up dedicated to creating high-quality natural oils. Even during a simple massage you will be offered a choice of oils designed to create a variety of moods.

CHOOSING A SPA

There is an extensive range of spas in Bali. They cater for a wide variety of budgets and preferences. It is worth shopping around. Most spa resorts offer combination packages – these are particularly suitable for first-time visitors, who would like to sample the range of treatments available.

The **Four Seasons Resort** in Jimbaran has a multi-million-dollar spa facility that has won many international awards. A full menu of local and Western treatments is available. One of its specialities is a massage in which water is sprinkled from above, simulating a calming, warm rainshower. Another is a *jamu* (natural remedies) bar where local herbal recipes are prepared.

The **Nusa Dua Spa**, at the Nusa Dua Beach Hotel, was one of the first spas on Bali. It is still one of the biggest. Simple beauty treatments and massages are offered in private rooms, and residents at the hotel who want the full package may enjoy treatments in their villas. Also in Nusa Dua, **The Spa at the Balé** offers Thai massage, hot stone massage and a special treatment for sunburn.

Thalasso, located at the Grand Mirage Resort, is a French treatment centre.

JAVANESE LULUR TREATMENT

The *lulur* treatment is a traditional beauty ritual which originated in the royal palaces of Central Java. It is the most popular therapy among the many offered by Balinese spas. It usually lasts two-and-a-half hours. A yellow paste is made from a fragrant blend of powdered turmeric, herbs, nuts, grains and other ingredients: this is first spread over the body and then rubbed off to remove dead skin. The

skin is then moisturized with splashes of cool yoghurt. This stage is followed by a shower and a scented bath before a long, slow, relaxing massage is performed. There are a number of variations to this treatment, with ingredients ranging from coffee to ginger and spices.

The Javanese *lulur* treatment – a rejuvenating treat for the skin

Natural sea water is used in many of its therapies.

The spa at the luxurious **Four Seasons Resort** in Sayan is modern and air-conditioned, and features Ayurvedic treatments. Also recommended is the **Intercontinental Resort Bali** in Jimbaran. Treatment pools are among the facilities here. Eastern and Western massage techniques and spa products are offered in beautifully appointed private rooms.

Bodyworks in Seminyak is a small, privately run spa with comfortable rooms and a full range of treatments, ranging from hair colouring to manicures, pedicures and facials. Bodyworks has another salon, larger and more luxurious, in Peti Tenget.

Prana Spa, part of The Villas Bali Hotel & Spa in Seminyak *(see p173)*, offers hot and cold plunge pools, reflexology, Ayurvedic treatments and

herbal steam rooms. Also in Seminyak is the **Oberoi** *(see p173)*, which specializes in *lulur* and body mud wrap treatments, and **Martha Tilaar**, the only spa offering *ken dedes*, which involves "smoking" the body.

Mandara Spas has taken over the running of some of the best spas; locations include **Padma Resort Bali, Nikko Bali** and **Ayodya Resort Bali**.

Nur Salon was one of the first salons to operate in Ubud; it is still traditional in style and very inexpensive. **Bali Hati** boasts pristine massage rooms with a steam room and outdoor jacuzzi. Prices are quite reasonable. The **Como Shambala** is pricier, with open-air treatment rooms bordering lush forest. **Bagus Jati Resort**, just north of Ubud, has a jacuzzi overlooking a

Mandara Spa's signature treatment performed by two therapists

stunning gorge. It offers Ayurvedic and Balinese treatments in a luxurious setting.

Espace is a trendy, white-themed spa offering massage, body treatments and facials. Check out the relaxing, mineral-rich Flores Island Sea Mud exfoliating body scrub.

The Yoga Barn is a rustic, environmentally-friendly space dedicated to yoga, movement and healing. In addition to a wide range of yoga classes, it offers holistic retreats.

DIRECTORY

GENERAL INFORMATION

PHRI (Bali branch)
Villa Rumah Manis,
Jalan Nakula, Seminyak.
Tel (0361) 730 606.

PRIVATE VILLAS

BHM
www.bhmvillas.com

Elite Havens
883 Jalan Raya Semer,
Banjar Semer, Kerobokan.
Tel (0361) 731 074.
www.elitehavens.com

Prestige Bali Villas
Jl Laksmana 22, Seminyak.
Tel (0361) 733 320.
www.prestigebalivillas.
com

Private Homes and Villas
www.phvillas.com

SPAS AND SPA RESORTS

Bagus Jati Resort
Banjar Jati Sebatu, Ubud.
Tel (0361) 978 885.
www.bagusjati.com

Bali Hati
Jalan Raya Andong, Ubud.
Tel (0361) 977 578.
www.balihati.com

Bodyworks
Jalan Raya Seminyak 63,
Seminyak.
Tel (0361) 730 454.
Kayu Jati 2, Peti Tenget.
Tel (0361) 733 317.

Como Shambala
Uma, Ubud.
Tel (0361) 972 448.
www.uma.como.biz

Espace
Jalan Raya Seminyar, BR
Basangkasa, Seminyak.
Tel (0361) 730 828.
www.espacespabali.com

Four Seasons Resort, Jimbaran
Jimbaran Bay.
Tel (0361) 701 010.
www.fourseasons.com/
jimbaran

Four Seasons Resort, Sayan
Sayan, Ubud.
Tel (0361) 977 577.
www.fourseasons.com/
sayan

Intercontinental Resort Bali
Jalan Uluwatu 45, Jimbaran.
Tel (0361) 701 888.
www.bali.
intercontinental.com

Mandara Spa at Ayodya Resort Bali
Jalan Pantai Mengiat,
Nusa Dua.
Tel (0361) 771 102.
www.ayodyaresortbali.
com

Mandara Spa at Nikko Bali
Jl Raya Nusa Dua, Selatan.
Tel (0361) 773 377.
www.nikkobali.com

Mandara Spa at Padma Resort Bali
Jalan Padma 1, Kuta.
Tel (0361) 752 111.
www.padmaresortbali.
com

Martha Tilaar
Jalan Raya Basangkasa
30a, Keminyak, Kuta.
Tel (0361) 731 463.

Nur Salon
Jalan Hanoman 29,
Padang Tegal, Ubud.
Tel (0361) 975 352.
Fax (0361) 974 622.

Nusa Dua Spa
Nusa Dua Beach Hotel,
Nusa Dua.
Tel (0361) 771 210.

Oberoi
Seminyak, Kuta.
Tel (0361) 730 361.
www.oberoihotels.com

Prana Spa
The Villas, Jalan Kunti
118x, Seminyak, Kuta.
Tel (0361) 730 840.
www.thevillas.net

The Spa at the Balé
Jalan Raya Nusa Dua
Selatan, Nusa Dua.
Tel (0361) 775 111.
www.thebale.com

Thalasso
Grand Mirage Resort,
Jalan Pratama 74,
Tanjung Benoa.
Tel (0361) 771 888.
Fax (0361) 772 148.

The Yoga Barn
44 Jalan Hanoman, Ubud.
Tel (0361) 971 236
or 970 992.
www.theyogabarn.com

Choosing a Hotel

Bali and Lombok's hotels cover the spectrum from luxurious resorts to simple *losmen*. Most *losmen (see p166)* do not take advance bookings, and are best chosen on arrival. They are not listed here. During high seasons (mid-December to mid-January, July and August), hotel rates may be higher. Discounts may apply in low season.

PRICE CATEGORIES
Hotel prices (in US dollars) for a standard double room per night, inclusive of service charges and any additional taxes, but not breakfast.
$ Under $50
$$ $50–$100
$$$ $100–$200
$$$$ $200–$300
$$$$$ Over $300

SOUTH BALI

CANGGU Hotel Tugu Bali
Jl Pantai Batu Bolong, Canggu Beach **Tel** *(0361) 731 701* **Fax** *(0361) 731 708* **Rooms** *22*   **Map** *C4*
$$$$$

This boutique hotel and spa is a living museum of priceless antiques and rare cultural artifacts, set between ricefields and the quiet, rugged beach of Canggu. Two suites contain replica studios of famous painters who discovered Bali in the 1930s; dining facilities include a 300-year-old temple. **www.tuguhotels.com**

JIMBARAN Intercontinental Resort Bali
Jl Uluwatu 45, Jimbaran, 80361 **Tel** *(0361) 701 888* **Fax** *(0361) 701 777* **Rooms** *425*   **Map** *C5*
$$$$

There are six restaurants, including a Japanese fine-dining restaurant, at this palatial beachfront resort boasting Balinese architecture, pools, fountains, a wealth of local artifacts, and numerous recreational and business facilities. There is also a stylish spa, kids' club and a luxurious VIP area within the resort. **www.bali.intercontinental.com**

JIMBARAN Jimbaran Puri Bali
Jl Uluwatu, Jimbaran **Tel** *(0361) 701 605* **Fax** *(0361) 701 320* **Rooms** *41*   **Map** *C5*
$$$$

Set within private walled gardens, this is a beachfront boutique hotel of cottages. Balinese touches such as stone carvings, hand-woven fabrics and intricately carved decorative wood abound. There is a luxurious swimming pool, two restaurants (one right on the beach), a library and an open-air, sand-floored bar. **www.pansea.com**

JIMBARAN Ayana Resort & Spa
Jl Karang Mas Sejahtera Jimbaran, 80364 **Tel** *(0361) 701 555* **Fax** *(0361) 702 750* **Rooms** *322*   **Map** *C5*
$$$$$

Amenities at this lavish, multi award-winning resort include five restaurants, a private beach, two glass wedding pavilions, pools, a library, a shopping mall, tennis courts and a children's club. The Thalasso spa includes one of the world's largest Aquatonic seawater pools. **www.ayanaresort.com**

JIMBARAN Four Seasons Resort at Jimbaran Bay
Jimbaran, 80361 **Tel** *(0361) 701 010* **Fax** *(0361) 701 020* **Rooms** *147*   **Map** *C5*
$$$$$

These luxurious and spacious villas, with thatched roofs, courtyard gardens and plunge pools, are set within the confines of stone courtyard walls. The resort also features five restaurants, a library and lounge, a multi award-winning spa, meeting facilities, tennis courts, an activities centre and a cooking school. **www.fourseasons.com**

JIMBARAN Jamahal Private Resort & Spa
Jl Uluwatu 1 **Tel** *(0361) 704 394* **Fax** *(0361) 704 597* **Rooms** *11*   **Map** *C5*
$$$$$

The luxurious accommodation here is scattered along a concealed pathway and bordered by a meandering lagoon pool. This intimate spa retreat presents individual suite-villas and a delightful spa. The room service menu offers fine cuisine, and there is also private transport to the beach just five minutes away. **www.jamahal.net**

KUTA Un's Hotel
Jl Bene Sari 16 **Tel** *(0361) 757 409* **Fax** *(0361) 758 414* **Rooms** *30*   **Map** *C5*
$

In the heart of Kuta, this peaceful oasis is just a stone's throw from the beach. The spacious rooms offer the option of a fan or air-conditioning, and are bordered by wide communal balconies and terraces set around a swimming pool in a pretty garden. Guests can order room service from the Balcony Restaurant. **www.unshotel.com**

KUTA Yulia Beach Inn
Jl Pantai Kuta 43 **Tel** *(0361) 751 893* **Fax** *(0361) 751 055* **Rooms** *34*   **Map** *C5*
$

This friendly hotel is located very close to Kuta Beach, in the midst of all the bustle, shopping and nightlife, so it can be a bit noisy. It offers a choice of simple and basic accommodation, including some bungalows. It also has a small restaurant and a swimming pool. **www.yuliainns.com**

KUTA Poppies Cottages
Jl Pantai, Gang Poppies **Tel** *(0361) 751 059* **Fax** *(0361) 752 364* **Rooms** *20*   **Map** *C5*
$$

These romantic, traditional-style cottages are set within an enchanting garden; each features a thatched roof, a courtyard bathroom with an open-air sunken bathtub, one double and two single bedrooms, and a large balcony. The two swimming pools have landscaped sunbathing terraces. **www.poppiesbali.com**

Key to Symbols *see back cover flap*

KUTA Alam KulKul $$$$

Jl Pantai Kuta **Tel** *(0361) 752 520* **Fax** *(0361) 766 861* **Rooms** *80*   **Map** *C5*

Located just across the road from Kuta Beach, this chic resort offers a choice of luxuriously fitted rooms and small private villas set among lovely old banyan trees. It also incorporates the Jamu Spa, a children's daycare centre, an Indonesian speciality restaurant and the famous Papa's Restaurant serving Italian cuisine. **www.alamkulkul.com**

KUTA Hard Rock Hotel $$$$

Jl Pantai, Banjar Pande Mas **Tel** *(0361) 761 869* **Fax** *(0361) 761 868* **Rooms** *418*   **Map** *C5*

The first Hard Rock Hotel in Asia covers a prime site beside Kuta Beach. This holiday resort with a rock-culture theme has eight restaurants and bars, live music venues, a megastore, a nursery/crèche, a large swimming pool, health club, spa, beauty salon and business centre. **www.hardrockhotels.net**

LEGIAN Three Brothers $

Jl Legian, Three Brothers Lane **Tel** *(0361) 751 566* **Fax** *(0361) 756 082* **Rooms** *93*   **Map** *C5*

Nestled between the beach and the shopping street of Jalan Legian, this budget accommodation of sprawling, ramshackle brick bungalows is shaded by banyan trees. The rooms are spacious; most of them are fan cooled. There is also a swimming pool and poolside café. **www.threebrothersbungalows.com**

LEGIAN All Seasons Resort $$

Jl Padma Utara **Tel** *(0361) 767 688* **Fax** *(0361) 768 180* **Rooms** *113*   **Map** *C5*

This large, modern hotel is part of the Accor group and aimed at young budget travellers, so it is a good place to meet people. It is located very close to Legian Beach in a large garden with a swimming pool and a great-value restaurant. All rooms are air-conditioned and have cable TV. **www.accorhotels.com/asia**

LEGIAN Legian Beach Hotel $$$

Jl Melasti **Tel** *(0361) 751 711* **Fax** *(0361) 752 652* **Rooms** *218*   **Map** *C5*

Set in a prime location right beside Kuta Beach, this family resort features generously sized, thatched Balinese-style bungalows and hotel rooms in extensive gardens. Guests can enjoy two swimming pools, massage services, a spa, beauty salon, fitness centre, watersports facilities, restaurants and cultural shows. **www.legianbeachbali.com**

LEGIAN Padma Resort Bali $$$

Jl Padma 1 **Tel** *(0361) 752 111* **Fax** *(0361) 752 140* **Rooms** *405*   **Map** *C5*

This stylish hotel, next to Kuta Beach, has undergone massive renovations and offers spacious accommodation and tasteful decor complemented by Balinese artwork. The large sports complex includes tennis and squash courts. There is also a Mandara Spa, three restaurants and a swimming pool. **www.padmaresortbali.com**

NUSA DUA Ayodya Resort Bali $$

Jalan Pantai Mengiat PO Box 46, Nusa Dua, 80363 **Tel** *(0361) 771 102* **Fax** *(0361) 771 616* **Rooms** *537* **Map** *C5*

This huge international resort with quintessential Balinese architecture is housed in six-storey blocks in large gardens with lagoons and a large swimming pool, beside a white-sand beach. There is also a spa, tennis and squash courts, a kids' club, conference rooms and watersports facilities. **www.ayodyaresortbali.com**

NUSA DUA Grand Hyatt Bali $$$

PO Box 53, Nusa Dua **Tel** *(0361) 771 234* **Fax** *(0361) 772 038* **Rooms** *457*   **Map** *C5*

Bali's largest resort rests within 40 acres (16 ha) of landscaped gardens and is designed to resemble a Balinese water palace. Bordered by a white sand beach, Grand Hyatt Bali has six swimming pools, six restaurants, conference facilities, two deluxe beachfront hotel villas and the self-contained Hyatt Grand Club. **www.hyatt.com**

NUSA DUA Nusa Dua Beach Hotel $$$

Nusa Dua **Tel** *(0361) 771 210* **Fax** *(0361) 772 617* **Rooms** *381*   **Map** *C5*

This large and lovely resort is owned by the Sultan of Brunei. The hotel accommodation is made up of suites and bungalows set in gorgeous landscaped gardens right beside the white-sand beach. There is a swimming pool, tennis and squash courts, an enchanting spa, kids' club and three restaurants. **www.nusaduahotel.com**

NUSA DUA Nikko Bali Resort & Spa $$$$

Jl Raya Nusa Dua, Selatan, Nusa Dua **Tel** *(0361) 773 377* **Fax** *(0361) 773 388* **Rooms** *386*   **Map** *C5*

Built into the sheer face of a 40-metre (130-ft) cliff, above a beautiful white-sand beach, this is one of the most spectacular beachfront resorts in Bali. Facilities include swimming pools, restaurants, spa, kids' club, sports facilities, an exclusive star-watching facility, Balinese cooking classes and camel safari riding. **www.nikkobali.com**

NUSA DUA Amanusa $$$$$

Nusa Dua **Tel** *(0361) 772 333* **Fax** *(0361) 772 335* **Rooms** *33*   **Map** *C5*

One of Bali's finest hotels, this chic hilltop resort features stunning architecture and elegant decor. Some villas overlook the Bali Golf and Country Club, with magnificent views across the Badung Strait. Amenities include a large swimming pool, two restaurants, tennis courts and a private beach club. **www.amanresorts.com**

NUSA DUA The Balé $$$$$

PO Box 76, Jl Raya Nusa Dua Selatan, 80363 **Tel** *(0361) 775 111* **Fax** *(0361) 775 222* **Rooms** *18*   **Map** *C5*

This intimate and peaceful sanctuary, promoting responsible and sustainable tourism and alternative therapies, uses Zen-inspired minimalist architecture and rich brown salak wood for its self-contained pool villas, each with an open-air veranda. Gourmet restaurant. Does not cater for children under 16. **www.thebale.com**

NUSA DUA St Regis Bali Resort

Kawasan Pariwisata, Nusa Dua **Tel** *(0361) 847 8111* **Fax** *(0361) 847 8099* **Rooms** *123*   **Map** *C5*

This spectacular resort presents opulent oversized suites, private villas and two exclusive residences, as well as restaurants and bars, an intimate wedding chapel, lagoon pool and signature spa. The design is a bold mixture of classic and modern, with rich fabrics, indigenous materials and cultural artifacts. **www.stregisbaliresort.com**

NUSA DUA The Westin Resort

Nusa Dua **Tel** *(0361) 771 906* **Fax** *(0361) 771 908* **Rooms** *355*   **Map** *C5*

Formerly the Sheraton Nusa Indah, and still part of the same group, this extensive resort is attached to a large convention centre. There is a wide choice of rooms and suites, an air-conditioned lobby, three swimming pools featuring waterfalls, a beach club, kids' club, tennis courts and restaurants. **www.westin.com/bali**

NUSA LEMBONGAN Hai Tide Huts

Nusa Lembongan **Tel** *(0361) 720 331* **Fax** *(0361) 720 334* **Rooms** *20*   **Map** *E4*

Lumbung-style thatch and bamboo huts, each with the bedroom accessed by a ladder, plus stylish furnishings, air-conditioning and room service, transform this traditional accommodation into ethnic chic. Bathrooms are shared and a short walk from the huts. Swimming pool and beach club. **www.balihaicruises.com/hai-tide-huts.html**

NUSA LEMBONGAN Nusa Lembongan Resort

Sanghyang Bay **Tel** *(0361) 725 864* **Fax** *(0361) 725 866* **Rooms** *12*   **Map** *E4*

This picturesque resort with a laid-back ambience rests above a beautiful white-sand beach and crystal clear waters. The luxurious bungalows are furnished with antiques, and feature marble bathrooms. Facilities include a swimming pool, library and gourmet restaurant. Activities include diving and snorkelling. **www.nusa-lembongan.com**

SANUR Hotel Segara Agung

Jl Duyung No 43 Semawang **Tel** *(0361) 288 446 / 286 804* **Fax** *(0361) 286 113* **Rooms** *16*   **Map** *D4*

This hotel features traditional Balinese architecture, a pretty garden full of flowers, a swimming pool and restaurant. There are four choices of accommodation, including family rooms. Some rooms are fan-cooled with cold water, and others are air-conditioned with hot water. A few minutes' walk from the beach. **www.segaraagung.com**

SANUR Mercure Resort

Jl Mertasari **Tel** *(0361) 288 833* **Fax** *(0361) 287 303* **Rooms** *189*   **Map** *D4*

A beachside resort presenting superior, deluxe and family rooms in Balinese-style cottages grouped within attractive gardens. Amenities include a special lounge for use after checking out. There are also conference facilities, tennis and badminton courts, and an open-air restaurant. **http://mercuresanur.com**

SANUR Griya Santrian Hotel

Jl Danau Tamblingan 47 **Tel** *(0361) 288 181* **Fax** *(0361) 288 185* **Rooms** *90*   **Map** *C5*

This family-run resort offers accommodation in private seaside bungalows, linked by meandering paths in a large garden. All bungalows have a private terrace, with garden or ocean views. A full range of facilities includes two pools, two restaurants and thoughtful touches for children. **www.santrian.com/gs-index.htm**

SANUR Hotel Sanur Beach

Jl Danau Tamblingan **Tel** *(0361) 288 011* **Fax** *(0361) 287 566* **Rooms** *425*   **Map** *D4*

Owned by Garuda airlines, this large hotel was built in 1974 as a successor to Bali's early guesthouses. Its gorgeous gardens are dotted with some of the most majestic trees in the area. The hotel also boasts the largest swimming pool in Sanur, tennis courts, fitness centres, a business centre and a spa. **www.sanurbeachhotelbali.com**

SANUR La Taverna

Jl Danau Tamblingan 29 **Tel** *(0361) 288 497* **Fax** *(0361) 287 126* **Rooms** *36*   **Map** *D4*

A historic hotel on the seafront, La Taverna has been stylishly renovated but it still maintains its traditional Balinese charm. It features thatched bungalows and classic double-storey buildings, a beach restaurant serving Indonesian and Italian cuisine, a swimming pool, spa services and gorgeous tropical gardens. **www.latavernahotel.com**

SANUR Puri Santrian

Jl Danau Tamblingan **Tel** *(0361) 288 009* **Fax** *(0361) 287 101* **Rooms** *182*   **Map** *C5*

This Balinese family-owned beachfront hotel has been flourishing for over 30 years. It has a wide choice of accommodation including self-contained bungalows and the sophisticated Santrian Club. There are three swimming pools, a wonderful spa and a classy Thai restaurant. **www.santrian.com/puri**

SANUR Tandjung Sari Hotel

Jl Danau Tamblingan 41 **Tel** *(0361) 288 441* **Fax** *(0361) 287 930* **Rooms** *26*   **Map** *D4*

Exceptionally romantic, this lovely old hotel has been beautifully maintained and is furnished with local artifacts and antiques. It offers a choice of traditional Balinese bungalows or villas with sitting rooms and pavilions. There is a swimming pool and a beachside restaurant shaded by magnificent trees. **www.tandjungsarihotel.com**

SANUR Bali Hyatt

PO Box 392 Sanur **Tel** *(0361) 281 234 / 288 271* **Fax** *(0361) 287 693* **Rooms** *389*   **Map** *C5*

This large beachside family resort is famous for its gorgeous gardens – designed by the acclaimed landscape artist Made Wijaya – rolling all the way down to the beach. Amenities include restaurants, swimming pools, a spa, children's club, convention centre and watersports facilities. **www.bali.resort.hyatt.com/hyatt/hotels/index.jsp**

Key to Price Guide *see p.170* **Key to Symbols** *see back cover flap*

SEMINYAK Bali Agung Village
🍴 ▨ ▤ $$

Jl Abimanyu (Dhyana Pura) **Tel** *(0361) 730 367* **Fax** *(0361) 730 469* **Rooms** *32*
Map *C4*

Located in the heart of Seminyak, these pleasant rooms are housed in two-storey buildings and cottages character-ized by Balinese architecture, thatched roofs and garden terraces. Facilities include a restaurant serving European, Chinese and Indonesian food, and Balinese dance performances. **http://bali-agung.com**

SEMINYAK Puri Naga Seaside Cottages
▨ ▤ $$

Jl Double Six **Tel** *(0361) 730 761* **Fax** *(0361) 730 524* **Rooms** *26*
Map *C5*

These traditional Balinese brick cottages are just a stone's throw from the trendy Seminyak Beach, where locals and visitors gather every evening to watch the sunset from the beachside cafés. The pleasant rooms all have balconies, and there is a small swimming pool. **www.purinagahotel.com**

SEMINYAK Hotel Vila Lumbung
🍴 ▨ ▤ $$$

Jl Raya Petitenget 1000X **Tel** *(0361) 730 204* **Fax** *(0361) 731 106* **Rooms** *30*
Map *C4*

A boutique resort with one-, two- and three-bedroomed villas and bungalows. The villas feature ground floor and upper floor bedrooms, with the larger ones boasting private courtyard gardens. There is a restaurant, and a large, free-form swimming pool is enhanced with bridges, a waterfall-cave and an island. **www.hotellumbung.com**

SEMINYAK The Royal Beach Seminyak
▨ 🍴 ▨ 🏊 ▤ 🛎 $$$

Jl Abimanyu (Dhyana Pura) **Tel** *(0361) 730 730* **Fax** *(0361) 730 545* **Rooms** *145*
Map *C5*

A very stylish beach resort, set within extensive tropical gardens. Accommodation ranges from rooms to villas with either a jacuzzi or pool. The highly acclaimed Husk restaurant serves Thai cuisine. Within walking distance of trendy Seminyak village. **www.accorhotels.com**

SEMINYAK Anantara
▨ 🍴 ▨ 🏊 🛎 ♿ $$$$

Jl Abimanyu (Dhyana Pura) **Tel** *(0361) 737 773* **Fax** *(0361) 737 772* **Rooms** *59*
Map *C5*

This luxurious hotel is located on the beachfront; a few minutes walk from the shops and nightlife of Seminyak. The large, modern and elegant suites have hi-tech amenities, balconies with coastal views and alfresco jacuzzis. The restaurant offers poolside and indoor dining, and there is a spa, a gym, and three swimming pools.

SEMINYAK The Legian
▨ 🍴 ▨ ▤ 🛎 $$$$$

Jl Laksmana **Tel** *(0361) 730 622* **Fax** *(0361) 730 623* **Rooms** *79*
Map *C4*

This exceptional all-suite boutique hotel on Seminyak Beach has an elegant, contemporary decor, a world-class restaurant, a deluxe spa, a gym and a stunning swimming pool that merges with the ocean. It also incorporates The Beach House, a luxurious one-bedroomed property with pool. **www.ghmhotels.com**

SEMINYAK The Oberoi
🍴 ▨ ▤ $$$$$

PO Box 3351 Denpasar **Tel** *(0361) 730 361* **Fax** *(0361) 730 791* **Rooms** *74*
Map *C4*

The oldest hotel in the area, The Oberoi has been impeccably maintained. It exudes luxury and romance, and was designed to resemble a Balinese palace. Located right beside the beach, it comprises rooms, villas, pool villas, a spa, two restaurants and a swimming pool evocative of an ancient Balinese bathing place. **www.oberoihotels.com**

SEMINYAK Villa Kubu
▨ ▤ $$$$$

Seminyak **Tel** *(0361) 731 129* **Fax** *(0361) 731 129* **Rooms** *15*
Map *C5*

A complex of romantic villas, each in an individual style, embraces the tropical, open-air living concept, complemented by butler service, hi-tech amenities, antique furnishings and a private swimming pool. Sample the superb menu delivered by room service, or personally prepared in-villa by a top-class chef. **www.villakubu.com**

SEMINYAK The Villas Bali Hotel & Spa
🍴 ▨ ▤ $$$$$

Jl Kunti 118X **Tel** *(0361) 730 840* **Fax** *(0361) 733 751* **Rooms** *50*
Map *C5*

The product of a company that pioneered the concept of the villa complex, with private facilities and a five-star standard of service, this hotel offers luxurious villas characterized by rustic architecture and open-air living spaces beside private pools. It is all complemented by the Mogul-inspired fantasy-styled Prana Spa. **www.thevillas.net**

TANJUNG BENOA Aston Bali Resort & Spa
▨ 🍴 ▨ 🏊 ▤ 🛎 $$$

Jl Pratama 68X, 80363 **Tel** *(0361) 773 577* **Fax** *(0361) 774 954* **Rooms** *187*
Map *C5*

With spacious guest rooms, five restaurants, a great programme of entertainment, activities and watersports, kids' club, a dedicated ladies' floor, spa, meeting rooms and a large swimming pool located right next to the beach, this family resort draws guests back year after year. **www.astonbali.com**

TANJUNG BENOA Novotel Bali
▨ 🍴 ▨ 🏊 ▤ 🛎 $$$

Jl Pratama **Tel** *(0361) 772 239* **Fax** *(0361) 772 237* **Rooms** *197*
Map *C5*

Quirky architecture, coconut wood and natural materials are used throughout this delightful hotel. The luxurious spa is complemented by breezy, open-air pavilions overlooking the golden beach of Tanjung Benoa. There are three restaurants, a boutique, kids' club and a large tennis complex. **www.novotelbalibenoa.com**

TANJUNG BENOA The Conrad Bali Resort & Spa
▨ 🍴 ▨ 🏊 ▤ 🛎 $$$$

Jl Pratama 168, Tanjung Benoa **Tel** *(0361) 778 788* **Fax** *(0361) 773 888* **Rooms** *305*
Map *C5*

This classy, contemporary resort and spa, with three guest service wings, a sparkling lagoon pool and a wide range of facilities, is generously spread throughout a tropical beachside oasis. There are three restaurants, a kids' club, a games zone, a state-of-the-art conference centre and flood-lit tennis courts. **www.conradhotels.com**

TUBAN Febri's
⬛⬛⬛ ⑤

Jl Kartika Plaza **Tel** *(0361) 754 575* **Fax** *(0361) 754 560* **Rooms** *67* **Map** *C5*

Situated in the heart of Tuban, close to the beach, shopping centres, Waterbom Park and numerous other family facilities, the focus of this budget hotel is on families, with the inclusion of 20 very large family rooms. It also features a large central swimming pool, an excellent spa and a restaurant. **www.greenbali.com**

TUBAN Bali Dynasty
⬛⬛⬛⬛⬛⬛⬛ ⑤⑤⑤

Jl Kartika Plaza Tuban **Tel** *(0361) 752 403* **Fax** *(0361) 752 402* **Rooms** *312* **Map** *C5*

This large, four-star family resort showcases contemporary Balinese architecture, and is set within beautiful gardens close to the beach. Amenities include a children's playground and club, restaurants and bars, meeting rooms and banqueting facilities. There is a choice of three pools. **www.bali-dynasty.com**

TUBAN Kupu Kupu Barong
⬛⬛⬛ ⑤⑤⑤⑤

Jl Wana Segara, Tuban **Tel** *(0361) 753 780* **Fax** *(0361) 753 781* **Rooms** *11* **Map** *C5*

This chic boutique hotel has thatched pavilions housing luxurious suites, each with Indonesian decor, local artifacts and a wide veranda or private balcony. Facilities include the superb Ma Joly Restaurant, an open-air bar, a large swimming pool and 24-hour personal butler service. **www.kupubarong.com**

ULUWATU Blue Point Bay Villas & Spa
⬛⬛⬛ ⑤⑤⑤⑤

Jl Lubuansit **Tel** *(0361) 769 888* **Fax** *(0361) 769 889* **Rooms** *29* **Map** *B5*

A villa-style hotel, complete with spa and restaurant, situated on top of the cliff close to Uluwatu Temple. There are four different standards of accommodation and two large pools – one overlooking the southern cliff, the other terraced – among the villas. **www.bluepointbayvillas.com**

ULUWATU Banyan Tree Ungasan
⬛⬛⬛⬛⬛⬛ ⑤⑤⑤⑤⑤

Jl Melasti, Banjar Kelod, Ungasan **Tel** *(0361) 300 7000* **Fax** *(0361) 300 7777* **Rooms** *9* **Map** *B5*

Set amid the rocky splendour of the Bukit Peninsula, Banyan Tree offers views over the Indian Ocean, contemporary Balinese architecture and beautifully landscaped gardens. Guests can enjoy treatments at the signature Banyan Tree Spa, dine at a choice of restaurants or laze on a private white sand beach. **www.banyantree.com/en/bali_ungasan**

ULUWATU Bulgari Hotels & Resorts, Bali
⬛⬛⬛⬛ ⑤⑤⑤⑤⑤

Jl Goa Lempeh, Banjar Dinas Kangin, Uluwatu **Tel** *(0361) 847 1000* **Fax** *(0361) 847 1111* **Rooms** *59* **Map** *C5*

Bali is privileged to have been chosen as the site for only the second Bulgari property in the world. This all-villa cliffside retreat is chic and exclusive, with private pool villas, a spa, a stunning swimming pool, two restaurants and uninterrupted ocean views. There is lift access to the pristine beach. **www.bulgarihotels.com**

CENTRAL BALI

AYUNG RIVER GORGE Alila Ubud
⬛⬛⬛⬛⬛ ⑤⑤⑤⑤

Desa Melinggih Kelod Payangan, Gianyar, 80572 **Tel** *(0361) 975 963* **Fax** *(0361) 975 968* **Rooms** *64* **Map** *C3*

This romantic, luxury resort comprises rooms and private villas, perched high on the Sayan Ridge with breathtaking views of the steep river valley and distant volcanoes. The gorgeous swimming pool has been voted one of the "50 most spectacular pools in the world". The resort also features a Mandara Spa. **www.alilahotels.com**

AYUNG RIVER GORGE Amandari
⬛⬛⬛ ⑤⑤⑤⑤⑤

Kedewatan **Tel** *(0361) 975 333* **Fax** *(0361) 975 335* **Rooms** *30* **Map** *C4*

A beautiful boutique hotel with sumptuous private pavilions, each with a veranda and a pool within a walled garden. The spectacular infinity pool takes its inspiration from a Balinese rice terrace. The hotel also boasts breathtaking views, a gift shop, a spa and a fine-dining restaurant. **www.amanresorts.com**

AYUNG RIVER GORGE Como Shambala Estate at Begawan Giri
⬛⬛⬛⬛⬛ ⑤⑤⑤⑤⑤

PO Box 54, Ubud, Gianyar, 80571 **Tel** *(0361) 978 888* **Fax** *(0361) 978 889* **Rooms** *15* **Map** *C3*

A unique residential health retreat nestling on a venerated spur of land at the confluence of two rivers, this resort features five remarkable residences, each reflecting the diverse architecture of Indonesia, plus several pool villas, two restaurants, and exceptional spa facilities hosting retreat programmes and seminars. **www.comoshambala.bz**

AYUNG RIVER GORGE Four Seasons at Sayan
⬛⬛⬛⬛⬛⬛ ⑤⑤⑤⑤⑤

Sayan, Ubud **Tel** *(0361) 977 577* **Fax** *(0361) 977 588* **Rooms** *60* **Map** *C3*

This unique resort is approached via a solid teak bridge leading to a huge, elliptical lotus pond which rests on the rooftop of a central three-storey building. The complex of villas cascades down through 18 acres (7 ha) of terraced hillside. There are also two restaurants and an award-winning riverside spa. **www.fourseasons.com**

AYUNG RIVER GORGE Kayumanis
⬛⬛⬛ ⑤⑤⑤⑤⑤

Sayan **Tel** *(0361) 770 777* **Fax** *(0361) 972 660* **Rooms** *9* **Map** *C3*

Set on the edge of the magnificent river valley, this intimate, private sanctuary consists of luxury villas amid bountiful gardens. One-, two- and three-bedroomed units each have a private swimming pool, a landscaped garden and barbeque area. The restaurant and 24-hour villa service offers Thai and Western cuisines. **www.kayumanis.com**

Key to Price Guide *see p.170* **Key to Symbols** *see back cover flap*

AYUNG RIVER GORGE Puri Wulandari Boutique Resort

$$($$($$($$($$($$(

Kedewatan **Tel** *(0361) 980 252* **Fax** *(0361) 980 253* **Rooms** *34* **Map** *C3*

You will find this luxurious boutique hotel encompassed by blinding green ricefields. All the villas have private swimming pools and marble bathrooms. The tranquil spa blends Balinese tradition with natural, ancient beauty and health rituals. The two restaurants serve international and Mediterranean-Italian cuisine. **www.puriwulandari.net**

AYUNG RIVER GORGE Royal Pita Maha

$$($$($$($$($$($$(

Kedewatan **Tel** *(0361) 980 022* **Fax** *(0361) 980 011* **Rooms** *52* **Map** *C3*

Owned by Ubud's royal family and richly decorated by local craftsmen, the Royal Pita Maha has private pool villas capturing magical views of the river gorge. A holy spring-fed Balinese bathing pool, health centre, two restaurants, bars and water sports facilities are spread around the grounds. **www.royalpitamaha-bali.com**

LAPLAPAN Natura Resort & Spa

$$($$($$($$($$(

Banjar Laplapan, Ubud, 80571 **Tel** *(0361) 978 666* **Fax** *(0361) 978 222* **Rooms** *14* **Map** *D3*

These luxury villas are situated on the steep banks of the Petanu River, with secluded garden-courtyards, open-air bathrooms and plunge pools, and spacious wooden decks. The resort also has a restaurant, a spa and a swimming pool, plus a separate infinity pool that appears to overflow into the valley below. **www.naturaresortbali.com**

NAGI The Viceroy

$$($$($$($$($$(

Jl Lanyahan, Nagi, Ubud **Tel** *(0361) 971 777* **Fax** *(0361) 970 777* **Rooms** *11* **Map** *D3*

Luxury private villas are combined with all of the amenities of an elite hotel in a setting that is second to none. Communal facilities, including a fine-dining restaurant and a spa, are at the top of a remote hill, with the villas nestled on the river slopes. There is a helipad for quick airport transfers. **www.theviceroybali.com**

PAYANGAN Nandini Bali Jungle Resort & Spa

$$($$($$(

Banjar Susut, Payangan **Tel** *(0361) 982 777 / 780 1611* **Fax** *(0361) 982 727* **Rooms** *18* **Map** *C3*

Designed by the acclaimed Balinese architect Popo Danes, this rainforest retreat clings to the side of a sheer escarpment above the Ayung River, offering affordable luxury in grass-roofed chalets with spectacular views. A bamboo funicular conveys guests down to the swimming pool and spa. **www.nandinibali.com**

PAYANGAN Ubud Hanging Gardens

$$($$($$($$($$(

Buahan, Payangan **Tel** *(0361) 982 700* **Fax** *(0361) 982 800* **Rooms** *38* **Map** *C3*

This intimate retreat is dramatically suspended on a terraced hillside with a spectacular jungle backdrop. The pool villas, riverside spa, free-form swimming pool and other facilities are easily accessed by a private funicular, with views of a remarkable temple on the opposite side of the Ayung River Gorge. **www.ubudhanginggardens.com**

SANGGINGAN Uma Ubud

$$($$($$($$(

Jl Raya Sanggingan, Banjar Lungsiakan, 80571 **Tel** *(0361) 972 448* **Fax** *(0361) 972 449* **Rooms** *29* **Map** *C3*

Providing a beautiful inland retreat designed to maximize the awesome views of the borderless ricefields, jungle, volcano and Tjampuhan valley, the Shambala retreat centre here is characterized by a dreamy pool and private treatment area. The Balinese-inspired cuisine incorporates local organic produce. **www.uma.como.bz**

TEGALLALANG Alam Sari Keliki

$$($$($$(

Tromol Pos 03, Tegallalang Gianyar, 80561 **Tel** *(0361) 981 420* **Fax** *(0361) 981 421* **Rooms** *10* **Map** *D3*

This enchanting hotel offers rooms, family units and suites in a gorgeous garden setting, surrounded by coconut groves. It also features a natural stone swimming pool and a restaurant serving healthy cuisine, and presents a wonderful range of activities, including numerous handicraft classes for children. **www.alamsari.com**

TENGKULAK The Chedi Club at Tanah Gajah

$$($$($$($$($$(

Tanah Gaja, Tengkulak, Ubud **Tel** *(0361) 975 685* **Fax** *(0361) 975 686* **Rooms** *20* **Map** *D3*

The Chedi offers the ultimate in holiday indulgence, within an exclusive private estate. Accommodation, with butler service, comprises self-contained suites, spa villas and pool villas. Communal facilities include a restaurant serving organic local cuisine, a spa, a yoga studio, a large pool, gym and tennis courts. **www.ghmhotels.com**

UBUD Siti Bungalows

$$($$(

Jl Kajeng No. 3 **Tel** *(0361) 975 699 / 974 271* **Fax** *(0361) 975 643* **Rooms** *8* **Map** *C3*

These garden cottages are owned by the family of the late, well-known Dutch painter, Han Snel, who lived in Ubud for many years. Accommodation is in bungalows, complemented by a pool, restaurant and bar, set in a quiet compound beside a river gorge just five minutes' walk from the town. **www.hansnelbungalow.com**

UBUD Tegal Sari

$$($$(

Jl Hanoman, Padang Tegal **Tel** *(0361) 973 318* **Fax** *(0361) 970 701* **Rooms** *21* **Map** *C3*

This romantic hotel rests within an enviable, peaceful location in the middle of ricefields, just outside the centre of Ubud. It features rooms and duplex bungalows, each one different. There is also a swimming pool, a massage pavilion, an open-air fitness arena, dining pavilions, lotus ponds and a restaurant. **www.tegalsari-ubud.com**

UBUD Tjampuhan Hotel

$$($$(

Campuhan **Tel** *(0361) 975 368 / 9* **Fax** *(0361) 975 137* **Rooms** *67* **Map** *C3*

The former home of the German artist, Walter Spies, forms part of this hotel and sleeps four people. The remainder of the property is made up of shared bungalows in a wonderful riverbank garden overlooking the confluence of Sungai Wos and Campuan. There is a spring-fed, hillside swimming pool and a restaurant. **www.tjampuhan.com**

UBUD Waka Namya

🍴 🏊 🖥 $$$

Jl Raya Penestanan **Tel** *(0361) 975 719* **Fax** *(0361) 975 719* **Rooms** *15*   **Map** *C3*

This intimate, luxury boutique hotel has the immaculate signature style of the Waka Resorts, with natural furnishings and interesting artwork. The two-bedroomed villas are constructed in the style of a traditional thatched rice barn, with opulent bathrooms featuring sunken tubs. There is also a restaurant. **www.wakanamya.com**

UBUD Ibah Luxury Villas

🍴 🏊 🖥 $$$$

Campuhan **Tel** *(0361) 974 466* **Fax** *(0361) 974 467* **Rooms** *15*   **Map** *C3*

Owned by Ubud's Royal Family, this boutique hotel rests in a beautiful setting overlooking the Wos River Valley and the picturesque Pura Gunung Lebah Temple. The spacious individual suites showcase local artifacts. Facilities include a Mandara Spa and a Balinese bathing pool carved into the side of the hill. **www.ibahbali.com**

UBUD Maya Ubud Resort & Spa

🛏 🍴 🏊 🖥 🚻 $$$$

Jl Gunung Sari Peliatan, PO Box 1001, 80571 **Tel** *(0361) 977 888* **Fax** *(0361) 977 555* **Rooms** *108*   **Map** *D3*

Spread throughout 4 acres (1.5 ha) of hillside garden between the river valley and the ricefields, the accommodation here includes pool villas, garden villas and rooms. It also has three restaurants, a lounge bar, a main swimming pool and an enchanting spa with pavilions that literally overhang the fast-flowing Petanu River. **www.mayaubud.com**

UBUD Komaneka Resort

🍴 🏊 🖥 $$$$$

Jl Monkey Forest, 80571 **Tel** *(0361) 976 090* **Fax** *(0361) 977 140* **Rooms** *20*   **Map** *C3*

A peaceful oasis in the heart of town beside the ricefields, the deluxe rooms, suites, and garden and pool villas here have private plunge pools and private verandas. The decor is contempary and elegant, using natural materials. There is also a restaurant, pool, spa, massage services, boutique and fine art gallery. **www.komaneka.com**

EAST BALI

AMED Good Karma Bungalows

🍴 $

Selang **Tel** *(081) 2368 9090* **Rooms** *17*   **Map** *F2*

These simple, beachside thatched bungalows are owned by a colourful Balinese character called Baba who sings to his guests and promotes ecological awareness. Each bungalow has its own open-air bathroom and veranda facing the beach. There is a friendly, backpacker atmosphere, making it popular with Bali's expats.

AMED Onlyou

🏊 🖥 $$

Desa Bunutan, Jl Raya Amed **Tel** *(0363) 23 595* **Fax** *(0363) 23 570* **Rooms** *3*   **Map** *F2*

Onlyou consists of three private villas – two accommodating four guests and one accommodating two – each with private swimming pool and in-villa dining service. From these luxury holiday homes, guests can enjoy glorious views, not to mention a beach with a beautiful coral reef right on their doorstep. **www.onlyou-bali.com**

AMED Santai

🍴 🏊 🖥 $$

Bunutan **Tel** *(0363) 23 487* **Fax** *(0363) 23 585* **Rooms** *10*   **Map** *F2*

This lovely beachside boutique hotel offers traditional Balinese bungalows with four-poster beds, open-air bathrooms, and a loft area with an extra bed. There is also a meandering swimming pool surrounded by flowering shrubs, and a restaurant serving fresh seafood as well as Mediterranean and Indonesian specialities. **www.santaibali.com**

CANDI DASA Temple Café & Seaside Cottages

🍴 🖥 $

Jl Raya Candi Dasa. **Tel** *(0363) 41 629* **Fax** *(0363) 41 629* **Rooms** *15*   **Map** *F3*

There is a choice of accommodation at this immaculate complex, with the bungalows ranging from the simple fan-cooled variety with cold water to the ocean-front Seaview Superior De-luxe, with air-conditioning and hot water plus sitting room and kitchenette. The Temple Café features a few German dishes. **www.balibeachfront-cottages.com**

CANDI DASA Candi Beach Cottage

🍴 🏊 🚣 🖥 🚻 $$$

Mendira beach, Sengkidu, Karangasem **Tel** *(0363) 41 234* **Fax** *(0363) 41 111* **Rooms** *64*   **Map** *F3*

Characterized by traditional Balinese architecture and set within a coconut grove garden beside a white-sand beach, this superb complex features comfortable cottage-style bungalows and rooms, a beachside restaurant, two swimming pools and blissful massage pavilions. Numerous tours and activities. **www.candibeachbali.com**

CANDI DASA Puri Bagus Candi Dasa

🍴 🏊 🖥 $$$

Jl Raya Candi Dasa **Tel** *(0363) 41 131* **Fax** *(0363) 41 290* **Rooms** *46*   **Map** *F3*

The most upmarket option in Candi Dasa, this beautiful and luxurious seaside resort is hidden away in gracious gardens at the quiet, eastern end of the beach. There is a choice of elegant rooms or villas with open-air bathrooms, as well as an excellent restaurant, swimming pool and poolside cabanas. **www.puribagus.net**

CANDI DASA Watergarden

🍴 🏊 🖥 $$$

Jl Raya Candi Dasa. **Tel** *(0363) 41 540* **Fax** *(0363) 41 164* **Rooms** *14*   **Map** *F3*

In an enchanting setting within a water garden, complete with waterfalls and lotus ponds stocked with *koi* and large water lizards, some of these thatched roof cottages are fan-cooled, while others have air-conditioning. There is also a swimming pool, a library and a good value restaurant and bar. **www.watergardenhotel.com**

Key to Price Guide *see p.170* **Key to Symbols** *see back cover flap*

GUNUNG BATUR Hotel Puri Bening Heyato

Toya Bungkah **Tel** *(0366) 51 234* **Fax** *(0366) 51 248* **Rooms** *34*　　　　　　　　　　**Map** *D2*

Positioned beside the lake below Gunung Batur, this modern, three-storey hotel features rooms and bungalows with water drawn from the hot springs, which are fuelled by the volcano. There is a simple restaurant. The rooms are not air-conditioned – it is not necessary in the cool mountain climate. **www.hotelpuribeningbali.com**

GUNUNG BATUR Lakeview Restaurant & Hotel

Penelokan **Tel** *(0366) 51 394* **Fax** *(0366) 51 464* **Rooms** *20*　　　　　　　　　　**Map** *D2*

This hotel is perched on the rim of an ancient caldera, with breathtaking views of the active volcano, Gunung Batur, and the crater lake. Rooms are spacious and comfortable, and the restaurant, which serves buffet lunches, is a popular destination for daytime tour groups. Breakfast is included. **http://lakeviewhotel.info**

MANGGIS Alila Manggis

Buitan, Karangasem, 80871 **Tel** *(0363) 41 011* **Fax** *(0363) 41 015* **Rooms** *54*　　　　　**Map** *E3*

Famous for its cooking school, this boutique resort and spa is set in a coconut grove garden that gently rolls on to Buitan Beach. Each room has a balcony with a cushioned daybed for total relaxation. The two suites have a dining room and a spacious living area opening on to a sundeck. There is a superb restaurant. **www.alilahotels.com**

MANGGIS Amankila

Karangasem **Tel** *(0363) 41 333* **Fax** *(0363) 41 555* **Rooms** *33*　　　　　　　　　　**Map** *E3*

A spectacular Aman resort featuring three, tiered, swimming pools which cascade down the side of a mountain to the sea. The pavilions have views of the Badung Strait Islands, and are characterized by thatched roofs and terraces, king-size canopied beds, and luxurious bathrooms with sunken tubs. **www.amankila.com**

PADANG BAI Hotel Puri Rai

Jl Silayukti **Tel** *(0363) 41 385* **Fax** *(0363) 41 386* **Rooms** *30*　　　　　　　　　　**Map** *E3*

The only hotel in Padang Bai with a swimming pool, this one-star hotel beside the beach offers a choice of air-conditioned or fan-cooled rooms, including four family fan rooms housed in a two-storey building, and all equipped with hot and cold showers. There is also a restaurant, bar and transport services. **www.puriraihotel.com**

TULAMBEN Tauch Terminal Resort

Tulamben **Tel** *(0361) 774 504* **Fax** *(0361) 778 473* **Rooms** *18*　　　　　　　　　　**Map** *F2*

A five-star diving school and resort built around a deep pool. Most of the deluxe and super-deluxe rooms have balconies with ocean views. It offers the facilities, equipment and tuition for every level from beginners upwards, in a unique environment with the shipwreck of the *SS Liberty* just offshore. **www.tauch-terminal.com**

NORTH AND WEST BALI

BEDUGUL Bali Handara Kosaido Golf & Country Club

Bedugul **Tel** *(0362) 22 646* **Fax** *(0362) 23 048* **Rooms** *77*　　　　　　　　　　**Map** *C2*

Set against a backdrop of mountains, forest and the peaceful Lake Buyan, the 18-hole golf course is a masterpiece of natural beauty. The luxury accommodation is reminiscent of wooden mountain chalets, with log fires and awe-inspiring views. Facilities include restaurants, tennis courts and a karaoke lounge. **www.balihandarakosaido.com**

BEDUGUL Pacung Mountain Resort

Jl Raya Pacung, Baturiti, 82191 **Tel** *(0368) 21 038 / 039* **Fax** *(0368) 21 043* **Rooms** *35*　　　　**Map** *C2*

This hillside resort is the only hotel in the area with a swimming pool; it also boasts a beautiful vista of the valley and Gunung Batukau. Accommodation incudes charming thatched cottages with balconies. A gondola transports guests from their rooms to the pool. There is also a restaurant, but no air-conditioning in this cool climate.

LOVINA Kubu Lalang

Tukad Mungga **Tel** *(0362) 42 207* **Rooms** *5*　　　　　　　　　　**Map** *B1*

Kubu Lalang means "small house of long grass" and is a collection of charming, elevated bungalows modelled on traditional rice barns. Each bungalow has a main bedroom plus a small loft bedroom with ceiling fan, and an open-air bathroom. Some have hot water and bathtubs, others only have cold water. **www.kubulalang.com**

LOVINA Lovina Beach Resort

Jl Raya Sererit, Kalibukbuk **Tel** *(0362) 41 237* **Rooms** *20*　　　　　　　　　　**Map** *B1*

This hotel presents two-storey thatched-roof cottages with private terraces, grouped in lush gardens dotted with fruit trees. There are lovely views of the bay, a breezy beachside restaurant and plenty of watersports facilities, including dolphin-watching by jet boat. **www.lovina-beach-resort.com**

LOVINA Rini Hotel

Jl Ketapang, Kalibukbuk **Tel** *(0362) 41 386* **Fax** *(0362) 41 386* **Rooms** *30*　　　　　　　　　　**Map** *B1*

This immaculately maintained hotel is hidden away on Kalibukbuk's quieter street. It offers simple accommodation with pleasant furnishings and a choice of fan-cooled rooms with cold water, or huge, air-conditioned rooms with hot water. There is a saltwater pool and also a small restaurant. **www.rinihotel.com**

LOVINA Puri Bagus Lovina
🍴 ≋ 🗏 $$$

Jl Singaraja-Seririt **Tel** *(0362) 21 430* **Fax** *(0362) 22 627* **Rooms** *40*   **Map** *B1*

Part of a locally-owned group of hotels, Puri Bagus Lovina offers comfortable villa-style accommodation with spacious bedrooms, verandas, and large bathrooms with both indoor and outdoor showers. There is an attractive garden and a large, free-form swimming pool, a café and restaurant. **www.puribagusdiscovery.com**

LOVINA Sunari Villas & Spa Resort
🍴 ≋ 🗏 $$$

Jl. Raya Lovina **Tel** *(0362) 41 775* **Fax** *(0362) 41 659* **Rooms** *129*   **Map** *B1*

A long driveway leads to this seaside resort with a variety of bungalows spread throughout a lush garden. Some boast private plunge pools, and others have jacuzzis, but the standard accommodation is much cheaper. There is a pool with lovely sea views, a spa, restaurant and 24-hour coffee shop. **www.sunari.com**

LOVINA Damai
🍴 ≋ 🗏 $$$$

Jl Damai Desa, Kayu Putih **Tel** *(0362) 41 008* **Fax** *(0362) 41 009* **Rooms** *14*   **Map** *B1*

There is a wonderful restaurant at this Danish-owned gourmet retreat perched high on a mountainside. The self-contained bungalows have romantic four-poster beds and bubbling jacuzzis in outdoor bathrooms. The attractive swimming pool has a poolside café and bar. **www.damai.com**

MENJANGAN Menjangan Jungle & Beach Resort
🍴 ≋ 🗏 $$$

Desa Pejarakan, Kabupaten Buleleng Singaraja **Tel** *(0362) 94 700* **Fax** *(0362) 94 708* **Rooms** *14*

Bordered by the West Bali National Park, this eco-resort of clifftop villas overlooks beautiful Bajul Bay and the tiny, uninhabited Menjangan Island. It also features a high tower with a restaurant offering panoramic views. Activities include bird-watching, kayaking, snorkelling, diving and horse-riding. **www.menjanganresort.com**

MENJANGAN Mimpi Resort
🍴 ≋ 🗏 $$$

Menjangen, Banyuwedang **Tel** *(0362) 94 497* **Fax** *(0362) 94 498* **Rooms** *50*

This luxury dive resort beside the beach, 15 minutes by boat from Menjangan Island, provides gorgeous villas complemented by courtyard bathrooms with bathtubs fed by hot water piped from the neighbouring hot springs. Some have private plunge pools and lagoon views. **www.mimpi.com**

MUNDUK Puri Lumbung Cottages
🍴 $$

Munduk **Tel** *(0362) 92 810* **Fax** *(0362) 92 514* **Rooms** *18*

Surrounded by lily ponds and ricefields, and with wonderful views all the way to the coast, this cluster of cottages on stilts is friendly and welcoming. Activities include trekking, and dance, handicraft and cookery classes. The restaurant serves delicious local dishes using produce from the neighbouring forest. **www.purilumbung.com**

PEMUTERAN Taman Sari Bali Cottages
🍴 ≋ 🗏 $$

Pemuteran, 81155 **Tel** *(0362) 93 264* **Fax** *(0362) 93 264* **Rooms** *29*

This beachfront hotel has on-site diving facilities and offers a choice of rooms and suites ranging from simple to luxurious. The suites are decorated with antiques, have garden bathrooms and either wide terraces or a second floor with wonderful ocean and mountain views. There is also a beachside restaurant. **www.balitamansari.com**

PEMUTERAN Matahari Beach Resort
🍴 ≋ 🗏 $$$$

Pemuteran **Tel** *(0362) 92 312* **Fax** *(0362) 92 313* **Rooms** *32*

An impressive, French-managed, beachside resort with four categories of accommodation. Some rooms have garden views and others have ocean views. There is also an excellent restaurant, tennis court and a luxurious spa. Excursions can be arranged to the nearby Menjangan Island. **www.matahari-beach-resort.com**

PEMUTERAN Puri Ganesha Villas
🍴 ≋ 🗏 $$$$$

Pantai Pemuteran, Gerokgak, Singaraja, 81155 **Tel** *(0362) 94 766* **Fax** *(0362) 93 433* **Rooms** *4*

The four enchanting, thatched beachside villas here are modelled on the traditional two-tiered Balinese *wantilan* (village meeting place). Each villa has two bedrooms, a garden bathroom, indoor and outdoor dining areas, kitchen and private saltwater swimming pool. Restaurant and personal butler service. **www.puriganesha.com**

PUPUAN Cempaka Belimbing Guest Villas
🍴 ≋ 🗏 $$$

Br Suradadi, Belimbing, Pupuan, Tabanan **Tel** *(0361) 745 1178* **Fax** *(0361) 745 1179* **Rooms** *16*   **Map** *B3*

These award-winning luxury villas are in a spectacular setting of rice terraces and fruit trees against a mountain backdrop. Each villa features traditional Balinese architecture and uses local materials. There is also a good restaurant, swimming pool, boutique and a spa offering traditional massage. **www.cempakabelimbing.com**

SERIRIT Zen Resort
🍴 ≋ 🗏 $$

Puri Jati, Desa Ume Anyar **Tel** *(0362) 93 578* **Fax** *(0362) 93 579* **Rooms** *14*   **Map** *A1*

Set on a hill overlooking the Sea of Java, this resort offers magnificent views of ricefields, vineyards and central mountains, and is a short walk from a quiet beach. Rooms are comfortable and air-conditioned with ocean views; the restaurant serves healthy gourmet food. Large yoga and meditation pavilion. **www.zenresortbali.com**

TABANAN Waka Gangga
🍴 ≋ 🗏 $$$

Banjar Yeh Gangga, Dusun Sudimara, Tabanan **Tel** *(0361) 416 257* **Fax** *(0361) 416 353* **Rooms** *10*   **Map** *B4*

Positioned on a cliff above the Indian Ocean, the concept here is "back to nature" and spiritual harmony. This unique sanctuary is ideal for meditation, with bungalows, spa, restaurant and pool in a magical setting amid cascading ricefields and lotus ponds, all under the gaze of the mighty Gunung Batukau. **www.wakaexperience.com**

TANAH LOT Pan Pacific Nirwana Bali Resort ⊞⊞⊞⊞⊞⊞ $$$$

Jl Raya Tanah Lot, Kedin **Tel** *(0361) 815 900* **Fax** *(0361) 815 901* **Rooms** *278*   **Map** *B4*

This luxury golf resort blends into the contours of the coastline, with unobstructed views across the water to the wave-lashed sea temple of Tanah Lot. Rooms and suites are modern with plush furnishings. There is also a spa, health club, two restaurants, three pools and two tennis courts. **www.panpacific.com**

LOMBOK

GILI ISLES Hotel Gili Air ⊞⊞⊞ $$

Gili Air **Tel** *(0370) 643 580* **Fax** *(0370) 634 435* **Rooms** *31*

The comfortable cottages here face the beach on the north coast of the island, and feature terraces and open-air bathrooms. All the rooms have either air-conditioning or a fan, and hot water. There is also a bar and a restaurant. **www.hotelgiliair.com**

GILI ISLES Villa Nautilus ⊞⊞ $$

Gili Meno **Tel** *(0370) 642 143* **Rooms** *5*

A small group of luxurious bungalows, generously spaced within a neat garden beside the beach. Each boasts immaculate decor, a large living area, a timber sundeck with gorgeous sea views, and bathrooms with hot and cold freshwater showers. The on-site café serves Indonesian and Western dishes. **www.villanautilus.com**

GILI ISLES Desa Dunia Beda Beach Resort ⊞⊞ $$$

Gili Trawangan **Tel** *(0370) 641 575* **Fax** *(0370) 641 585* **Rooms** *7*

This coconut grove resort is reminiscent of a small Javanese village. The traditional, wooden houses feature raised verandas, open shutters and garden bathrooms. Each breezy bedroom is furnished with a four-poster bed built into the central funnel of the roof. There is also a large swimming pool, restaurant and spa. **www.desaduniabeda.com**

GILI ISLES Hotel Vila Ombak ⊞⊞⊞ $$$

Gili Isles **Tel** *(0370) 642 336* **Fax** *(0370) 642 337* **Rooms** *110*

This hotel offers luxurious bamboo grass-roofed houses following the design of traditional rice barns. There is also a three-tiered swimming pool, a bodyworks centre and a diving academy. Limited resources on the Gilis means saline water is used in the showers, with jars of fresh water for rinsing off. No hot water. **www.hotellombak.com**

KUTA Novotel Coralia Lombok ⊞⊞⊞ $$$

Pantai Putri Nyale, Pujut **Tel** *(0370) 653 333* **Fax** *(0370) 653 555* **Rooms** *100*

Decorated in faded desert colours, the eccentric fairytale architecture of this quirky resort draws inspiration from traditional Sasak villages. The rooms are simply furnished in natural tones and enhanced with indigenous artifacts. Facilities include two beachfront restaurants and three swimming pools. **www.novotel-lombok.com**

MANGSIT Puri Mas Boutique Hotel ⊞⊞⊞ $$

Pantai Mangsit, Senggigi **Tel** *(0370) 693 831* **Fax** *(0370) 693 023* **Rooms** *17*

The hotel here has a small collection of thatched bungalows, rooms and suites, each in a different architectural style. One of Lombok's prettiest hotels, set right beside the beach within an enchanting garden of flowering shrubs, meandering paths, lily ponds, stone carvings and a shaded swimming pool. **www.purimas-lombok.com**

MANGSIT Puri Mas Village ⊞⊞ $$

Puri Mas Village Kerandangan, Senggigi **Tel** *(0370) 693 444* **Fax** *(0370) 693 596* **Rooms** *4*

These four villas, sleeping up to four people, are furnished with antiques and grouped around an exotic swimming pool, bordered by tall coconut palms and Hindu stone-carved waterspouts. This unique property is set against a dramatic backdrop of jungle-clad hills, with a romantic spa and room-service menu. **www.purimas-lombok.com**

SENGGIGI Holiday Resort Lombok ⊞⊞⊞⊞⊞⊞ $$

Jl Raya Mangsit, Senggigi **Tel** *(0370) 693 444* **Fax** *(0370) 693 023* **Rooms** *188*

Offering a collection of modern apartments, houses and beach bungalows, this beachside hotel features contemporary furnishings, balconies, sunlit private outdoor bathrooms, garden terraces, and sea and garden views. There are two restaurants, a children's pool and ample sports facilities. **www.holidayresort-lombok.com**

SENGGIGI Sheraton Senggigi Beach Resort ⊞⊞⊞⊞⊞⊞ $$$

Jl Raya Senggigi, Senggigi **Tel** *(0370) 693 333* **Fax** *(0370) 693 140* **Rooms** *154*

This five-star, town-centre resort offers a great range of facilities for adults and children, with rooms, suites and villas, including two beachfront villas with private pools. Other facilities include a lagoon pool, restaurants, bars, tennis courts, a fitness centre with sauna, steam room and gym, and spa treatments. **www.starwoodhotels.com**

TANJUNG The Oberoi Lombok ⊞⊞⊞⊞ $$$$$

Medana Beach, Tanjung, PO Box 1096, Mataram, 83001 **Tel** *(0370) 638 444* **Fax** *(0370) 632 496* **Rooms** *50*

A secluded, multi-award-winning paradise hideaway, set within coconut palm-studded gardens and bordering an exclusive beach, offers a cluster of luxurious single-storey pool villas and terrace pavilions plus a magnificent 40-m (130-ft) swimming pool, which merges with the sea and reflective ponds. **www.oberoihotels.com**

WHERE TO EAT

From local food at *warung* and *rumah makan* to international restaurant cuisines, Bali and Lombok cater for all tastes. Good food is available over a wide price range. As the number of visitors has increased, many new establishments have opened, and generally they show a high level of skill and confidence. The range is particularly wide in the more developed

Chilli, a spice often used in local food

parts of Bali – the options in remoter parts of the island, and in Lombok, are more limited. Credit cards are accepted in more sophisticated restaurants and cafés. Prices on menus may be expressed in US dollars, although payment in rupiah is always accepted. Restaurants will accommodate disabled visitors, although most do not make any specific provisions.

Barbecued seafood being prepared in a hotel kitchen

EATING HOURS

The Balinese have no set meal times and most places will be happy to serve guests throughout the day. However, there are not many dining options before 7am or after midnight.

LOCAL FOOD

The everyday Balinese diet consists of a couple of meals based on rice with a little meat, vegetables and the occasional egg. The combination is known as *nasi campur (see p182)*. This and other Balinese dishes are served in most restaurants.

For the "genuine" – and often tastier – article, try the *warung* (food stalls) or *rumah makan* (eating houses) where locals eat when away from home. The food here is cheap, fresh and spicier than in restaurants. Lining the streets and parked at night markets are *kaki lima* (food carts), which are not recommended as the standard of hygiene is often questionable.

INTERNATIONAL RESTAURANTS

Bali offers the world on a plate, from the entire complement of Asian cuisines to traditional Western food. A large number of foreign chefs have been attracted to Bali by the hotel chains, and some have started up their own operations. In turn they have trained many local chefs in foreign food preparation. French, Italian and other Mediterranean cuisines are all part of the enormous range offered in the island's restaurants, and standards are generally high. The prices are very reasonable by international standards. Some very good Japanese food can be enjoyed in Bali for a fraction of what it would cost in most other places.

HOTEL DINING

Many hotels in Bali offer excellent meals in surroundings more luxurious than those encountered in most other tourist destinations. The best

are often featured in international food and travel magazines. The Aman resorts have an excellent reputation for hiring young chefs with signature styles, as do the Four Seasons Resorts and the GHM hotels – the Legian, and the Chedi Club at Tanah Gajah *(see pp173–5)*. The major chain hotels all offer the full range of dining styles from coffee shops to cafés and restaurants. It is often possible to eat in the open air. Hotel bars and restaurants are open to the public as well as to hotel guests *(see pp170–79 and pp184–91)*.

Eating in hotels will generally be more expensive than in restaurants outside, and menus in hotel restaurants are often priced in US dollars.

Warung selling rice and a variety of Indonesian dishes

CAFES AND COFFEE SHOPS

Since the 1970s when surfers and independent travellers put Bali on the tourist map, the island has embraced the idea of casual eating. Bars and beach-side eateries serving fairly simple fare are common sights. They serve

Al fresco dining at Senggigi Beach, on the west coast of Lombok

nasi goreng (fried rice), the ubiquitous banana pancake, fresh local fruit juices and grainy Bali coffee. However, growing demand from visitors and increased awareness among locals have fired up the café scene. Particularly in the artistic village of Ubud, European-style cafés with espresso machines are common, as are, increasingly, up-market coffee houses serving gourmet blends of freshly-roasted Indonesian coffee varieties. Accompaniments include everything from tiramisu to the delicious *bubur hitam* (black rice pudding). In fashionable Seminyak, north of Kuta, many new establishments have opened. Here the modern coffee house can be seen in all its varieties from French patisseries to espresso bars offering Italian-style sandwiches and fresh salads.

FAST FOOD AND TAKEAWAYS

Bali has seen the rapid establishment of fast-food chains, and McDonald's, Pizza Hut, Kentucky Fried Chicken, Starbuck's and Dunkin' Donuts can be found in tourist and city areas. Most restaurants will do *bungkus* (takeaways) and many will deliver.

ALCOHOL

It would be a pity to visit Bali and Lombok without sampling the local alcohol, especially since imported alcohol attracts high duties and is very expensive. Bintang is a popular, refreshing lager; Bali Hai, while cheaper, is not as good. A local wine called Hatten's is being produced – this is light, dry, inexpensive and fairly drinkable. *Arak* cocktails, made with palm brandy, are a popular choice.

Alcohol is available almost everywhere in Bali, even in small *warung* outside tourist areas. In Muslim Lombok, alcohol is available only in tourist areas and up-market hotels, and should be consumed within the premises.

CHILDREN

The restaurant scenes in Bali and Lombok do not generally cater specifically to children, but it is easy to find something children will eat. Some restaurants will serve a half-portion, and have high chairs available on request; others will not. The larger hotels often offer buffet breakfast free to children under 12.

VEGETARIAN FOOD

There is a wonderful range of tasty and nutritious vegetarian dishes in Bali and Lombok. *Tahu* (tofu) and *tempe* (cakes made of compressed, fermented soy beans) are popular and plentiful, as is *bubur sayur bayam* (rice porridge with spinach leaves, chilli, coconut shavings and coconut milk).

Many restaurants include a variety of vegetarian dishes on their menus. Those with Chinese-style dishes usually offer a wider range. It is possible to get vegetarian versions of non-vegetarian dishes on request. Just make sure your order is stated clearly.

Dining in the courtyard of the Hard Rock Hotel in Kuta *(see p184)*

RESTAURANT ETIQUETTE

Many Balinese still eat with the right hand and no cutlery (the left hand is never used), and well-dressed locals can often be seen eating in this traditional way.

Food will often appear in random order. It is best simply to start rather than wait until everyone is served.

Casual clothing is accepted everywhere, but people tend to be more smartly dressed in up-market restaurants. Most restaurants are open-air, so smoking is generally allowed, although an increasing number now have a non-smoking area.

Tipping is more common than it once was; expensive places tend to add a service charge anyway. Staff in cheaper local restaurants will be happy with a token tip.

View of Jimbaran Bay from PJ's at Four Seasons Resort *(see p184)*

The Flavours of Bali and Lombok

Many of this region's distinctive tastes and cooking styles were influenced by early Chinese, Indian, Arabic and Dutch traders and settlers. Flavoursome curries rely on freshly ground spices, and common seasonings include ginger, lemongrass, kaffir lime leaves and tamarind. Sauces feature coconut milk and the essential trio of fresh coriander, pepper and garlic. A paste of salted and fermented shrimp is also used to enliven and add depth to dishes. Hot fresh chilli appears in fiery accompanying sauces called sambals, and peanuts are typically present as a garnish, or ground into a paste to form a sweet and spicy sauce.

Peanuts

Fresh chillies, a key ingredient in the cuisine of Bali and Lombok

BALI'S HARVEST

The chain of mountains that divides Bali is responsible for different climatic conditions and soil types, which yield a huge variety of crops. The southern-central plains are dominated by terraced ricefields, while the inland regions support onions, cabbages, papayas, spinach, lettuce, potatoes, carrots, coffee, cloves and peanuts. Fruit, including strawberries, is grown in the cool mountain area of Bedugul. Kintamani is famed for oranges and the Buleleng Regency for its durians. In Tejakula there are acres of mango plantations. The *wani*, found in the Singaraja area, is a white mango with a distinctive smell, which is cherished by the Balinese. The farmers in the hot and arid northern-coastal region cultivate dry-land crops such as maize, cassava, beans and, surprisingly, grapes, a fruit that has been nurtured here since the early 20th century.

JIMBARAN BAY SEAFOOD

Every morning at dawn, the Jimbaran fishermen return to shore in their gaily painted

Durian
Star fruit
Mango
Watermelon
Pineapple
Pomelo
Passion fruits
Papaya

Selection of luscious tropical fruit from the islands of Indonesia

REGIONAL DISHES AND SPECIALITIES

Everyday Indonesian fare comprises rice, vegetables, egg and perhaps a little meat or fish. Known as *nasi campur*, it is usually cooked in the early morning and eaten whenever the need arises. In Bahasa Indonesia the word *lombok* means chilli pepper, and the Lombok people use home-grown hot chillies liberally in their cooking. Traditional white rice is the staple of Sasak food and is served with curries or soup made from vegetables, fish, and a little meat, but no pork. *Taliwang* dishes feature fried or grilled ingredients with a chilli sauce, and anything with *pelecing* in the name is also served with chilli sauce.

Ginger, lemongrass, kaffir lime and lime leaves

Gado gado *is a warm salad of blanched mixed vegetables, tofu and egg, with a sweet and spicy peanut sauce.*

Selecting the best fruits on offer at an Indonesian market

vessels to trade at the bustling Kedonganan fish market. At sunset the beach becomes the scene of a daily ritual as hundreds of visitors take their seats in the many *warung* – the simple seafood cafés that run virtually the length of the bay and serve up the catch of the day. The fish is displayed on ice at the back of the café, and guests are invited to select the seafood of their choice – mainly whole red and white snapper, barracuda, squid, giant prawns and lobster (the latter two served in their shells). The feast includes a bamboo steamer of rice, along with tasty steamed Balinese water spinach, delicious home-made garlic, tomato and chilli sauces, baked potatoes and a simple dessert of fresh pineapple, watermelon and banana.

PADANG CUISINE

Padang food, from the Minangkabau region of West Sumatra, is to be found in the Rumah Makan Padang eating-houses. Glass-fronted cabinets showcase platters

Fish, straight from the ocean to a Kedonganan market stall

and pots filled with cold vegetables, meats and fish. The food is of Indian origin and is typically spicy, featuring plenty of chilli and meat curries. Customers choose a selection of dishes to make up a composite meal. These might include classic dishes such as beef rendang, but also items like *perkedel* (potato cakes), deep-fried corn cakes, the sesame-dipped and deep-fried bean curd known as *tempe*, hardboiled eggs, liver, brains, lungs, fried chicken, tuna steaks, aubergine (eggplant), cassava leaf and water spinach – all served with rice, curried sauces and chilli sambals.

RIJSTAFEL

The name Rijstafel, literally meaning "rice-table", originated with the Dutch plantation owners, who liked to sample selectively from Indonesian cuisine. Steamed white or yellow rice is always the centrepiece, often presented in a cone and capped with a banana leaf. It is accompanied by a range of different meat, poultry, seafood and vegetable dishes, which are often served in handmade coconut pots on a banana leaf plate. These boiled, grilled, roasted, steamed, wok-fried or deep-fried dishes are complemented by *krupuk* (rice crackers), *acar* (pickled sour vegetables) and a range of chilli and onion sambals and spicy sauces.

Sate lilit *may be minced meat or fish, infused with coconut and grilled on a lemongrass skewer.*

Bebek bututu *is duck stuffed with spices, wrapped in banana leaves and cooked in an earth oven.*

Kue dadar *are little crêpe parcels, filled with a mixture of palm sugar, vanilla and grated fresh coconut.*

Choosing a Restaurant

Bali and Lombok's restaurants serve a wide range of cuisines, generally at reasonable prices. Several hotels *(see pp170–79)* have good restaurants, although these are often a little more expensive. The recommendations in this guide have been chosen for their value, exceptional food and interesting location.

PRICE CATEGORIES
Restaurant prices (in *rupiah*) for a three-course meal for one, including service charges, excluding drinks.

(Rp) Under Rp75,000
(Rp)(Rp) Rp75,000–Rp150,000
(Rp)(Rp)(Rp) Rp150,000–Rp250,000
(Rp)(Rp)(Rp)(Rp) Rp250,000–Rp350,000
(Rp)(Rp)(Rp)(Rp)(Rp) Over Rp350,000

SOUTH BALI

CANGGU The Beach House
Jl Pura Batu Mejan (Echo Beach) **Tel** *(0361) 738 471*   **Map** C4

The Beach House bar and restaurant has tables spilling out on to a beachside bluff, with an extensive drinks list, friendly staff and great sunsets. The simple international menu includes Indonesian dishes and snacks. Live music is complemented by a seafood barbeque on Sunday evenings when it can get very busy. Attracts a bohemian crowd.

CANGGU Waroeng Tugu
Jl Pantai Batu Bolong **Tel** *(0361) 731 707 / 731 702*   **Map** C4

Hotel Tugu has successfully recreated the ambience of the Majapahit Hindu Kingdom with this rustic, open-sided restaurant flanked by a simple brick kitchen. Here, Iboe Soelastri, the Javanese cook, skilfully prepares authentic sauces, cooking traditional Balinese and Javanese dishes in a hot clay oven fuelled by coconut husks.

DENPASAR Rasa Sayang
Jl Teuku Umar, Denpasar **Tel** *(0361) 262 006*   **Map** C4

This is one of the best Chinese restaurants in Denpasar. The extensive menu includes a wide range of fish, poultry, meat and vegetable dishes. Delicacies include fish-head soup, mud crab, frogs' legs, lettuce buns, raw lobster with *wasabi*, deep-fried squid in Worcester sauce and sliced beef with Chinese broccoli.

JIMBARAN Jimbaran Seafood Cafés
Kedonganan & Jimbaran Beach   **Map** C5

A plethora of simple beachside cafés serves fresh seafood such as snapper, barracuda, giant prawns, squid and lobster. Plastic chairs and tables lit by flickering candles spill out on to the sand. Guests may select the seafood of their choice, and the feast will include a bamboo steamer of rice, vegetables, homemade sauces, and fresh fruit.

JIMBARAN PJ's
Four Seasons, Jimbaran Bay **Tel** *(0361) 701 010*   **Map** C5

The Four Seasons Resort restaurant is right on the beach and accessible from the road without going through the hotel entrance. It provides alfresco dining in breezy seaside pavilions. The menu has an ethnic island theme and offers Mediterranean-inspired dishes and dips, super fresh seafood, wood-fired pizzas and wicked desserts.

KUTA Aromas
Jl Legian, Kelod **Tel** *(0361) 751 003*   **Map** C5

An extensive menu of local and international vegetarian dishes, salads and dips, from India, Thailand, the Middle East, Mexico and Europe, is offered at this long-established vegetarian restaurant. The large, open air pavilion is surrounded by shrubs, water and fountains, a pleasant retreat from the bustle and traffic of busy Jalan Legian.

KUTA The Balcony
Jl Benesari 16, Kuta **Tel** *(0361) 757 409*   **Map** C5

This semi open-air Mediterranean restaurant serves fresh, warm, home-baked caraway bread, generous salads, pasta dishes and main courses such as roasted rosemary chicken, beef *entrecôte* and the house speciality of seafood and meat *brochettes*. It also features an extensive tapas menu, and classy desserts.

KUTA Hard Rock Café
Jl Pantai, Kuta **Tel** *(0361) 755 661*   **Map** C5

The walls of this American, rock 'n' roll-themed, live music venue and family restaurant are covered with music memorabilia. American fast food is served by waiters and waitresses selected for their friendly, outgoing personalities. The music begins as soon as the doors open; the food is consistently good and the portions are huge.

KUTA Kopi Pot
Jl Legian 139, Kuta **Tel** *(0361) 752 614*   **Map** C5

A pretty, tiered garden restaurant and bar, famous for its coffee and cakes and black rice pudding. Dishes include soups, salads, as well as sausage and mash with onion gravy. Indonesian specialities include *ayam betutu* (tender pieces of chicken in a spicy Balinese sauce), and *ikan balado* (chunks of fresh mackerel in a Sumatran chilli sauce).

Key to Symbols *see back cover flap*

KUTA Kori Restaurant & Bar
Gang Poppies II, Kuta **Tel** *(0361) 758 605*

Map C5

Encompassed by a lotus pond, this open pavilion restaurant serves delights such as Thai-style salad of fresh blue swimmer crab meat, tossed in Bali mango, papaya, red onion, lemongrass and coriander. Other favourites include chargrilled bangers and mash, and warm sticky-toffee date pudding with butterscotch sauce.

KUTA Maccaroni
Jl Legian 52, Kuta **Tel** *(0361) 754 662*

Map C5

The architecture (by Giovanni D'Ambrosio) at Macaroni features polished grey concrete and tubular metal, comprising a series of intimate spaces flanked by cascading green vines. The innovative menu bursts with Italian classics, seafood and exciting new creations from the Italian chef. Cool ambience and sophisticated music.

KUTA Made's Warung I
Jl Pantai, Kuta **Tel** *(0361) 755 297*

Map C5

Kuta's oldest and most famous restaurant was established in 1969 as Bali's first *warung* to serve Western food. It offers a selection of Indonesian, Japanese and Western dishes, followed by European desserts. Classic Indonesian dishes include Nasi Campur Special, Nasi Goreng à la Mode, *gado gado* and *satay*. Gets very busy.

KUTA Nero Bali
Jl Legian 384, Kuta **Tel** *(0361) 750 756*

Map C5

The creation of architectural designer Giovanni D'Ambrosio, this ultra avant-garde restaurant and cocktail bar was nominated as one of the 25 most beautiful restaurants in the world. The extensive menu offers Mediterranean fare, including kebabs, seafood, pasta, pizza and tapas. There is also a sushi bar. Open daily for lunch and dinner.

KUTA Papa's Café
Jl Pantai, Kuta **Tel** *(0361) 755 055*

Map C5

Papa's Café serves high quality, authentic Italian and Asian food, including pasta and pizzas. There is a choice of dining areas and the Asian kitchen offers dishes from all over the continent such as curry, bento box, *bebek betutu*, and *tum be pasih*. The ginger and date pudding in butterscotch sauce is a must.

KUTA Poppies Restaurant
Gang Poppies I, Kuta **Tel** *(0361) 751 059*

Map C5

This romantic garden restaurant is so famous that it has even had two lanes named after it. A Kuta landmark since 1973, Poppies offers a selection of Asian and western dishes, from fresh fish and seafood, pasta and steaks to classic Indonesian specialities and vegetarian curries. Reservations recommended. Open until 11pm daily.

KUTA TJ's
Gang Poppies I, Kuta **Tel** *(0361) 751 093*

Map C5

A Kuta institution established in 1984, this thatched, open-air pavilion has a colourful decor and a garden setting. It serves superb, authentic Californian-Mexican cuisine such as buffalo wings, tacos, enchiladas, fajitas, salads and baked potatoes, followed by desserts such as mango cheesecake with raspberry sauce.

KUTA Un's Restaurant
Off Gang Poppies I **Tel** *(0361) 752 607*

Map C5

Renowned for its Entrecôte Café de Paris, Un's Restaurant serves fine European cuisine and Indonesian specialities. There is sashimi-grade tuna medallions, beef Stroganoff, veal cutlets in *porcini* sauce, potato-wrapped snapper fillet, beef *rendang*, and *crème catalan*. Traditional Balinese-style architecture around an open courtyard.

LEGIAN Poco Loco
Jl Padma Utara, Legian **Tel** *(0361) 756 079*

Map C5

Set back from the road and on two different levels, this colourful open-air Mexican restaurant and bar offers a good variety of all the usual Californian-style Mexican dishes, including enchiladas, tortillas and "create your own" fajitas. Also good salmon steaks and grills, a delicious "muddy mud pie", tequila shots and jugs of margarita.

LEGIAN Drops
Casa Padma Suites, Jl Padma **Tel** *(0361) 753 073*

Map C5

The concept at this stylish restaurant at Casa Padma Suites Hotel is one of contemporary International and classic Balinese cuisine. A varied menu includes sandwiches, pizza, pasta, *nasi campur*, sweet and spicy roasted duck salad, steaks, spare ribs, butterfish mozzarella, pork schnitzel and banana spring rolls.

NUSA DUA Nampu at Grand Hyatt Bali
Nusa Dua **Tel** *(0361) 771 234*

Map C5

Try Japanese fine-dining at the Grand Hyatt. The choice of classic dining experiences includes a *teppanyaki* room, private *tatami* rooms, and a sophisticated dining room with an open kitchen. High quality sashimi, sushi, charcoal grilled dishes, and much more. Desserts include black sesame custard with *yuzu* sorbet. Wide selection of sake.

NUSA DUA Sorrento at Melia Bali
Melia Bali Villas & Spa Resort, Nusa Dua **Tel** *(0361) 771 510*

Map C5

This fine restaurant has a Mediterranean-Spanish theme. Candlelit dining takes place under the palm trees, or within the air-conditioned comfort of the classy interior, which has a dramatic, painted ceiling. Ingredients include Serrano ham, *chorizo* sausages and fresh seafood. Authentic dishes include superb *gazpacho* and steaming hot *paella*.

NUSA DUA Tetaring at Kayumanis

Kayumanis Private Villa & Spa, Nusa Dua **Tel** *(0361) 770 777*

Map C5

The architecture here is industrial and minimalist, with black obsidian marble complemented by glass and pebbles. The cuisine is Western and Southeast Asian with a modern twist. Gastronomic delights include poached lobster salad, Javanese fish curry, roasted duck breast, and frozen passion-fruit *sabayon* with banana and honeycomb sauce.

NUSA LEMBONGAN JoJo's Restaurant

Nusa Lembongan Resort **Tel** *(0361) 725 864*

Map E4

The menu here includes plenty of fresh seafood, pizza, stir-fries and vegetable tempura, plus dishes such as seafood grilled in banana leaves, and a salad of pan fried scallops with baby potatoes. JoJo's is within an idyllic beachside resort set on the edge of a secluded coral bay.

SANUR Kafe Wayang

Komplex Pertokoan Sanur Raya No. 12–14, Jl By Pass Ngurah Rai **Tel** *(0361) 287 591*

Map C4

This modern, spacious restaurant and bakery serves a fusion of Asian and Mediterranean cuisine, including salads, soups, pasta, rice and noodles, imported steaks, grilled food, sandwiches and snacks. Popular dishes include cheese samosa, tequila mussels, chicken breast *piemontese* and the ultimate tamarind salmon.

SANUR Stiff Chilli

Jl Kesumasari 11, Semawang **Tel** *(0361) 288 371*

Map D4

Italian cuisine with an Asian twist is on offer at this simple, open-air restaurant beside the beach. Famous for its crispy-skinned, grilled sausages, freshly baked *ciabatta* bread, Thai-style pumpkin soup and authentic Italian pizzas, there is also tri-coloured *fettuccine* topped with rich sauces such as creamy, smoked marlin.

SANUR Café Batu Jimbar

Jl Danau Tamblingan 75 **Tel** *(0361) 287 374*

Map C4

This popular streetside café has a spacious forecourt for eating out under the trees. The Italian and Mexican dishes on the menu include pasta and *quesadillas*, plus salads, homemade breads and cakes, herbal teas and fruit juices. Organic vegetables and herbs are from the owner's farm near Bedugul.

SANUR Jazz Bar & Grille

Komplex Pertokoan Sanur Raya No. 15–16, Jl By Pass Ngurah Rai **Tel** *(0361) 285 892*

Map C4

Regular live entertainment is performed here by well-respected jazz bands from Bali and beyond. The restaurant offers everything from sandwiches, snacks and pizzas, to four-course meals. Western and Indonesian classics include Jazz Grille nachos, black 'n' blue tuna, Mongolian lamb chops, *sop buntut, gado gado* and pecan pie. Dinner only.

SANUR Massimo Il Ristorante

Jl Danau Tamblingan 206 **Tel** *(0361) 288 942*

Map C4

There is always a great atmosphere at this popular Italian restaurant, serving high quality, authentic regional dishes in an attractive, open pavilion surrounded by a garden. The extensive menu offers *bruschetta*, salads, deep-fried mozzarella, risotto, pasta and pizza, chicken, duck and fish specialities, and the best Italian ice cream in Bali.

SANUR Pepper's Latino Grill & Bar

Hotel Sanur Beach, Jl Danau Tamblingan **Tel** *(0361) 288 011*

Map D4

Latin-American food in an interior reminiscent of a wine cellar. There is also an outdoor veranda with decorative wrought iron archways and a pergola dripping with passion-fruit vines. Delights include *gazpacho*, nachos, steaks, *paella*, Cuban roasted pork loin, lobster, and mango ice cream topped with pina colada pulp. Dinner only.

SANUR Pergola

Jl Danau Toba 2, Sanur **Tel** *(0361) 288 462*

Map C4

Pergola's menu offers a combination of Eastern and Western cuisine, with English influences. It attracts regular customers, especially families, with Sunday roast and spectacular *flambé* tableside cooking. Dishes include English Stilton cheese, "Summerset" Pork Chop, sizzling stir-fries, sherry trifle and banana *flambé*.

SANUR The Mezzanine

Jl Danau Tamblingan 63 **Tel** *(0361) 270 624*

Map D4

Housed in a grand building with breezy terraces, The Mezzanine offers an extensive menu of Thai, Japanese, Chinese and western fare. Specialities include teppanyaki *hotate*, made with rich, creamy grilled scallops, Chinese claypot of braised seafood and the Thai *gaeng phed ped* (duck in red curry). Open for dinner daily.

SEMINYAK/KEROBOKAN Baku Dapa

Jl Abimanyu (Dhyana Pura) 11A, Seminyak **Tel** *(0361) 731 148*

Map C5

Renowned for its *sop buntut* (oxtail soup), this simple streetside *warung* is open 24 hours. The menu includes *nasi goreng* special, chicken *satay, gado gado* with peanut sauce, fried soybean, and piping-hot fried tofu, accompanied by a selection of fresh and fiery home-made chilli *sambals*, and followed by banana fritters with honey.

SEMINYAK/KEROBOKAN Ryoshi

Jl Raya Seminyak 15, Seminyak **Tel** *(0361) 731 152*

Map C5

This authentic and efficient Japanese fast-food restaurant features Japanese-style low tables and cushions or chunky wooden tables and chairs, and an extensive menu. Dishes include sashimi and sushi sets, miso soup, hot mixed mushroom salad, plus house sake. Regular live jazz music.

Key to Price Guide *see p184* **Key to Symbols** *see back cover flap*

SEMINYAK/KEROBOKAN Sate Bali
Jl Laksmana/Oberoi No. 22a **Tel** *(0361) 736 734*   **Map** *C4*

A rustic eatery specializing exclusively in authentic Balinese dishes. Delicious food is presented in traditional style using lemongrass skewers, banana leaves, frangipani flowers and clay pots. This is a great place for large groups as guests will be indulged with a magnificent Balinese Rijstafel – a banquet comprising 10 different dishes.

SEMINYAK/KEROBOKAN Zula
Jl Abimanyu (Dhyana Pura) No. 5, Seminyak **Tel** *(0361) 732 723*   **Map** *C5*

This colourful vegetarian café presents healthy dishes rich in vitamins and minerals, plus energy enhancing and immune system boosting fruit and vegetable juices. The Mediterranean Platter is a treat from the Middle East created with an authentic blend of flavours and spices, and the Planet Platter is based on macrobiotic principles.

SEMINYAK/KEROBOKAN Khaima
Jl Laksmana **Tel** *(0361) 742 3925*   **Map** *C4*

Enjoy a Moroccan experience created by Moghul architecture, coloured glass lanterns and mellow Arabic-infused music, mint tea, ornate shisha pipes and belly dancers. The authentic menu includes salads, *briwattes*, soups, bread, *tagines*, couscous and *mechoui*. Desserts include flourless orange cake and almond custard pastille.

SEMINYAK/KEROBOKAN La Sal
Jl Drupadi II, No. 100, Seminyak **Tel** *(0361) 780 0681*   **Map** *C5*

La Sal offers Spanish food and a vibrant Spanish atmosphere, with tables spilling out into the garden. The menu presents a plethora of traditional and fusion tapas dishes, including batter-coated sardines, octopus salad, *croquetas*, stuffed mussels, prawns, fried squid and much more. Also serves great salads and some creative desserts.

SEMINYAK/KEROBOKAN Naughty Nuri's Warung
Jl Batubelig 41, Kerobokan **Tel** *(0361) 847 6722*   **Map** *C4*

An Ubud institution, Naughty Nuri's also has a Kerobokan branch. This streetside café with wooden tables and benches offers gargopen-air and garden dining. One of the main draws is the daily BBQ of pork ribs, sashimi-grade tuna and other delights. The place is also renowned for its potent martinis. Reservations recommended.

SEMINYAK/KEROBOKAN Queen's Tandoor
Jl Raya Seminyak 73 (Gallery Seminyak) **Tel** *(0361) 732 770*   **Map** *C5*

The extensive menu here features no less than 30 dishes hot from the tandoor and 25 *bageeche se* from the vegetable garden, together with chicken, lamb, fish and prawn curries. There are also a few hot vegetarian dishes from the south, such as *masala dosa* and *sambhar*, plus a wide selection of traditional breads from the clay oven.

SEMINYAK/KEROBOKAN Cocoon Beach Club
Jl Double Six, Blue Ocean Boulevard, Seminyak **Tel** *(0361) 731 266*   **Map** *C5*

Complete with swimming pool, sunset roof terrace with ocean views, and several lounge and bar areas, this chic split-level beach club offers a cuisine inspired by the food-sharing philosophy of the Mediterranean. Graze on gourmet tapas accompanied by cocktails in a VIP cabana beside the pool.

SEMINYAK/KEROBOKAN Gado Gado
Jl Abimanyu (Dhyana Pura) 99, Seminyak **Tel** *(0361) 730 955*   **Map** *C5*

This lovely, up-market restaurant offers seriously fine dining in a stunning and very romantic location overlooking the ocean. The spacious lounge bar extends on to a wide, open-air terrace shaded by leafy trees. The enticing lunch and dinner menus offer beautifully presented, exotic dishes with plenty of seafood and luscious desserts.

SEMINYAK/KEROBOKAN La Lucciola
Kaya Ayu Beach, Temple Petitenget, Kerobokan **Tel** *(0361) 261 047*   **Map** *C4*

An open-sided, two-storey, breezy thatched beach house with fabulous ocean views is the venue for an inspired Italian and Mediterranean menu featuring great breakfasts. There is a wonderful terrace for sunset cocktails. Dishes include pasta, salads, char-grilled chicken, swordfish steaks, tropical fruit sorbets, chocolate soufflé and much more.

SEMINYAK/KEROBOKAN Nutmegs at Hu'u Bar
Jl Petitenget, Kerobokan **Tel** *(0361) 736 443*   **Map** *C4*

This chic restaurant and lounge-club attracts a hip crowd and is famous for its lychee martinis and tapas. Dishes such as oriental duck pancakes, braised beef *tagine*, and *pandan crème brulée* are offered. Zen-inspired minimalist architecture is complemented by a stunning swimming pool. Late-night DJs raise electronic sounds to an upbeat pitch.

SEMINYAK/KEROBOKAN Sarong
Jl Petitenget 19x, Seminyak **Tel** *(0361) 737 809*   **Map** *C4*

The menu at this popular restaurant features the great cuisines of Southeast Asia, namely Thai, Chinese, Malaysian, Indian and Indonesian. Hawker food – for example, betel leaf parcels of raw tuna, shallots, chilli, lemongrass and basil – is elevated to fine dining levels. The restaurant comprises two open pavilions.

SEMINYAK/KEROBOKAN Ku De Ta
Jl Laksmana 9, Kerobokan **Tel** *(0361) 736 969*   **Map** *C4*

Bali's famous beachfront restaurant and sophisticated hot spot is the place to see and be seen, with wonderful breakfasts, an excellent grazing menu and intimate dining at night. Contemporary Australian cuisine includes shucked oysters, classic rack of lamb with soft polenta, white chocolate *tiramisu* and Australian cheese platter.

SEMINYAK/KEROBOKAN Métis

Jl Petitenget 6, Kerobokan **Tel** *(0361) 737 888*   **Map** *C4*

This stylish restaurant offers alfresco dining on a terrace overlooking the ricefields. The fine French Mediterranean cuisine includes dishes such as crispy pork belly with Swiss chard and Granny Smith apples poached in white wine. Desserts include passionfruit soufflé. Reservations recommended. Closed Sun lunch.

SEMINYAK/KEROBOKAN Sardine

Jl Petitenget 21, Kerobokan **Tel** *(0361) 738 202*   **Map** *C4*

Sardine is a gourmet seafood and fish restaurant, with dishes such as crab bisque, barramundi, smoked sardines and miso sea bass served with soba noodles. This delightful open-air restaurant is housed in a pavilion crafted entirely from bamboo, with a stunning view over a beautifully lit ricefield. Reservations recommended. Closed Mon.

TANJUNG BENOA Bumbu Bali

Jl Pratama Matahari Terbit **Tel** *(0361) 774 502*   **Map** *C5*

Created by the former executive chef of Grand Hyatt Bali, this famous establishment presents authentic Balinese cuisine and is the venue of Balinese cooking classes and dance performances. The restaurant is a series of Balinese *wantilan*-style pavilions built around an open courtyard.

TANJUNG BENOA Spice

The Conrad Bali Resort & Spa, Jl Pratama 168 **Tel** *(0361) 778 788*   **Map** *C5*

Gourmet restaurant serving exotic, modern Asian cuisine based on recipes from the Middle, near and Far East. The elegant third-floor dining room has views of the water garden and Indian Ocean. The menu includes a mixed entrée plate, Mandarin Pancakes stuffed with crispy duck and flourless chilli chocolate cake with *crème* Chantilly.

TUBAN Blue Fin

Complex Kuta Sidewalk on Jl Kartika Plaza, Tuban **Tel** *(0361) 764 100*   **Map** *C5*

Featuring four distinct dining areas, this funky Japanese fusion restaurant has an extensive menu which blends traditional Japanese ingredients with cooking styles from around the world. The menu includes innovative fusion rolls with fun and fancy names such as Rolls Royce, Rock & Roll, Jalan Jalan Roll, Rose Blossom and Volcano Roll.

TUBAN Ma Joly

Jl Wana Segara, Tuban **Tel** *(0361) 753 780*   **Map** *C5*

You will get eye-popping coastline views at this enchanting beachfront restaurant serving classy French cuisine. Beautifully presented dishes include fresh seafood, premium cuts of imported meat and tasty vegetarian delights, complemented by home-baked bread, homemade sauces and a selection of fine wines.

CENTRAL BALI

AYUNG RIVER GORGE Ayung Terrace at Four Seasons Sayan

Four Seasons Resort at Sayan, Gianyar, Ubud **Tel** *(0361) 977 577*   **Map** *C3*

Built into the side of the river gorge at Four Seasons Resort, the Ayung Terrace has a panoramic open-air vista of the Ayung River coiling its way through the chasm below. The menu offers Asian-Pacific cuisine with flair, including such dishes as seared scallop and papaya in paper rolls, spicy South Indian vegetable curry, and carrot cake.

AYUNG RIVER GORGE The Restaurant at Alila Ubud

Alila Ubud, Desa Melinggih Kelod Payangan **Tel** *(0361) 975 963*   **Map** *C3*

Alila Ubud offers a harmonious balance of Balinese, Indonesian, Asian and Mediterranean specialities, including the regional cuisine of Ubud and featuring slow-cooked duck and Balinese Rijstaffel – a collection of dishes typical of a ceremonial meal. Vegetarians will enjoy "Cuisine Au Naturel", with the best and freshest local market ingredients.

NAGI CasCades at The Viceroy

The Viceroy Bali, Jl Lanyahan, Nagi, Ubud **Tel** *(0361) 972 111*   **Map** *D3*

Acclaimed as one of the best in Asia, it is not just the breathtaking setting on the ridge of a valley that makes this restaurant exceptional. The menu includes *foie gras*, truffle and morel *velouté*, Beluga caviar and roasted duck breast on barley risotto with licorice sauce, climaxing with "Orgasme de Chocolat".

PAYANGAN Beduur at Ubud Hanging Gardens

Ubud Hanging Gardens, Buahan, Payangan **Tel** *(0361) 982 700*   **Map** *C3*

This wonderful, fine-dining restaurant at Ubud Hanging Gardens is dramatically suspended above the Ayung River, with views of a remarkable floodlit temple. The French cuisine includes duck *foie gras* terrine, pan-fried lamb fillet with maple syrup, caramelized apple tart and lime cheesecake.

SANGGINGAN Naughty Nuri's

Jl Raya Sangiggan, Ubud **Tel** *(0361) 977 547*   **Map** *C3*

This streetside, open-air, *warung*-style hangout is reminiscent of an English pub and well-patronized by Ubud's expat community, always busy, and famous for martinis. There is a daily barbeque of steaks, lamb chops, ribs and sausages. Chicken, *nasi goreng*, *nasi campur* and vegetable curry are also on the menu, washed down with plenty of cold beer.

SANGGINGAN Mozaic

Jl Raya Sanggingan, Ubud **Tel** *(0361) 975 768* **Map** *C3*

Be prepared for dazzling, eclectic cuisine at the only restaurant in Indonesia to have received the exceptional honour of entry in the refined worldwide guide of *Les Grandes Tables du Monde*. Tables spill out into a romantic candlelit garden. Expect an evening of culinary discovery with bold, enticing and intriguing visual creations.

TEGALLALANG Kampung Café

Ceking, Tegallalang **Tel** *(0361) 901 201* **Map** *D3*

The concise-yet-varied menu here combines fresh ingredients to create dishes such as seared tuna on *arugula* with *wasabi* and ginger, spicy chicken with lemongrass and water spinach, fillet of *mahi mahi* on *fettuccine*, and delicious flourless orange and almond cake.

UBUD Café des Artistes

Jl Bisma 9x **Tel** *(0361) 972 706* **Map** *C3*

This pretty, Belgian-owned restaurant is tucked away off the main road. The extensive menu offers a selection of international dishes, including Belgian specialities, Italian pasta dishes and a few Indonesian and Thai dishes. Belgian beers are also available. Tables are on an open pavilion spilling out onto a garden terrace.

UBUD Dirty Duck (Bebek Bengil)

Padang Tegal **Tel** *(0361) 975 489* **Map** *C3*

An Ubud institution, this sprawling open-air garden restaurant and bar is surrounded by ricefields with numerous cosy and intimate spots for dining and drinking. It promotes popular local dishes and European-style home cooking. There is an extensive menu, including imported steaks and old-fashioned apple crumble.

UBUD Tut Mak

Jl Dewi Sita **Tel** *(0361) 975 754* **Map** *C3*

This friendly, café-style restaurant was one of the first places in Ubud to serve gourmet coffee. It serves hearty breakfasts and is renowned for its omelettes. It also offers a wide variety of sandwiches, burgers, dips, snacks and full meals, including Indonesian specialities. Children's menu available.

UBUD Batan Waru

Jl Dewi Sita **Tel** *(0361) 977 528* **Map** *C3*

This colonial-style hangout offers a fine selection of authentic Indonesian dishes, plus international cuisine and wholesome breakfasts. The cooking features premium and organic ingredients, and freshly made sauces. Desserts include the "Klappertart" – Dutch Colonial bread pudding with young coconut, raisins and vanilla rum cream.

UBUD Casa Luna

Jl Raya Ubud **Tel** *(0361) 973 283* **Map** *C3*

Owned by Janet De Neefe, famous for her Balinese cooking classes and organizer of the annual Ubud Writers' & Readers' Festival, this restaurant is renowned for Sunday brunch, breakfast and cakes. Look out for vegetarian spring rolls, smoked marlin salad, spiced coconut fish and delectable offerings from the Honeymoon Bakery.

UBUD Indus

Jl Raya Sanggingan **Tel** *(0361) 977 684* **Map** *C3*

With views of the Campuan River Valley and Mount Agung, Indus presents semi-open-air dining and alfresco terraces on two levels. The menu offers healthy Asian cuisine, with dishes such as Chinese spring rolls, Indonesian *nasi campur*, Balinese smoked duck, vegetarian Indian curry, booster juices and delicious home-baked desserts.

UBUD Terrazo

Jl Suweta **Tel** *(0361) 978 941* **Map** *C3*

The atmosphere is casual and hip at this popular hangout. Signature dishes include double-baked goat's cheese soufflé and braised Moroccan lamb shank with tomato and lentils served over couscous pilaf or mash. There are also stone-baked gourmet pizzas, soups and salads. The chocolate *dégustation* plate is pure seduction.

UBUD Lamak

Monkey Forest Road, Ubud **Tel** *(0361) 974 668* **Map** *C3*

Flamboyant designer Made Wijaya has created a vibrant dining space – slightly whimsical, but blended with tradition and wit. Dining is alfresco or within chic, air-conditioned comfort. Dishes are based on recipes from the south of France and Asia, and include curried yogurt-coated smoked butterfish and Pacific *ketu* salmon caviar.

EAST BALI

AMED Restaurant Gede

Lipah Beach **Tel** *(0363) 23 517* **Map** *F2*

Surrounded by flowers on the hill overlooking Lipah beach, this rustic little café-style restaurant boasts a large menu dominated by fresh seafood, plus jaffles, sandwiches, omelettes and some Chinese and Indonesian dishes. Favourites include prawn salad served in a pineapple boat, chicken mandarin, spare ribs, and green papaya curry.

CANDI DASA The Watergarden Café

Jl Raya Candi Dasa **Tel** *(0363) 41 540*

Map F3

Great value European and Asian cuisine – salads, seafood, sandwiches and burgers – is served semi-alfresco beside a cool watergarden. Favourites include Thai fish cakes, antipasto platter, Mexican wraps, fish and chips, Indian chicken korma and beef fillet. Vegetarians are well-catered for with spring rolls, guacamole, tempura and samosas.

GUNUNG BATUR Lakeview

Lakeview Hotel, Kintamani **Tel** *(0366) 51 394*

Map D2

This hotel restaurant is perched on the ridge with awesome views of the puffing volcano, Gunung Batur, and its crater lake. A narrow terrace offers alfresco dining in the crisp mountain air. A popular stop-off for large tour groups, it serves banana fritters for breakfast and a traditional Indonesian buffet from 11am daily. Evening à la carte menu.

MANGGIS The Restaurant at Alila Manggis

Alila Manggis, Buitan **Tel** *(0363) 41 363*

Map E3

A cool and breezy thatched pavilion in the coconut-grove garden of Alila Manggis is the venue for freshly-picked produce from the resort's organic garden. Choose between vegetarian dishes, a five-course tasting menu, and an à la carte range of international and local cuisine including delicious fresh fish.

PADANG BAI Puri Rai Restaurant & Bar

Jl Silayukti **Tel** *(0363) 41 396*

Map E3

One of numerous restaurants lining the beach and overlooking the harbour, this one is attached to a hotel and renowned as being the best on the strip. Typical beach and backpackers' fare includes Western and Indonesian classics, fish and chips, fresh seafood and vegetarian options. The innovative drinks list includes arak coffee.

TULAMBEN Tunkung at Mimpi Resort

Mimpi Resort, Tulamben **Tel** *(0366) 21 642*

Map F2

One of only a few restaurants in the area, this one is located at an up-market resort. An open-air bamboo pavilion nestles beneath shady trees beside the swimming pool, with lovely views of the ocean and the black, volcanic beach of Tulamben Bay. Enjoy the laid-back ambience and a menu of high quality International and Indonesian cuisine.

NORTH AND WEST BALI

BLIMBING Star Fruit Café (Café Blimbing)

Banjar Suradadi

Map B3

Located high above the road on the slopes of Gunung Batukau, Star Fruit Café has a magnificent, panoramic view of some of the island's most spectacular rice terraces, surrounded by coffee and clove plantations. The charming and simple open-air café serves high quality Indonesian and Western food, salads, snacks and fresh fruit juices.

LOVINA Khi Khi

Jl Raya Singaraja, Kalibukbuk, **Tel** *(0362) 41 548*

Map B1

An old favourite, this long-established, large seafood restaurant is very popular with the locals. It serves Indonesian and Japanese cuisine, including sushi, *mie goreng, nasi goreng*, grilled fresh fish, prawns and calamari, and a variety of Chinese specialities including sweet and sour fish, sweet chilli dishes and plenty more.

LOVINA Sea Breeze

Jl Bina Ria **Tel** *(0362) 41 138*

Map B1

As the name implies, this is right on the beach, with uninterrupted views of the pretty black-sand bay. The menu features tempting Indonesian and Western café-style food: superb breakfasts, sandwiches and snacks, healthy salads, the freshest seafood and delicious desserts. It's also a great spot for enjoying an ice-cold Bintang beer at sunset.

LOVINA Saraswati Restaurant at Puri Bagus Hotel

Puri Bagus Hotel, Lovina **Tel** *(0362) 21 430*

Map B1

This elegant restaurant is in an open-air thatched pavilion beside the hotel pool, overlooking the lovely gardens. There are authentic Balinese and Indonesian dishes such as *gado gado, nasi goreng, bebek betutu* (roasted duck), *pepes ikan* (spiced fish in banana leaf parcels), plus grilled fresh fish and Asian-influenced Western dishes.

LOVINA The Restaurant at Damai Villas

Damai Villas, Jl Damai, Kayu Putih **Tel** *(0362) 41 008*

Map B1

Rated one of the top restaurants in South East Asia, Damai Villas nestles on the side of a mountain with boundless views extending across the ocean. The five-course set dinner menu changes daily and showcases Balinese desserts. Lunchtime and à la carte innovations include cold Bloody Mary soup served with a tomato sorbet.

MUNDUK Ngiring Ngewedang Restaurant

Munduk Village, North Bali **Tel** *(8123) 807 010*

Map B2

Enchanting, family-run, open-air restaurant and coffee house perched way up above the road with spectacular views as far as the northwest coast and volcanoes of East Java. Robusta and Arabica coffee beans from the neighbouring forests are processed and sold here. Worth a visit for the best fried noodles and banana fritters on the island.

Key to Price Guide *see p184* **Key to Symbols** *see back cover flap*

PEMUTERAN Warung Sehat at Puri Ganesha

Puri Ganesha Villas, Pantai Pemuteran, Gerokgak **Tel** *(0362) 94 766*

Owner Diana Von Cranach creates healthy gourmet food, including Balinese dishes inspired by her mother-in-law's recipes. Every day the blackboard displays an ever-changing menu which makes use of organic produce, home-grown vegetables, the freshest fish and no red meat. There is also a "living food" menu of vegetarian and vegan raw foods.

LOMBOK

GILI ISLES Tir Na Nog

Mainstrip, Gili Trawangan **Tel** *(0370) 639 463*

This lively Irish restaurant and bar beside the beach serves enormous portions of fish and chips and Irish stew, in addition to sandwiches, seafood barbeques, loaded nachos, Indonesian dishes and puddings such as apple crumble and banoffi pie. Also provided are personal DVD pavilions with individual TVs and a choice of 550 movies.

GILI ISLES The Beach House

Main strip, Gili Trawangan **Tel** *(0370) 642 352*

Providing a popular and lively venue for nightly seafood and steak barbeques, the open-sided Beach House offers soups, pasta, fresh antipasto platter, chicken liver pâté with gherkins and croutons, *nasi goreng*, chargrilled sirloin with gravy and mash, Vietnamese calamari salad with beansprouts, papaya and prawn salad and much more.

GILI ISLES Waves Restaurant at Hotel Vila Ombak

Hotel Vila Ombak, Gili Trawangan **Tel** *(0370) 642 336*

Gili Trawangan's most upmarket hotel is home to this classy two-storey restaurant with cosy corners and a beach terrace. Serving international, Asian and fusion cuisine, fresh seafood, salads, wood-fired pizzas and burgers, it also showcases local arts and crafts. Enjoy a balmy evening dining alfresco at a table on the beach or beside the pool.

KUTA Empat Ikan at Novotel

Novotel Coralia Lombok, Mandalika, Kuta **Tel** *(0370) 653 333*

The exotic Novotel Coralia hosts the romantic-looking Empat Ikan restaurant, with its tapering thatched roof and Sumbanese statues beside the white sandy beach of Putri Nyale. The French cordon bleu cuisine here includes succulent fresh lobster, beautifully prepared fish dishes and Australian beef fillet with wild mushrooms.

MANGSIT Puri Mas Restaurant

Puri Mas Boutique Hotel, Pantai Mangsit, Senggigi **Tel** *(0370) 693 831*

Beside Mangsit Beach and with views across the Lombok Strait to Gunung Agung in Bali, this romantic boutique hotel restaurant specializes in fresh seafood, such as the exquisitely presented seafood platter, laden with grilled lobster, prawns, snapper and squid. Delicious desserts include good old-fashioned apple crumble.

SENGGIGI Lotus Bayview

Jl Raya Senggigi **Tel** *(0370) 693 758*

Come to enjoy the sunset at Lotus Bayview, a charming beachside restaurant hidden behind the old art market in the town centre. It features lotus flower tile-topped tables and an Italian menu that also includes international dishes such as cheese samosas, salads, pasta, shrimp cocktails, excellent fresh fish and wood-fired pizzas.

SENGGIGI Papaya

Jl Raya Senggigi **Tel** *(0370) 693 616*

Located in the heart of Senggigi, set back from the main street, this funky restaurant is characterized by natural wood and tribal art. Papaya specializes in seafood, plus Chinese, Indonesian and Western cuisine, and you get the choice of ordering small, medium or large portions, with dishes designed for sharing. Regular live music is scheduled.

SENGGIGI Asmara

Jl Raya Senggigi **Tel** *(0370) 693 619*

Asmara is a German-owned, large and airy two-storey, thatched restaurant, renowned for being the best in town. It specializes in fresh seafood, and also serves high quality steaks, pasta, European dishes and traditional dishes from Lombok. Vegetarians are well catered for. There is also a billiard table, a library, and a children's pool and play area.

SENGGIGI Taman Restaurant

Jl Raya Senggigi **Tel** *(0370) 693 842*

This breezy, crescent-shaped, two-storey restaurant is surrounded by flowering shrubs and greenery in the centre of town. There are fresh sandwiches, burgers and fresh seafood as well as innovative pasta dishes, generous salads, imported Australian steaks and Indian curries. It also has Senggigi's only rotisserie, offering hot roasted chicken.

TANJUNG Lumbung at The Lombok Oberoi

The Oberoi Lombok, Medana Beach, Tanjung **Tel** *(0370) 638 444*

The best restaurant in Lombok is set within the coconut-grove garden of the beautiful Oberoi Hotel. Dining takes place alfresco or in romantic gazebos overlooking reflective ponds. The fine selection of international dishes and seafood includes goat's cheese and artichoke soufflé, king prawn salad and luscious desserts.

SHOPPING IN BALI AND LOMBOK

Visitors unused to bargaining may find shopping in Bali and Lombok a frustrating experience, but the temptations can be quite irresistible – in fact, many people travel to the islands just to buy goods for export. Many things easily available in Bali are fashionable elsewhere, and purchasing these direct at the source can be very rewarding. There are many products with "designer" labels on sale. Some are copies, hard to distinguish from

Bamboo and timber table lamp

the real thing. Others are genuine, produced under licence in Indonesia. Almost everything produced in Bali and Lombok is available in the busier shopping areas of Kuta, Sanur and Ubud. In general, the better presented the shop, the more one pays for the items on offer. Shops selling similar goods, for example basketware, fabrics, furniture, jewellery and paintings, will quite often be grouped together, which is useful for comparing prices.

Kuta Square – a popular shopping destination for visitors

SHOPPING HOURS

Shopping hours vary from area to area, but most shops are open from around 10am until at least 6pm (10pm in Kuta). Markets generally start very early and close before the shops – the stalls usually begin to pack up around 3pm. Shopping in Bali and Lombok can be tiring – it is best to avoid the heat in the middle of the day.

HOW TO PAY

Many shops catering to tourists price their goods in US dollars, but rupiah will be accepted. Major international credit cards, such as American Express, Visa and MasterCard, can be used in most upscale shops and major department stores. Some shops will add a surcharge (usually 3–5 per cent) for credit card payments. Cash is preferred in smaller shops.

BARGAINING

Except in more expensive shops, where prices are clearly marked, bargaining is the normal practice. Begin by asking the shopkeeper for his price, then make an initial offer, usually a third to two-thirds of the asking price, before then moving towards a sensible compromise.

HAWKERS

The hawkers on the streets can be aggressive and aggravating. Many of the goods they sell are of poor quality, and not always cheap. Unless you are interested, avoid eye contact and ignore them completely. In some areas of Bali hawkers are now required to wear coloured shirts with serial numbers. If they are causing trouble, take down their number and report them to the police. Just telling them you will do this is often enough to send them away.

Street hawkers selling goods to a tourist

Entrance to Matahari, the biggest chain store in Bali

DEPARTMENT STORES AND SHOPPING CENTRES

Department stores and shopping centres are air-conditioned and comfortable, and sell both local and imported goods at excellent prices. Shoes, cosmetics and clothes are popular buys. The biggest chain is **Matahari**, with three stores located in Denpasar and Kuta. **Ramayana** is around the corner from Matahari in Denpasar, and has a variety of speciality shops. **Mal Bali Galeria** at Simpang Siur in Kuta has two bookshops, numerous clothing and music shops, and a large duty-free shop. Bali's three major shopping centres are: Kuta Square, with sports shops and designer boutiques; Discovery Mall in front of Discovery Kartika Plaza in Kuta; and Kuta Galleria, with many restaurants and surf shops.

Bamboo and cane products on display at Pasar Ubud

MARKETS

Markets are crowded and sometimes airless, but it is worth searching in them for local handicrafts. **Kumbasari Market** in Denpasar is a dense warren of small shops selling goods sourced from around Indonesia. **Pasar Ubud** in Ubud *(see p89)* sells traditional fabrics, clothes, homewares and all manner of bric-à-brac. **Sukawati Art Market** in Gianyar is loud and claustrophobic, but an excellent source of locally produced crafts. In Lombok, the **Sweta Market**, located at the busy bus station on the eastern side of Sweta *(see p154)* is packed with colourful stalls selling all kinds of handicrafts made in Lombok, including *ikat* and *songket* fabrics, baskets and pottery.

SUPERMARKETS

The biggest supermarket on the islands is **Makro** between Benoa and Kuta. Besides local products, it also sells a full range of Western food. **Bintang** in Seminyak has fresh produce and a large range of local and imported food. In Lombok, **Pacific Supermarket** in Mataram has a wide-ranging stock. Bintang is the major supermarket in Ubud and **Hardy's** is the biggest and best in Sanur.

DELIS AND BAKERIES

For visitors in need of a change from local cuisine, there are a number of excellent delis. The following patisseries are recommended for their excellent breads, cakes and deli items: **Bali Deli** in Seminyak and **Roti Segar** in Kerobokan; **Le Bake, Bali Bakery** and **Dijon Deli** in Kuta; **The Pantry** in Sanur; and **Casa Luna** and **Kakiang Bakery** in Ubud.

TEXTILES

There are numerous tailors in Bali, and many visitors rush to have clothes custom-made. For textiles, the main centre is **Jalan Sulawesi** in Denpasar *(see p60)*. Here you will find everything from traditional fabrics to saris, silks, cottons, velvet, lace, wools and rayon in every colour. For fine silks, lace and linens, **Duta Silk**, located beside Matahari in Denpasar, though small, is very popular. **Klungkung** textile market is the best place for traditional textiles. **Threads of Life** in Ubud supports a weaving cooperative.

CLOTHES

Boutiques in Kuta Square and along the main road in Legian and Seminyak are among the best places for women's fashion. Recommended shops are **Paul Ropp** and **Body & Soul** in Kuta and Seminyak, and **Mama and Leon** in Renon. Also worth visiting are the boutiques in the Sheraton Nusa Indah in Nusa Dua and the Novotel in Tanjung Benoa. Balinese garments such as finely embroidered *kebaya* and silk sarongs can be found at **Wira's** in Kuta.

CHILDREN'S WEAR

Children's wear in department stores is often very good value. **Kuta Kidz** sells printed lycra outfits, surf

Threads of Life, which supports sustainable textile art

styles, swimwear, accessories, jewellery, shoes, bags and bedding; **Rascals** has a good range of colourful kids' clothing and batiks. **Kiki's Closet** features trendy Bali-style clothing.

Teenage girls will love the casual and surf clothes at **Surfer Girl**, Kuta, while teenage boys can get authentic surf labels at **Billabong** and **Rip Curl**, also in Kuta.

Casual wear and surfing gear for sale in a shop in Kuta

JEWELLERY

Silver jewellery comes mainly from the village of Celuk *(see p82)*, in Central Bali. **Suarti**, which offers a large, diverse range and up-to-date styles, has outlets around the island and a large factory in Celuk. In Kuta, **Jonathan Silver** and **Yusuf Silver** offer a good selection. In Ubud, **Treasures** at Ary's Warung has a large range of designer jewellery. **Perlu** is a newer jewellery outlet in Seminyak and worth a visit.

Gold jewellery with intricate designs created from very bright, 24-carat gold is favoured by the Balinese. Gold is generally priced by weight, with a premium added if a lot of work has gone into the piece. The place to go is **Jalan Hasanudin** in Denpasar, where there are many outlets. Prices are good.

LEATHER GOODS

Handmade leather clothing and shoes are popular and inexpensive items to buy in Bali. There are many shops along **Jalan Padma** and **Jalan Werkudara** in Legian which are good places to purchase leather jackets, skirts, shoes and boots.

PUPPETS

Puppets used in *wayang kulit* (shadow puppet) performances are skilfully fashioned from leather which is painstakingly cut into intricate lacy panels.

The best place to purchase puppets is the Babakan neighbourhood near the Pasar Seni markets in Sukawati, or in art and antique shops. Try **Wayan Mardika** and **Wayan Narta** in Sukawati, where it is possible to see puppets being made. Javanese *wayang golek* puppets, which

A *wayang golek* puppet

perform in front of the screen and are used in Java to enact old folktales, are popular with visitors. **Wayan Wija** in Peliatan specializes in animal puppets.

BASKETWARE

Two main types of basketware are available: those from the Balinese village of Tenganan *(see pp110-11)*, and those from Lombok *(see p37)*. Baskets from Tenganan, made of rattan, are intricately and tightly woven. Prices can be high, and visitors should consider buying direct from the village. Rattan baskets made in Lombok are mostly cheaper. A good place to buy them is Sweta Market *(see Markets)*.

WOOD AND STONE CARVINGS

The village of Mas is the traditional centre of woodcarving in Bali and here the streets are lined with the carvers' workshops.

The greatest concentration of soft stone carving is in the village of Batubulan and the villages around Singapadu. In South Bali, the shops lining Jalan Bypass Ngurah Rai and Jalan Raya Kerobokan, as well as **Jimbaran Gallery**, are all excellent sources of stone works from all over the island.

Workshop in Seminyak selling furniture made mostly from teak

POTTERY

Lombok's pottery is still formed the traditional way and fired in pits in the earth to a strong brick-red *(see p37)*. The use of paints and various other finishes is a quite recent innovation. The **Lombok Pottery Centre** has branches in Kuta (South Bali) and in Mataram (Lombok).

In Jimbaran, South Bali, **Jenggala Keramik** makes an attractive range of stoneware and porcelain. Here, visitors can test their own skills at making and painting pots.

PAINTINGS

There are many highly gifted painters at work in Bali and the standard is high. Paintings in many styles can be bought in the small galleries lining the streets of Ubud. Paintings are also sold at the **Neka Art Museum**, **ARMA** and Pendet Museum in Nyuh Kuning village. Exhibitions at **Ganesha Gallery**, at the Four Seasons, Jimbaran, and the Alila in Kedewaten, are worth visiting. For contemporary art try **Komaneka** in Ubud or **Tony Raka** in Mas.

Balinese painting with a floral theme

FURNITURE

Indonesian teak furniture is internationally fashionable. There are not many genuine antiques. Sometimes old wood is combined with new pieces to replace those which have been lost or broken. The result can be good, but close inspection is needed. If buying new furniture ensure the wood is sustainably produced and carries a Forest Stewardship Council certificate.

Along the main road north of Seminyak is a busy furniture centre with many shops offering a full range of new and old furniture and home accessories. **Warisan** is one of the best – and most expensive. You can see a wider range at their Sempidi factory. **Lio Collection** on Jalan Raya Kerobokan offers excellent value for money. The other main area for furniture is Jalan Bypass Ngurah Rai, between Sanur and Kuta; the most popular places here are **Nostalgia** and **Victory**.

Changes in moisture, such as exposure to a drier climate or an air-conditioned room, affects wood. Newly manufactured furniture made from wood that has not been properly dried may crack later. Buy from a reputable dealer and be prepared to pay extra for a quality product that will last. Use a good shipping company, such as **MSA Cargo**, **CSA** or **PAL** to ensure furniture arrives in good condition.

DIRECTORY

DEPARTMENT STORES

Mal Bali Galeria
Jalan Bypass I Gusti
Ngurah Rai, Simpang
Dewa Ruci, Kuta.

Matahari
Jalan Dewi Sartika,
Denpasar.
Kuta Square, Kuta.

Ramayana
Mal Bali, Jalan
Diponegoro, Denpasar.
Tel (0361) 246 306.

MARKETS

Kumbasari Market
Jalan Gajah Mada,
Denpasar.

Pasar Ubud
Jalan Raya Ubud, Ubud.

Sukawati Art Market
Sukawati, Gianyar.

Sweta Market
Jalan Sandubaya,
Sweta, Lombok.

SUPERMARKETS

Bintang
Jalan Raya Seminyak,
Seminyak.
Tel (0361) 730 552.
Jalan Raya Sangginen 45,
Ubud. *Tel (0361) 972 972.*

Hardy's
Jalan Danau Tamblingan
193, Sanur.
Tel (0361) 285 807.

Makro
Jalan Bypass Ngurah Rai
222x, Sesetan, Denpasar.
Tel (0361) 723 222.

Pacific Supermarket
Jalan Langko, Mataram.
Tel (0370) 623 477.

DELIS AND BAKERIES

Bali Bakery
Jalan Iman Bonjol, Kuta.
Tel (0361) 755 149.

Bali Deli
Jalan Kunti 117x,
Seminyak.
Tel (0361) 733 555.

Casa Luna
Jalan Raya Ubud, Ubud.
Tel (0361) 977 409.

Dijon Deli
Kuta Poleng Art and
Antique Mall, Blok A1–A2,
Jalan Setiabudi, Kuta.
Tel (0361) 759 636.

Kakiang Bakery
Jalan Pengosekan,
Pengosekan.
Tel (0361) 978 984.

Le Bake
Jalan Griya Anyari, Kuta.
Tel (0361) 753 979.

The Pantry
Jalan Danau Tamblingan
75a, Sanur.
Tel (0361) 281 008.

Roti Segar
Jalan Bumbak Kerobokan.

TEXTILES

Duta Silk
Next to Matahari, Den-
pasar. *Tel (0361) 232
818.*

Jalan Sulawesi
Denpasar. Shops on street.

Klungkung Market
Main crossroads
Semarapura, Klungkung.

Threads of Life
Jalan Kajeng 24, Ubud.
Tel (0361) 972 187.

CLOTHES

Body & Soul
Kuta Square and
Jalan Legian 162, Kuta.
Tel (0361) 756 297.

Mama and Leon
Renon.
Tel (0361) 288 044.

Paul Ropp
Jalan Raya Seminyak 39,
Seminyak.
Tel (0361) 731 208.

Wira's
Jalan Raya Kuta, Kuta.
Tel (0361) 763 863.

CHILDREN'S WEAR

Billabong
Kuta Square, Kuta.
Tel (0361) 756 296.

Kiki's Closet
Jalan Raya Seminyak 57,
Seminyak.
Tel (0361) 746 4892.

Kuta Kidz
Bemo Corner, Kuta.
Tel (0361) 755 810.

Rascals
Kuta Square, Kuta.
Tel (0361) 754 253.

Rip Curl
Jalan Legian, Kuta.
Tel (0361) 757 404.

Surfer Girl
Jalan Legian, Kuta.
Tel (0361) 752 693.

JEWELLERY

Jalan Hasanudin
Denpasar. Shops on street.

Jonathan Silver
Jalan Legian 109, Kuta.
Tel (0361) 754 209.

Perlu
Jalan Laksmana, Seminyak.
Tel (0361) 780 2553.

Suarti
Jalan Raya Celuk 100X,
Celuk.
Tel (0361) 751 660.

Treasures
Ary's Warung, Ubud.
Tel (0361) 976 697.

Yusuf Silver
Jalan Legian, Kuta.
Tel (0361) 758 441.

LEATHER GOODS AND PUPPETS

Jalan Padma & Jalan Werkudara
Legian. Shops on street.

Wayan Mardika
Banjar Babakan, Sukawati.
Tel (0361) 299 646.

Wayan Narta
Jalan Padma, Sukawati.
Tel (0361) 299 080.

Wayan Wija
Banjar Kalah, Peliatan.
Tel (0361) 973 367.

WOOD AND STONE CARVINGS

Jimbaran Gallery
Jalan Bypass Ngurah Rai,
Jimbaran.
Tel (0361) 774 957.

POTTERY

Jenggala Keramik
Jalan Uluwatu II, Jimbaran.
Tel (0361) 703 310.

Lombok Pottery Centre
Jalan Kartika Plaza 8X,
Kuta.
Tel (0361) 753 184.
Jalan Sriwijaya 111A,
Mataram, Lombok.
Tel (0370) 640 351.

PAINTINGS

ARMA
Jl Pengosekan, Peliatan.
Tel (0361) 975 742.

Ganesha Gallery
Four Seasons, Sayan.
Tel (0361) 977 577.

Komaneka Gallery
Jl Monkey Forest, Ubud.
Tel (0361) 977 140.

Neka Art Museum
Jl Raya Campuhan, Ubud.
Tel (0361) 975 074.

Tony Raka Gallery
Jalan Raya Mas, Mas 88.
Tel (0361) 974 538.

FURNITURE AND SHIPPING

CSA
Jalan Ngurah Rai 109x,
Suwung Kauh, Denpasar.
Tel (0361) 720 525.

Lio Collection
Jalan Raya Kerobokan 2.
Tel (0361) 780 0942.

MSA Cargo
Jalan Hayam Wuruk 238,
Denpasar.

Nostalgia
Jalan Bypass Ngurah Rai,
Sanur. *Tel (0811) 395 082.*

PAL
Jalan Sekar Jepun 5,
Gatsu Timor, Tohpati.
Tel (0361) 466 999.

Victory
Jalan Bypass Ngurah Rai,
Sanur. *Tel (0361) 722 319.*

Warisan
Jl Kerobokan, Seminyak.
Tel (0361) 731 175.

What To Buy in Bali and Lombok

Batik shoes

Decorative art and craft products are probably the best buys in Bali and Lombok. They are sold in all the major tourist centres. More adventurous visitors may choose to buy products in the villages where they are made. Woven textiles, including *songket* and *ikat*, are produced chiefly in East Bali. Jewellery is made in Celuk, south of Ubud. Good basketware, pottery and textiles can be bought in Lombok. Surfwear and other casual clothing is widely available, particularly in the resort areas of South Bali.

Carvings
Craftsmen work with a variety of materials including paras *(a soft, volcanic stone), ceramics, wood and silver. Small figurines include Garudas and Buddhas.*

Masks
Characters from Balinese mythology are skilfully represented by woodcarvers; the masks are used in theatrical performances.

Woodcarving   Paras carving

Puppets from Bali and Java
Many attractive puppets are made or sold in Bali, including the hand-painted puppets made of tanned hide used in Balinese wayang kulit (see p31), *and these Javanese-style puppets.*

Lombok Pottery
This distinctive, brick-red or black pottery, widely available in Bali and Lombok, is exported all over the world. Most retailers will pack fragile items and arrange shipping.

Lontar Engravings
The village of Tenganan (see pp110–11) is known for these engravings on the leaves of lontar palms.

Furniture
Modern and reproduction pieces are made from teak and mahogany. Dutch colonial-style furniture is popular though there are few antiques. Not all new furniture is made with materials from sustainable harvests, but some shops use recycled timber.

Teak chair   Bamboo table   Carved wood panel

Kites
During kite season in Bali (see p41), local communities collaborate in making kites by hand. Mass-produced kites, made of bamboo and nylon, are also attractive.

Bracelets

Silver pendant

Earrings

Necklace

Jewellery
Celuk is the jewellery centre of Bali. Gold and silver pieces are designed, made and sold here and the level of craftsmanship is high. Designs are contemporary and traditional.

Ikat

Textiles
The most commonly produced cloth is endek, *for which a single* ikat *dye process is used. Ikat in earthy tones can be found in the markets. Double-ikat geringsing, made in Tenganan, is unique to Bali. Songket is embellished with gold and silver thread.*

Child's outfit

Sash

Fabrics and Custom-made Clothes
Made-to-measure clothes are very affordable – there are many tailors in Bali. Fabrics are mostly rayon but there are imported cottons. The best place to buy fabrics is Jalan Sulawesi in Denpasar.

Batik dress

Lombok Basketware
Rattan baskets can be purchased directly in the villages where they are made or at many local markets.

Luggage
Bali produces finely woven rattan bags and handmade, durable leather goods which are sold in shops and markets. The decoration is usually geometrical.

Leather bag

Woven bag

Star fruit

Nutmeg

Mango

Preserved Fruits and Nuts
Dried fruits and nuts are inexpensive and palatable local snacks that can be bought ready-packaged at supermarkets. The local markets and some warung *sell strips made up of more than one fruit such as mango, papaya and pineapple. Flavours range from sweet to spicy or tart.*

Papaya

Pineapple

Salak

ENTERTAINMENT

Entertainment for the Balinese has traditionally been associated with religious festivals and ceremonies, a major component of which is the performance of dances accompanied by music. Most traditional dances and music are associated with religious ceremonies; however, some have entered the secular arena, and are regularly staged

Carved theatrical mask

for tourists. Western-style nightlife is concentrated in the tourist areas, especially in South Bali, which is packed with discos and bars catering to all age groups, musical tastes and budgets. Seminyak's scene is more fashionable than Kuta's. Sanur is more laid-back, as is Nusa Dua, and Ubud has good live music and theatre.

INFORMATION SOURCES

Excellent entertainment listings can be found in *Hello Bali*, *The Beat* and *Bali Advertiser*. *FRV Travel* and *The Yak* magazines, and the English-language daily *Jakarta Post* provide good information, and so do the hotels and notices outside various establishments.

BUYING TICKETS

It is not difficult to find Balinese dances, as there are performances nearly every night at almost all the tourist centres. Prices start at around Rp50,000. Trips to these performances booked through agents will cost much more, although the price will usually include transport.

The best places to buy tickets for performances on the public stages are the hotel tour desks, and the tour operators and moneychangers to be found throughout Bali's tourist centres. Payment is usually made by cash in rupiah, although US dollars are also accepted.

Dancers with elaborate costumes and masks in Denpasar

TRADITIONAL DANCE

Most of the Balinese dances staged for tourists are not entirely authentic. Many offer a smorgasbord of extracts and highlights of a variety of traditional dances. Standards, however, are generally very high, and visitors are given an explanatory leaflet which usually comes in a several languages, including English, Japanese, French and German. There are no seat

reservations, so it is a good idea to turn up early.

Ubud, generally regarded as the artistic heartland of Bali, is the place to go for dance, and most visitors to Ubud spend a good part of their evenings at one of the numerous shows staged every night. One of the best venues is **Puri Saren** (*see p90*), the outer courtyard of the royal palace, creating a spectacular backdrop. The main dances performed are the *Ramayana* ballet and the *legong*; the latter is a highly stylized dance performed by two young girls. Tickets at Puri Saren can be purchased through a tour operator or at the door. Nightly performances begin at 7:30pm.

The village of Batubula (*see p82*) has several stages on which dances are performed. Daily Barong and Keris performances (*see p25*) by the celebrated Denjalan troupe are staged at 9:30am at the **Pura Puseh**. The Stage Sila Budaya at the **Stage Sila Anom Tegehe Batubulan** is an outdoor theatre that features Barong and Keris dances daily at 9:30am, and the *kecak* (*see p30*) and fire dances nightly at 6:30pm. It is generally not necessary to buy tickets in advance.

The **Taman Werdhi Budaya** (*see p61*) in Denpasar has numerous events scheduled throughout the year; its programme can be found in the *Bali Post*. There are often special events on Saturday nights. The Taman Werdhi Budaya is the main venue for the Bali Arts Festival, Bali's premier cultural event, which takes place in June and July.

Legong dancers in gold-painted *prada* costumes

A *gamelan* orchestra accompanying a dance in Ubud

TRADITIONAL MUSIC

Every traditional Balinese dance is accompanied by music, but the *gamelan* orchestra (*see pp32–3*) is now heard more widely. Many hotels engage musicians for *gamelan* performances. The music is loud, percussive and intriguing, and it is generally enjoyed by foreigners as much for its showmanship as for the music itself.

A temple is one of the best places to see a *gamelan* orchestra perform; visitors are always welcome to watch and listen. Local tourist offices, hotels and guides can provide details of places and dates.

In Ubud, performances by **Semara Ratih** in Kutuh and **Cudamani** in Pengosekan demonstrate superb musicality. The latter also provide classes for local children and visitors.

PUPPET THEATRE

The shadow puppet play, or *wayang kulit*, is prominent in Balinese life. Delicately cared for and finely gilded leather figures are one-dimensional representations of the gods and myriad characters in the ancient Hindu epics, the *Ramayana* and the *Mahabharata*. Performed behind a screen by a *dalang* or puppeteer, and illuminated by a flickering candle, the *wayang kulit* is loved by the Balinese. It is rarely staged in its entirety for tourists as these full performances regularly last for hours. Neither is it staged for tourists in traditional authentic form, as this is difficult to follow. However, the *wayang kulit* is sometimes staged at hotels with an emphasis on its dramatic

aspects. A more authentic *wayang kulit* performance can be seen at **Oka Kartini's** in Ubud on Wednesdays and Saturdays at 8pm.

Wayang kulit is performed at Balinese family and temple celebrations. Special performances by **Wayan Mardika**, **Wayan Wija** and **Nyoman Sumandhi** can be arranged.

A relatively modern innovation is *wayang listrik*, named after its use of lighting and giant shadow images.

ENTERTAINMENT FOR CHILDREN

An elaborately painted puppet

The Balinese love children and will pay them a great deal of attention. The larger holiday resorts often have very good in-house children's programmes, and some will accept children of non-guests for a fee. The **Westin Resort Nusa Dua**'s facilities (open to non-guests) are highly recommended. The **Conrad Bali**, **Nikko Bali** (*see p171*) and the **Intercontinental Resort Bali** (*see p170*) also have great kids' clubs.

Children will also love the colour and pageantry of the more dramatic Balinese dances, which are staged at most hotels in Bali.

Two of the more spectacular venues in Bali are the Budaya Cultural Theatre at **Nusa Dua Beach Hotel** (*see p171*) and the **Grand Hyatt**'s

Pasar Senggol, where for an all-in price you choose a meal from the many food stalls and enjoy the show over dinner.

Rafting, trekking and cycling tours are well supervised, safe and fun for older kids.

Camel rides beside the Nikko in Nusa Dua are also popular choices for older children. **Bali Adventure Tours** and **Sobek** are excellent operators. The former also organizes white-water rafting and mountain biking trips for kids. At **Pemuteran Stables** and **Umalas Stables**, horse-riding lessons for children and supervised riding tours are available.

A number of water and nature parks are designed for families. The most popular is the **Waterbom Park & Spa**. The park is well-managed, and safety is a major consideration. To really let the kids run off steam, visit the **Bali Treetop Adventure Park** (*see p141*), which is fun for all ages and skill levels. South of Ubud, the **Bali Bird Park** (*see pp84–5*), with over a thousand birds, and the **Bali Reptile Park** (*see p82*) are good family attractions. North of Ubud, the **Elephant Safari Park** (*see p207*) offers a wonderful day out, while south of Gianyar, the **Bali Safari & Marine Park** is home to more than 50 species of animals.

Fun for people of all ages at the Waterbom Park & Spa in Tuban

NIGHTLIFE

Bali has been a party island since the first surfers arrived in the early 1970s, and the large resorts all offer some kind of in-house entertainment. Outside of the resorts, however, organized nightlife is found only in the major tourist areas.

Each area's character is reflected in its entertainment. Some of Kuta's oldest night-clubs are still doing great business selling jam-jars full of the local *arak* (distilled palm brandy) to revellers. More sophisticated and elegant night spots have emerged to meet the demands of 5-star travellers. Nightlife is concentrated mainly in the tourist areas of Kuta, Sanur, Seminyak, Ubud and Nusa Dua. The dance bars in Seminyak start getting busy at around 11pm, while Kuta tends to start earlier. Most of the bars in Sanur and Ubud close at midnight.

In Kuta, **Kori**, **Peanuts**, **The Bounty**, **TJ's**, **Sky Garden Lounge** and **Eikon** are popular places for a drink or chat. **Maccaroni** serves sophisticated cocktails. Along Poppies Lanes I and II are bars that are simple hangouts for relaxation, offering cheap beer, videos and the like. Most are catering to budget travellers.

The **Hard Rock Hotel** has a good cocktail bar with acoustic bands, while **Hard Rock Café** offers an excellent line-up of local and foreign bands after 11pm; there is always a good crowd, and its bar upstairs is a lively meeting place. **M-Bar-Go**, **88 Club Bali**, **Apache Reggae Bar** and

The Bounty, one of the many large clubs in South Bali

Paddy's are good nightclubs in Kuta. In Tuban, **Deejay Café** is open all night.

The best pub in Sanur is **Arena**, which attracts the expat crowd. **The Jazz Bar & Grille** hosts live music nightly, and **Blue Eyes** is a dance club.

In Seminyak, along the beach from **Padma Resort** to **La Lucciola**, sunset is a great time for volleyball, snacks and cold beers. Visitors almost invariably then head back to the hotel for a shower and move on to one of Seminyak's many restaurants for dinner. The famous **Ku De Ta** is a fine-dining restaurant and party venue incorporating Kuve, a rooftop lounge with a tapas-style menu and trail-blazing cocktails. **Santa Fe** and **Jaya Pub** have a relaxed, casual atmosphere.

Bali Jo, **Mixwell** and **Facebar** are where the late night gay scene is to be found. **Double**

Six is a well-known dance club, complete with a 50-m (164-ft) bungy jump. Much of the action in Seminyak also happens in places like **JP's**, **Mannekepis** and **Obsesion**, which are good for live and DJ music. **SOS Lounge** at Anantara Resort hosts international guest DJs and singers.

There are no real late-night haunts in Ubud apart from **Ozigo**, a dance club with live bands and DJ music. **Jazz Café** has live music from Tuesday to Saturday, while **Indus** hosts Latin music on Monday nights.

Lovina has locally run bars with passable reggae and standard cover bands. The strip leading down to the beach is the setting for the happy-hour wars – choose a bar you like the look of, sit back and enjoy a cold Bintang beer.

The **Four Seasons Resort** at Sayan, near Ubud, has a spectacularly located bar, well worth the price of a drink. For those in search of a little luxury, the **Alila** and **Amankila** at Manggis are great places to spend an evening.

Nusa Dua's resorts have cocktail bars, beach bars where the sunset can be enjoyed, and often in-house nightclubs. There are usually beach parties at full moon – late at night, and tending to trance dance music best suited to the young.

Peanuts, one of Kuta's most popular bars

DIRECTORY

TRADITIONAL DANCE

Pura Puseh
Jl Raya, Batubulan, Gianyar.
Tel (0361) 298 038.

Puri Anom Tegehe Batubulan
Jl Raya Batubulan, Gianyar.
Tel (0361) 298 505/092.

Puri Saren
Jalan Raya Ubud, Ubud.
Tel (0361) 975 057.

Taman Werdhi Budaya
Jl Nusa Indah, Denpasar.
Tel (0361) 222 776.

TRADITIONAL MUSIC

Cudamani
Jl Raya Pengosekan, Ubud.
Tel (0361) 977 067.
www.cudamani.org

Semara Ratih
Banjar Kutuh, Ubud.
Tel (0361) 973 277.

PUPPET THEATRE

Nyoman Sumandhi
Jalan Katrangan Lane 5B/6, Denpasar.
Tel (0361) 742 3981.

Oka Kartini's
Jalan Raya Ubud, Ubud.
Tel (0361) 975 193.
www.okakartini.com

Wayan Mardika
Banjar Babakan, Sukawati.
Tel (0361) 299 646.

Wayan Wija
Banjar Kalah, Peliatan.
Tel (0361) 973 367.

ENTERTAINMENT FOR CHILDREN

Bali Adventure Tours
Adventure House, Jl Bypass Ngurah Rai, Pessanggaran.
Tel (0361) 721 480.
www.baliadventuretours.com

Bali Bird Park
Jalan Serma Cok Ngurah Gambir, Singapadu, Batubulan, Gianyar.
Tel (0361) 299 352.

Bali Reptile Park
Jalan Serma Cok Ngurah Gambir, Singapadu, Batubulan, Gianyar.
Tel (0361) 299 344.

Bali Safari & Marine Park
Jl Bypass Prof Dr Ida Bagus Mantra, Km 19,8, Gianyar.
Tel (0361) 950 000.
www.balisafari
marinepark.com

Bali Treetop Adventure Park
Kebun Raya Botanical Gardens, Jl Raya, Bedugul.
Tel 081 338 306 898.
www.balitreetop.com

Conrad Bali
Jalan Pratama Raya 168.
Tel (0361) 778 788.

Elephant Safari Park
Taro. **www**.baliadventure
tours.com

Grand Hyatt
Nusa Dua.
Tel (0361) 771 234.

Pemuteran Stables
Jalan Singaraja, Gilimanuk.
Tel & Fax (0362) 92 339.

Sobek
Jalan Tirta Ening 9, Sanur.
Tel (0361) 287 059.
www.balisobek.com

Umalas Stables
Banjar Umalas, Kerobokan.
Tel (0361) 731 402.

Waterbom Park & Spa
Jalan Kartika Plaza, Tuban.
Tel (0361) 755 676.

Westin Resort Nusa Dua
Nusa Dua, Bali.
Tel (0361) 771 906.
www.westin.com/bali

NIGHTLIFE

Alila
Manggis. **www**.alilahotels.com/manggis

Amankila
Manggis, near Candi Dasa.
Tel (0363) 41 333.

Apache Reggae Bar
Jalan Legian 146, Kuta.
Tel (0361) 761 213.

Arena
Jalan Bypass, Sanur.
Tel (0361) 287 255.

Bali Jo
Dhyana Pura Street Arcade 8, Jl Abimanyu, Seminyak.
Tel (0361) 730 931.

Blue Eyes
Jalan Bypass Ngurah Rai 888, Sanur.
Tel (0361) 780 7478.

The Bounty
Jalan Legian, Kuta.
Tel (0361) 754 040.

Deejay Café
Jalan Kartika Plaza, Tuban.
Tel (0361) 753 188.

Double Six
Jl Double Six, Seminyak.
Tel (0361) 731 266.

88 Club Bali
Jalan Pantai Kuta, Kuta.
Tel (0361) 767 540.

Eikon
Jalan Legian 178, Kuta.
Tel (0361) 750 701.

Facebar
Dhyana Pura Street Arcade 9, Jl Abimanyu, Seminyak.
Tel (08179) 701 883.

Four Seasons Resort
Sayan, Ubud.
Tel (0361) 977 577.

Hard Rock Hotel and Café
Jalan Pantai, Kuta.
Tel (0361) 755 661.

Indus
Jl Raya Sanggingan, Ubud.
Tel (0361) 977 684.

Jaya Pub
Jalan Raya Seminyak, Seminyak.
Tel (0361) 730 973.

The Jazz Bar and Grille
Jl Bypass Ngurah Rai 15–16, Sanur. *Tel (0361) 285 892.*

Jazz Café
Jl Sukma 2, Tebesaya, Ubud. *Tel (0361) 976 594.*

JP's
Jl Abimanyu 6, Seminyak.
Tel (0361) 731 622.

Kori
Poppies Lane II, Kuta.
Tel (0361) 758 605.

Ku De Ta
Jalan Kayu Aya 9, Seminyak.
Tel (0361) 736 969.

La Lucciola
Jalan Kayu Aya, Kayu Aya Beach, Seminyak.
Tel (0361) 261 047.

Maccaroni
Jalan Legian 52, Kuta.
Tel (0361) 751 631.

Mannekepis
Jalan Raya Seminyak 2, Seminyak.
Tel (0361) 847 5784.

M-Bar-Go
Jalan Legian, Kuta.
Tel (0361) 756 280.

Mixwell
Dhyana Pura Street Arcade 6, Jl Abimanyu, Seminyak.
Tel (0361) 736 864.

Obsesion
Jalan Dhyana Pura, Seminyak.
Tel (0361) 730 269.

Ozigo
Jl Sanggingan, Ubud.
Tel (0361) 974 728.

Paddy's
Jalan Legian 166, Kuta.
Tel (0361) 758 555.

Padma Resort
Jalan Padma 1, Legian.
Tel (0361) 752 111.

Peanuts
Jalan Raya Kuta, Kuta.
Tel (0361) 752 364.

Santa Fe
Jl Dhyana Pura, Seminyak.
Tel (0361) 731 147.

Sky Garden Lounge
Jalan Legian, Kuta.
Tel (0361) 755 423.

SOS Lounge & Bar
Anantara Resort, Jl Abimanyu, Seminyak.
Tel (0361) 737 773.

TJ's
Poppies Lane I, Kuta.
Tel (0361) 751 093.

OUTDOOR ACTIVITIES

The range and quality of outdoor activities available in Bali and Lombok are exceptional; they are among the best in the world. In addition to the established favourites, such as surfing, fishing, sailing, snorkelling, trekking and diving, there are "adrenalin" sports such as bungy-jumping, skydiving, paragliding, kayaking and ocean and white-water rafting. The energetic visitor can ride surfboards on the waves, horses along the beach, elephants in the jungle and

Windsurfing, a popular water sport in Bali

motorbikes into the unknown. Reptiles and birds are there to be observed; there are dolphin cruises, cycling trips into the hills and adventure tours off the beaten track. Tennis and golf are both available in luxurious, 5-star surroundings in Bali's Nusa Dua resort area. In this respect as in others, Lombok is much less developed and more informal than Bali. Its main outdoor attractions are surfing, snorkelling and trekking.

Surfboards available for rent on the beach at Legian

SURFING

Bali is a very popular centre for surfing, offering almost perfect year-round conditions for both beginners and more experienced veterans. Boards and gear can be bought or rented at most beaches. Well-managed surf schools in Sanur and Kuta, such as the popular **Rip Curl School of Surf**, charge by the day or by the hour for private instruction. Also recommended is **Bali Learn to Surf** at the Hard Rock Hotel. The liveliest scenes are around Kuta. For more on the best surfing sites see pp208–209.

DIVING AND SNORKELLING

Organized tours with experienced guides are a good way to explore the waters off Bali and Lombok. Besides day trips, there are live-aboard trips that include diving off nearby islands, such as Komodo and Sumbawa, are popular. A valid licence

must be produced for dive trips; PADI (Professional Association of Diving Instructors) certification is generally recognized. Most dive operations are professionally run. Good rental equipment is available. **Bali Marine Sports, Dream Divers, Geko Dive, Reef Seen Aquatic, Aquamarine Diving Centre** and the 5-star **Reefseekers Dive Centre** offer a range of trips. For more detailed information on diving sites, see pp210–11.

WINDSURFING AND WATER-SKIING

Sanur is the place in Bali to go for windsurfing; the lagoon (see pp64–5) offers good protection from the ocean swells. Here, as elsewhere in Bali and Lombok, most beach-front hotels will have boards for rent.

The facilities of the **Blue Oasis Beach Club** in Sanur are the best on the island. In addition to windsurfing, it also offers water-skiing. Trick skis and wakeboards are available for rent. All staff are professional and qualified.

A number of windsurfing courses, conducted by Asian windsurfing champions, are available for all ability levels. Courses last 4–6 hours.

FISHING

Several tour operators such as **Bali Fishing** and **Moggy Offshore Cruising Catamaran** specialize in deep-sea fishing trips; they have offices in the

Kuta-Legian area (see pp68–9), in the east around Padang Bai and Candi Dasa (see p108) and in the north at Singaraja (see p146). There are boats from Padang Bai, Candi Dasa, Amed, Tulamben, Singaraja and Sanur, but most leave from Benoa Harbour (see p72), and trips usually start early and last all day.

Some companies offer yachts and fishing boats with guides for game fishing charters; the aim is to catch tuna, mai-mai, mackerel and marlin. Cod, snapper and coral trout can be found on reef-fishing trips.

Depending on your budget, you can choose to go fishing in an outrigger, a small boat or a state-of-the-art Black Watch fishing vessel with experienced crew, full insurance and all electronics and safety gear. Extended charters to the waters off Lombok and islands further east can be arranged.

Outriggers offering game fishing trips off Lombok

Benoa Harbour, the best-equipped marina in the area

CRUISES

There is a range of sailing and yachting options off Bali and Lombok. Cruise options include day trips to offshore islands and remote reefs, or sunset dinners aboard a modern cruise liner, a traditional Bugis schooner or a yacht.

Scheduled sailing cruises ranging from 3 to 14 days depart from Benoa Harbour, the main port of call, and here it is also easy to book daily cruises. Major sailing and yachting companies use this as a home base; it is an interesting place for the boat-lover to explore and a well-stocked bar overlooks the pontoons. From Benoa, it is possible to sail by tall ship to the west coast of Lombok to explore the Gili Isles (see p156) and the waters off Senggigi (see p156), or charter a luxury yacht for a once-in-a-lifetime wedding cruise. Most people, however, prefer to spend a day sailing to the islands of Nusa Lembongan or Nusa Penida (see p75).

Quicksilver Cruises organizes day trips to Nusa Penida on its 37-metre (122-ft) catamaran. It also offers a dinner cruise as well as a voyage in a purpose-built submarine, and fun banana boat rides. **Bali Hai Cruises** offers sailing trips to Nusa Lembongan aboard luxury catamarans fully equipped for snorkelling. On the islands, a full holiday experience is provided, with beach clubs, restaurants, pools and diving and snorkelling equipment (the latter at extra cost). They also have a sailing boat that goes to Lembongan. **Bounty Cruises** has dinner sunset cruises around Nusa Dua, as well as journeys to Lembongan. On most cruises, children under 14 receive a 50 per cent discount.

If you prefer to be in charge of your own craft, dinghy rentals are available from Sanur, Nusa Dua and Jimbaran. Alternatively, charter a yacht or schooner with 2–16 cabins, an experienced crew and a tour guide.

WHITE-WATER RAFTING, OCEAN RAFTING AND KAYAKING

There is a number of white-water rafting companies offering trips through rapids ranging over Grades 2–4 (from fairly easy to rigorous). Safety standards are generally high, and the environmental impact of these river activities is kept to a minimum.

Sobek, established in 1989 as the first adventure tour company of its kind, is still one of the best. It offers world-class guides and Grade 3 rapids. The Ayung River, northwest of Ubud (see pp96–7), and the Unda River, north of Klungkung (see p105), are the most popular starting points. Trips organized by Ayung River Rafting last from 3 to 4 hours. The Telaga Waja River in East Bali near Muncan and Sidemen (see p105) is also becoming popular. When planning, allow for transfer time from and back to your hotel. **Bali Adventure Tours'** package includes changing rooms, hot showers, towels and food and drinks. Their trip takes you along 8 km (5 miles) of white water against a backdrop of unspoiled rainforest, towering gorges and terraced rice paddies. It includes Grade 2 and 3 rapids.

Always take a change of clothes, a hat and plenty of sun-screen. The price for a rafting trip should include hotel transfers, full instruction, qualified guides, lunch and insurance.

River kayaking, also offered by Ayung River Rafting, is an exciting development. Hurtling through the rapids in a two-person inflatable kayak is a much more intense experience than rafting.

Lake kayaking, a more relaxed option, is offered by Sobek at Lake Tamblingan (see pp140–41).

White-water rafting on the Ayung River

A ride on a banana boat in South Bali

SWIMMING

Beaches in Bali and Lombok can be superb for swimming, with secluded bays and crystal-clear seas. However, it is important to take note of any warnings posted regarding bad rips and strong currents as the waters, especially along the south coasts, can be very dangerous. A safer option for swimming is the hotel pool.

Many of the major international hotels and luxury resorts located in Nusa Dua in Bali (see p73) and Senggigi in Lombok (see p156) have good swimming facilities.

Club Med in Nusa Dua offers an all-day guest ticket (valid until 5pm) which includes access to the pool plus a range of other sports activities. It also includes an Asian and Western lunch buffet with unlimited wine, beer and soft drinks.

Kuta's **Waterbom Park & Spa** is home to 16 state-of-the-art water slides.

GOLF AND TENNIS

There are five spectacular golf courses in Bali, all open to non-members for a fee, where you can play against a backdrop of ocean views or mountain scenery. Nusa Dua is home to the 18-hole **Bali Golf and Country Club**, while close by, on the Bukit Peninsula, is the **New Kuta Golf Club**, with ocean views. In Sanur is a 9-hole course at the Grand Bali Beach Hotel. Near the shores of Lake Bratan, high in the hills near Bedugul (see p141), is **Bali Handara Kosaido Country Club**, an award-winning 18-hole golf-resort. The most dramatic golf course in Bali is the 18-hole **Nirwana Bali Golf Club** near Tanah Lot in Tabanan.

Most of the larger hotels provide excellent tennis facilities with floodlit courts, expert coaching, playing partners and racket rental.

Wreathed hornbill

ECO-TOURS

Eco-tourism has caught on in Bali and Lombok, and a number of operators are now starting to cater to visitors who prefer ecologically based holidays and activities.

Perhaps the most innovative eco-tours in Bali are led by **JED** (Jaringian Ekowisata Desa or Village Eco Tourism Network). Their packages include a trek to a local village, where a traditional lunch is prepared by, and shared with, the local people. Profits from the tours benefit the whole village.

Dolphin-watching has become popular for a day out, and involves four-hour trips into the waters off South Bali. **Bali Hai Cruises** provides early morning high-speed cruises along the Nusa Dua and Uluwatu coastline, while **Ena Dive Centre** offers dolphin-watching tours and water sports.

Off the shores of Lovina in the north of Bali (see p147), small, traditional fishing boats, known as outriggers, are used for dolphin-watching. As dolphins are wild animals, the certainty of actually seeing one on a trip can never be guaranteed.

Bird-watching is a little more predictable. The **Bali Bird Park** (see pp84–5), near Singapadu, gives an excellent view of bird life in Bali and elsewhere in the tropics. The **Bali Reptile Park** (see p82) is just next to the Bali Bird Park.

A boat trip at Lake Bratan near the Bali Handara Kosaido Country Club

For visitors looking for birds in the wild, bird-watching trips can be arranged to the **Taman Nasional Bali Barat** *(see pp136–7)*. Guided tours to other parts of Bali and Lombok are available by prior arrangement. Morning bird walks around Ubud can be arranged with **Bali Bird Walks**. Bird-watching and trekking around Lake Tamblinga *(see pp140–41)* and the adjacent high forest can be arranged through **Puri Lumbung**.

For a totally different perspective on Bali, try **Treetop Adventure Centre**, where you can walk through the treetops of Eka Karya Botanical Gardens (wearing a safety harness). There are 65 challenges here at all skill levels.

Bottlenose dolphins frolicking in the waters off South Bali

WALKING, TREKKING AND CAMPING

Sightseeing on foot reveals the unspoilt Bali and Lombok. Trips range from full- and half-day visits to overnight treks to the top of Gunung Rinjani in Lombok *(see pp158–9)*.

Keep Walking Tours offers paddy field and temple treks, and **Herb Walks in Bali** will take you for a leisurely stroll through the hills of Ubud to discover how the Balinese use plants for healing.

Guides are important in remote areas; but well-worn hill paths such as those around Manggis *(see p108)* and north of Tenganan in East Bali *(see p109)*, Ubud *(see pp94–5)*, and the Ayung River Gorge *(see pp96–7)* are safe for the unaccompanied.

Traditional villages such as the Bali Aga villages of Tenganan *(see pp110–11)*, and Trunyan on the shores

Exploring rural Bali on foot, one of the most rewarding ways

of Lake Batur *(see p121)*, can also be interesting.

Try camping in North Bali at Air Sanih *(see p147)* or the national parks, such as Taman Nasional Bali Barat or Gunung Rinjani *(see pp136–7 and 158–9)*.

MOUNTAIN TREKKING

Lovers of mountains, and particularly of volcanoes, can undertake treks on Bali's Gunung Agung *(see p114)* and Gunung Batur *(see pp120–21)*, as well as on Lombok's Gunung Rinjani *(see pp158–9)*. During the wet season from October to April, mountains can be very dangerous places and not suitable for climbing. All trips to volcanoes should be accompanied by professional guides. Reliable tour operators, such as **Mandalika Tours**, organize an interesting variety of trips including walks through the rainforest around Gunung Batukau *(see p133)*. **Bali Sunshine Tours** offers a sunrise trek over the volcanic caldera of Gunung Batur. **Puri Agung Inn Trekking** takes you to the slopes of Bali's highest mountain, Mount Agung.

CAR AND BIKE TOURS

Organized four-wheel-drive tours are ideal ways to escape from more developed areas. The price for these day-trips should cover lunch, drinks and transfers. **Waka Land Cruise** offers tours by Land Rover to the Waka Louka rainforest camp high in the mountains. If you prefer, you can rent your own car and

explore at your leisure. Check out **SDR Car Rentals** for details. Maps are easy to buy (although not always very detailed or reliable) and roads are generally good. However, driving in Indonesia can be dangerous. People and animals walk into traffic with apparent lack of concern. Always check you are fully insured when driving.

Exploring by motorcycle is enjoyable, although accidents are common. Always inspect the bike and helmet, and insist on insurance. Also watch out for potholes and gravel on the road.

Bike Adventure Tours organizes off-road trail-bike trips. This is an exciting, and safer, alternative to battling with the island's traffic. **Bali Adventure Tours** takes you by car to the rim of Mount Batur, and you can then hop on a bicycle and cycle down.

Touring by bike along the scenic route beside Lake Batur

CYCLING

Organized cycling trips on mountain bikes are great for seeing the spectacular scenery in Bali around Ubud, Gunung Batur *(see pp120–21)* and Sangeh *(see p132)*. **Bali Adventure Tours** offers mountain cycling through Bali's central highlands. Safety equipment is provided as well as drinks, picnic boxes, towels, transfers and insurance. This activity is not suitable for children under ten.

HORSE RIDING

In Bali you can ride a horse along a deserted beach, through the surf at sunset, or through lush, green paddy fields in the central hills. **Umalas Stables** and **Pemuteran Stables** offer idyllic horse-riding experiences for beginners as well as for experienced riders.

The horses come in various heights – from small ponies to large horses. You can ride with a guide leading your horse, or ride unassisted. Wear long trousers and a pair of shoes (not sandals), and bring lots of sunblock.

Ride on an elephant in the Elephant Safari Park

ELEPHANT SAFARIS

The ultimate in tropical outdoor activities has to be an elephant safari in the hills and jungles of central Bali. The **Elephant Safari Park** (see p99) is located about 20 minutes north of Ubud in beautifully landscaped gardens at Desa Taro. It offers the opportunity to hand-feed, touch, and interact with these amazing animals. The park's reception centre has a full-size mammoth skeleton, and an extensive graphic display explaining the elephant's natural history.

Elephant rides are available, and there are special rides for children. Prices usually include entrance fees, lunch, hotel transfers and insurance. Bookings can be made through their parent company **Bali Adventure Tours**.

Thrill in mid-air bungy jumping in Kuta

The Safari Park includes an impressive Elephant Museum, with over 1,000 exhibits, including fossils dating back 5 million years, prehistoric horns, century-old mammoth tusks, and bone carvings. The museum entrance displays the skeleton of a 30-year-old Sumatran Elephant.

The Indonesian elephant is an endangered species so the Safari Park also helps to raise awareness of conservation issues as well as supporting the relocation of wild elephants to special reserves where breeding programmes can take place. Proceeds from the gift shop, which offers an extensive range of elephant paintings, carvings, souvenirs and jewellery, also help to support the park's Elephant Foundation.

The Asian Elephant Art and Conservation Project was set up in 1999 and has been a spectacular success. Its aim has been to teach elephants at the Safari Park to paint artworks using their trunks. The paintings are then sold to raise more funds for elephant conservation.

BUNGY-JUMPING

Extreme sports are firmly established in Bali, with world-famous New Zealander A. J. Hackett bringing the sport of bungy-jumping into the public eye.

A J Hackett Company has a spectacular jump off an Australian-manufactured tower that is 48 m (156 ft) high. The tower is located on Legian beach close to the centre of Kuta, and jumps take place over a massive 5-metre (16-ft) deep pool. There is a lift to take you to the top of the jumping tower, which has spectacular views in all directions over Bali and the ocean.

There are jumps every afternoon and evening from noon until 8pm, and on Fridays and Saturdays you can even jump at night between 2am and 5am.

PARAGLIDING AND PARASAILING

Paragliding off the windy cliffs at Uluwatu in the south of Bali (see p76) is a spectacular experience available only in the afternoons, subject to weather conditions. All instructors are fully trained and experienced, and will accompany first-time fliers on a 20-minute tandem ride. **Exofly** is a professional paragliding club. Paragliding is not suitable for children under ten.

Tanjung Benoa (see p72) is the best place for parasailing. **Bali Hai Cruises** offers 10-minute parasailing trips.

Parasailing over the scenic Lake Bratan in the central mountains

DIRECTORY

SURFING

Bali Learn to Surf
Hard Rock Hotel, Kuta.
Tel *(0361) 761 869 ext 8116.*

Rip Curl School of Surf
Jl Arjuna, Seminyak, Kuta.
Tel *(0361) 735 858.*

DIVING AND SNORKELLING

Aquamarine Diving Centre
Jalan Raya Seminyak 2A, Seminyak.
Tel *(0361) 730 107.*
www.aquamarine.com

Bali Marine Sports
Jalan Bypass Ngurah Rai, Blanjong Sanur.
Tel *(0361) 270 386.*
www.bmsdivebali.com

Dream Divers
PT Samudra Indah Diving, Lombok.
Tel *(0370) 692 047.*
www.dreamdivers.com

Geko Dive
Jalan Silayukti, Padang Bai, Klungkung.
Tel *(0363) 41 516.*
www.gekodive.com

Reef Seen Aquatic
Jalan Raya Pemuteran, North Bali.
Tel *(0362) 92 339.*
www.reefseen.com

Reefseekers Dive Centre
Gili Air Harbour, Lombok.
Tel *(0370) 541 008.*

WINDSURFING & WATER-SKIING

Blue Oasis Beach Club
Sanur Beach Hotel, Sanur.
Tel *(0361) 288 104.*
www.blueoasisbeach
club.com

FISHING

Bali Fishing
Jalan Candi Dasa 007, Candi Dasa, Karangasem.
Tel *(0361) 774 504.*
www.bali-fishing.com

Moggy Offshore Cruising Catamaran
Bali International Marina, Jalan Pelabuhan, Benoa Harbour, Denpasar.
Tel *(0361) 723 601.*

CRUISES

Bali Hai Cruises
Benoa Harbour.
Tel *(0361) 720 831.*
www.balihaicruises.com

Bounty Cruises
Benoa Harbour.
Tel *(0361) 726 666.*
www.balibounty
cruises.com

Quicksilver Cruises
Jalan Kerta Dalem 96, Sidhakarya, Denpasar.
Tel *(0361) 727 946.*
www.quicksilver-bali.com

WHITE-WATER RAFTING, OCEAN RAFTING AND KAYAKING

Ayung River Rafting
Jalan Diponegoro T508-29, Denpasar.
Tel *(0361) 238 759.*
www.ayungriver
rafting.com

Bali Adventure Tours
Adventure House, Jl Bypass Ngurah Rai, Pesanggaran.
Tel *(0361) 721 480.*
www.baliadventure
tours.com

Sobek
Jalan Tirta Ening 9, Sanur.
Tel *(0361) 287 059.*
www.balisobek.com

SWIMMING

Club Med
Lot N-6, Nusa Dua.
Tel *(0361) 771 521.*

Waterbom Park & Spa
Jalan Kartika Plaza, Tuban.
Tel *(0361) 755 676.*
www.waterbom.com

GOLF

Bali Golf & Country Club
Nusa Dua. **Tel** *(0361) 771 791.* www.baligolfand
countryclub.com

Bali Handara Kosaido Country Club
Pancasari Village, Bedugul.
Tel *(0362) 221 182.*

New Kuta Golf Club
Pecatu, Jimbaran.
Tel *(0361) 848 1333.*
www.newkutagolf.com

Nirwana Bali Golf Club
Jalan Raya Tanah Lot, Kediri, Tabanan.
Tel *(0361) 815 970.*

ECO-TOURS

Bali Bird Park
See p201.

Bali Bird Walks
Tel *(0361) 975 009.*

Bali Hai Cruises
See Cruises.

Bali Reptile Park
See p201.

Ena Dive Centre
Jalan Tirta Ening 1, Sanur.
Tel *(0361) 288 829.*
www.enadive.co.id

JED
Jalan Pengubengan Kauh St 94, Kerobokan-Kuta.
Tel *(0361) 735 320.*
www.jed.or.id

Puri Lumbung
Munduk Village, Banjar District, Buleng Regency.
Tel *(0362) 929 101.*
www.purilumbung.com

Taman Nasional Bali Barat
Jalan Raya Gilimanuk, Cekik.
Tel *(0361) 61 060.*

Treetop Adventure Centre
See p201.

WALKING, TREKKING AND CAMPING

Bali Sunshine Tours
Jalan Pondok Indah Raya III/1, Gatsu Barat, Denpasar.
Tel *(0361) 414 057.*

Herb Walks in Bali
Jalan Jembawan, Ubud.
Tel *(0361) 975 051.*

Keep Walking Tours
Jalan Hanoman 44, Ubud.
Tel *(0361) 970 581.*

Mandalika Tours
Jalan Hang Tuah Raya 11, Sanur.
Tel *(0361) 287 129.*

Puri Agung Inn Trekking
Tirta Gangga.
Tel *(0366) 23 037.*

CAR, CYCLING AND BIKE TOURS

Bali Adventure Tours
See White-Water Rafting.

Bike Adventure Tours
Ubud. **Tel** *(0361) 978 052.*

SDR Car Rentals
Jalan Mertasari 9, Kerobokan.
Tel *(0361) 735 258.*

Waka Land Cruise
Jalan Pandang Kartika 5x, Denpasar.
Tel *(0361) 426 972.*

HORSE RIDING

Pemuteran Stables
Jalan Raya Pemuteran, North Bali.
Tel *(0362) 92 339.*

Umalas Stables
Jalan Lestari 9x, Umalas Kauh, Kuta.
Tel *(0361) 731 402.*

ELEPHANT SAFARI

Bali Adventure Tours
See White-Water Rafting.

Elephant Safari Park
Taro, Tegallalang, Gianyar.
Tel *(0361) 721 480.*

BUNGY-JUMPING

A J Hackett Company
Jalan Arjuna, Legian Beach.
Tel *(0361) 731 149.*

PARAGLIDING AND PARASAILING

Bali Hai Cruises
See Cruises.

Exofly
Tel *(081) 139 3919.*
www.exofly.com

Surfing and Beach Culture

Sea shell

Bali and, to a lesser extent, Lombok, have a vibrant beach culture. Surfers made Bali a popular destination from the 1960s onwards, and for many visitors the beaches are still the most alluring features of both islands. The whole range of beach activities is available – from surfing, windsurfing and water-skiing to less energetic options such as sunbathing and a beach massage. Conditions for beach life, including surfing, are best during the months from May to September. For those who cannot take their own gear, watersports equipment can be rented on all the more popular beaches, particularly those of South Bali.

Surfboards for rent on Kuta Beach

Canggu Beach *offers high-performance surfing popular with locals and visitors. Best before midday, the swells roll in over the rock-bottom forming peaks that split left and right.*

WINDSURFING

Bali offers good surf on many of its beaches, with Sanur and Tanjung Benoa considered the best places for windsurfing with world-class waves and fast, good-sized breaks.

The sail enables the wind to lift the board over waves, as well as move forward.

The windsurfing board, made of fibreglass, has a mast and a sail.

TOP SURFING AREAS

Surfers off Bali and Lombok make most use of the south-facing beaches. These catch the ocean swells arriving from the directions of southern Africa and western Australia. Tide charts are available at surf shops and a local magazine, *Surf Time*, provides information on surfing competitions and other events.

BALI SEA

BALI

LOMBOK

Canggu •
Kuta • • Sanur
• • Pulau Serangan
Padang-padang

• Desert Point

Maui • • Gerupuk

INDIAN OCEAN

0 kilometres   75

0 miles   50

Beach massage services *are common to most of Bali's popular beaches. Prices are generally low and negotiated by the hour.*

Parasailing, *seen here at Tanjung Benoa, has become a very popular activity. Other options include jet-skiing, banana boating, ocean rafting, fly fishing, water-skiing and windsurfing.*

Kuta Beach *is the birthplace of Bali's surfing tradition. The sand-bottom beach wave breaks with thin lips attract surfers of all levels of skill – this is a good place for beginners. Watch out for rip tides.*

Bali's wave breaks give opportunities for acrobatics.

SAFETY PRECAUTIONS

• Not all beaches have visitor or medical facilities.
• Remember that lifeguards are found only on popular beaches such as Kuta and Nusa Dua.
• Keep between the safety flags, if there are any.
• Use high-protection sunscreen.
• Wear sunglasses and a hat.
• Pack a first-aid kit.

On Sanur Beach, *sailing boats can be rented. Shown here is a hobie cat, a small catamaran notable for its speed. Boats of this kind flip easily, so caution needs to be exercised in high winds or lively seas, conditions sometimes encountered here.*

Diving in Bali and Lombok

Bali's dive sites are rich in marine life, lush coral gardens and reef walls. There are several shipwrecks. Top sites include Menjangan Island *(see p138)* for its variety of soft and hard coral; Tulamben, site of the *Liberty* wreck; and Nusa Penida and Nusa Lembongan *(see pp74–5)* for sightings of the ocean sunfish. Lombok offers good diving and snorkelling off the Gili Isles. The PADI (Professional Association of Dive Instructors) system of certification is generally recognized. The greatest concentration of diving-trip operators is in the South Bali resort areas *(see p57)*.

Butterfly fish

Diving instruction *off Pemuteran, where the current is minimal, and visibility is good. There are many such diving schools on Bali where PADI certification can be obtained.*

The reef wall is a haven for many forms of marine life.

The black spotted puffer fish *can be found in the coral gardens off Menjangan Island, where walls dominate the reef structure.*

Apparatus can be rented from the many PADI-certified organizers of diving trips.

DIVE SITE RATINGS

There is a good variety of sites around these islands. Divers should know the level of experience required in any dive site before braving the waters.

	Snorkelling	Novice Diving	Advanced Diving	Expert Diving
Candi Dasa ④	●		●	■
Gili Isles ⑧	●	■	●	■
Menjangan Island ①	●	■	●	■
Nusa Dua ⑦	●	■	●	■
Nusa Penida ⑤			●	■
Pemuteran ②	●	■	●	■
Sanur ⑥	●	■	●	■
Tulamben ③	●	■	●	■

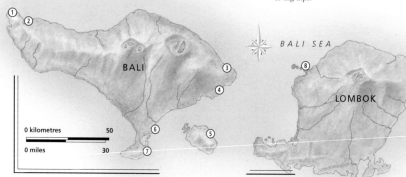

BALI SEA

BALI

LOMBOK

0 kilometres   50

0 miles   30

A diver's platform *is attached to the rear of a boat. It is often used to facilitate the training of novice divers, who can explore shallow depths of around 15 m (50 ft) at the most.*

GETTING TO THE REMOTER DIVE SITES

Most organized diving trips include transport and there are some live-aboard trips available through hotels. For those travelling independently, **Menjangan Island** *and* **Pemuteran** *are best reached by car or motorcycle.* **Tulamben** *and* **Candi Dasa** *are closer to South Bali and a bemo is an option. The* **Gili Isles**, *off Lombok, are reached most easily from* **Senggigi***.*

The coral hawkfish *can sometimes be seen in the waters off Nusa Penida, where marine life includes jacks, tuna, manta rays, reef sharks and, on rare occasions, whale sharks.*

MARINE LIFE

The rare ocean sunfish, known in Bali as the "mola mola", migrates through Balinese waters in great numbers from November to February. It is a memorable sight. The absence of a distinct tail fin gives the fish a "chopped off" appearance.

A correctly equipped diver *can explore marine and coral life in safety provided due regard is given to strong currents in some areas.*

Fish of the Gobiidae family *dwell in the crevices and branches of coral. There are many hundreds of species of these fish living in the Indo-Pacific region and they are easily observed by divers in the waters of Bali and Lombok.*

SURVIVAL
GUIDE

PRACTICAL INFORMATION 214–225

TRAVEL INFORMATION 226–229

PRACTICAL INFORMATION

Bali and Lombok, like the rest of Indonesia, have been undergoing profound and rapid changes since the end of the Suharto regime in 1998. The furious pace of development exerts continuous pressure on the social and physical landscape. Visitors should be prepared for unexpected changes in prices, regulations, facilities, phone numbers, office hours, street names, and even attitudes. Check websites *(see p217)* for the latest information.

Bali is generally more developed than Lombok. There is an international

Tourism Development Project logo

airport at Denpasar. The tourism infrastructure is most developed in the beach resorts of South Bali, in Ubud, the "cultural heartland" of Bali, and increasingly in the north and east. Tourism in Lombok is concentrated on the north-west coast around Senggigi; outside this area, tourism services are scarce. Most visitors go to Bali first, to savour its busy nightlife, absorb its charming culture and get accustomed to the warm climate. They then move on by sea or air to Lombok, to enjoy its quieter pace and unspoiled natural beauty.

WHEN TO GO

High seasons in Bali and Lombok, with attendant crowds and higher prices, are from mid-December to mid-January (Christmas–New Year period), and in July and August. The weather is most pleasant from May to September *(see pp40–43)*.

VISAS AND PASSPORTS

To enter Indonesia, your passport must be valid for at least six months after the date of departure. Airport immigration officials may ask to see a ticket out of Indonesia, or proof of funds for the duration of your stay and for onward travel, without which you may be refused entry.

Tourist visas are only valid for 30 days, and they are non-extendable. Visitors coming from 11 countries, mainly in the Far East, do not need a visa, and those from 63 other countries (including the USA, the UK, Australia and Japan) may purchase a visa on arrival. Check with your local Indonesian consulate because citizens of some countries need to apply for a visa in their home country prior to travelling.

Be sure to keep the white immigration card (attached to your passport upon entering the country), as you will need to return it to immigration officials when you leave.

DRIVING PERMITS

If you plan on driving in Indonesia, you must have an International Driving Permit, which can best be obtained in your own country if you already have a valid driver's licence.

If you plan to drive a motorcycle, ensure that your International Driving Permit includes a motorcycle permit – this is better than going through the laborious process of obtaining a motorcycle permit in Bali.

IMMUNIZATION AND HEALTH PRECAUTIONS

While there are no legal medical requirements for visitors from most countries, cholera, hepatitis A, typhoid and polio inoculations are recommended, and tetanus shots should be up to date. Dengue fever has been reported in Bali and Lombok, and malaria is a real risk in Lombok, so consult your physician about preventive and emergency medication before you begin your trip.

WHAT TO TAKE

Casual clothes in lightweight natural materials are recommended, with at least one set of smarter conservative clothes *(see pp218–19)*, should you need to visit a government office. A wide range of sports equipment

Surfboards available for rent on the beach at Sanur

for diving, golf, surfing, snorkelling and tennis can easily be rented or bought at most sports locations.

Most medicines are available in the major towns, but if you require special medication, it is wise to bring a full supply in the original packaging. You may also wish to bring some first-aid items such as antiseptic

Casual clothes are acceptable in resorts and tourist areas

◁ **Colourful outrigger boats lining Sanur beach, South Bali** cream, aspirin, sticking plaster, diarrhoea medication and insect repellent. If you wear prescription spectacles, bring a spare set.

It is possible to exchange rupiah in and outside Indonesia. Visitors are advised to purchase some rupiah before entering the country, at least enough for taxi fare from the airport and spending for the first day.

Two-pin plug of the type used in Bali and Lombok

ELECTRICITY AND ELECTRICAL APPLIANCES

Electricity generally runs at 220V–240V AC. In some rural areas, the system still runs on 110V, and some remote areas do not have electricity at all. Power supplies may be unstable.

You may need a plug adaptor with two-pronged, parallel pins. You should buy an adaptor if necessary before you travel.

CUSTOMS AND DUTY-FREE

Indonesian customs regulations allow foreign nationals to import 200 cigarettes (or 50 cigars or 100 grams of tobacco) and 1 litre of alcohol. Visitors may be asked to declare photographic and electronic equipment. There are restrictions on the import and export of products such as ivory and turtle shell, on things made from endangered species, and on the export of antiquities and certain cultural objects. Check with an Indonesian embassy or consulate for details. There are duty-free shops in Bali and in the departure area of the airport. Import or export of rupiah is limited to Rp100,000,000 per person.

Duty-free shop logo

FACILITIES FOR DISABLED TRAVELLERS

Provisions for disabled people are, as in much of Asia, inadequate. Facilities for the disabled that are available are not as sophisticated as they are in the United States and in Europe.

The terrain is often hilly, and there are stairs and steps everywhere. Wheelchair access is very rare. Pavements rarely have slopes to aid getting on or off them; most are high and uneven. Many public places are accessed by steps; very few have ramps, and wheelchair users will find public transport inaccessible.

The more up-market hotels, however, are slowly becoming increasingly aware of the needs of disabled travellers. Some of the more modern 5-star hotels have wheelchair access, and villas usually have spacious bathrooms and extensive grounds, suitable for wheelchair users.

Steps to temple hindering wheelchair access

FACILITIES FOR CHILDREN

In Bali and Lombok, children are treated with great respect and appreciation. In fact, small children are likely to be greeted (in some places) with far more enthusiasm by hotel staff than by fellow guests. Some hotels have special rates, facilities and activities for children of various ages, so ask your hotel. Because Indonesian children are constantly attended and

Child enjoying herself in a pool with a rubber ring

included in general society, no special safety measures are taken for them, and there are few facilities outside of resorts specifically for children. Parents of small children need therefore to be especially alert to environmental hazards such as stairs, unguarded edges and traffic.

Paraphernalia for infant care are available in department stores and most pharmacies.

Children will find much to keep themselves happily occupied in Bali and Lombok. There is an enormous range of activities available: water-based activities in beaches, pools and water parks; jungle rides, trekking, rafting and mountain-biking; and music and dance performances. For more information on activities suitable for children, see p199 and pp202–7.

THE LAW

For drivers, motor insurance is both obligatory and highly recommended. You must tell the police (see p220) if you intend to spend more than 24 hours in a private home. Notify your consulate if you are arrested for a crime. Inform the police and your consulate if you are in an accident where someone is injured or there is property damage; if your passport is lost or stolen; if you are the victim of any other crime; if you give birth; or if someone in your party dies.

> ### WARNING
>
> Indonesian law prescribes the death penalty for trafficking in illegal drugs, and heavy penalties for possession of weapons.

TOURIST INFORMATION AND SERVICE CENTRES

There are government-run tourist information offices (*Dinas Pariwisata Pemerintah Propinsi Daerah Tingkat I Bali*) in each regional capital; in some towns there may be several branches. These offices offer a range of brochures on major tourist sites. Some of the offices in outlying areas away from the main tourist hubs are not as efficient as you would expect, especially when dealing with telephone enquiries.

Tourist areas also have information centres. Opening hours are normally 7:30am–3pm from Mondays to Thursdays and 7:30am–2pm on Fridays. Offices in major tourist sites, such as those in Kuta, Sanur and Ubud, have longer opening hours.

Another good source of local information is the many small businesses in tourist areas, which also offer some

Locals starting their day early at the morning market at Sidemen

or all of the following services: telephone, fax, e-mail, tours, car and bicycle rentals, airline bookings, cargo packing and shipping, currency exchange, video rental, film processing, postal service and *post restante*, and sale of tickets for cultural performances.

TIME

Bali and Lombok are eight hours ahead of Greenwich Mean Time (GMT), in the same time zone as Perth; Jakarta is seven hours ahead. Because of the proximity to the equator, days and nights are of almost equal length and vary little throughout the year. Night falls very quickly, at around 6–7pm.

Open (*buka*) and closed (*tutup*) signs

OPENING HOURS

For farmers and market vendors, the day begins before dawn – in Muslim Lombok, with prayers amplified from the mosques. By two in the afternoon, it is time to rest. Banks, government offices and many small businesses mostly follow this pattern. Businesses catering to tourists keep hours more like their guests, opening mid-morning and closing mid-evening, every day except major public holidays (*see p43*).

Tourist sites, such as temples, are open during daylight hours every day. Museum hours and opening days vary. Government office hours are 8am–4pm, although some places may close earlier, especially on Fridays. Banks are generally open from 8:30am to 3pm from Mondays to Fridays, although some are open on Saturday mornings.

CHRISTIAN WORSHIP FOR VISITORS

The dominant religion in Bali is Hinduism, while that in Lombok is Islam. However, there are several Christian churches offering services in English, such as **Bali Legian Church**. Some hotels, such as the **Nusa Dua Beach Hotel** and the **Grand Bali Beach Hotel** in Sanur also offer services on demand on Sundays at which both hotel guests and non-residents are welcome.

A tourist information centre offering a variety of services

CAGAR BUDAYA NASIONAL (NATIONAL HERITAGE SITE)

Keep an eye out for small white signs with black lettering marked "Cagar Budaya Nasional"; they indicate a national heritage site. In Bali, some of these are historic sites, but many are temples. Until the 1990s, most temples were open to anyone as long as you wore a temple sash. That is no longer the case. Except for very important temples, those not designated as "Cagar Budaya Nasional" are likely to be closed, except during their anniversary festivals, when anyone who is correctly dressed and not in a taboo condition (*see p219*) may visit. Cagar Budaya Nasional sites generally have a visitors' kiosk with a guest book and donation box – a few thousand rupiah is enough – and there are sarongs and sashes which you may borrow to fulfil temple dress requirements. Some sites may charge an admission fee.

A Cagar Budaya Nasional sign marking a national heritage site

Balinese-style toilet signs in a restaurant

CONVERSION CHART

Imperial to Metric
1 inch = 2.54 centimetres
1 foot = 30 centimetres
1 yard = 0.9 metres
1 mile = 1.6 kilometres
1 ounce = 28 grams
1 pound = 454 grams

Metric to Imperial
1 centimetre = 0.4 inches
1 metre = 3 feet 3 inches
1 metre = 1.11 yards
1 kilometre = 0.6 miles
1 gram = 0.04 ounces
1 kilogram = 2.2 pounds
1 litre = 0.22 gallons
1 litre = 1.8 pints

PUBLIC TOILETS

Public toilets are scarce in Bali and Lombok, except at major tourist stops. Hygiene is poor and toilet paper rare. Toilets *(kamar kecil)* consist of a "squat" toilet and a large bin of water *(bak mandi)*, with which you flush the toilet and cleanse yourself. Toilet signs – *"wanita"* (female) or *"pria"* (male) – are often elaborate woodcarvings at tourist areas.

Fabric sold by length in a textile shop

DIRECTORY

USEFUL PHONE NUMBERS

Ngurah Rai International Airport Information
Tel (0361) 751 011.

USEFUL WEBSITES

www.baliblog.com
www.expat.or.id/info/bali.html
www.bali-paradise.com
www.bali-portal.com
www.balibagus.com
www.http://balivillas.com
www.lombok-network.com

TOURIST INFORMATION SERVICES

Badung
Badung Tourism Authority (South Bali, Java, West Nusantara and Lombok), Jalan Raya Kuta 2, Kuta.
Tel & *Fax* (0361) 756 176.
www.lbadung.go.id

Denpasar
Regional Office of Tourism, Art and Culture, Jalan Raya Puputan Niti Mandala, Denpasar.
Tel (0361) 225 649.
Fax (0361) 233 474.
www.bali.go.id/tourism

Denpasar
Bali Toursim Authority (DIPARDA), Jalan S Parman Niti Mandala, Denpasar.
Tel (0361) 222 387.
Fax (0361) 226 313.
www.balitourism authority.net

West Nusa Tenggara
Provincial Tourist Service, Jalam Langko 70, Ampenan, Lombok.
Tel (0364) 21 730.
Regional Office of Tourism, Art and Culture, West Nusa Tenggara, Jalan Singosari 2, Mataram, Lombok.
Tel (0370) 632 723 or (0370) 634 800.
Fax (0370) 637 233.

FOREIGN CONSULATES

Australia
(also represents Canada, New Zealand, and other Commonwealth countries in emergencies.)
Jalan Hayam Wuruk 886, Denpasar.
Tel (0361) 241 118.
Fax (0361) 221 195.
www.dfat.gov.au/bali

Great Britain
Jalan Tirtanadi 20, Sanur.
Tel (0361) 270 601.
Fax (0361) 287 804.

United States
Jalan Hayam Wuruk 188, Renon, Denpasar.
Tel (0361) 233 605.
Fax (0361) 222 426.

IMMIGRATION OFFICES

Airport
Kantor Imigrasi Ngurah Rai Tuban, Jalan Raya I Gusti Ngurah Rai, Tuban.
Tel (0361) 751 038.

Denpasar
Kantor Imigrasi Denpasar, Jalan Di Panjaitan, Niti Mandala, Renon.
Tel (0361) 265 030.

Lombok
Kantor Imigrasi Lombok, Jalan Udayana 2, Mataram, Lombok.
Tel (0370) 632 520.

CHRISTIAN WORSHIP

(English-language services.)

Bali Legian Church
(Interdenominational.)
Jalan Patimura.
Tel (0361) 754 255.

Christian City Church
Jalan Diponegoro 148, Denpasar.
Tel (0818) 567 802.

Eastern Orthodox Church Service
(Divine liturgy.)
Mykonos Restaurant, Jalan Laksmana 52.
Tel (0813) 3874 3782.

Sanur
(Interdenominational.)
Grand Bali Beach Hotel, Sanur (6:30pm Sun).
Tel (0361) 286 022.

St Joseph Church
(Catholic holy mass.)
Jalan Kepundung, Denpasar.
Tel (0361) 233 729.
St Franciscus Xaverius, Jalan Kartika Plaza, Kuta (6pm Sat & 8am Sun).

Etiquette

Visitors behaving with due courtesy will generally be made welcome in Bali and Lombok. Indeed the greatest pleasure of travelling in Indonesia is getting to know its very hospitable and gracious people. The Balinese are an extroverted, cheerfully self-confident people; the Sasaks of Lombok are more reserved. The inhabitants of both islands will treat tourists well, especially those with a little knowlege of local manners.

Balinese dressed up in formal attire for a ceremony

WHAT TO WEAR

The dress code at resorts is very relaxed, and shorts and bare arms and shoulders are generally accepted. Upper-end hotels may require "smart casual" dress in the evenings. However, most Indonesians may be offended by immodest attire and visitors should be sensitive to this when entering towns and villages.

Within tourist enclaves, dress is very casual. A hat or cap and comfortable shoes that slip off easily are best for touring – Indonesians generally remove their shoes before entering a home.

When visiting a government office, conservative dress is obligatory: for men, long trousers and long-sleeved shirt, shoes and socks; and for women, a knee-length dress or skirt, a blouse that covers the upper arms, and shoes. Rubber flip-flops are considered "not polite" by Indonesians in general.

Outside tourist areas, especially in Lombok, conservative dress is a sign of courtesy. Ubud's dress code is more conservative than that of beach resort areas. Some Ubud visitors adopt the sarong.

LANGUAGES

Most locals who deal with tourists speak some English, and there are guides trained in Japanese and major European languages.

Bahasa Indonesia is the national language of Indonesia. It is based largely on Malay, for centuries the trading language of the archipelago, and uses the Latin alphabet. Verbs take suffixes and prefixes, making it difficult to look up a word in a phrasebook without knowing its root form. It is easy to master a simplified form of Bahasa Indonesia that is widely used with visitors.

The Balinese and the Sasaks of Lombok maintain their indigenous languages which share a common base with Javanese, and are written with a Sanskrit-based alphabet. There is a complex system of parallel vocabularies to reflect status rankings, and mistakes can cause offence.

The lotus, a symbol of grace in Bali

Tourists at a temple wearing the required sarong and waist sash

SOCIAL BEHAVIOUR

In Bali and Lombok, certain social rules are observed, which, if followed by visitors, will open up a warm exchange; and if ignored, may cause embarrassment or even seriously offend.

Always give and receive things with the right hand, never the left. Avoid pointing with the index finger, especially at a person: this gesture may be taken as a physical challenge. If you must point at something, only use the thumb of your right hand. To be very polite, do so while cupping your right elbow. Never point to anyone or anything with your foot.

Avoid touching anyone's head, even a child's – a person's head is considered the most sacred part of the body – and do not stand next to someone who is sitting down. If you need to walk past someone who is sitting on the ground, it is best to bend from the waist and murmur something apologetic (*"Maaf"* or *"Sorry, sorry"*).

In a social situation with Indonesians where refreshments are served, wait until you are invited before you begin drinking or eating. (Indonesians wait until they are bidden several times before they do so.) Similarly, do not sit down until you are directed to a place; spatial placement holds a significant social code for Indonesians.

As far as possible, do not express anger or behave in a confrontational manner. Any extravagant displays of emotion will make you look foolish. As in much of Asia, it is considered coarse to call attention to oneself unnecessarily, especially while in public. Gracious behaviour is much appreciated by Indonesians and will get better results than an angry outburst.

Indonesians frown on public displays of private affection – these are considered embarrassing to others and therefore rude.

SOCIAL ENCOUNTERS

It is usual to greet people whether you know them or not, and to acknowledge those nearby with a smile and a nod when you arrive or leave a place. Polite conversation often takes the form of an exchange of questions. Westerners may find these intrusive – the best solution is to ask questions in return.

Visitor taking off his shoes before entering a Balinese home

PLACES OF WORSHIP

Hindus in Bali and Lombok observe strict rules in regard to their temples, which they believe must be observed by everyone, including visitors, for safeguarding the spiritual hygiene of sacred places. These rules mainly concern dress requirements and conditions of *sebel* (taboo).

A waist sash, and in many places a sarong, is the dress required of anyone entering a temple or other holy ground, whether or not there is a ceremony in progress. These may be borrowed at temples that regularly accept tourists, but it is easy to buy your own almost anywhere.

There is no moral censure attached to being in a state of *sebel*; on the contrary, to acknowledge this state is a mark of self-awareness. These rules should be observed, even if they conflict with your religious beliefs.

Conditions of *sebel* are: menstruation or having an open wound – this relates to a prohibition on shedding blood in a temple; bringing food into a temple as it clashes with offerings; being physically or mentally ill, or in a state of psychic disturbance; being in a state of bereavement (for the Balinese, up to 42 days from the date of the death of a close relative); and having given birth within the past 42 days (thought to attract attention from spirits).

There are other rules that should be observed when entering temples, especially during festivals.

Ask permission before entering a courtyard, as some gates are reserved for priests and holy objects. It is best to stay quietly at the back of a courtyard until invited. Do not walk in front of anyone who is praying, or a priest performing a ritual.

Photography is restricted in some temples, so check with temple attendants before using a camera.

Temple offerings should also not be touched, and temple walls and shrines must never be climbed. It is considered sacrilegious to do so unless one is a priest.

There are rules that should be observed when entering mosques: visitors should take off their shoes before going into a mosque, and cover up shoulders, arms and legs; women should cover their heads with a scarf, and must not enter when menstruating.

BARGAINING

Except for up-market shops and department stores, most shops do not have fixed prices and shopkeepers expect customers to bargain before

Bargaining for a straw bag at a market

finalizing a sale. Indonesians consider it fair that tourists pay higher prices than the (usually much poorer) locals. Be realistic. To get a good price, learn the prices of goods elsewhere before making a purchase, then disarm the vendor by being polite.

UNWELCOME ATTENTION

If you do not wish to buy something from a street or beach peddler, or accept the offer of "transport", it is usually enough to say quietly "No, thank you".

Avoid giving money to children. If you have a small gift for them, give it to their parents instead.

Women are regarded with respect in Indonesia, and it is rare for foreigners to be bothered by sexual harassment. However, dressing modestly helps.

Hawkers peddling their wares to a potential buyer

Personal Security and Health

Visitors to Bali and Lombok generally face no greater personal danger than sunburn and perhaps a day or two of digestive upset. It is important, however, to bear in mind that visitors are operating in a "parallel economy" which is conspicuously richer than that of the largely poor, local population; that it takes some time for visitors from temperate areas to adjust to the tropical climate; and that the sanitation and medical infrastructure is not yet as complete as in developed countries. In general, tourists should follow the same precautions they take when visiting their own local cities.

Cycling down a one-way street in Kuta, a convenient way to travel

LOOKING AFTER YOUR PROPERTY

Violent crime in Bali and Lombok is rare; but tourist areas attract delinquents, and you should treat your belongings with care.

Most hotels offer some form of lock-up storage. Use it. To leave valuables lying around unattended is to invite theft. Put valuables and important documents in your hotel safe. Lock the doors and windows of your hotel room when you are not there. Be on guard against pickpockets, who usually operate in crowded places such as public transport vehicles and airport terminals. At banks and especially at moneychangers, count cash carefully at the counter and put it immediately in your wallet before leaving the premises. Do not let the moneychanger handle the money after you have counted it.

Make a note of the serial numbers of your camera, computer or other equipment, and keep photocopies of documents such as your passport data and visa pages, credit cards and driving licence – these will come in useful in the event of a police report or an insurance claim.

PERSONAL SAFETY

Tourists in Bali and Lombok are generally treated as valued guests. If you travel alone late at night off the beaten track, you will certainly attract attention from local people, but probably in the form of concern for your welfare. Women travelling alone should exercise the usual precautions.

In places such as Kuta where there is a developed nightlife, be alert, as you would in any other country.

Some cases of armed robbery have been reported in the remoter parts of Lombok, especially around Gunung Rinjani. You should seek local advice before travelling in this area alone.

If you are pestered by someone, immediately seek out a crowded place. Be aware that if you are robbed and you call out for help, this may arouse an entire village, who could well enact "street justice" on the spot, with tragic consequences for any person accused, so be cautious about accusing anyone.

The 2002 terrorist attacks in Indonesia resulted in travel warnings from some countries. Check your government's travel advice for most recent information. It is also advised not to get involved in political demonstrations while in Bali.

A police patrol car

An ambulance

MEDICAL FACILITIES

There are 24-hour clinics in the major tourist areas for minor illnesses and first-aid. The fact that they cater mainly to tourists is reflected in their prices. The clinics include the **Bali International Medical Centre**, the **Bali Nusa Dua Emergency Clinic**, the **SOS Clinic**, the **General Hospital** and the **Ubud Clinic**. There is an extra charge for house calls.

The local equivalents to these clinics are the Puskesmas, not always staffed round the clock, and not as well equipped. Major hotels have doctors on call. There are public hospitals (*rumah sakit umum*) in every regional capital – the best is in Sanglah, Denpasar. There are a few private hospitals. Visitors are strongly advised to take out medical evacuation insurance before travelling.

COMMON AILMENTS

The most common health problems for visitors are over-exposure to sun, digestive troubles, infections arising from untreated surface cuts and motorcycle mishaps.

Use a sunblock and renew it after you swim; avoid the beach (sunny or not) between 11am and 2pm; and wear a hat.

Bottled water

Resist the temptation to make a motorcycle tour in your bathing suit – not only will you look silly (crash helmets are obligatory), your skin will be scorched by both sun and wind. Wear protective clothing, and beware of the exhaust pipe, which can give your leg a deep, slow-to-heal burn.

Tropical ulcers are infections that can arise when surface wounds such as cuts, blisters or scratched mosquito bites go unattended. Even very minor wounds should be washed with soap and water and treated with antiseptic powder or cream.

Treat stomach upsets with a mild diet (boiled rice and black tea is an effective remedy). Severe diarrhoea must be followed with a rehydration treatment; neglect

Hats and shades for sun protection

of this can be fatal for infants. The water of a young coconut is also effective. If you suspect cholera, see a doctor.

To minimize digestive problems, avoid fresh fruit that you do not peel yourself. Drink only bottled water, checking first that the seal is intact. Food at local food stalls is always fresh, but it is highly spiced and hygiene is questionable. In some tourist places, on the other hand, excessive faith in refrigeration can result in food being stored too long. In cases of serious doubt, plain rice with a little salt is generally safe.

APOTIK ANGKASA
(NO. SIA : PO. 00. 02. SIA . RA.VII. 98 2915)
JL. KEMAYORAN . BANDARA NGURAH RAI
TELP. 763102

A street sign indicating a local pharmacy (*apotik*)

PHARMACIES

Pharmacies are known as "*apotik*" and are generally abundant in towns. There is usually a qualified pharmacist on hand who speaks some English and can advise you on medications. Imported, branded medications are relatively expensive; cheaper, generic equivalents are often easily available.

SNAKES AND INSECTS

Snakes (*ular* in Bahasa Indonesia, *lelipi* in Balinese) can sometimes be seen – Bali still has field and water snakes. Most are harmless. The brilliantly coloured green tree viper has a poisonous bite which can be fatal to small children and the physically weak. It inhabits ricefields and trees. Do not go into thick vegetation without adequate protection, and make warning noises. Cobras have been sighted in gardens in South Bali.

Scorpions and centipedes sometimes lurk in quiet corners; their bite is not generally dangerous, but can be very painful. Mosquitoes are prevalent in coastal areas. Use repellents and protective

clothing, and burn mosquito coils (*obat nyamuk*), available in most hotels and restaurants.

ENVIRONMENTAL HAZARDS

The tropical sun is deceptively strong; so too are the currents of the Indian Ocean on the south coasts of Bali and Lombok. Not all beaches have lifeguards or markers. Drownings are common. Rivers which cross beaches and empty into the sea have traversed towns where sanitation can be poor or even non-existent. For this reason, and because of mudslides, avoid even upstream rivers for bathing.

Banking and Local Currency

An old *kepeng* coin from the past

Since the 1997 financial crisis, exchange rates between Indonesian and other currencies have fluctuated wildly, as have prices encountered by visitors. Modern banking and exchange facilities are available in the bigger towns and tourist centres. Major international credit cards are widely accepted. Although cash and traveller's cheques in other major currencies can be exchanged, US dollars are most widely welcomed. Many tourist services are priced in US dollars. Local currency will often be used for giving change.

An automatic teller machine or ATM at a bank

A branch of BCA, an Indonesian bank, in Kuta

BANKING SERVICES

The only foreign banks in Bali are **ABN Amro** and **Citibank**. In Bali, the main offices of the major Indonesian banks are in Denpasar, with branch offices in the regional capitals, as well as in Kuta, Sanur and Ubud, and in major hotels. Major banks in Lombok are in Mataram. Most banks in tourism areas have facilities for exchanging foreign currency. It is possible to wire money directly to a bank in Indonesia.

TRAVELLER'S CHEQUES AND MONEYCHANGERS

Traveller's cheques, not normally accepted in place of cash in Bali and Lombok, may be cashed at most banks and moneychangers, usually for less favourable rates than currency. Bring your passport for identification. Exchange facilities are widely available in Bali and in major tourist areas in Lombok. Elsewhere, visitors should carry cash. Authorized moneychangers are found in abundance in tourist centres. Elsewhere, rates may be disadvantageous. Abuses have been reported, so exercise normal precautions.

AUTOMATIC TELLER MACHINES (ATMS)

Electronic banking has grown rapidly and ATMs can be found at banks in tourist areas such as Sanur, Kuta, Denpasar and Ubud, and at the airport's international and domestic arrival halls. Major international credit cards are widely accepted.

A moneychanger in Seminyak

DIRECTORY

CREDIT CARDS	BANKING SERVICES	Bank Lippo	

CREDIT CARDS

American Express
c/o Pacto, Ltd, Grand Bali Beach Hotel, Sanur.
Tel (0361) 288 449 or *(0361) 288 511*, ext. *1111* (for traveller's cheques).

BCA Card Centre
(for BCA, Visa, Master-Card and JCB Cards)
Jalan Raya Kuta 55XX, Kuta.
Tel (0361) 759 010 or *(0361) 759 011* (for lost or stolen Visa cards).
Tel (001) 803 65 6576 (toll-free).

BANKING SERVICES

The major banks in Indonesia are used to dealing with foreign exchange, credit card advances and telegraphic transfers. Normal weekday banking hours are 8am–3pm and on Saturdays 8–11am.

ABN Amro
Jalan Teuku Umar 10, Denpasar.
Tel (0361) 244 277.

Bank Danamon
Jalan Raya Legian 87, Kuta.
Tel (0361) 761 620.

Bank Lippo
Jalan M.H. Thamrin 59, Denpasar.
Tel (0361) 436 047.

Bank Mandiri
Jalan Danau Tamblingan 59, Sanur.
Tel (0361) 283 885.

Bank Negara Indonesia
Grand Bali Beach Hotel, Sanur.
Tel (0361) 288 511.

Jalan Gajah Mada 30, Denpasar.
Tel (0361) 263 304.

Jalan Langko 64, Mataram, Lombok.
Tel (0370) 636 046.

Jalan Legian 359, Kuta.
Tel (0361) 751 914.

Jalan Raya Ubud, Ubud.
Tel (0361) 975 986.

Jalan Surapati 52A, Singaraja.
Tel (0362) 22 648.

Nusa Dua Beach Hotel, Nusa Dua.
Tel (0361) 771 906.

Citibank
Jalan Teuku Umar 208, Denpasar.
Tel (0361) 269 999.

CREDIT CARDS

Major international credit cards (such as American Express, Visa and MasterCard) are accepted at most establishments which cater for visitors in Bali and Lombok, and they are becoming more widely used by Indonesians. Cash advances on credit cards are available at most banks, but this is usually subject to a commission fee and a maximum withdrawal. Inform your bank before travelling to avoid problems using your card.

LOCAL CURRENCY

The Indonesian currency unit is the rupiah. The currency fluctuates, so be sure to check the latest rates. Carry an adequate amount of currency in small denominations: people may often not be able to give change for large notes. Some old notes are still in circulation. Be cautious when receiving soiled or damaged notes. The current import and export limit is Rp100,000,000 per person.

Banknotes
Notes come in the following denominations: Rp1,000, Rp2,000, Rp5,000, Rp10,000, Rp20,000, Rp50,000 and Rp100,000.

1,000 rupiah

2,000 rupiah

5,000 rupiah

10,000 rupiah

20,000 rupiah

50,000 rupiah

100,000 rupiah

Coins
Coins come in denominations of Rp25 and Rp50 (rare and virtually worthless), Rp100, Rp200, Rp500 and Rp1,000. Some coins from earlier designs are still in circulation.

100 rupiah   200 rupiah   500 rupiah   1,000 rupiah

Communications

Wartel Aifa logo

Communications with the rest of the world are good in the major tourism centres, and steadily improving throughout Bali and Lombok. Telkom is the government-owned telephone utility, and offers Internet service; Indosat is a major telecom service-provider. *Wartel* (from "*warung telkom*", or "telecom shops") are public telecom service outlets run by local businesses. International phone rates are among the highest in the world, especially if you make calls chargeable to your hotel bill.

Wartel office providing phone services

TELECOMMUNICATIONS IN BALI AND LOMBOK

Telephone offices known as *wartel* and branded *Wartel Telkom* or *Wartel Aifa* may be used for local and international calls, although long-distance and international calls are expensive. There are very few public telephones available on the street.

Prepaid "Hello" cards, for use on landlines, are available at many Internet shops and offer a cheaper rate if you plan on making a lot of calls. Some local phonecard services also accept "Hello" cards; check details with the vendor before buying. Prices for "Hello" cards start at around $20.

Mobile phones are common among most Indonesians. Mobile phones in Indonesia use GSM or CDMA phone systems. Check whether your mobile phone operator has an agreement with one of the GSM or CDMA operators in Indonesia, such as Simpati, or Pro-XL. If so, you will be able to buy phonecards for topping up your mobile phone. There are shops and kiosks on nearly every street selling these, and they offer good value for money as well as convenience. The card may cover a limited area, all of Indonesia or international coverage, so check the details before buying.

If you do not own a mobile phone, or if you forget to bring one with you, another option is to rent one for the duration of your stay. This can easily be done in Bali, where some companies helpfully arrange to deliver the phone to, and collect it from, your hotel. Visit www.balidiscovery.com/phones for more information on this service.

Fax services are available at *wartel* offices, business centres and Internet cafés. Charges are made for sending and receiving faxes, and they are based on phone rates, plus the number of pages sent. Be aware that the rates vary widely.

REACHING THE RIGHT NUMBER

Indonesian telephone numbers are composed of the country code (62), an area code, and a 5- or 6-digit number. When making an *interlokal* call to other places within Indonesia, a zero is added before the area code.

AREA CODES

South Bali
Badung regency: **361**
Central Bali
Gianyar regency: **361**
East Bali
Bangli regency: **366**
Klungkung regency: **366**
Karangasem regency: **363**
North Bali
Buleleng regency: **362**
West Bali
Tabanan regency: **361**
Jembrana regency: **365**
Lombok: 370

POSTAL SERVICES

The Indonesian post office provides all the services you would normally expect. International delivery normally takes 8–10 days. There are many informal postal-service outlets at tourist shops where you may buy stamps and post letters. The central post office is on the main road in Renon in Denpasar. Post offices in Ubud, Kuta and Singaraja have *poste restante* services. For mailing packages, it is more secure to go through an established courier service such as **DHL**, **FedEx** or **UPS**.

Telephone at a *wartel* office for placing international calls

COURIER

Major international courier services have offices in Bali and Lombok. Most are based in Denpasar, although FedEx, DHL and **Elteha** have branches in Ubud. You may have to take your package to one of their offices. Elteha also delivers packages within Indonesia.

INTERNET

Indonesia has more than 50 Internet Service Providers (ISPs). Users should check with their services for international access numbers. The simplest way to access the Internet is through **Telkom**'s dial-up number, which offers free access with no registration.

Internet cafés can be found throughout Bali and Lombok. A few offer broadband connections, but most are still quite slow. Recommended Internet cafés include **Xtreme Café Bali**, **Roda Internet Café**, **Bali3000**, **Millennium Internet**, **Highway**, **Wi Fi Connection** and **Bali@Cyber Café**.

TELEVISION

Satellite television is widespread in urban Indonesia and is found in all major hotels. Indonesia has more than ten private TV channels and the government-run TVRI. Bali TV has numerous cultural programmes with lots of music and traditional dancing. All the channels are in the Indonesian languages, although they offer some American programmes and foreign films.

Hello Bali **magazine**

NEWSPAPERS AND MAGAZINES

English-language daily newspapers – primarily the American *International Herald Tribune* and the *Jakarta Post* – are available in tourist outlets and (at slightly higher prices) from many street vendors.

English-language magazines include *Hello Bali*, a free monthly magazine for tourists available at hotels and dining outlets, and the monthly *Bali and Beyond*, a tourism, art and culture magazine that covers events and happenings in Bali and Lombok. The quarterly *Yak* and *Bud* focus on the Seminyak and Ubud areas.

The free biweekly newspaper *Bali Advertiser* is aimed at the expatriate community, but has good information about restaurants, tours and activities that may be of interest to short-term visitors.

The Beat is a free entertainment and gig guide. It is published every two weeks and is widely available.

DIRECTORY

USEFUL DIALLING CODES

Local Directory Enquiries
Tel 108.

National Directory Enquiries
Tel 0809 108 108.

International Directory Enquiries
Tel 102.

Operator-assisted International Calls
Tel 101.

International Direct Dialling
Tel 001, 017 or 008.

POSTAL SERVICES AND COURIERS

DHL
Jalan Bypass Ngurah Rai, Tuban.
Tel (0361) 768 282.

Jalan Bypass Ngurah Rai 155, Sanur.
Tel (0361) 283 818.

Jalan Legian Kaja 451, Kuta.
Tel (0361) 762 139.

Jalan Raya Ubud 16, Ubud.
Tel (0361) 972 195.

Elteha
Jalan Pengosekan, Ubud.
Tel (0361) 977 773.

Elteha Lombok
Jalan Koperasi 8, Mataram, Lombok.
Tel (0370) 631 820.

FedEx
Jalan Bypass Ngurah Rai 72, Jimbaran.
Tel (0361) 701 727.

Jalan Raya Ubud 44, Ubud.
Tel (0361) 977 575.

United Parcel Service (UPS)
Jalan Bypass Ngurah Rai 2005.
Tel (0361) 764 439 or (0361) 766 676.

INTERNET

Bali 3000
Jalan Raya Ubud.
Tel (0361) 978 538.
www.bali3000.com

Bali@Cyber Café
9 Kompleks Sriwijaya, Jalan Patih Jelantik, Kuta.
Tel (0361) 761 326.

Highway
Jalan Raya Ubud.
Tel (0361) 972 107.
www.highwaybali.com

Millennium Internet
Opp. Papaya Restaurant, Senggigi, Lombok.

Roda Internet Café
Jalan Bisma 3, Ubud.
Tel (0361) 973 325.

Telkom
Free Internet access with no registration.
Tel 0809 89 999.
In dialogue box, key in username "telkomnet@instan" and password "telkom".
Tel 162 (Information).

Wi Fi Connection
Bali Deli, Jalan Kunti 117x, Seminyak.
Tel (0361) 738 686.

Xtreme Café Bali
Jalan Kerobokan 388x, Kuta.
Tel (0361) 736 833.

COMPUTER SALES & RENTAL

Adi Computer
Jalan Tukad Yeh Penet 2, Renon, Denpasar.
Tel (0361) 236 531 or (0361) 238 430.

Harry's Computer
Jalan Teuku Umar 173, Denpasar.
Tel (0361) 232 470 or (0361) 266 773.

PC Mac
Jalan Iman Bonjol 266D, Denpasar.
Tel (0361) 489 747.

Rimo Complex
Jalan Diponegoro, Denpasar.
Tel (0361) 233 206.

TRAVEL INFORMATION

Bali is one of the main gateways into Indonesia. Its international airport, Ngurah Rai Airport, serves many airlines from around the world, and its harbour is equipped with customs and immigration officers to handle international arrivals. Lombok's

Logos of
Indonesian airlines

airport handles international arrivals only from Singapore, on Silkair. It is also possible to reach Bali and Lombok from within Indonesia by bus and ferry. Transport from the airport is handled by airport taxis and hotel shuttle buses. An airport tax is levied upon departure.

Aircraft arriving at Ngurah Rai Airport in Bali

FLYING TO BALI

The Ngurah Rai International Airport in Bali is located in Tuban, south of Kuta, but the destination is referred to as Denpasar.

Major international airlines currently serving Denpasar include **Garuda Indonesia**, Indonesia's national carrier, **Air Asia Indonesia**, **Cathay Pacific**, **China Airlines**, **EVA Air**, Japan Airlines, Korean Air, **Malaysia Airlines**, **Jetstar Airways**, Qatar Airways, **Singapore Airlines**, **Thai Airways International** and Transaero.

There are frequent direct flights from Australia and some countries in East Asia, such as Singapore, Thailand and Japan.

Other carriers go no further than Jakarta, but they may make onward connections to Denpasar via Garuda Indonesia.

There are numerous flights between Jakarta and Denpasar every day. Many travellers from Europe fly to Singapore, from where there are several daily direct flights to Denpasar on Garuda and Singapore Airlines.

Carriers from Taiwan (China Airlines) and Hong Kong (Cathay Pacific Airways) stop in their own capital cities.

AIRFARES AND TAXES

Fares are highest during the high season, but this varies according to the airline. For instance, "high season" for Jetstar includes the southern hemisphere summer holidays in December.

The airport levies a nominal departure tax on domestic flights. Taxes on international flights are higher.

GETTING TO AND FROM THE AIRPORT

The Ngurah Rai Airport is about a 45-minute drive from Kuta, Nusa Dua and Sanur, and about 90 minutes from Ubud. Traffic moves well once you get outside the centres.

Transport from the airport is restricted to special airport taxis, hotel shuttle buses and private vehicles. Several car-rental companies (see p229) have facilities at the airport.

To get a taxi, go to the taxi kiosk just outside the airport building exit. Fares are posted and range from about Rp50,000 (for Kuta Beach) to about Rp195,000 (for Ubud). A levy of 30 per cent extra is placed on out-of-town services. Purchase a voucher at the kiosk, and you will be guided to your assigned taxi. This system eliminates touting and gives all drivers a fair chance to obtain fares. When you arrive at your destination, give your voucher to the driver.

An airport taxi

Fares are in rupiah. There are moneychangers just inside the exit door, and exchange rates are usually quite favourable at the airport. There are ATMs in the international and domestic terminal buildings which accept major credit cards.

For transport to the airport, there are, apart from taxis, cheap tourist shuttle buses from the most popular tourist centres (see pp228–9).

A tourist information outlet offering tickets and reservations

TRAVELLING TO ISLANDS OFF BALI

The island of Nusa Penida is not usually considered a tourist destination, except for the most rugged and intrepid travellers. It can be reached by small boats from Sanur Beach, from Kusamba Beach or Padang Bai. Nusa Lembongan, off the northwest coast of Nusa Penida, is developing as a destination for day trips and overnight trips. Companies such as **Bali Hai Cruises**, **Bounty Cruises** and **Island Explorer Cruises** offer day trips to the island. **Ombak Putih** goes to the eastern islands in a schooner.

FLYING TO LOMBOK

Bali's airport is a major terminal for Indonesian domestic flights, and it is served by a number of domestic airlines. Air travel between Bali and Lombok's airport at Mataram is handled by **Merpati Nusantara Airlines**, Air Indonesia Transport and **Lion Air**. Schedules are subject to change depending on demand, but currently there are about ten daily flights. Flight time is about 25 minutes, and there is a departure tax for each leg of the trip.

TRAVELLING TO LOMBOK BY SEA

The cheapest way to cross the Lombok Straits is by ferry, although the voyage takes nearly a whole day. Ferries travel from Padang Bai in East Bali to Pelabuhan Lembar (Lembar Harbour) in Lombok at 60- to 90-minute intervals. The crossing takes four hours (or longer, depending on conditions). Seasoned travellers get to Padang Bai well in advance in order to choose one of the newer and safer ferries. A first-class ticket buys a seat in an air-conditioned saloon; however, this is not as pleasant as being on the deck. Note that there is an extra charge for bicycles, motorcycles and

Ferries at Pelabuhan Lembar (Lembar Harbour)

cars. Tickets are purchased at the harbour.

There are alternatives to the ferry. The **BlueWater Express**, operated by BlueWater Safaris, offers daily fast boat facilities. There is also a flight to Mataram from Denpasar that will get you from door to door in less than 30 minutes. Perama Shuttle offers a bus and boat ride to Senggigi daily at 6am for about $25. The bus leaves Kuta for Padang Bai, and the passage is on Perama's own boat.

An alternative is to take their bus from either Kuta or Ubud at 9am to catch the regular ferry to Lembar.

TRAVELLING TO ISLANDS OFF LOMBOK

The most convenient way to get to the Gili Isles from Senggigi is by a shuttle boat. This can be arranged in advance from Bali. You can also charter an outrigger boat from Senggigi or Bangsal. Cruise options are also available. **Bounty Cruises** offers daily excursions to the Gili Isles.

DIRECTORY

FLYING TO BALI

Air Asia Indonesia
Tel (021) 5050 5088.
www.airasia.com

Cathay Pacific Airways
Tel (0361) 766 932.
www.cathaypacific.com

China Airlines
Tel (0361) 757 298.
www.china-airlines.com

EVA Air
Tel (0361) 751 011.
www.evaair.com

Garuda Indonesia
Garuda Call Centre.
Tel 080 418 07807.
www.garuda-indonesia.com

Jetstar Airways
Tel 001 8036 1691.
www.jetstar.com

Malaysia Airlines
Tel (0361) 757 299.
www.malaysiaairlines.com

Singapore Airlines
Tel (0361) 768 388.
www.singaporeair.com

Thai Airways International
Tel (0361) 288 141.
www.thaiair.com

FLYING TO LOMBOK

Lion Air
Tel (0361) 236 666.
www.lionair.co.id

Merpati Nusantara Airlines
Denpasar. *Tel (0361) 235 358.*
Lombok. *Tel (0370) 36 745.*
www.merpati.co.id

TRAVELLING TO THE ISLANDS

Bali Hai Cruises
Benoa Harbour, Bali.
Tel (0361) 720 331.

BlueWater Express
Serangan. *Tel (0361) 895 1082.*
www.bluewaterexpress.com

Bounty Cruises
Benoa Harbour, Bali.
Tel (0361) 726 666.
www.balibountycruises.com

Island Explorer Cruises
Suwung, Badung.
Tel (0361) 728 088.

Ombak Putih
Kuta. *Tel (0361) 766 269.*

The BlueWater Express fast boat, travelling to Lombok

Travelling by Road

The only means of land travel within Bali or Lombok is by road. Getting around Bali, especially in the south and in Ubud, is becoming increasingly hectic as cars and motorcycles become more numerous. Inexpensive public transport, such as *bemo* and buses, is available throughout Bali and Lombok. However, many people prefer to rent a car with a driver. Tourist shuttles are also good alternatives.

A road map of Bali

PUBLIC TRANSPORT

Public transport in Bali and Lombok is cheap, but not always convenient for visitors, since it becomes scarce after dark, and the routes are designed to serve the needs of the local population rather than tourists.

Bemo are minivans that drive along pre-determined routes. Small *bemo* service a town while large *bemo* travel between towns, such as from Denpasar to Ubud or Kuta. Fares are low (less than Rp5,000 within a town and less than Rp10,000 between towns), but it may take several hours to cover a distance of 15 km (10 miles), and tourists are sometimes overcharged. *Bemo* are often very crowded.

Buses, used mainly by locals, operate long-distance inter-city and inter-island routes. With fewer stops, buses generally have shorter journey times than *bemo*. Main routes are from Denpasar to Singaraja, Denpasar to Amlapura and Sweta to Labuhan Lombok. Fares (non-negotiable) are paid to

the driver or the conductor. Tickets cannot be bought in advance except for inter-island trips.

The main terminals in South Bali are around Denpasar: at Batubulan in the north; at Kereneng in central Denpasar; and at Ubung in the west.

TAXIS

In South Bali, metered taxis with air-conditioning can be flagged down or called by phone. Sometimes drivers will try to negotiate a flat fee; it is usually better to use the meter. Some drivers are reluctant to go to Ubud at night because it is hard for them to find a fare for the return trip. Usually a 20% surcharge is added to the fare.

Bahasa Indonesia and Balinese road signs

TOURIST SHUTTLES

Tourist shuttles – minivans or minibuses that travel between tourist destinations at regular intervals – are very convenient. They are popular with backpackers and a good way to meet other travellers. Several companies run services between the major tourist

destinations on a regular schedule for reasonable, posted fares (Rp40,000–200,000). It may be necessary to book in advance.

CAR AND MOTORCYCLE RENTAL

Car rental is popular in Bali and Lombok, and many international agencies are represented. Good self-drive rates can be negotiated with local agencies. As road conditions become more crowded, it is well worth paying a little extra to have the services of a driver, who will act as a guide as well.

Rental options range from the charter of a minivan to the rental of a luxury car, complete with a chauffeur and multi-lingual guide.

The major tourism centres are lined with local agencies that rent cars and motorcycles. Vehicles for rent range from a Volkswagen Safari to a BMW. The most popular are the Suzuki Jimny (ideal for two people) and the Toyota Kijang (good for up to eight people).

You may negotiate directly yourself, or ask your hotel to arrange a rental for you. Be sure to clarify whether the price includes fuel and insurance. Insurance is obligatory, and helmets are compulsory for motorcyclists. Check that the vehicle's lights, brakes, signals and horn are in good working order before you drive off.

You should obtain your International Driving Permit in your home country before your arrival in Bali or Lombok (*see p214*).

Motorcycle was once the most popular way of getting around and motorcycle hire is still widely available in tourist

A taxi

A *bemo*

A tourist shuttle

centres, but traffic conditions make biking increasingly hazardous. It is not recommended in crowded South or Central Bali or in towns.

DRIVING IN BALI AND LOMBOK

Indonesians drive on the left-hand side of the road. Traffic rules and regulations and driving conventions in practice do not always coincide: motorbikes overtake on either side; drivers pull out into traffic without looking – they expect you to avoid them. Right of way belongs to whoever is bigger or flashes his lights first. As the pavements (sidewalks) are scarce and narrow, pedestrian traffic flows onto the roads including livestock, pushcarts, religious processions and cyclists going the wrong way.

Motorcycles in Singaraja – the most popular form of transport for locals

Rice drying on the road – an obstacle to watch out for

In Lombok, traffic is much lighter, but you must watch out for pony carts.

It is the general practice to sound the horn briefly before overtaking. Traffic lights are scarce: at intersections where you are going straight ahead rather than turning, hazard lights should be used. In towns, one-way systems are increasingly common.

Parking in towns and at markets is supervised by a parking attendant who collects a small fee (generally Rp500–1,000 depending on the vehicle) and helps you get back on to the road.

Driving just after dark is generally inadvisable because of poor visibility and, in particular, the inadequate lighting on bicycles and motorcycles. Drivers should watch out for piles of black sand on the road (dumped

there for the next day's building activities). Motorcyclists in particular should avoid driving at dusk because of the number of flying insects.

Indonesians are generally glad to help anyone in trouble on the road. It is customary in such circumstances to offer some small compensation in return.

Pony carts, a hazard for drivers in rural areas

DIRECTORY

TERMINALS

Batubulan Terminal
Batubulan.
Tel (0361) 298 526.

Kereneng Terminal
Jalan Hayam Wuruk,
Denpasar.
Tel (0361) 226 906.

Mandalika Terminal
Sweta, Lombok.

Tegal Terminal
Jalan Imam Bonjol,
Denpasar.
Tel (0361) 980 899.

Ubung Terminal
Jalan Cokroaminoto,
Denpasar.
Tel (0361) 427 172.

TAXI SERVICE

Bali Taxi (Bluebird)
Tel (0361) 701 111.

Ngurah Rai Taxi
Tel (0361) 724 724.

Praja Taxi
Tel (0361) 709 566.

TOURIST SHUTTLES AND SERVICES

Danasari
Poppies Lane 1, Kuta.
Tel (0361) 755 125.

Perama
Jalan Legian 39, Kuta.
Tel (0361) 751 875.

Jalan Hanoman, Ubud.
Tel (0361) 974 722.

VEHICLE RENTAL

Avis Rent-a-Car
Danan Tam Blingan 27,
Sanur. *Tel (0361) 282 635.*
www.avis.com

Bali Limousine
Banjar Nyuh Kuning,
Dusun Mas, Gianyar.
Tel (0361) 744 7877.
www.balilimousine.com

Hertz
Grand Bali Beach Hotel,
Area Cottage 50, Sanur.
Tel (0361) 266 962.
www.hertz.com

SDR Car Rental
Jalan Mertasari 9,
Kerobokan.
Tel (0361) 735 258.

General Index

Page numbers in **bold** type refer to main entries.

A

Adat 28
Adil Artshop 86
Agung Rai 96
Agung Rai Gallery 96
Agung Rai Museum of Art (ARMA) 96, 194, 195
Air Asia Indonesia 226, 227
Air Panas Banjar 139
Air Sanih 147
Airlangga 45
Airlines **226–7**
Airports 226
AJ Hackett Company 206, 207
Alam Sari Keliki (Tegallalang) 175
Alam Kul Kul (Kuta) 171
Alang alang grass 94
Alas Kedaton 132
Albino cattle 99
Alcohol 181, 215
Alila Manggis 177, 200
Alila Ubud (Ayung River Gorge) 174
All Seasons Resort (Legian) 171
Amandari (Ayung River Gorge) 174
Amankila (Manggis) 177, 200, 201
Amanusa (Nusa Dua) 73, 171
Ambron, Emilio 105
Amed 102, **113**
Amlapura **112**
Ampenan 48, 155
Anak Wungsu, King 45, 99
Anantara (Seminyak) 173
Ancestor worship 24, 114
Ancient cults **22**
Andong 96
Andoya Resort (Nusa Dua) 173
Animism 22, 24
Anom, I B 86
Apache Reggae Club (Kuta) 200, 201
Apotik 221
Arab merchants 50, 60, 155
Archaeological Museum, Cekik 135
Archaeological Museum, Pejeng 97
Arena Club (Kuta) 200
Arja 30
ARMA *see* Agung Rai Museum of Art
Aroma's (Kuta) 184
Aromatherapy 168
Art 17, **34–5**, 91, 92–3, 96, 105, 106
Ary's Warung (Ubud) 88
Asmara Restaurant (Senggigi) 191
Aston Bali Resort & Spa (Tanjung Benoa) 173
Automatic teller machine (ATM) 222
Ayana Resort and Spa (Jimbaran) 170
Ayodya Resort Bali (Nusa Dua) 169, 171
Ayung River Gorge 10, 79, **96–7**, 203
Ayung Terrace Restaurant (Ayung River Gorge) 188

B

Badung kingdom 47, 49, 57
Bagan 154
Bagus Jati Resort 169
Baha 129
Bahasa Indonesia 50, 218
Balcony, The (Kuta) 185
Balé, The (Nusa Dua) 172
Bale agung 26
    Pura Gunung Raung 99
    Tenganan 110

Bale banjar 28
    Batu Jimbar 64
    Batubulan 82
    Teges 86
Bale dangin 29
Bale daub 29
Bale gede 29
Bale gong 26
    Pura Ulun Danu Batur 123
Bale Kambang 106–7
Bale London 112
Bale meten 29
Bale Petemu Tenganan 110
Bale piasan 27
Bale sekenam 29
Bale tajuk 77
Bali Adventure Tours 199, 201, 203, 205, 206, 207
Bali Advertiser 198, 225
Bali Aga 46, 101
    villages 55, **110–11**, 121, 139, 147
Bali Agung Village (Seminyak) 173
Bali and Lombok
    Bali and Lombok at a Glance 54–5
    Discovering Bali and Lombok 10–11
    map 12–13
Bali Arts Centre 41, 57, **61**, 198, 201
Bali Arts Festival 30, **41**, 198
Bali Bakery (Kuta) 193, 195
Bali Bird Park 54, 80, 82, **84–5**, 199, 201, 204, 207
Bali Bird Walks 205
Bali Collection Mall 73
Bali Deli 193, 195
Bali Dynasty (Tuban) 174
Bali Golf and Country Club 73, 204, 207
Bali Hai 74
Bali Hai Cruises 203, 204, 206, 207, 227
Bali Handara Kosaido Country Club (Lake Bratan) 141, 177, 204, 207
Bali Hati 169
Bali Hyatt (Sanur) **65**, 169, 173
Bali International Convention Centre 73
Bali Jo (Seminyak) 200, 201
Bali Kite Festival **41**
Bali Museum 10, 54, 57, **62–3**
Bali Padma (Legian) 169, 171, 200, 201
Bali Plus 198
Bali Post 61
Bali Reptile Park 80, **82**, 199, 201, 204, 207
Bali Safari & Marine Park 199, 201
Bali starling 54, 84, **137**
Bali Treetop Adventure Park 141, 199, 201
Balian Beach 129
Balinese calendar 38, **39**
Balinese Market (Sobrat) 93
Balinese painting **34–5**, 62–3, 93
Balinese Stone-Craftsmen Working (Madia) 35
Balinese temple architecture **26–7**
Bamboo furniture 86
Bamboo instruments 32, 33, 140
Banana boats 72, 204, 209
Bangko Bangko **163**
Bangli 47, 49, 101, **104**
Banjar (community association) 28
Banjar **139**
Banjar suka duka 28
Banjar War 139
Banks **222–3**
Banyan Tree Ungasan (Uluwatu) 174
Banyu Penaruh 39

Banyumulek 36, **154**
Banyuwedang 138
Bargaining **192**, 219
Baris gede **30**, 122
Barong **25**, 45, 82, 198
Basketware **194**, 197
    Lombok 15, **37**, 161
    Tenganan 109, 110
Basuki 108
Bat cave 108
Batan Waru (Ubud) 189
Batara Sakti Wawu Rauh 76
Bateson, Gregory 88
Batik 97
Battle of Marga **132**
Batu Bolong 156
Batuan 34, **83**
Batuan, I Dewa Nyoman 34
Batubulan **82**, 194, 198
Batur 115, 120, **122–3**
Batur Volcano Museum 121
Bau Nyale 11, 42
Beach House, The (Canggu) 184
Beach House, The (Gili Isles) 191
Beaches
    Air Sanih 147
    Balian 129
    Candi Kusuma 135
    Canggu 64
    Jimbaran 74
    Klating 129
    Kuta (Bali) 73
    Kuta (Lombok) 162
    Legian 73
    Lovina 147
    Mawun 162
    Medewi 134
    Nusa Dua 73
    Nusa Lembongan 74
    Padang Bai 108
    Pantai Gondol 138
    Pemuteran 138
    Rening 134–5
    Sanur 65, 73
    Seminyak 67
    Senggigi 156
    Tanjung Aan 162
    Tejakula 147
    Tuban 67
Beadwork 97
Beat, The 198
Bebandem 109
Bedaulu legend **87**, 110
Bedugul 126, **141**
Bedulu 79, **87**
Bedur at Ubud Hanging Gardens (Payangan) 188
Beggar's Bush (Ubud) 200, 201
Belaganjur 33
Blimbingsari 135
Belo, Jane 88
Bemo 228
Bemo Corner 67, 69
Benoa Harbour 58, **72**, 125, 202
Bertais Market *see* Sweta Market
Berutuk festival 121
Besakih Temple Complex 27, 40, 41, 47, 55, 101, **116–17**
Betara Luhur Ing Angkasa shrine 148, 149
Betara Tengah Segara 128
Bhairava Buddhism 97
Bhatari Mandul, Queen 45
Bhikku Giri Rakhita 139
Bhima statue 67

Bhima Swarga narrative, 106
Biastugal 108
Billabong 193, 195
Bima 202
Bintang Bali Resort (Kuta) 200, 201
Bintang Supermarket 193, 195
Bird market **61**
Bird-watching 204
Birds Dancing the Gambuh (Sali) 92
Blahbatuh **83**
Blayu **132**
Blega 86
Blue Eyes (Sanur) 200, 201
Blue Fin (Tuban) 188
Blue Point Bay Villas & Spa
 (Uluwatu) 174
BlueWater Express 227
Boat rental 226–7
 Benoa Harbour 72
 Jimbaran 74
 Lake Bratan 141
 Lake Buyan 141
 Pemuteran 138
 Tulamben 113
Body & Soul 193, 195
Bodyworks spa 169
Boma heads 128
Bona 86
Bone carvings 99
Bonnet, Rudolf 35, 88, 92
The Bounty (Kuta) 67, 200, 201
Bounty Cruises 227
Boutique hotels 64, 166
Boutiques 193
Brahma Vihara Ashrama 23, 139
Brahmana Siwa clan 47
Brahmans 86, 139
Bronze inscriptions 61, 104
Bualu 73
Budakling 109
Buddhism 22, **23**, 83, 87, 139
Budiana, I Ketut 93
Buffalo races 41, 134
Bugis 72, 125, 134, **135**, 144, 163
Bukit Demulih 109
Bukit Peninsula 57, 58, **74**, 75
Buleleng 47, 48, 125, 146
Bulgari Hotels & Resorts (Uluwatu) 174
Bumbu Bali (Tanjung Benoa) 188
Bungy-jumping 206
Bunutin 104
Buses 228
Busungbiu 125
Buta kala 24
Butterfly park **129**, 205, 207

C

Café Batujimbar (Sanur) 186
Café Lotus (Ubud) 88
Cafés and coffee shops **180–81**
Café des Artistes (Ubud) 189
Cakranegara 155
Camel safari 73, 199
Camping **205**
Campuhan 91, 94
Candi 99, 131
Candi Beach Cottage (Candi Dasa) 176

Candi bentar **27**
 Nusa Dua Beach Hotel 73
 Pura Luhur Uluwatu 77
 Pura Meduwe Karang 148
 Pura Sada 128
 Pura Taman Ayun 131
Candi Dasa 11, **108**
Candi Kusuma 135
Canggu **64**, 208
Cape Rening 135
Car and bike tours **205**
Car rental 205, **228**, 229
Casa Luna (Ubud) 189, 193, 195
CasCades at the Viceroy 188
Catholic cathedral, Palasari 23
Catur Muka **61**
Cavehouse 74
Caves
 Goa Gajah 87
 Goa Karangsari 75
 Goa Lawah 108
 Gondang 157
 Gunung Lesong 141
Ceiling paintings **106–7**
Cekik 135
Celuk **82**, 193
Celukang Bawang, 144
Cempaka Belimbing Guest Villas
 (Pupuan) 178
Cepuk 75
Chaplin, Charlie 61
Chedi Club (Tengkulak) 175
Children
 activities **199**
 facilities **215**
 hotels **167**, 170–79
 restaurants **181**
Children's wear **193**, 195, 197
Chinese 23, 45, 72, 144
 apothecaries 60
 merchants 50, 144, 155
Chinese New Year 42
Chinese temples
 Singaraja 144
 Tanjung Benoa 72
 Vihara Amurva Bhumi Blahbatuh 83
Christians **23**, 125, 135, 216
Cidomo 163
Circumcision rites, 23
Climate 40–43
Clothes **193**, 195, 197, 214, **218**, 219
Clove growing 140
Club Double Six 66
Club Med (Nusa Dua) 169, 204, 207
Cock-fighting 111
Cocoon Beach Club (Seminyak) 187
Coffee growing 140
Colonial rule **49–50**, 125, 146
Communications **224–5**
Community of Artists, Pengosekan **34**
Como Shambala (Ayung River Gorge)
 169, 174
Computer, rental and services 225
Conrad Bali Resort & Spa
 (Tanjung Benoa) 173, 199
Consulates 217
Conversion charts **217**
Cooking classes 83, 167
Coral reefs 19, 75, 113, 138, **156**, 162,
 210
Cosmic Circle (Batuan) 34
Cottage industry 16–17, 36
Cotton growing 75, 157
Courier services **225**
Covarrubias, Miguel 88

Coward, Noel 61
Crafts and textiles **36–7**
Credit cards 192, 222, **223**
Cremations 38, 41
Crime 220
Cruises **203**
CSA 194, 195
Cudamani 199, 201
Currency **222–3**
Customs and duty-free **215**
Cycling 140, **205**

D

Da Tonta 121
Damai Lovina Villas (Lovina) 177
Damai Villas Restaurant (Lovina) 190
Danau Segara Anak 11, 55, **158**
Death of Abhimayu 34, 44
Deblog, I Gusti Made 92
Deejay Café (Kuta) 200
Deer 137, 138
Delis and bakeries **193**, 195
Denjalan troupe 82, 198
Denpasar 10, 15, 54, 57, 58, **60–63**
Department stores **192**, 195
Desa Dunia Beda (Gili Isles) 179
Desert Point 163
Dewa Agung 47
Dewa Ratu Gede Pancering Jagat 121
Dewi Danu 141
Dewi Sri 20, **25**, 92
Dewi Ulun Danu, Ida Betari 121, 123
Dharmaswami (Gelgel), 92
Diah, Jero Dalang 146
Dijon Deli (Kuta) 193, 195
Dipanagara, Prince 48
Dirty Duck (Bebek Bengil) (Ubud)
 189
Disabled travellers **215**
Diving 167, 202, **210–11**
 Amed 113
 Candi Dasa 108
 Gili Isles 156
 Menjangan Island 138
 Nusa Lembongan 74
 Nusa Penida 75
 Padang Bai 108
 Pantai Gondol 138
 Pemuteran 138
 Sanur 65
 Senggigi 156
 Tulamben 113
Djedeng, Ketut 92
Djelantik, Gusti Bagus 112
Dokar 67
Dolphins 147, 204
Dong-son culture 97
Double *ikat* 37, 105, 110
Double Six (Seminyak) 200, 201
Dress code 218, 219
Driving, driving permits 214, 228, 229
Drops (Legian) 185
Drums
 gamelan 132
 kecimol 157
 Lombok **33**, 157
 Pejeng Moon 97
 slit-log 28
Durga 83
Duta Silk 193, 195
Dutch colonial rule 48–51
Duty-free **215**
Dwijendra 86
 see also Nirartha, Dang Hyang
Dyes 161

E

Earthquakes 101, 112, 116
Eco-tours **204–5**
Economic development 16
Egrets 97
88 Club Bali (Kuta) 200, 201
Eikon (Kuta) 200
Eka Dasa Rudra 115
Eka Karya Botanic Gardens 141
Electricity, electrical appliances **215**
Elephant Cave 87
Elephant Safari Park 10, **99**, 199, 201, 206, 207
Empat Ikan at Novotel (Kuta, Lombok) 191
Endek 37
Entertainment **198–201**
Environmental hazards **221**
Eruption of Gunung Agung (Rai) 115
Espace Spa 169
Etiquette 181, **218–19**
Expatriates 17, 50, 88, 91, 225

F

Facebar (Seminyak) 200, 201
Fast food 181
Fax services 224
Febri's (Tuban) 174
Ferry 226–7
   Benoa Harbour–Lombok 227
   Gilimanuk–Java 135
   Labuhan Lalang–Menjangan Island 138
   Lombok–Sumbawa 161
   Nusa Penida–Nusa Lembongan 75
   Padang Bai–Lombok 108, 227
Festivals and holy days **38–9**
Fighting Horses (Rundu) 34
Fire dances 198
Fishing trips **202**
   Bangko Bangko 163
   Sanur 65
   Tanjung Benoa 72
Flutes 33
Forests **18**, 133, 136, 140–41
Four Seasons Resort (Sayan, Ayung River Gorge) 169, 174, 200, 201
Four Seasons Resort (Jimbaran) 74, 168, 169, 170, 193, 194
Four-wheel-drive tours 205
FRV Travel magazine 198
Furniture 64, 67, 86, **194**, 195, 196

G

Gabeleran, I Made 83
Gado Gado (Seminyak) 66, 187
Gajah Mada 46, 87
Galungan 39, 43
Gambuh performances 83
Gamelan 26, **32–3**, 199
   Krambitan 129
   Negara 134
   Peliatan 96
   Pura Jagat Natha 146
   Pura Ulun Danu Batur 123
Ganesha Gallery 194, 195
Gangsa 32
Gardens
   Bali Hyatt Hotel 65
   Eka Karya Botanic Gardens 141
   Narmada 154
   Oberoi Hotel 67
   Pura Taman Ayun 130–31
   Pura Taman Saraswati 90

Garuda 31, 36, 57, 73, 122, 147
Garuda Vishnu Kencana 73
Gedong Kertya **146**
Gelgel 46, 101, 105, **108**
Gelgel, Ida Bagus 92
Geography 12–13, 15, 19, 54
Geringsing 37, 63, 105, 110
Gerupuk **162**
Gesing 141
Gianyar 47, 49, 79, **86**
Gili Air 156
Gili Air, Hotel (Gili Isles) 179
Gili Gede 154
Gili Isles 11, 15, 152, **156**, 210, 227
Gili Meno 156
Gili Nanggu 154
Gili Trawangan 156
Gilimanuk **135**
Giri, Sunan 47
Gitgit **147**
Glass-painting 146
Goa Gajah **87**
Goa Karangsari 75
Goa Lawah **108**
Goldsmithing 36, 37, 82
Golf 73, 141, **204**
Gondang 157
Gondol Cape 138
Gongs **32**, 33, 83
Good Karma Bungalows (Amed) 176
Grand Bali Beach Hotel (Sanur) **64**
   golf course 204
Grand Hyatt (Nusa Dua) 171, 199
Grand Mirage Resort (Tanjung Benoa) 169
Griya Santrian (Sanur) 172
Ground spirits 24
Gubug 140
Guerrilla war 51, 132
Gumung 109
Gunarsa, I Nyoman 35
Gunung Abang 115, 120, **121**
Gunung Agung 11, 55, 101, 102, 103, 113, **114**
   eruptions 51, 101, **115**, 116
Gunung Baru 158
Gunung Batukau 126, 128, **133**
Gunung Batur 11, 55, 101, 102, 115, **120–21**
Gunung Catur 141
Gunung Kawi Royal Monuments 41, 45, **99**
Gunung Lempuyang 109, **113**
Gunung Pengsong 154
Gunung Penulisan 115, 120
Gunung Puncak Manggu 141
Gunung Raung 99
Gunung Rinjani 11, 157, **158–9**, 160
Gunung Seraya 109
GWK 73

H

Hackett, A J 206
Hai Tide Huts (Nusa Lembongan) 172
Handphone hire 224, 225
Handicrafts 17, **36–7**, 83, 155
Hanoman 132
Hard Rock Hotel and Café (Kuta) 69, 171, 184, 200, 201
Hardy's Supermarket 193
Hari Raya Sumpah Pemuda 41
Hariti 87, 108
Hawkers 192
Health **214**, 220–21
   Hello Bali 198, 225

"Hello" cards 224
Hinduism **22**, 46
   Hindu-Buddhist kingdoms 45, 79
   Hindu New Year 40, 43
   Hindu temples *see Pura*
History, Bali and Lombok **45–51**
Holiday Inn Resort Lombok (Senggigi) 179
Holy days 43
Homestays **166**
Horse-drawn buggies
   cidomo 163
   dokar 67
Horse riding 199, 206
Hospital 220, 221
Hot springs *see* Springs
Hotels 64, 65, **166–79**
   boutique hotels 64, 166
   directory 170–79
   dining 180
   losmen and homestays **166**
   private villas 166, **167**
   reservations 167
   resorts **166–7**
   speciality hotels and resorts **167**
   travelling with children 167
Houses 16, **29**

I

Ibah Luxury Villas (Ubud) 94, 176
Ilda Betari Dewi Ulun Danu 121
Idiot Belog Who Became King, The (Togog) 340
Ijo Gading River 134
Ikat textiles 37, 75, 105, 110, 146
Immigration 214, 217
Immunization 214
Independence **50**, 132
Independence Day **41**, 43, 132
Independence Monuments 61, 145
Indonesian Hotel and Restaurant Association 166
Indonesian Observer 225
Indus (Ubud) 189
Industrialization 16
Inilah! 225
Inna Bali Hotel (Denpasar) **61**
Insects 18–9, 221
Intercontinental Resort Bali (Jimbaran) 169, 170, 199
International Herald Tribune 225
Internet 167, 225
Iseh **104**
Islam **23**, 43, 46, 47
Island Explorer 203
Iwo, Kebo 87

J

Jaba tengah 27
Jagaraga 48, **147**
Jakarta Post 198, 225
Jalan Bypass Ngurah Rai 59, 67
Jalan Dewi Sita, Ubud 89
Jalan Gajah Mada, Denpasar **60**
Jalan Hanoman, Ubud 89
Jalan Hasanudin, Denpasar 60, 193, 195
Jalan Legian, Kuta 67, 68
Jalan Padma, Legian 193, 195
Jalan Raya Ubud, Ubud 88, 90–91
Jalan Sulawesi, Denpasar 193, 195
Jalan Wanara Wana, Ubud **88**, 90–91
Jalan Werdukara, Legian 193, 195
Jamu 141, 168, 169
Japanese occupation 50
Jatiluwih 133

Java 45, 46, 48
Javanese lulur treatment **168**
Jayapangus, King 45
Jayaprana 22, 138
Jayaprana Ceremony (Kerip) 35
Jazz Bar and Grille (Sanur) 186
Jelantik, Gusti 48, 147
Jembrana 47, 48, 125
Jemeluk 113
Jenggala Keramik 194, 195
Jero tengah 77
Jeroan 26
Jeruk Manis waterfall 161
Jet catamarans 74
Jet-skiing 209
Jewellery 17, 37, 60, 82, 86, 147, **193**,
     195, 197
Jimbaran **74**
Jimbaran Gallery 194, 195
Jimbaran Puri Bali 170
Jimbaran Seafood Cafés (Jimbaran)
     74, 184
Jojo's Restaurant (Nusa Lembongan)
     186
Jonathan Silver 193, 195
JP's (Seminyak) 200, 201
Jukung 65, 108
Juwukmanis Temple 95

K

Kafe Wayang (Sanur) 186
Kahyangan tiga 26
Kaja-kelod 28
Kajeng Kliwon 61
Kakiang Bakery 193, 195
Kala 77
Kala Rau (Budiana) 93
Kaliasem 147
Kamasan 105
Kampung Café (Tegallalang) 98, 189
Kangkung 157
Kapal **128**
Kapitu 98
Karangasem 47, 48–9, 101, 112
Kastala 109
Kayaking **203**
Kebo Iwo 83, 87
Kebon 98
Kecak **30**, 70–71, 198,199
Kediri **129**
Kemenuh 83
Kencana Warga Mardika 155
Kenderan 98
Kepeng 45, 222
Kerip, I Nyoman 35
Keris 24, 25, 45, 82
     trance dance 82, 198
Kerobokan 67
Kerta Gosa **106–7**
Kertanegara, King 46
Ketut, Anak Agung Anglurah 112
Khaima (Seminyak) 187
Khi Khi Restaurant (Lovina) 190
Kiki's Closet 193, 195
Kintamani 11, **115**, 120
Kites 41, 68, 197
Klating Beach 129
Klenteng 83
Klungkung 75, 101, 102, **105–7**
     kingdom 47, 49, 79, 116
     market 193, 195
     puputan 49, 101, 105
Kokokan 97
Komaneka Gallery 195
Komaneka Resort (Ubud) 175

Komodo 72, 85, 202
Kopi Pot (Kuta) 184
Kori agung 26, 131
Kori Restaurant & Bar (Kuta) 185, 200
Krakas 157
Krambitan **129**
Krause, Gregor 50
Ku De Ta (Seminyak) 187
Kubu Lalang (Lovina) 177
Kulkul 27, 28
     Bali Museum 63
     Pura Kehen 104
     Pura Taman Ayun 47
Kumbasari Market 193, 195
Kuningan 39, 43
Kupu Kupu Barong (Tuban) 174
Kusamba 108
Kuta (Bali) 10, 17, 54, 57, 58, **66–9**
     beach 41, 58, 66, 68
     development 51
     nightlife 200
     Street-by-Street 68–9
     surfing 209
Kuta (Lombok) 17, 42, **152**
Kuta Art Market 69
Kuta Centre 192
Kuta Galleria 69
Kuta Kidz 193, 195
Kuta Reef 67
Kuta Square 69, 193
Kutri 83
Kuturan, Mpu 45, 72, 76, 108

L

La Lucciola Restaurant Bar Beach
     Club (Seminyak) 187, 200, 201
La Sal (Seminyak) 187
La Taverna (Sanur) 172
Labuhan Haji 147
Labuhan Lalang 138
Labuhan Lombok **160**
Lake Batur 11, 55, **120–21**, 122, 123
Lake Bratan 11, 140, **141**, 142–3, 206
Lake Buyan 11, 140, **141**
Lake goddess **123**, 141
Lake Tamblingan **140–41**
     kayaking 203
Lakeview Restaurant & Hotel
     (Gunung Batur) 177, 190
Lamak (Ubud) 189
Landscape **18–19**
Languages **218**
Law **215**, 220
Layonsari 138
Le Bake 193, 195
Le Mayeur, Adrien 64
Leather goods **193**, 195
Legend of Tenganan 110
Legian 58, **66**
Legian, The (Seminyak) 169, 173
Legian Beach Hotel 171
Legong 198
Lembar 152, **154**
Lempad, I Gusti Nyoman 34, 87, 90
     Lempad collection 96
Lempad House 89, **90**
Lesser Sunda Islands 72
Lewis, G P 50
Liberty 113, 210
Limestone temples 72
Lingsar **152**
Lio Collection 194, 195
Lipah 113
Local food 60, 86, 180, **182–3**
Lombok 11, 12, **150–63**, 227

Lombok Pottery Centre 155, 194, 195
Lontar engravings 196
Lontar palm goods 86
Lord of Kalianget 138
Losmen **164–5**, 166
Lotus Bayview (Senggigi) 191
Lotus throne *see Padmasana* shrine
Lovina 11, **147**, 200
Lovina Beach Resort 177
Loyok 161
Lulur treatment 168
Lumbung 21, 162
Lumbung Restaurant (Tanjung) 191

M

Ma Joly (Tuban) 188
Maccaroni (Legian) 200, 201
Maccaroni (Kuta) 185
Made's Warung I (Kuta) 66, 69, 185
Madia, I Nyoman 35
Magazines **225**
Magic **24**
Mahabharata 31, 44, 67, 106, 199
Majapahit **46**, 61, 79, 87, 101, 108, 128
Makam Jayaprana 22, **138**
Makro 193, 195
Mal Bali Galeria (Kuta) 192
Mama and Leon 193, 195
Mambal 132
Mandara Spas 169
Manggis 102
Manis Kuningan 43, 72, 86
Mannekepis 200, 201
Manuaba 98
Maps
     Bali, Dutch map 47
     Bali and Lombok 12–13
     Bali and Lombok at a Glance 54–5
     Bali Bird Park 84–5
     Bersakih Temple Complex 117
     Central Bali 80–81
     Denpasar 60–61
     Dive sites 210
     East Bali 102–103
     Gunung Agung 114
     Gunung Rinjani 158–9
     Indonesia and environs 13
     Kuta, Street-by-Street 68–9
     Kuta and Legian 66
     Lake Buyan 140–41
     Lake Tamblingan 140–41
     Lombok 12, 152–3
     Mataram 155
     North and West Bali 126–7
     Nusa Lembongan 75
     Nusa Penida 75
     Road map Back Endpaper
     Sanur Town and Beach 65
     Singaraja 146
     Singaraja, Street-by-Street 144–5
     South Bali 58–9
     Surfing areas 208
     Taman Nasional Bali Barat 136–7
     Taman Nasional Gunung Rinjani
          158–9
     Temples, main Balinese 27
     Tenganan 110–11
     Tenganan to Tirtagangga, walk 109
     Ubud 91
     Ubud, Street-by-Street 88–9
     Ubud, countryside walk 94–5
     Wallace's Line 19
Marga 51, **132**
Margarana Monument 132
Marine life, Gili Isles **156**

Markandya, Rsi 99, 116
Markets **193**, 195
  Bertais Market *see* Sweta Market
  Bird market 61
  Gianyar 86
  Kumbasari Market 193, 195
  Kuta Art Market 69
  Pasar Anyar 144, 145
  Pasar Badung 60
  Pasar Burung 61
  Pasar Seni Sukawati 83, 193, 195
  Pasar Ubud 89, 90, 193, 195
  Sweta Market 154, 193, 194, 195
Martha Tilaar 169
Mas 34, **86**, 97, 194
Masbagik Timur 36, 154
Masjid Agung Jamik 145
Masjid Nur 145
Mask and puppet theatre **31**
Maskerdam Building 112
Masks 31, 62, 196
Massage 168–9
Massimo's (Sanur) 186
Matahari Beach Resort and Spa
  (Pemuteran) 178
Matahari department store 67, 192, 195
Mataram 15, 152, **155**
Maui 163
Mawun beach 162
Mayadanawa, King 87
Maya Ubud (Ubud) 176
Mayura Water Palace 15, **155**
M-Bar-Go (Kuta) 200, 201
McPhee, Colin 88
Mead, Margaret 88
Mecaling, Ratu Gede 75, 90
Medewi Beach **134**
Medical facilities **220–21**
Medicinal plants 141, 168
Megawati Sukarnoputri 51
Mekepung 41, 134
Melangit River 79
Men Brayut 87
Mengwi 47, **128–31**
Menjangan Island 54, 136, **138**, 210
Menjangan Jungle & Beach Resort 178
Merajan 29
Mercure Resort (Sanur) 172
Merta, Ketut 145
Meru shrine 27
  Lake Bratan 141, 142–3
  Lake Tamblingan 141
  Pura Gunung Raung 99
  Pura Luhur Uluwatu 76
  Pura Penataran Agung 116
  Pura Rambut Siwi 134
  Pura Sada 128
  Pura Taman Ayun 130
  Pura Taman Sari 105
Métis (Kerobokan) 188
The Mezzanine (Sanur) 186
Mimpi Resort (Menjangan Island)
  138, 178
Mixwell (Seminyak) 200, 201
Mola mola 211
Moneychangers **222**
Monkey Forest Road, Ubud 88, 90–91
Monkey Forest Sanctuary **91**
Monkeys 18, 91, 132, 138, 161
Monsoons 42
Moojen, P J 62
Mosques
  Lombok 145, 150, 152
  Pengambangan 134
  Perancak 134

Mosques (cont.)
  Singaraja 145
  Tanjung Benoa 72
Motor insurance 215
Motorcycles 205
  rental 228
Mount Meru 27, 77
Mountain trekking **205**
  see also Trekking
Mozaic (Sanggingan) 189
MSA 194, 195
Munduk 125, **140**, 141
Museums and galleries
  Agung Rai Museum of Art (ARMA) 96
  Bali Museum 10, 54, 57, **62–3**
  Batur Volcano Museum 121
  Museum Daerah Semarapura
    105, 107
  Museum Le Mayeur **64**
  Museum Negeri **155**
  Museum Purbakala, Cekik 135
  Museum Purbakala, Pejeng 97
  Museum Puri Lukisan 10, 88, **92–3**
  Museum Subak 129
  Neka Art Museum 96
Musical instruments **32–3**
Muslims 23, 43, 47, 50, 144
  Bali 134, 147
  Lombok 151, 157

N

Nagasepaha 146
Nampu at Grand Hyatt Bali
  (Nusa Dua) 185
Nandini Bali Jungle Resort & Spa
  (Payangan) 175
Napoleonic Wars 48
Narmada 152, **154**
Natah 29
National parks
  Taman Nasional Bali Barat 11, 54,
    126, 135, **136–7**, 204, 205
  Taman Nasional Gunung Rinjani
    55, 153, **158–9**
Nationalism 50–51
Natura Resort & Spa (Laplapan) 175
Naughty Nuri's (Sanggingan) 188
Naughty Nuri's Warung (Kerobokan)
  187
Negara 40, 41, 125, **134–5**
Neka, Sutéja 96
Neka Art Museum **96**, 194, 195
Nero Bali's Restaurant and Bar 185
New Kuta Golf Club 204, 207
New Order 51
Newspapers and magazines **225**
Ngiring Ngewedang Restaurant
  (Munduk) 190
Ngulesir, Dewa Ketut 108
Ngurah Rai, Gusti 51, 61, 132
Ngurah Rai International Airport 226
Nieuwenkamp, W O J 50, 149
Nightlife 64, **200**
Nikko Bali Resort & Spa (Nusa Dua)
  73, 169, 171, 199
Nirartha, Dang Hyang 46–7
  Pura Luhur Uluwatu 76, 77
  Pura Peti Tenget 67
  Pura Pulaki 138
  Pura Rambut Siwi 134
  Pura Sakenan 72
  Pura Taman Pule 86
  Pura Tanah Lot 128
Nirwana Bali Golf Club 204, 207
Njana Tilem Gallery 86

Nostalgia 194, 195
Novotel Benoa Bali (Tanjung Benoa)
  72, 173, 193
Novotel Coralia Lombok (Kuta)
  162, 179
Nur Salon 169
Nusa Dua 41, 57, 58, **73**, 166, 200
Nusa Dua Beach Hotel & Spa
  (Nusa Dua) 73, 168, 169, 171, 199
Nusa Lembongan 58, 72, **74**, 210
Nusa Lembongan Resort 172
Nusa Penida 58, **75**, 210
Nutmegs at Hu'u Bar 187
Nyale Fishing Festival 162
Nyale seaworm 42
Nyana, Ida Bagus 97
Nyepi **40**, 43
Nyoman Sumandhi 199, 201
Nyuh Kuning 91

O

Oberoi (Seminyak) 67, 169, 173
Oberoi Lombok (Tanjung) 169, 179
Ocean rafting **203**, 209
Octopus (Deblog) 92
Odalan 22, 26, **38**
Offerings
  lake goddess 123
  odalan 14, 38
  shrine 24, 25
  temple 23, 123
Ogoh-ogoh 40
Oleg tambulilingan 30
Ombak Putih 227
Onlyou (Amed) 176
Opium trade 48
Orchids 141
Outdoor activities **202–211**
Ozigo (Ubud) 200, 201

P

Pabean Harbour **145**, 146
Pacific Supermarket 193, 195
Pacung Mountain Resort (Bedugul) 177
Pacung, rice terraces 133
Padang Bai **108**
Padang Tegal 91
Paddy's (Kuta) 200, 201
Padma Resort (Legian) 200, 201
Padmasana shrine **26**, 47
  Pura Jagat Natha 146
  Pura Kehen 104
  Pura Penataran Agung 116
  Pura Taman Ayun 130
  Pura Taman Saraswati 90
Pagerwesi **39**
Painting 17, **34–5**, 194, 195
Pakrisan River 79
PAL 194, 195
Palace *see Puri*
Palasari 23, 135
Pan Pacific Nirwana Bali Resort
  (Tanah Lot) 179
Pande clan 37, 82
Panji Sakti 47, 135
Panji Tisna Mausoleum 147
Pantai Gondol 126, 138
Pantry 193, 195
Paon 29
Papa's Café (Kuta) 185
Papaya (Senggigi) 191
Paragliding 72, **206**, 209
Paras 82
Parasailing 141, **206**, 209
Pasar 28 *see also* Market

Pasar Anyar 144, 145
Pasar Badung **60**
Pasar Burung **61**
Pasar Seni Sukawati 83, 193, 195
Pasar Ubud 89, **90**, 193, 195
Pasifika Art Museum 73
Pasir Putih 108
Passports 214
Paul Ropp 193, 195
Payan 157
Payogan 94
Peanuts (Kuta) 200, 201
Pedawa 139, 140
Pegayaman 147
Pejaten **129**
Pejeng 79, 87, **97**
Pejeng Moon 97
Pejeng Vessel 97
Peliatan **96**
Pelinggih 26
Pemecutan palace **61**, 49
Pemuteran **138**
Pemuteran Stables 199, 201, 206, 207
Penelokan 115, 120
Penestanan 34, **97**
Pengambangan **134**
Pengosekan 34, 91, 199
Penjor 39
Penujak 36, **161**
Pepper's Latino Grill & Bar (Sanur) 186
Perancak 134
Peresehan 31
Pergola (Sanur) 186
Perlu 195
Persatuan Hotel dan Restaurant
    Indonesia (PHRI) 166, 169
Pesta Kesenian Bali
    see Bali Arts Festival
Petanu River 79
Petulu 97
Pharmacies 221
Phonecards 224
Pinisi 72, 74
Pita Maha association 34, **35**, 88
PJ's (Jimbaran) 184
Poco Loco (Legian) 185
Poleng cloth 25
Polok, Ni 64
Poppies Cottages (Kuta) 171
Poppies Lanes I & II **67**, 68–9, 200
Poppies Restaurant (Kuta) 185
Portrait of Sutéja Neka (Smit) 96
Postal services 224
Poste restante 224
Pottery
    Bali 128, 129, 194, 195
    Lombok 11, 17, 36, **154**, 161, 194,
        195, 196
Prada 37
Prapen, Sunan 47
Prasada 128
Prasasti Blanjong 65
Pratima 26
Preserved fruits and nuts 197
Pringgasela **161**
Private villas **167**
Public
    holidays **43**
    telephones 224
    toilets 217
    transport **228**
Pulau Serangan **72**
Pupawresti 31
Puppets 30, **31**, 37, 194, 195, 196
Pupuan **140**

Puputan 49
    Badung 49, 60, 61
    Banjar 139
    Jagaraga 48
    Klungkung 49, 101, 105
    Marga 51, 132
    Monument 60, 61, 105, 132
Pura 26
Pura Alas Kedaton 127, 132
Pura Arjuna Metapa 97
Pura Batu Bolong 128
Pura Batu Kuning 75
Pura Beji 147
Pura Belanjong 45, 65
Pura Besakih 11, **116–7**
Pura Bukit Dharma Kutri 83
Pura Bukit Sari 132
Pura Campuhan 91, 94
Pura Candi Dasa 108
Pura dalem 28, 45
Pura Dalem Agung 91
Pura Dalem Gubug 141
Pura Dalem Jagaraga 147
Pura Dalem Pengungekan 104
Pura Dalem Sangsit 147
Pura Dasar 108
Pura desa 28, 45
Pura Desa Batumadeg 75
Pura Desa Peliatan 78
Pura Desa Sanur **64**
Pura Galuh 128
Pura Gangga **133**
Pura Goa Lawah 27, 108
Pura Gomang 108
Pura Griya Sakti 98
Pura Gunung Kawi **98**
Pura Gunung Lebah 91
Pura Gunung Raung 99
Pura Jagat Natha, Singaraja **146**
Pura Jagatnatha, Denpasar 43, **61**
Pura Jero Kandang 128
Pura Kebo Edan 97
Pura Kehen 27, 42, 43, 104
Pura Lempuyang Luhur 113
Pura Lingsar 42, 55, 154
Pura Luhur Batukau 133
Pura Luhur Uluwatu 27, 54, 57, **76–7**
Pura Maospahit 41, 46, **61**
Pura Meduwe Karang 27, 54, **148–9**
Pura Meru **155**
Pura Panarajon 115
Pura Ped 75
Pura Pejenenang 95
Pura Pekemitan Kangin 141
Pura Pekendungan 128
Pura Penataran 108
Pura Penataran Agung, Besakih 116–17
Pura Penataran Agung, Bunutin 104
Pura Penataran Sasih 42, 97
Pura Pengastulan 80, 87
Pura Penulisan **115**
Pura Penyimpenan 104
Pura Petitenget 67
Pura Pulaki 41, 138
Pura puseh 28, 45
Pura Puseh Batuan 83
Pura Puseh Batubulan 82, 198, 201
Pura Pusering Jagat 97
Pura Rambut Siwi 134
Pura Ratu Pande 117
Pura Sada 108
Pura Sakenan Dang Hyang 43, 72
Pura Samuan Tiga 40, 87
Pura Segara 41, 65
Pura Silayukti 108

Pura Sukawana 115
Pura Taman Ayun 27, 40, 47, 54, 129,
    130–31
Pura Taman Pule 42, 43, 86
Pura Taman Saraswati 88, **90**
Pura Taman Sari 105
Pura Tanah Lot 11, 27, 47, 124, **128**
Pura Tegeh Koripan 41, 45, **115**
Pura Telagamas 113
Pura Tirta Empul 27, 41, 45, **99**
Pura Ulun Carik 95
Pura Ulun Danu Batur 27, 40, 41,
    122–3
Pura Ulun Danu Bratan 11, 141, 142–3
Pura Ulun Danu Tamblingan 140
Pura Ulun Sui 95
Puri 28
Puri Agung 36, 112
Puri Agung Wisata 129
Puri Anom Tegehe Batubulan 198, 201
Puri Anyar 129
Puri Bagus Candi Dasa (Candi Dasa)
    176
Puri Bagus Lovina (Lovina) 178
Puri Bening Heyato, Hotel (Gunung
    Batur) 177
Puri Ganesha (Pemuteran) 190
Puri Ganesha Villas (Pemuteran) 178
Puri Gede 112
Puri Gianyar 50, 79, 86
Puri Kelapa Garden Cottages (Sanur)
    172
Puri Kertasurahe 112
Puri Lumbung Cottages (Munduk) 178
Puri Mas Boutique Hotel (Mangsit) 179
Puri Mas Restaurant (Mangsit) 191
Puri Mas Village (Mangsit) 179
Puri Nagi Seaside Cottages
    (Seminyak) 173
Puri Pemecutan 49
Puri Rai (Padang Bai) 177, 190
Puri Saren, Ubud 10, 89, **90**, 198, 201
Puri Sinar Nadiputra 146
Puri Taman Ujung 112
Puri Wulandari Boutique Resort
    (Ayung River Gorge) 175
Purnama 40–43
Puskesmas 221
Putung 104

Q
Queen's Tandoor (Seminyak) 187

R
Raffles, Thomas Stamford 48
Rai, Ida Bagus Nyoman 115
Rainfall 40–43, **42**
Ramadan **43**
Ramayana 31, 132, 148, 199
Ramayana ballet 198
Ramayana department store 92, 195
Rangda **25**, 134
Rasa Sayang (Denpasar) 184
Rascals 193, 195
Rawana 132
Reefseekers Dive Centre 202, 207
Rejang 31
Relief carvings 83, 87, 107, 147, 149
Religions **22–3**, 24–5, 30, 32, 38–9,
    40–43, 45, 46, 47
Rembitan **162**
Rening 134–5
Resorts **166–7**
Restaurant at Alila Ubud, The
    (Ayung River Gorge) 188

Restaurant at Alila Manggis 190
Restaurant Gede (Amed) 189
Restaurants 72, 74, **180–91**
  alcohol 181
  directory 184–91
  etiquette 181
  local food 182–3
Rice **20–21**
  barns 21, 162
  ceremonies 20
  cultivation and harvesting 20–21,
    45, 64, 95, 101, 102, 110, 127, 129
  goddess 20, **25**, 92, 95
  terraces 16, 19, 21, 80, 104, 133
Rini Hotel (Lovina) 177
Rip Curl (Kuta) 193, 195
Rites of passage 23, **38**
Ritual and trance **30**
Rivers and ricefields, ecology **19**
Roda, Nyoman 3
Roti Segar 195
The Royal Beach Seminyak 173
Royal Pita Maha (Ayung River Gorge)
  175
Rudana Museum 96
Rumah Manis (Seminyak) 173
Rundu, I Gusti Ketut 34
Ryoshi (Seminyak) 186

S

Sacred River 129
Sade **162**
Sai 131
Sail Sensations 227
Sailing **209**
St Regis Bali Resort (Nusa Dua) 172
Salak 104, 197
Sali, Ida Bagus 92
Salt production 100, 108, 113
Sangeh **132**
Sanggah 29
Sanggingan **96**
Sanghyang 30
Sangsit 147
Sangupati, Pangeran 47
Santa Fe (Seminyak) 200, 201
Santai Cottages (Amed) 176
Santai, Hotel (Sanur) 172
Sanur 10, 17, 50, 57, 58, **64–5**, 200
  art **34**
  watersports 202, 208, 209
Sanur Beach Hotel 172
Sapit **160**
Saraswati **39**, 43, 90
Sarcophagi 97, 135
Sardine (Kerobokan) 188
Sarong (Seminyak) 187
Sasaks 11, 16, 42, 49, 151
  dances 30, 31, 153
  religion 22, 23, 46, 47
Sate Bali (Seminyak) 187
Sawan 147
SDR Car Rentals 205, 207
Sea Breeze (Lovina) 190
Seaweed farming 75, 162
Sebatu **98**
Security **220–21**
Segara Agung Hotel (Sanur) 172
Segara Village Hotel (Sanur) 65
Segenter **157**
Sekala niskala 24
Sekotong 154
Selong Blanak **163**
Semara Ratih 199, 201

Semarapura 105
Sembalun 159, **160**
Sembiran Bali Aga village 147
Seminyak 10, 66, **67**, 194, 200
Senaru **157**
Sendanggile Waterfalls 157
Sendratari 30
Senggigi 17, 55, 151, 152, **156**, 204
Senggigi Beach Hotel (Lombok) 169
Seniwati Women's Art Gallery 89, 90
Servant-clowns 31
Setra 28
Sexual harassment 219
Shadow puppet play 30, **31**, 83, 199
Shallot growing 160
Sheraton Senggigi Lombok (Senggigi)
  179
Shipwrecks 48, 49, 113, 128, 210
Shopping **192–7**
  credit cards 192, 222, 223
  hawkers 192
  markets 193
Siadja & Son 86
Sibetan 104
Sidatapa 139
Sidemen **105**
Sidha Karya Gong Foundry 83
Silversmithing 36, 37, 82
Singapadu 194
Singaraja 54, 125, 126, **144–7**
Singsing Waterfall 147
Siti Bungalows (Ubud) 175
Siwa Latri **42**
Sky Garden Lounge (Kuta) 67, 200
Slave trade 48
Sleeping Woman (Nyana) 97
Smit, Arie 35, 97
Snakes 221
Snorkelling 167, **202**, 210–11
  Candi Dasa 108
  Lovina 204
  Menjangan Island 138
  Nusa Lembongan 74
  Padang Bai 108
  Pantai Gondol 138
  Pemuteran 138
  Senggigi 156
  Tulamben 113
Sobek 199, 201, 203, 207
Sobrat, Anak Agung Gede 93
Social behaviour **218–19**
Soka Beach 129
Songket 37, 105, 161
Sorrento at Melia Bali (Nusa Dua) 185
SOS Clinic (Kuta) 221
SOS Lounge & Bar (Seminyak)
  200, 201
Spa at the Balé 169
Spas **168–9**
Speciality hotels and resorts **167**
Spice (Tanjung Benoa) 188
Spice growing 140
Spies, Walter 35, 64, 88, 91, 104
Spirits 24, 25
Split gate *see Candi bentar*
Springs
  Air Panas 139
  Air Sanih 147
  Angsri 133
  Banyuwedang 138
  Goa Gajah 87
  Krakas 157
  Pura Gunung Kawi 98
  Pura Tirta Empul 99
  Telaga Waja 98

Springs (cont.)
  Tirtagangga 112
  Toya Bungkah 121
  Yeh Panas 133
Stage Sila Budaya 198
Star Fruit Café (Blimbing) 190
Stiff Chilli (Sanur) 186
Stone carving **36**, 82, 194, 195, 196
Street-by-Street maps
  Kuta 68–9
  Singaraja 144–5
  Ubud 88–9
Styles, Balinese painting **34–5**
Suarti 193, 195
Subak **20**, 95, 129
Subali 132
Suharto 51
Sukarara **161**
Sukarno 50, 51
Sukawati 79, **83**
Sukawati, Cokorda Gede Agung
  35, 90, 92
Sukawati Art Market 83, 193, 195
Suling 33
Sumbawa 161, 202
Sunari Villas (Lovina) 178
Sunfish 75, 210, 211
Sunshine 41
Supermarkets **193**, 195
Surabrata 129
Surf schools 202
Surf Time 208
Surfer Girl 193, 195
Surfing 202, **208–9**
  Balian Beach 129
  Bangko Bangko 163
  Canggu 64, 208
  Desert Point 163, 208
  Gerupuk 162, 208
  Kuta (Bali) 10, 66, 208
  Kuta (Lombok) 162
  Kuta Reef 74
  Nusa Dua 73
  Medewi Beach 134
  Maui 163, 208
  Padang Padang 208
Susilo Bambang Yudhoyono 51
Suwungwas 72
Sweta **154**
Sweta Market 154, 193, 194, 195
Swimming 199, **204**, 214, 221

T

Tabanan 125, **129**
  kingdom 47, 49
Taman Gili 55, 102, 105, **106–7**
Taman Kupu Kupu 129
Taman Nasional Bali Barat 11, 54,
  126, 135, **136–7**, 204, 205
Taman Nasional Gunung Rinjani
  55, 153, **158–9**, 205
Taman Puputan 60, **61**
Taman Restaurant (Senggigi) 191
Taman Sari Bali Cottages (Pemuteran)
  178
Taman Werdhi Budaya 41, 57, **61**,
  198, 201
Tampaksiring 99
Tandjung Sari (Sanur) 173
Tanjung **157**
Tanjung Aan 162
Tanjung Benoa **72**, 206, 208, 209
Tanjung Luar **163**
Tantra Gallery 86
Tantri stories 106

Tantri Stories (Lempad) 34
Taro 99
Tauch Terminal Resort (Tulamben) 177
Taxis 226, 228
Tebesaya 91
Tegal Sari (Ubud) 175
Tegallalang 97, **98**
Tejakula **147**
Tektekan 129
Telaga Waja River 98, 203
Telephone services **224**
Television **225**
Telkom 224
Teluk Terima 138, 139
Temperature 43
Temple Café & Seaside Cottages
  (Candi Dasa) 176
Temples **26–7** *see also Pura*
  architecture and layout 26–7
  etiquette 219
  festivals 22, 38, 40–43
Tenganan Bali Aga Village 11, 55,
  102, 109, **110–11**
  weaving, textiles 37, 63, 110
Tennis **204**
Terazo (Ubud) 188
Tetaring at Kayumanis (Nusa Dua) 186
Tetebatu 152, **161**
Textiles 17, **37**, 63
  buying 60, 193, 195, 197
  East Bali **105**, 110
  Gianyar 86
  Klungkung 105
  Lombok 154, **161**, 162
  Nusa Penida 75
  Singaraja 146
  Tenganan 63, 105, 110
Thallasso Spa 169
Theatrical performance **30**
Three Brothers (Legian) 171
Three Dancers (Gunarsa) 35
Tide charts 208
Tilem 43
Tilem Kapitu 42
Time differences, time zones 216
Tir Na Nog (Gili Isles) 191
Tirtagangga 101, 102, 109, **112**
Tiu Kelep waterfall 157
Tiu Pupas waterfall 157
TJ's (Kuta) 185
Tjampuhan Hotel and Spa
  (Ubud) 91, 175
Tobacco growing 157, 161
Togog, Ida Bagus Made 34
Toko Saudara 60
Tombs 99
Tony Raka Gallery 195
Topeng **31**, 83, 86
Tourism 16, **17**, 50, 51, 214, 216, 217
Tourist information centres 216, 217
Tourist shuttles 228
Toya Bungkah 121
Toyapakeh 75
Traditional
  beauty treatments 168
  beliefs **24–5**
  dance and drama **30–31**, 198
  hand-woven textiles **37**
  music **32–3**, 199
Trail-bike trips 205
Trance possession 24, 30
Travellers' cheques **222**
Travelling **226–9**
  by road 228–9
  with children 167

Treasures 193, 195
Trekking **205**, 207
  Gunung Agung 114
  Gunung Batur 120–21
  Gunung Rinjani 157–60
Trip, I Made 140
Trunyan Bali Aga village 115, **121**
Tuak 109
Tuban 66, **67**, 74
Tugu Bali, Hotel (Canggu) 64, 170
Tukadmungga 147
Tukang banten 38
Tulamben 102, **113**, 210
Tumbal 24
Tumbal (Magical Amulet) (Sobrat) 24
Tumpek 39
Tumpeng 147
Tumuwuh, Sang Hyang 133
Tunkung at Mimpi Resort (Tulamben)
  190
Turtle Island **72**
Turtles 19, 72, 138, 156
Tut Mak (Ubud) 188

U
Ubud 10, 17, 54, 79, 80, **88–95**, 200
  art 34, 194
  dance 198
  expatriates 17, 50, 88
  gamelan 199
  Tourist Information Centre 89, **90**
Ubud Hanging Gardens (Payangan) 175
Udayana, King 45
Ujung **112**
Uluwatu 206
Uma Jero 140
Uma Ubud (Sanggingan) 175
Umalas Stables 199, 201, 206, 207
Un's (Kuta) 170, 185
Unda River, white-water rafting 203
United East India Company (VOC) 48

V
Vegetarian food 181
Viapi (Kuta) 200
Viceroy, The (Nagi) 175
Victory 194, 195
Vihara Amurva Bhumi Blahbatuh 83
Vila Ombak, Hotel (Gili Isles) 179
Villa Agencies 169
Villa Kuba (Seminyak) 173
Villa Lumbung (Seminyak) 173
Villa Nautilus (Gili Isles) 179
Village and village life **28–9**
  structure and layout 16, 28
  temple system 28, 45
Villas Bali Hotel (Seminyak) 173
Visas 214
Volcanoes 18, 114, 120–21
  eruptions 51, 115, 120, 123, 158

W
Waisak **40–41**, 43
Waka Gangga (Tabanan) 178
Waka Land Cruise 205
Waka Namya (Ubud) 176
Waka Nusa (Nusa Lembongan) 172
Waka Shorea (Menjangan Island) 178
Walks, Walking **205**
  Gunung Batur **120–21**
  Lake Buyan 141
  Lake Tamblingan **140–41**
  Taman Nasional Bali Barat 136
  Tenganan to Tirtagangga **109**
  Ubud Countryside **94–5**

Wallace, Alfred Russel 19
  Wallace's Line 19
Wanasari 129
Wantilan 28
  Pura Griya Sakti 98
  Tenganan 110
  Ubud 89
War of Independence memorial 132
Warisan (Seminyak) 187, 200, 201
Waroeng Tugu (Canggu) 184
Wartel 224
Warung 28
Warung Sehat at Puri Ganesha
  (Pemuteran) 191
Wasantara Net 225
Waterbom Park & Spa 67, 199, 201,
  204, 207
Waterfalls
  Jeruk Manis 161
  Munduk 140
  Sendanggile 157, 158
  Singsing, Gitgit 147
  Tiu Kelep and Tiu Pupas 157
Watergarden (Candi Dasa) 176
Water-skiing **202**
  Lake Bratan 141
  Tanjung Benoa 72
Waturenggong, King 46
Waves Restaurant (Gili Isles) 191
Wayan Mardika 194, 195, 199, 201
Wayan Narta 194, 195
Wayan Wija 194, 195, 199, 201
Wayang kulit **30**, 31, 83, 199
Wayang listrik 199
Wayang painting style 34, 106
Wayang wong 31, 83, 86, 147
Weaving 36, **37**
  Pringgasela 161
  Rembitan 162
  Sade 162
  Sukarara 161
Weddings 38
West Bali National Park
  see Taman Nasional Bali Barat
Westin Resort (Nusa Dua) 172, 199
Wetu Telu 23, 47, 157
White-water rafting 80, 97, 199, **203**
Wianta, Made 35
Widhi Wasa, Sang Hyang 61
Wijaya, Made 65
Wijaya, Raden 46
Wildlife **18–19**, 136–7, 140, 204–205
Wilhelmina, Queen 112
Windsurfing 156, **202**, 208
Wira's 193, 195
Woodcarvings 17, 81, 86, **97**, 194,
  195, 196
  Kemenuh 83
  Mas 97
  Nyuh Kuning 91
  Peliatan 96
  Sebatu 98
  Tegallalang 97, 98
Wos Barat River 94
Wos Timur River 94

Y
Yak magazine 198
Yeh Panas **133**
Yeh Pulu 87
Young Artists School **35**, 97
Yulia Beach Inn (Kuta) 170
Yusuf Silver 193, 195

Z
Zen Resort (Sererit) 178
Zula (Seminyak) 187

Acknowledgments

Dorling Kindersley would like to thank the following people whose contributions and assistance have made the preparation of this book possible.

Main Contributors
Andy Barski is a motorcycle enthusiast and writer who has written extensively on travelling around the Indonesian archipelago, where he has been based since 1987.

Bruce Carpenter first came to Bali in 1974. He has written numerous books and articles on Balinese art and culture.

John Cooke taught zoology at Oxford University before becoming a wildlife filmmaker, photographer and writer.

Jean Couteau settled in Bali in 1979. He writes short stories and art criticism in French, English and Indonesian.

Diana Darling is a freelance writer and editor who has lived in Bali since 1981. She is the author of *The Painted Alphabet: a Novel* (1992), based on a Balinese tale.

Sarah Dougherty arrived in Bali in 1993 to become editor of *Bali Echo* magazine. She contributes to many international publications and is working on a cookbook.

Tim Stuart is a travel writer, photographer and teacher of business communication. With his wife Rosa, he publishes Lombok's only English-language travel magazine, *Inilah!*.

Tony Tilford is a wildlife photographer and writer with wide experience of Indonesian flora and fauna. An avid traveller, he is in search of common and exotic subjects.

Additional Contributors Rachel Lovelock.

For Dorling Kindersley
MANAGING EDITOR Anna Streiffert
PUBLISHING MANAGER Kate Poole
SENIOR PUBLISHING MANAGER Louise Lang
DIRECTOR OF PUBLISHING Gillian Allan
PUBLISHER Douglas Amrine
PRODUCTION Marie Ingledew, Michelle Thomas
DTP Vinod Harish, Vincent Kurien, Azeem Siddiqui,
MAP CO-ORDINATORS Uma Battacharya, Mohammed Hassan, Jasneet Kaur, Casper Morris, Dave Pugh,

Design and Editorial Assistance
Helle Amin, Emma Anacootee, Claire Baranowski, Tessa Bindloss, Christine Chua, Lydia Halliday, Victoria Heyworth-Dunne, Hoo Khuen Hin, Kok Kum Fai, Rachel Lovelock, Helen Partington, Pollyanna Poulter, Marisa Renzullo, Patricia Rozario, Sands Publishing Solutions, Dora Whitaker, Karen Villabona.

Additional Photography
Luis Ascui, Rucina Ballinger, Koes Karnadi, Rachel Lovelock, Ian O'Leary, Rough Guides/Martin Richardson.

Fact Checking
Rucina Ballinger, Anak Agung Gede Putra Rangki, Anak Agung Oka Dwiputra, Rachel Lovelock.

Proof Reading and Indexing
Kay Lyons.

Special Assistance
Edi Swoboda of Bali Bird Park; Ketty Barski; Steve Bolton; Georges Breguet; Georjina Chia and Kal Muller; Lalu Ruspanudin of DIPARDA, Mataram; Justin Eeles; Peter Hoe of evolution; Ganesha Bookshop; David Harnish; Chris Hill; Jean Howe and William Ingram; Rio Helmi of Image Network Indonesia; I Wayan Kicen; Lagun Sari Indonesia Seafood Pte Ltd; Peter and Made of Made's Warung; M Y Narima of Marintur; Rosemarie F Oei of Museum Puri Lukisan; Jim Parks; David Stone; The Vines Restaurant; Bayu Wirayudha, Made Widana and Luh Nyoman Diah Prihartini.

Photography Permissions
The publisher would like to thank all the parks, temples, museums, hotels, restaurants, shops, galleries and sights for their kind permission to photograph at their premises.

Picture Credits
Key: a-above; b-below/bottom; c-centre; f-far; l-left; r-right; t-top.

The publisher would like to thank the following individuals, companies and picture libraries for permission to reproduce their photographs and drawings:

AIFA WARTEL: 224tl. ALAMY IMAGES: Ace Stock Limited 183c; Ian Dagnall 10bl; imagebroker/Manfred Bali 64br; redbrickstock.com/Patria jannides 88tr; Jochen Tack 182cl; travelib 69cra.
BALI HYATT: 65tl. BES STOCK: 208cla, 208–209c, 210tl, 210–211c, 211bl, 212–213; © Alain Evrard 14, 43cla, 209tl; © Globe Press 24cr; BLUE MARLIN DIVE CENTER, LOMBOK: © Clive Riddington 156bc.

EDITIONS DIDIER MILLET: 3c, 20br, 22cl, 25tl, 28tr, 30tl, 32tr, 45bc, 45bcl, 46bl, 47clb, 48cb, 51tl, 83tr, 88bl, 165c, 167tl, 167crb, 167br, 194tl, 199tr, 202cla, 203t; © Gil Marais 23bl; © Tara Sosrowardoyo 45ca, 46bc, 46br.
FOUR SEASONS RESORT: 168cl, 181bl.

A.A. GEDE ARIAWAN: 88cb; GETTY IMAGES: Photographer's Choice/Steve Satushek 183tl; Riser/Marc Romanelli 11bl; Science Faction/Louie Psihoyos 11tl.

HARD ROCK HOTEL: 181cr; HEMISPHERES IMAGES: Romain Cintract 11cr; Patrick Frilet 10cr.

PHOTO AND PRINT COLLECTION OF THE KONINKLIJK INSTITUUT VOOR TAAL-, LAND- EN VOLKENKUNDE (KITLV), LEIDEN: Woodbury & Page, Batavia 48br, Neeb 49tl, 50tc.
LONELY PLANET IMAGES: Tom Cockrem 68tr.

MANDARA SPA: 169tr; KAL MULLER: 19crb, 19br, 210tr, 210cla, 211tl, 211cra, 211crb; MUSEUM PURI LUKISAN: 16c, 24br, 34cla, 34bcl, 34br, 34–35c, 35cr, 35bl, 35br, 87br, *Bubuk Sah and Gagak Aking* I Cokot (1935) 88cla, 92tr, 92cla, 92bl, 92bc, 93cr, 93cr, 93bl, 97tr.

NASA: Image STS068-160-53 13br; NEKA ART MUSEUM: 34tr, 35tr, 44, 96cr, 115tl; THE NIEUWENKAMP FOUNDATION, VLEUTEN: 9c, 49br, 213c; NOVOTEL BENOA BALI: 168bc.

© PHOTOBANK/TETTONI, CASSIO AND ASSOCIATES PTE LTD: 1, 2–3, 8–9, 18cla, 18cra, 18bl, 18crb, 22tr, 22c, 27br, 30tr, 30cl, 30bcl, 30br, 31tr, 31cla, 31cra, 31clb, 31crb, 31bl, 32–33c, 33tl, 33cr, 33bl, 33br, 36tr, 37cra, 37clb, 37br, 38cl, 38bl, 38–39c, 48tc, 49crb, 52–53, 56, 57b, 70–71, 78, 79b, 89tl, 91tr, 100, 106cl, 118–119, 124, 125b, 153tr, 153cr, 159bl, 164–165, 198tc, 198c, 198bl, 199tl, 200tr, 200bl, 202br, 209tr, 209br; PRIMA FOTO: 30cra, 205cl; PT MEDIA WISATA DEWATA: 224tl.

REEFSEEKERS DIVE CENTRE: 136cla; ROBERT HARDING PICTURE LIBRARY: © Gavin Hellier 142–143.

© MORTEN STRANGE/FLYING COLOURS: 136br.

© TC NATURE: 18tr, 19bl, 81br, 84tl, 84tr, 84cl, 84c, 84cr, 84bl, 85tl, 85tr, 85bc, 85br, 94tl, 94tr, 94clb, 94bc, 95tr, 95crb, 109cla, 109crb, 109bc, 110bl, 136tl, 136tr, 136clb, 137ca, 137bl, 138tl, 140crb, 140bl, 141br, 148tl, 204c, 205tc; © John Cooke 19cra, 54tl, 109tc, 121tl; © Tony Tilford 19clb, 54tl, 85bl, 137br; THREADS OF LIFE: 193bc.

ADRIAN VICKERS: 50bl.

ZFL PRCO: 74tl.

Front Endpaper: All special photography except © PHOTOBANK: tl, tlc, cra, bl.

Jacket Front – ALAMY IMAGES: Philippe Roy; Back – AWL IMAGES:Gavin Hellier tl, Travel Pix Collection bl; DORLING KINDERSLEY: Jamie Marshall cla, clb; Spine – ALAMY IMAGES: Philippe Roy t.

Further Reading

History

Bali in the 19th Century Ide Anak Agung Gde Agung (Jakarta: Yayasan Obor Indonesia, 1991)

Bali Profile: People, Events, Circumstances (1001–1976) Willard A Hanna (American Universities Field Staff, 1976)

Bali at War: a History of the Dutch-Balinese Conflict of 1846–49 Alfons van der Kraan (Monash Asia Institute, 1995)

In Praise of Kuta: From Slave Port to Fishing Village to the Most Popular Resort in Bali Hugh Mabbett (January Books, 1987)

Lombok: Conquest, Colonization, and Underdevelopment, 1870–1940 Alfons van der Kraan (Heinemann Educational Books, 1980)

Negara: the Theater State in 19th Century Bali Clifford Geertz (Princeton University Press, 1981)

Society and Culture

Adat and Dinas: Balinese Communities in the Indonesian State Carol Warren (Oxford University Press, 1993)

The Changing World of Bali: Religions, Society and Tourism Leo Howe (Routledge, 2005)

Bali: A Paradise Created Adrian Vickers (Tuttle, 1997; first published 1989)

Bali: Cultural Tourism and Touristic Culture Michel Picard (Archipelago Press, 1998)

Bali, Morning of the World Luca Invernizzi Tettoni and Nigel Simmonds (Periplus, 1997)

Bali: Rangda and Barong Jane Belo (University of Washington Press, 1949)

Bali: Sekala and Niskala F B Eiseman (Periplus, 1989)

Bali: Studies in Life, Thought, and Ritual (Foris Publications, 1984)

Bali Today: Real Balinese Stories Jean Couteau with Usadi Wiratnaya et al (Spektra Communications, 2005)

The Balinese Hugh Mabbett (January Books, 1985)

Being Modern in Bali: Image and Change ed Adrian Vickers (Yale University Southeast Asia Studies, 1996)

The Food of Bali ed Wendy Hutton (Periplus World Food Series, 1999)

Island of Bali Miguel Covarrubias (Periplus, 1999; first published 1937)

The Peoples of Bali Angela Hobart, Urs Ramseyer and Albert Leeman (Blackwell, 1997)

Perfect Order: Recognizing Complexity in Bali J Stephen Lansing (Princeton University Press, 2006)

A Sacred Cloth Religion: Ceremonies of the Big Feast Among Wetu Telu Sasak Sven Cederroth (Nordic Institute of Asian Studies, 1991)

Arts and Architecture

The Art And Culture of Bali Urs Ramseyer (Oxford University Press, 1977/1987)

At Home in Bali Made Wijaya, photography Isabella Ginannesch (Abbeville Press, 1999)

Bali: the Imaginary Museum Michael Hitchcock and Lucy Norris (Oxford University Press, 1996)

Bali Modern: The Art of Tropical Living Gianni Francione, photography Luca Invernizzi Tettoni (Tuttle, 1999)

Bali Sketchbook watercolours Graham Byfield, text Diana Darling (Archipelago Press, 1998)

Bali Style Rio Helmi and Barbara Walker (Times Editions, 1995; Thames & Hudson, 1995; Vendome Press, 1996)

Balinese Dance in Transition: Kaja and Kelod I Made Bandem, Frederik Eugene Deboer (Oxford University Press, 1995)

Balinese Dance, Music and Drama I Wayan Dibia, Rucina Ballinger (Periplus Editions, 2005)

Balinese Gardens photography Luca Invernizzi Tettoni, text William Warren et al (Periplus/Thames and Hudson, 1996/2000)

Balinese Music Michael Tenzer (Periplus, 1991/1994)

Balinese Textiles Brigitta Hauser-Schublin, Marie-Louise Nabholz-Kartaschoff and Urs Ramseyer (Periplus, 1991/1997)

Dancing Out of Bali John Coast (Periplus Editions, 2005)

The Epic Of Life: A Balinese Journey Of The Soul Idanna Pucci (Alfred van der Marck Editions, 1985)

The Folk Art of Bali Joseph Fischer and Thomas Cooper (Oxford University Press, 1998)

Kecak: The Vocal Chant Of Bali I Wayan Dibia (Hartanto Art Books, 1996)

The Language of Balinese Shadow Theater Mary Sabine Zurbuchen (Princeton University Press, 1987)

Masks of Bali: Spirits of An Ancient Drama Judy Slattum, photography Paul Schraub (Chronicle, 1992)

Monumental Bali A J Bernet Kempers (Periplus, 1991/1997; first published 1977)

Music in Bali Colin McPhee (Da Capo Press, 1976; first published 1966)

W O J Nieuwenkamp: First European Artist in Bali Bruce W Carpenter (Archipelago Press, 1998)

Perceptions of Paradise: Images of Bali in the Arts Garrett Kam (Dharma Seni Museum Neka, 1993)

Pre-War Balinese Modernists 1928–1942 Dr F Haks et al (Ars et Amimatio, Haarlem, the Netherlands)

Ulat-ulatan, Traditional Basketry in Bali Fred B Eiseman Jr (White Lotus, 1999)

Vessels Of Life: Lombok Earthenware Jean McKinnon (Saritaksu, 1996)

Nature

Bali – Periplus Action Guide Wally Singian, David Pickel (Periplus, 2000)

The Birds of Java and Bali Derek Holmes, illustrations Stephen Nash (Oxford University Press, 1989)

Butterflies of Bali Victor Mason (Saritaksu Publications, 2005)

Diving and Snorkeling Guide to Bali and the Komodo Region Tim Rock (Pisces, 1996)

The Ecology of Java and Bali Tony Whitten et al (Oxford University Press, 1997)

Flowers of Bali Fred Eiseman (Periplus, 1994)

Fruits of Bali Fred Eiseman and Margaret Eiseman (Periplus, 1994)

Travelogues and Memoirs

Bali: the Last Paradise Hickman Powell, photography André Roosevelt (Oxford University Press, 1930/1989; Dodd, Mead, 1936)

Bali: People and Art Gregor Krause (White Lotus, 2000; first published in German 1926)

The Birthmark: Memoirs of a Balinese Prince A A M Djelantik (Periplus, 1998)

A House in Bali Colin McPhee (Tuttle/Periplus, 2000; first published 1946)

A Little Bit One O'Clock William Ingram (Ersania Books, 1998)

The Night of Purnama Anna Matthews (Jonathan Cape, 1965)

Our Hotel In Bali: ... A Story Of The 1930s Louise G Koke (January Books, 1987)

Stranger In Paradise: the Diary of an Expatriate in Bali 1979–80 Made Wijaya (Wijaya Words, 1984)

Travelling to Bali: Four Hundred Years of Journeys Adrian Vickers (Oxford University Press, 1995)

Fiction

Bali Behind the Seen: Recent Fiction From Bali trans and ed Vern Cork (Darma Printing, 1996)

The Edge of Bali Inez Baranay (Angus & Robertson, 1992)

The Painted Alphabet: a Novel Based on a Balinese Tale Diana Darling (Tuttle, 2001; Graywolf, 1992; Houghton Mifflin, 1992)

The Sweat of Pearls: Short Stories About Women of Bali Putu Oka Sukanta, trans Vern Cork (Darma Printing, 1999)

A Tale from Bali Vicki Baum (Tuttle/Periplus, 2000; first published 1937)

Books for Children

Bye, Bye, Bali Kai Harriett Luger (Browndeer, 1996)

The Dancing Pig Judy Sierra (Gulliver, 1999)

The Haughty Toad, And Other Tales From Bali Victor Mason, illustrations by artists Of Pengosekan (Bali Art Print/Hamlyn, 1975).

Rice Is Life Rita Golden Gelman (Henry Holt, 2000)

Glossary

ARCHITECTURE

atap: palm-leaf thatched roof
bale: pavilion
candi bentar: split gate
gedong: enclosed pavilion
kori: roofed gate
kori agung: grand gate
kulkul: drum tower
meru: multi-tiered shrine
padmasana: tall shrine to the
   Supreme Deity
pelinggih: shrine, spirit house
pura: temple
puri: palace, house of nobility
rumah: house
wantilan: public pavilion with
   double roof
warung: coffee stall, small shop

ARTS AND CRAFTS

geringsing: warp- and weft-dyed
   textile, "double ikat"
ikat: warp resist-dyed textile
kayu: wood
lontar: type of palm; palm-leaf
   book
lukisan: painting
mas: gold
pande: metalsmith
paras: volcanic stone used for
   building and statuary
patung: statue
perak: silver
prada: gilt-painted cloth
songket: textile with
   supplementary weft thread,
   often gold or silver
tapel: mask
tenunan: weaving

MUSIC AND DANCE

arja: Balinese opera
baris: classical solo male dance
baris gede: a sacred dance for
   rows of male dancers
Barong: large sacred effigy
   danced by two men
belaganjur: processional
   percussion orchestra
gambuh: ancient court dance
gamelan: percussion orchestra
gangsa: bronze-keyed
   instrument
kebyar: vigorous style of gamelan music; vigorous solo dance
kendang: drum
keris: sacred wavy-bladed
   dagger
legong: classical dance for three
   females
prembon: mixed programme
Rangda: sacred demonic effigy,
   consort of the Barong
rejang: sacred dance for rows of
   female dancers
suling: bamboo flute
tari: dance

topeng: masked dance based on
   geneological tales
trompong: bronze instrument
   with 8 to 12 kettle gongs
wayang kulit: shadow puppet
   theatre
wayang wong: masked dance
   based on Hindu epics

DRESS

baju: shirt, dress
baju kaus: T-shirt
destar: head cloth for Balinese
   males
gelungan: ornate headdress
jilbab: head cloth for Muslim
   females
kain: cloth; long hip cloth,
   unsewn
kebaya: traditional jacket for
   females
peci: hat for Muslim males
sarong: sewn long hip cloth
selendang: ceremonial temple
   sash
sepatu: shoes

RELIGIONS AND COMMUNITY

banjar: village association
hari raya: any religious holiday
karya: work, especially
   collective ritual work
mesjid: mosque
odalan: temple festival
pedanda: high priest
pemangku: temple priest
penjor: festooned bamboo pole
pura dalem: temple of the
   netherworld
pura desa: village temple
pura puseh: temple of origins
sebel: taboo
sunat: Islamic ritual
   circumcision
tirta: holy water
yadnya: Hindu ritual (generic)

FOOD

air minum: drinking water
ayam: chicken
babi guling: roast pig
babi: pork
bakar: grilled
bebek tutu: smoked spicy duck
buah-buahan: fruit
cumi-cumi: squid
daging: meat
gado-gado: vegetarian dish with
   peanut sauce
garam: salt
goreng: fried
gula: sugar
ikan laut: fish
jeruk nyepis: lime
jeruk: orange; citrus
kelapa: coconut
kopi: coffee

makan: eat
mie: noodles
minum: drink
nasi: food; rice; rice meal
pedas: hot (spicy)
pisang: banana
roti: bread
sambal: spicy condiment
sapi: beef
sate, sate lilit: small skewers of
   barbecued meat
susu: milk
teh: tea
telur: egg
udang: prawn, shrimp

NATURE AND LANDSCAPE

bukit: hill
burung: bird
danau: lake
gunung: mountain
hujan: rain
jalan: road
laut: sea
mata hari: sun
pantai: beach
pohon: tree
sawah: ricefield
subak: irrigation co-operative
sungai: river, stream
taman: garden, park
tanah: ground, earth, soil

TRAVEL AND TRANSPORT

bemo: public minibus
cidomo: rubber-tyred pony cart
   (in Lombok)
dokar: pony cart
jukung: outrigger sailing canoe
mobil: car
sepeda motor: motorcycle

MISCELLANEOUS

adat: customary law
bagus: good, handsome
baik: good
Bapak: polite term of address for
   a man
bayar: pay
cantik: pretty
dingin: cold
Ibu: polite term of address for
   a woman
mahal: expensive
murah: inexpensive
panas: hot, warm
pariwisata: tourism
puputan: suicidal
   fight-to-the-end
roko: cigarette
sakit: hurt; sick
selamat jalan: farewell ("on your
   journey")
terima kasih: thank you
tidak: no, not
tidur: sleep
uang: money

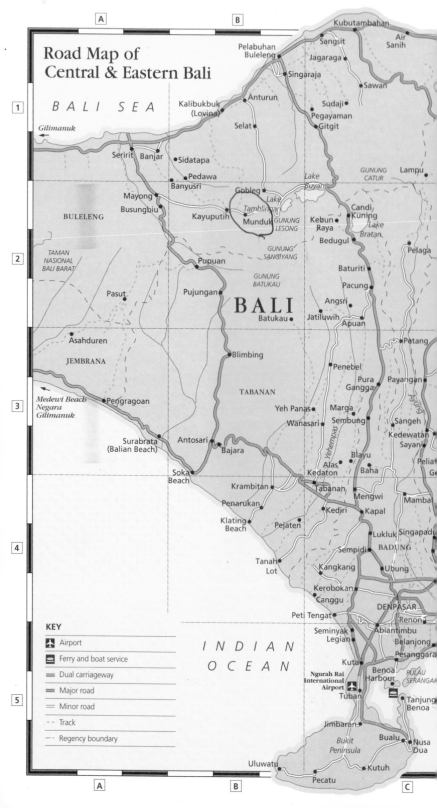